Praise for *VSTO for Mere Mortals*™

"This is the book I wish I'd had when I was first introduced to VSTO and the .NET Framework. It will be invaluable not only to those considering VSTO, but for anyone transitioning from Office VBA to Visual Basic.NET. The wide range of subjects covered provides an entry point for the more in-depth, developer-oriented documentation available on MSDN and elsewhere."

—Cindy Meister, MS Word MVP

"*VSTO for Mere Mortals*™ does a great job of building a bridge between the worlds of VBA and VSTO. Kathleen and Paul show how a VBA developer can have the richness of Office and also the power, maintainability, and security of Visual Studio. They succeeded in writing a book that is approachable, understandable, and compelling."

—KD Hallman, General Manager, Microsoft, Developer Division

"This book is an excellent choice for VBA developers looking to make the switch to .NET development for Office using Visual Studio Tools for Office. In many instances VB.NET code is presented alongside equivalent VBA code to help illustrate key conceptual and usage differences."

—Steve Hansen, OfficeZealot.com,
author of *Mastering Excel 2003 Programming with VBA*
and coauthor of *Mastering Excel 2000 Premium Edition*

"Visual Studio 2005 Tools for Office is the way to go for building managed Office applications. If you're moving from VBA to managed code, this book shows you the way."

—Ken Getz, Senior Consultant, MCW Technologies, LLC

"This book is highly recommended for VBA developers who are interested in doing Office programming using the rich power of Visual Studio and .NET."

—Mei Liang, Software Design Engineer in Test, Microsoft

"Kathleen McGrath has stuffed *VSTO for Mere Mortals*™ with in-depth code samples that demonstrate VSTO in an easy-to-understand way. From simple how-to's to advanced functionality, it's all here. I learned a great deal from reading this book."

—Justin Whitney, Technical Journalist

"This book provides an instantly accessible resource for VBA and Office developers to become familiar with the powerful new Office development platform, but even goes beyond that, providing a number of 'worth the purchase of the book' tips, fully functional examples, and elegant methods from someone who has obviously spent a lot of time with these tools to help the mortal on the path to becoming a guru."

—Rory Plaire, Solutions Architect, DigitalCommons LLC

"For the Office VBA developer interested in programming in .NET or the .NET programmer looking to move to the Office platform, this book is worth its weight in gold. If you are looking for a complete, well-written source to quickly get you up to speed to develop and program Office solutions in Visual Studio 2005, I believe this book is a must-have."

—Frank Rice, Programming Writer, Microsoft Office Developer Center

"With this book, VBA developers have access to a great resource that will help them understand essential concepts of managed code and best practices to migrate VBA solutions to Visual Basic 2005 and Visual Studio 2005 Tools for Office. This book goes beyond an introduction to VSTO to introduce the new world of VSTO 2005 SE and the 2007 Microsoft Office system."

—Erika Ehrli Cabral, Site Manager,
MSDN Office Developer Center, Microsoft

"Kathleen and Paul have been involved with VSTO in one way or the other from its very beginnings, and it shows. Their depth and breadth of knowledge is reflected in this detailed and authoritative book. I highly recommend it for any professional developer making the transition from VBA to managed code."

—Eric Lippert, Software Design Engineer, Microsoft

VSTO
for Mere
Mortals™

VSTO

for Mere

Mortals™

*A VBA Developer's Guide to
Microsoft Office Development Using
Visual Studio 2005 Tools for Office*

Kathleen McGrath
Paul Stubbs

✦Addison-Wesley

Upper Saddle River, NJ ▪ Boston ▪ Indianapolis ▪ San Francisco

New York ▪ Toronto ▪ Montreal ▪ London ▪ Munich ▪ Paris ▪ Madrid

Capetown ▪ Sydney ▪ Tokyo ▪ Singapore ▪ Mexico City

Many of the designations used by manufacturers and sellers to distinguish their products are claimed as trademarks. Where those designations appear in this book, and the publisher was aware of a trademark claim, the designations have been printed with initial capital letters or in all capitals.

The authors and publisher have taken care in the preparation of this book, but make no expressed or implied warranty of any kind and assume no responsibility for errors or omissions. No liability is assumed for incidental or consequential damages in connection with or arising out of the use of the information or programs contained herein.

The publisher offers excellent discounts on this book when ordered in quantity for bulk purchases or special sales, which may include electronic versions and/or custom covers and content particular to your business, training goals, marketing focus, and branding interests. For more information, please contact:

U.S. Corporate and Government Sales
(800) 382-3419
corpsales@pearsontechgroup.com

For sales outside the United States, please contact:

International Sales
international@pearsoned.com

 This Book Is Safari Enabled

The Safari® Enabled icon on the cover of your favorite technology book means the book is available through Safari Bookshelf. When you buy this book, you get free access to the online edition for 45 days.

Safari Bookshelf is an electronic reference library that lets you easily search thousands of technical books, find code samples, download chapters, and access technical information whenever and wherever you need it.

To gain 45-day Safari Enabled access to this book:

• Go to http://www.awprofessional.com/safarienabled

• Complete the brief registration form

• Enter the coupon code 19GZ-BRHF-QKB5-ZTF1-DHJL

If you have difficulty registering on Safari Bookshelf or accessing the online edition, please e-mail customer-service@safaribooksonline.com.

Visit us on the Web: www.awprofessional.com

Library of Congress Cataloging-in-Publication Data

McGrath, Kathleen.
  VSTO for mere mortals : a VBA developer's guide to Office development using Visual studio 2005 tools for Office / Kathleen McGrath and Paul Stubbs.
     p. cm.
  Includes bibliographical references and index.
  ISBN 0-321-42671-1 (pbk. : alk. paper)
  1. Microsoft Visual studio. 2. Microsoft Office. I. Stubbs, Paul R., 1969- II. Title. III. Title: Visual Studio Tools for Office for mere mortals.
  TK5105.8885.M57M375 2006
  005.5—dc22

                                                                                          2006034309

ISBN 0-321-42671-1
Text printed in the United States on recycled paper at RR Donnelley in Crawfordsville, Indiana.
First printing, December 2006

For Mark
—Kathleen

For my sons
—Paul

Contents

Foreword

If you are familiar with VBA and you are thinking about dipping a toe into the world of Office development with Visual Basic 2005 and Visual Studio Tools for Office (VSTO)—look no further, this is the book for you.

Kathleen and Paul take a unique approach in this book as they describe VSTO with the VBA developer in mind. Let's face it, there are a lot of new things to learn as you move from VBA to Visual Basic 2005 and VSTO. The Visual Basic language has changed more than one would like and some of the old familiar language constructs are gone. Fortunately, this book describes the major changes you will encounter as you move from VBA development to Visual Basic 2005 development. The development environment of VSTO is also quite different than the VBA development environment. Once again, this book guides you through the new features of VSTO and helps you understand how to transfer your hard-earned VBA skills to the new Visual Studio based development environment.

In the end, is it worth making the switch from VBA to VSTO? I think you'll find it is. VSTO provides a much richer environment with a lot more power to use in your Office development projects. In the end, you'll write less code and get more done. Isn't that what it's all about?

Kathleen and Paul are great guides to take you on this journey into the new world of VSTO. Kathleen was a programming writer during the development of VSTO—in other words, she had to write about VSTO as we were developing it. I've found that writing about something is one of the best ways to validate the design of something—and sure enough, as Kathleen wrote about VSTO, she would come into my office and point out tons of things that were confusing or just plain wrong. In the end she made VSTO a much better product and she is in a unique position to understand and write about the features of VSTO.

I also have to mention the fantastic videos Kathleen put together about VSTO. If you are still wondering about trying out VSTO in your own projects, check out some of her videos and other contributions to the community she made as a contributor to the VSTO team blog:

http://blogs.msdn.com/vsto2/

Not only do you get Kathleen, you also get Paul's wisdom in this book. Paul was one of the early users of VSTO and he helped guide Microsoft through his participation in the early software design reviews of the VSTO product. He was so helpful, the VSTO team hired him and he continued his role as one of the "first users" of VSTO even after starting at Microsoft. If you search the forums and newsgroups, it will frequently be Paul responding to the difficult VSTO questions posted by developers.

As you might expect, both Paul and Kathleen have great blogs. Check them out here:

http://blogs.msdn.com/kathleen/

http://blogs.msdn.com/pstubbs/

As an early reviewer of this book, I loved how things were kept accessible and practical for a VBA developer. You won't find any C# in this book and that's a good thing. Visual Basic is the best language you can pick for Office development because Visual Basic grew up with Office and has features that make it much easier to use the Office object models. Also, I found some great tips and tricks in this book to make your experience with VSTO a great one—for example, Kathleen and Paul tell you how to set up your environment to make debugging much easier.

Finally, this is the first book that will give you a look at VSTO 2005 Second Edition and the wider range of Office applications you can now target, including Office 2007. I might also add that we are already working on the next generation of VSTO for Office 2007 and we are continuing to work to make VSTO simple and powerful. VSTO is here to stay and this is the book to help the VBA developer make the switch.

Eric Carter
Development Manager, Visual Studio Tools for Office
Microsoft Corporation

Preface

The target audience for Visual Studio Tools for Office (VSTO) is the "professional developer." This term has several meanings, but the most agreed-upon definition we've heard is "someone who gets paid to write code." In other words, it's his or her primary job. It's not the departmental developer—say, an accountant who writes Excel macros as part of his accounting tasks or an office worker who customizes Word to increase her productivity. Instead, it is the .NET developer who might be interested in using Microsoft Office as a development platform.

We believe that the traditional Office developer is also interested in VSTO. Before joining Microsoft, both of us worked as VBA developers, customizing Office applications, and we were very much interested in learning about managed code. We don't think we were unique in that respect. There are millions of VBA developers, and many of them are interested in learning about this next generation of Office development. Current books and documentation for VSTO typically are not written with VBA developers in mind; it's assumed that the developer is familiar with Visual Studio, object-oriented programming, and the .NET Framework. The focus is (understandably) more on the features of VSTO and how to work with the hefty Office object models.

We wanted to write a book for VBA developers. Although you might not be familiar with .NET programming, you have one important advantage: knowledge of the Office object models. As an Office developer, you most likely have power-user knowledge of the Office application and a lot of experience in manipulating the Office object models. We can't think of a better environment for learning about managed code than in the context of something you are already familiar with: Office development.

VSTO brings Office development to the .NET world, and it has both disadvantages and advantages compared with VBA. You can do some amazing things to customize Word, Excel, and Outlook using VSTO—for example, creating a customized task pane, adding smart tags to a document, and binding objects on a document to a data source. With VSTO 2005 SE, you can create add-ins for six Office applications, customize the new Ribbon feature of the 2007 Microsoft Office system, and create application-level custom task panes.

We've had the advantage of working with the folks who designed, coded, tested, and documented VSTO, and we have learned a great deal from all of them. We've had an insider view of VSTO, and we hope to convey that information to you in an understandable and enjoyable manner.

—Kathleen McGrath

—Paul Stubbs

Introduction

There are millions of Microsoft Office developers in the world. Most people who create Visual Basic for Applications (VBA) solutions do not think of themselves as Office developers, but they are. In fact, if you use VBA to customize Office documents, you're using one of the most popular development platforms out there.

You may have started your development career by recording macros in Word or Excel to automate a repetitive task. You then quickly moved on to adjusting your macros to get them to work exactly the way you needed them to. You may have experienced the excitement of being the office hero by getting an important document created for the boss on time. If you're like many people, you've dug further into VBA coding. You are now creating your VBA projects from scratch, and the number of lines of code has exploded. You may have even reached a point where you've discovered some limitations of VBA that prevent you from creating your solution exactly the way you want it.

You may have heard that Microsoft is not actively adding new features to the VBA language. That is not to say that Microsoft will stop supporting VBA. It does mean, however, that advances in new features will not be added—for example, Web services, XML, and other features such as code snippets. If you use Visual Studio 2005 Tools for Office (VSTO) and Visual Basic, though, you can take advantage of these new features.

You may have already started your transition to using VSTO for Office development and want to learn more. Maybe you are just now starting to kick the tires to try out VSTO and see what kinds of enhancements you can make to your solutions using managed code.

In short, no matter how far along you are in making the transition to a new level of productivity with VSTO and Visual Basic 2005, this book will help you get there.

Who Should Read This Book

We wrote this book with the VBA developer in mind. "VBA developer" is a broad term that can include anyone who has recorded a simple macro as well as professional developers who create enterprise solutions. This book was written for those people, from the novice VBA developer who understands a little bit about programming VBA to the higher-end developer who may already work with Visual Basic 6.0 or Visual Basic 2005.

This book is all about making the transition from VBA to Visual Basic 2005 and VSTO. You will learn how to create great Office solutions using Visual Basic 2005, which is arguably the best Office development language you can use.

The Purpose of This Book

Both of us come from a background of creating Office solutions with VBA, and we saw the need to help others make the transition to managed programming using Visual Studio 2005 and VSTO. Working on the VSTO team has given us a deep understanding of the features and capabilities of VSTO and Office development. We speak to many VBA developers who have questions about how to translate code that they've written in VBA to VSTO and Visual Basic 2005. Over the years, we started to see a pattern in the issues that VBA developers were having. We decided to write this book to address those needs.

How to Read This Book

We have written the chapters to be read in order. Each chapter builds upon concepts of the previous chapters. The complexity of the concepts also grows with each chapter.

In the beginning, we show you how to do the basics, like creating a project and running it. If you are new to VSTO or Visual Basic 2005, we recommend that you start at the beginning and work your way through the book. If you are familiar with Office and .NET programming, you may want to skip directly to the chapters that interest you.

We have also included advanced samples in the appendixes for your use when you feel comfortable with VSTO programming. Appendix A shows you how to create XML code snippets. These snippets allow you to insert your code into your solutions to make it easier and faster to create great applications. Appendix B shows you one way to create toolbars for Outlook Inspectors.

How This Book Is Organized

Here is a brief overview of each chapter.

Part I: Introduction to VSTO

Chapter 1, Getting Started with VSTO, introduces you to VSTO. The chapter shows you how to create solutions using the Visual Studio integrated development environment (IDE). This chapter also introduces you to some of the VSTO features that you will learn in detail in other chapters.

Chapter 2, The Programming Environment, shows you how to use some of the features of the IDE, including how to build, run, and debug your solutions. This chapter also shows you how to use the integrated Help system to easily find information about programming with VSTO.

Chapter 3, Introduction to Managed Code, teaches you the fundamentals of the .NET Framework, including a discussion of object-oriented programming and new Visual Basic 2005 features. In this chapter you will also explore features of the common language runtime and the Office primary interop assemblies (PIAs).

Chapter 4, Moving from VBA to VSTO and Visual Basic 2005, discusses the reasons for moving to Visual Basic from VBA and shows you new and powerful Visual Basic features that are not available in VBA. You will also see how to migrate key language features from VBA to Visual Basic 2005, such as moving from UserForms to Windows Forms.

Part II: Word and Excel

Chapter 5, Customizing Word and Excel Task Panes, introduces you to the Document Actions task pane. You will learn how to manage and design the actions pane. You will also learn how to create powerful context-aware solutions using XML and the actions pane.

Chapter 6, Customizing Word with VSTO, shows you how to create Word projects and explains the structure behind a project. You will also learn how to work with Word controls on documents to bind data and handle events.

Chapter 7, Customizing Excel with VSTO, shows you how to create Excel projects and explains the structure behind a project. You will also learn how to work with Excel controls on worksheets to bind data and handle events.

Chapter 8, Controls in Word and Excel, shows you how to add controls to your solutions. You will learn how to add controls to toolbars and menus, how to use Windows Forms controls on your document or workbook, and how to create controls at run time.

Chapter 9, Smart Tags in Word and Excel, teaches you how to create document-level VSTO smart tags in Word and Excel. You will learn how to recognize terms and expressions and how to handle the actions of a smart tag.

Part III: Outlook and Beyond

Chapter 10, Creating Add-ins for Outlook with VSTO, explains how to create application-level customizations for Outlook. You will be introduced to the Outlook object model and will learn how to customize the menus and toolbars. You will also learn how to secure and debug an Outlook add-in.

Chapter 11, Security and Deployment, introduces you to the VSTO security model and shows you how to secure and deploy your Word, Excel, and Outlook projects. You will see how to deploy using the Publish Wizard and Visual Studio Setup projects.

Chapter 12, Migrating VBA Solutions to VSTO, describes reasons to migrate VBA solutions to VSTO. You will learn some conversion strategies and will walk through a sample conversion.

Chapter 13, Advanced Topics in VSTO, discusses how to add a VSTO customization to (and remove it from) a document. This chapter also shows you how to access the data cache in VSTO documents on the server.

Chapter 14, VSTO 2005 SE and the 2007 Microsoft Office System, contains examples of using VSTO with Office 2007. You will learn how to program new features of Office 2007, such as application-level custom task panes, Office ribbons, and Outlook form regions.

Acknowledgments

I would like to thank my husband, Mark Shelton, for his support throughout this endeavor, for reviewing many of the chapters, and for his extreme patience during the time I spent focused on this project. Also a huge thanks goes to my coauthor, Paul Stubbs. Paul's technical expertise, commitment to completing this project, and sense of humor have been greatly appreciated.

—Kathleen McGrath

I would like to thank my family for supporting me through the long hours of writing and rewriting, and especially my wife for taking care of everything, enabling me to focus on writing the best book possible. I would also like to thank Kathleen for inviting me write a few chapters for the book. Kathleen has been great to work with and her passion for VSTO is what has made this book possible.

—Paul Stubbs

We would also like to thank our editor, Joan Murray, for giving us the opportunity to write this book and for walking us through the process. A special thanks to our series editor, Mike Hernandez, for allowing this book to be the first product-specific book in his Mere Mortals series.

Next we'd like to thank our technical editors and the production and marketing teams at Addison-Wesley, especially Kim Boedigheimer, John Fuller, Lara Wysong, Curt Johnson, and Eric Garulay. And a thank you and acknowledgment to all of the technical reviewers who provided us with valuable feedback, including Eric Carter, Mei Liang, Justin Whitney, Peter Jausovec, Rory Plaire, Joe Kunk, McLean Schofield, Thomas Quinn, and Frank Rice. Kudos to everyone on the VSTO product team for creating such a great product!

About the Authors

Kathleen McGrath is a programming writer at Microsoft. She has written documentation for Visual Studio 2005 Tools for the Microsoft Office System (VSTO), Visual Studio Tools for Applications (VSTA), and Visual Basic. Prior to joining Microsoft, she worked as a VBA developer customizing Word applications in the financial printing and legal industries. Kathleen has also created short video demonstrations of the features of VSTO and Visual Basic on her blog at http://blogs.msdn.com/kathleen.

Paul Stubbs works as a program manager with the Visual Studio Tools for Office (VSTO) team at Microsoft. In addition to VSTO, Paul works with the VSTA team developing a new managed code application programmability development tool for InfoPath 2007 and independent software vendors (ISVs). Paul has written for *MSDN Magazine* and has spoken at such events as TechEd and TechReady. Paul also participates in the developer community on the Microsoft forums and his blog at http://blogs.msdn.com/pstubbs.

Part I

Introduction to VSTO

Getting Started with VSTO

A journey of a thousand miles begins with a single step.
—CONFUCIUS

Topics Covered in This Chapter

What Is VSTO?

Why Use VSTO Instead of VBA?

Features of VSTO

Creating VSTO Solutions

How VSTO Integrates with Visual Studio

Summary

Review Questions

What Is VSTO?

Visual Studio 2005 Tools for Office (VSTO) enables you to extend Office 2003 applications—such as Word, Excel, InfoPath, and Outlook—using either Visual Basic 2005 or Visual C#. Instead of using Visual Basic for Applications (VBA) and the Visual Basic Editor (VBE) from within Office, you use the robust Visual Studio development environment to create your customizations. Whether you're creating a simple data entry application or complex enterprise solutions, VSTO makes it easy.

As the name suggests, VSTO is a toolset within Visual Studio for creating custom Office applications. To get the VSTO functionality in Visual Studio, you must install either the stand-alone edition of Visual Studio 2005 Tools for the Microsoft Office System or Visual Studio Team System.

To customize Office using VSTO, you start by creating a new Office project in Visual Studio. Five types of Office-related Visual Studio project templates are included in a default installation of VSTO: four project templates for creating document-level customizations for Word and Excel, and one project template for creating an application-level customization in the form of an Outlook add-in. VSTO also includes an optional template for InfoPath extensions. However, because this book is written for developers who are interested in moving from VBA to VSTO, InfoPath development is not described. InfoPath has never supported VBA and so a comparison cannot be made.

A *document-level customization* means that the code is associated with a particular document rather than the entire application. Keep in mind that the code does not reside in the document or a template, as is the case with VBA customizations. Instead, the code lives inside a code library called an *assembly* that is associated with the document. After you create a new VSTO project, you can access the objects in the Office object models via a *primary interop assembly* (PIA). The Office PIAs allow VSTO customizations to interact with the Office object model. You'll learn more about assemblies in Chapter 3, Introduction to Managed Code.

VSTO also provides enhanced Office objects that you can program against. For example, you'll find VSTO versions of an Excel workbook, worksheet, and range that have extended functionality not found in the native Excel object model. You can, for example, add .NET controls, known as *Windows Forms controls,* directly to an Excel spreadsheet or Word document and then bind data directly to the controls.

An *application-level customization* is available to the entire application. VSTO provides an add-in template for Outlook 2003. With Visual Studio 2005 Tools for the 2007 Microsoft Office System (VSTO 2005 SE), you can create add-ins for six applications in the 2007 release of Office and five applications in the 2003 release of Office. You will learn more about VSTO 2005 SE in Chapter 14.

Why Use VSTO Instead of VBA?

VSTO provides a professional development environment for developers who want to build applications that target Office. There are many reasons you might want to create solutions using VSTO, as well as some reasons VBA might be the better choice for your solution.

You might choose VBA to create an Office solution if you want to do the following:

- Create application-level customizations for versions of Office older than Office 2003 Professional

- Create application-level customizations for Office applications, such as Microsoft Access, that are not supported in VSTO or VSTO 2005 SE

- Create document-level customizations for Office 2003 (Standard Edition)

- Create application-level customizations for Word and Excel by using global templates

- Override native commands of Word, Excel, and Outlook by creating a macro that has the same name as the command you want to override

- Adhere to organizational requirements that prohibit deploying the .NET Framework to end-user computers

You might choose to use VSTO or VSTO 2005 SE to create an Office solution if you want to do the following:

- Easily add smart tags to your solutions

- Provide smart tags that are available only to a particular document

- Use a richer set of controls both on the document and on the task pane

- Store data in a document for offline use that can easily be updated the next time the document is online

- Create add-ins that have a stable loading and unloading mechanism

- Customize the task pane using only a few lines of code

- Easily customize the Ribbon in Office 2007

- Customize Outlook 2007 form regions

- Access the .NET Framework class libraries

- Use more robust debugging tools

- Gain access to the many tools in Visual Studio's integrated development environment (IDE), such as the Data Sources window and rich IntelliSense features

- Write your solution in managed code using a professional development language such as Visual Basic 2005 or Visual C#

- Use an easier method of maintaining code and updating deployed solutions, making code changes in one location (within a single assembly) rather than within multiple copies of a document or in a global template

- Reduce the possibility of macro viruses by preventing end users from deciding whether code is safe to run

- Gain data binding capabilities for objects on a document within your Office solutions

- Gain access to the events exposed on the extended Office objects that VSTO provides

For discussion of the main language differences between VBA and Visual Basic 2005, see Chapter 4, Moving from VBA to VSTO and Visual Basic 2005. For a description of how to migrate solutions from VBA to VSTO, see Chapter 12, Migrating VBA Solutions to VSTO.

Features of VSTO

VSTO provides a programming model that extends some of the common objects in Word and Excel, such as a bookmark or range. These objects now have data binding capabilities. For example, you can bind a field in a database to a cell in Excel. With data binding, you can automatically populate areas of your document with data and update the data in a database with user input.

The idea behind VSTO's programming model is to separate data from the presentation of the data. You now can directly access the data that resides in a data source without having to locate the object that displays the data in the document. Data sources can include a database, an Extensible Markup Language (XML) file, or even a text file.

Data binding is especially useful for server-side programming. VSTO enables you to store data in the document that is accessible from external applications (without the need to open the document). You do this by storing the data in an XML data island, or data cache. If you store your data in a data cache, you can then access the data cache on the server without having to open the document or install Word or Excel on the server.

Another way VSTO objects are extended is that they add events that are not available on the native object. For example, you can now program against the change event of a worksheet cell without having to traverse the object model and write numerous lines of code to figure out which cell has changed. When you add these extended objects to your document or worksheet, VSTO creates them as first-class .NET objects that you can program directly against. These objects are known as *host controls,* and the documents or worksheets to which you add the host controls are known as *host items.*

With VSTO 2005 SE, you can create application-level add-ins for Office 2003 and the 2007 Microsoft Office system. VSTO 2005 SE also enables you to customize the new UI of Office 2007, including the Ribbon, the custom task pane, and the Outlook form regions.

Host Items and Host Controls

As mentioned earlier, a host item is a class that represents the entry point into the Office object model. Four host items in Excel are created by default when you create an Excel solution: Workbook, Sheet1, Sheet2, and Sheet3. If you add more worksheets at design time, the new worksheets are created as host items. The host item extends the native Office document by enabling data binding and providing additional events.

One way to think of the host item is that it is the design surface of Word or Excel that acts as a container for controls. In the same way that you add controls to a UserForm in VBA, you can add Windows Forms controls as well as host controls to a host item. The exception to this rule is the workbook host item. The workbook can contain components, but not controls.

In Word, only one host item—the document—is automatically created when you create a Word solution in VSTO. In Excel, each worksheet, chartsheet, and workbook is considered a host item. If you add more worksheets at design time, VSTO creates them as host items in the project.

VSTO doesn't automatically create the worksheets as host items if they are added programmatically at run time. This means that if you programmatically add a worksheet to your workbook, the worksheet is created as a native Excel worksheet rather than a host item. Because the worksheet is not a host item, you do not get the worksheet's extended functionality, and you cannot programmatically add controls to it, as you can when the worksheet is created at design time. Controls can be added only to a host item worksheet.

VSTO provides a Controls collection for all the controls (host controls as well as Windows Forms controls) that you add to a document or worksheet. Whenever you add a control to a document, it is added to the document's Controls collection. In Excel, each worksheet contains its own Controls collection instance. Host controls can be created at design time or at run time. VSTO provides a number of helper methods (described in Chapters 6 and 7) that you can use to dynamically add host controls to your document.

VSTO extends three objects in the Word object model into host controls: the Bookmark, XMLNode, and XMLNodes controls. In addition to enabling data binding and events for these controls, VSTO improves the functionality of some of the objects. For example, assigning text to a VSTO bookmark does not cause the bookmark to be deleted (as it does when text is assigned to a native Word bookmark). Extended Excel objects include NamedRange, ListObject, XMLMappedRange, and Chart.

You can add the host controls to a document using Word's or Excel's native functionality. For example, if you select a Bookmark from the Insert menu in Word at design time, it is added as a host control. Some of these controls can be dragged from the Toolbox onto the document. The Toolbox contains all the controls that can be added to a design surface and is similar in concept to the toolbox in the VBE.

When the Excel workbook designer has focus, a NamedRange and ListObject control appears in the Toolbox on the Excel Controls tab. When a Word document has focus, a Bookmark control is available on the Toolbox in the Word Controls tab. Figure 1.1 displays the host controls on the Toolbox for Word and Excel.

Additional host controls exist for Word and Excel, but these host controls are not available on the Toolbox. These host controls include Excel's Chart and XMLMappedRange controls and Word's XMLNode and XMLNodes controls. In Chapters 6 and 7 you will learn more about how these controls can be added to a document.

In addition to data binding, the main functionality that is provided for extended Office objects is events. Many of the Office object model

Figure 1.1. *Host controls for Word and Excel on the Visual Studio Toolbox*

objects do not natively expose events. For example, the only way to determine whether a cell's value has changed in VBA is to first check the Change event of the entire worksheet. You then must determine whether the change occurred within a particular cell on that worksheet. With VSTO, you can write code directly in the Change event handler of the NamedRange control. In Word, you can now write code in the BeforeRightClick event handler of a Bookmark. For example, you could create a context menu that appears whenever text within a bookmark is right-clicked.

Windows Forms Controls

Word and Excel have a number of controls that can be added directly to a document and against which you can write code in VBA to respond to the control's events. These controls are not always stable on documents, and there is a limit to the number of controls available. Creation of these controls is not supported in VSTO. Instead, you can use Windows Forms controls.

VSTO lets you add Windows Forms controls to a document or worksheet. These controls have all the properties and events of regular Windows

Forms controls that you would normally add to a Windows Form, but there are some differences in the behavior of a control on a document versus the behavior of a control on a Windows Form. For example, you cannot set the tab order of the controls that reside on a document, because you cannot tab from control to control on a document.

You can add Windows Forms controls to the document at design time or at run time. As with host controls, you add Windows Forms controls to the Controls collection of the document or worksheet. The Windows Forms controls are not embedded directly in the document. Instead, they are embedded in an ActiveX control, which is embedded in the document. For that reason, you cannot programmatically add the control to the document in the same way you would add a control to a Windows Form. In VSTO, you must use helper methods to programmatically add controls to a document. There is even a generic AddControl method for adding controls that do not have helper methods specific to the desired control. Adding Windows Forms controls to documents is covered in more detail in Chapter 8.

Because of technical limitations, you cannot add some controls to a document when you're creating your solution (at design time). Therefore, VSTO adds only a subset of the Windows Forms controls to the Toolbox for use on Word and Excel documents. For example, you cannot drag a GroupBox control to a document in order to group related controls at design time, so the GroupBox control is not made available in the toolbox. Figure 1.2 displays all the supported Windows Forms controls that can be added to a Word document or Excel worksheet at design time.

In addition to support for host controls and Windows Forms controls on documents, VSTO has many other features. You can add smart tags to a document or worksheet, cache data in a document, customize the task pane, create managed add-ins, write more secure customization code, customize the UI in Office 2007, and work in a more robust developer environment.

Figure 1.2. *Windows Forms controls for Word and Excel on the Visual Studio toolbox*

Smart Tags

Creating smart tags for Word and Excel has never been easier. VSTO provides a SmartTag class that enables you to add smart tags to the document by specifying terms to recognize and actions to take when those terms are recognized. Note, however, that the smart tags are specific to a document rather than to the entire application. Thus, you can control the number of smart tag recognizers for a particular document. Smart tags are covered in more detail in Chapter 9.

Customizing Task Panes

Microsoft Office 2003 provided many of the UI elements of the application in the task pane, such as the Styles and Formatting task pane (Word) and the New Workbook task pane (Excel). There is no way to customize this task pane using VBA, but you can create a smart document using Visual Basic 6 or Visual Basic .NET, or by using XML. These methods of customizing the task pane are difficult at best, and it can be a challenge to identify errors in the required XML expansion pack. Additionally, you must implement the ISmartDocument interface, and that requires many lines of code just to add a single control to the task pane.

VSTO enables you to customize the Document Actions task pane with very little coding. VSTO provides an ActionsPane object that lets you add Windows Forms controls or custom controls to the Word or Excel task pane with one line of code. The VSTO actions pane is built upon existing ISmartDocument technology, but VSTO takes care of all the implementation details for you. For example, you do not need to create and attach an XML expansion pack. Chapter 5 has more about customizing the task pane for Word and Excel solutions.

The actions pane is available only to document-level customizations in Word and Excel. If you want to customize the new application-level custom task pane in Office 2007, you must add controls to the CustomTaskPane object. Chapter 14 has more about how to add controls to the custom task pane.

Caching Data in a Document

VSTO provides a data cache for storing data in a dataset inside the document, known as a *data island.* You can cache the data in the data island so that you still have access to the data when you are not connected to a network and can then update the data source after a connection has been reestablished.

This capability is also useful when the target document exists on a server. Running Word or Excel on a server is not a Microsoft-supported scenario. Instead, VSTO enables you to access data in a document without having to run Word or Excel on the server. Data caching in Word and Excel is described in Chapter 13, Advanced Topics in VSTO.

Managed Add-ins

VSTO provides an Outlook Add-in project template that enables you to create managed add-ins for Outlook 2003. VSTO 2005 SE enables add-in creation for the 2003 and 2007 releases of Office. Add-ins created with VSTO are more stable and have a simpler event model for loading and unloading the add-ins. Instead of the five events that are used in add-ins created with the IDTExtensibility2 interface, VSTO provides two: the Startup and Shutdown events. This is also consistent with the Startup and Shutdown event handlers that are provided in Excel and Word document-level solutions.

If you create an add-in using VSTO or VSTO 2005 SE, the add-in is loaded into an isolated execution space called an *application domain.* VSTO then ensures that the add-in is unloaded properly when the add-in is disconnected or when the application is closed. In Chapter 10 you'll find more information about creating managed add-ins for Outlook 2003 using VSTO, and Chapter 14 has more about creating managed add-ins with VSTO 2005 SE.

Security and Deployment

Because you use Visual Studio to customize Office applications, you have access to all the security features of the .NET Framework. End users can change the macro security settings of their Office applications so that all code runs or so that they are always prompted for permission to run the code. Typically, end users just click OK on a dialog box that asks whether they want to trust the code.

Instead of leaving this decision to the end user, VSTO uses the *code access security* (CAS) features of the .NET Framework. CAS determines whether code is safe to run based on criteria such as the location of the code, whether the code is signed, and the permissions that have been set by an administrator.

These security requirements make deployment more complex than that required to deploy a VBA solution, because you must set security to grant permissions to assemblies that you deploy. Gone are the days of sending end users an e-mail with an attached solution that just runs whenever the attachment is opened. But also gone are the days when an end user could accidentally run malicious code that was e-mailed in a document. Security and deployment are covered in more detail in Chapter 11.

Ribbon Support

The *Ribbon* is a new feature in Office 2007 that replaces the traditional menus and toolbars. Using VSTO 2005 SE, you can customize the Ribbon by adding tabs, groups, and buttons or by hiding existing UI elements on the Ribbon. You'll learn more in Chapter 14 about customizing the Ribbon.

Enhanced Development Environment

Because VSTO solutions are created in Visual Studio, you will have access to all the advanced tools available in the IDE, such as the Data Sources window. The enhanced development environment that is available to VSTO solutions developers is described in greater detail in Chapter 2.

Creating VSTO Solutions

Creating Office customizations with VBA has some similarities to creating Office solutions with VSTO, but there are many differences.

Creating Office Solutions with VBA

When you create a VBA solution, you start in the Office application. In Word and Excel, you can press ALT+F11 to open the Visual Basic Editor. Within the VBE, you have access to projects for any documents that are currently open, templates that the document is based on, and any globally accessible templates. You can choose to add your code in a module within the document, or in an attached or globally available template, such as Normal.dot.

When you add your code to ThisDocument or ThisWorkbook, or to a new module that you've added to the document project, that code will be available only to the document or workbook in which you've added the code. If you add the code to a template, the code will be available either to documents based on that template or, in the case of a global template, to any document that is opened using the application.

You can access the VBE from Outlook, but Outlook can support only one VBA project at a time. Typically, developers create Component Object Model (COM) add-ins for Outlook using the IDTExtensibility2 interface.

Creating Office Solutions with VSTO

When you create a VSTO solution, you start in the Visual Studio IDE. Here you can choose to create a document or template solution for Word or Excel, or an add-in solution for Outlook. If you create an Outlook add-in, it is available to the entire Outlook application. If you choose a Word or Excel document, the code is available only to that document. If you choose a Word or Excel template, the code is available to any document that is created from the template.

When you use VSTO to create a Word or Excel customization, you have full access to the Word or Excel application and object model from within Visual Studio. When you create an add-in, you have access to all the objects in the application through the Application object, but you don't have direct access to the application from within Visual Studio.

The code that you write for a VSTO document-level solution is stored in a code file associated with the document. This is often referred to as *code-behind* file because the code supports the document functionality behind the scenes in the form of an assembly, rather than in embedded code as VBA does. When the code file is compiled into an assembly (DLL), it is then associated with the document. This compiled code can be accessed only at the document level (and not at the application level).

You can also create a VSTO solution based on an Excel template or a Word template. In that case, whenever a document is opened based on that template, your VSTO customization code will run. You cannot create application-level customizations for Word 2003 and Excel 2003 using VSTO; however, you can create application-level add-ins for several Office applications (including Word 2003 and Excel 2003) using VSTO 2005 SE. You'll learn more about this in Chapter 14.

The application-level solutions of VSTO and VSTO 2005 SE are created in the form of an add-in that gets loaded whenever the application is started and is unloaded whenever the application is closed. A user can also manually load and unload the add-in. You can create add-ins that customize your application's user interface, such as adding new menus or menu items in Excel 2003, adding buttons to a Ribbon in Word 2007, or performing a particular action when an application event occurs.

Using VBA, you create application-level customizations in Word by adding code to a global template. This might be the Normal.dot template or a custom template that you make global to the application by storing the template in the Startup directory. This scenario is not supported in VSTO because VSTO creates customizations that are specific only to an individual document rather than every document that is opened in Word. If you create a VSTO customization using a Word template and then store it in the Startup directory, the customization code associated with the template is not available to all open documents; it runs only when a document based on the template is open. If you want to create an application-level customization for Word, you should create an add-in project using VSTO 2005 SE.

When you use VBA to customize Excel, you can create a type of application-level add-in that uses an Excel add-in file (.xla file). However, you cannot create a VSTO solution using an existing .xla file because this file type is not supported in project creation. Although you can create an Excel VSTO solution and then later save the file as an .xla file that runs the customization code, this scenario is not supported by Microsoft.

Project Types

When you open Visual Studio 2005 and create a new project, you will find a number of Office-related project templates available. The way in which these projects appear in the New Project dialog box differs depending on the environment settings you selected when you installed Visual Studio. In this book, we assume that you are using the Visual Basic profile. In Chapter 2 you'll learn more about the Visual Studio environment settings and ways you can change them.

With a default installation of VSTO, you can create a Word document, a Word template, an Excel workbook, an Excel template, or an Outlook add-in project. You can optionally install the InfoPath toolkit, making the InfoPath template available, as shown in Figure 1.3. To view these project templates, point to New on the File menu and then click Project. You can expand the Visual Basic node to reveal the project template categories. To display the VSTO project templates in the Templates pane of the New Project dialog box, click the Office node.

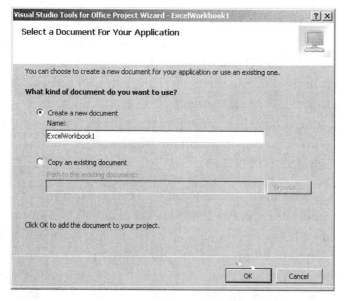

Figure 1.3. *VSTO templates in the New Project dialog box*

If you've installed VSTO 2005 SE on top of VSTO, additional templates are available in the New Project dialog box, as shown in Figure 1.4.

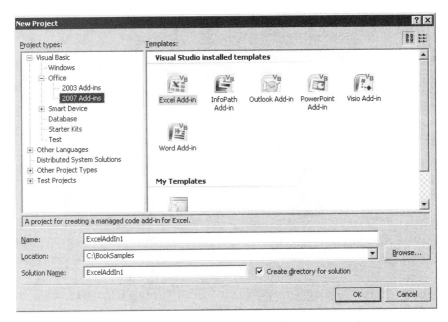

Figure 1.4. *VSTO 2005 SE templates in the New Project dialog box*

Notice that there are a number of add-in project templates for Office 2007 in the 2007 Add-ins node, as well as project templates for Office 2003 in the 2003 Add-ins node.

Excel Workbook

The Excel Workbook project template enables you to create a VSTO customization for an Excel workbook (.xls file). When you choose Excel Workbook in the New Project dialog box and click OK, Visual Studio 2005 presents you with the Visual Studio Tools for Office Project Wizard. Using this wizard, you can choose to customize a new workbook, or you can select an existing workbook, as shown in Figure 1.5.

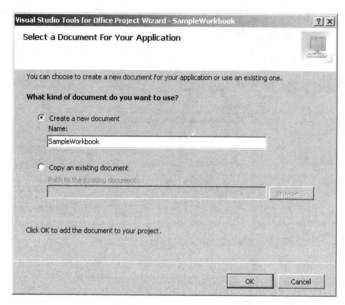

Figure 1.5. *VSTO Project Wizard*

To select an existing document, click Browse and navigate to the workbook that you want to create. Rather than use the selected workbook,
VSTO makes a copy and saves it in the same directory where your VSTO
solution is saved.

Excel Template

The Excel Template project template enables you to create a VSTO
customization for an Excel template (.xlt file). When you select Excel
Template, you can either create a new template or select an existing
one. To select an existing template, you must select a file that has an
.xlt extension. If you want to create a template based on an existing
workbook, you save the workbook as a template outside Visual Studio
before selecting it in the wizard. VSTO copies the template to the same
directory where your VSTO solution is saved.

Word Document

The Word Document project template lets you create a VSTO customization for a Word document (.doc file). When you select Word Document in the New Project dialog box and click OK, Visual Studio displays the Visual Studio Tools for Office Project Wizard. In this wizard, you either create a new document, or select an existing one. VSTO makes a copy of the selected document and saves it to the same directory where your VSTO solution is saved.

Word Template

The Word Template project template enables you to create a VSTO customization for a Word template (.dot file). When you select Word Template, you can create a new template or select an existing one. To select an existing template, you select a file that has a .dot extension. To create a template based on an existing document, you must first save the document as a template outside Visual Studio before selecting it in the wizard. VSTO copies the template to the same directory where your VSTO solution is saved.

Outlook Add-in

In the Outlook Add-in project template, you can create an add-in for Outlook using VSTO. When you select Outlook Add-in, Visual Studio opens the add-in project in code view, displaying the ThisApplication_Startup and ThisApplication_Shutdown event handlers. VSTO also creates a setup project for your Outlook solution. The setup project is used to register and deploy the Outlook add-in.

VSTO 2005 SE Add-ins

If you've installed VSTO 2005 SE, you will find additional project templates for creating add-ins for several Office 2003 and Office 2007 applications, including Word, Excel, Outlook, PowerPoint, Visio, and

InfoPath (2003 only). The architecture of these add-ins differs slightly from that of the VSTO Outlook add-in. When you create a VSTO 2005 SE add-in, Visual Studio opens the add-in project in code view, displaying the ThisAddin_Startup and ThisAddin_Shutdown event handlers.

How VSTO Integrates with Visual Studio

When you create a Word or Excel solutions, using VSTO, you can interact with the Word or Excel application directly from within Visual Studio. This is because VSTO is integrated with Visual Studio.

Word and Excel as Designers

After you have created a new Excel or Word document or template project, the document is available within the Visual Studio environment as a designer. In fact, the entire application is available to you right inside Visual Studio!

A *designer* is a container for the user interface of the application you are building. For example, if you create a UserForm in a Word VBA solution, the VBE displays the UserForm as a designer for your application. You can then add controls to the UserForm. This same experience is now available with Word and Excel solutions when you use VSTO to build your solution. The document is a designer on which you can add controls by dragging them from the Toolbox.

There are two types of controls that can be added to the designer: Windows Forms controls and host controls. These controls are described in Chapter 8, Controls in Word and Excel.

The designer is the visual representation of the application, and each designer is associated with a code file (as mentioned earlier, this code is sometimes referred to as a code-behind file). You can switch from designer view to code view in a number of ways. One way is to right-click the document and then click View Code on the shortcut menu.

When you're in code view, you can right-click the Code Editor and select View Designer from the shortcut menu to open the designer in Visual Studio, as shown in Figure 1.6. You can also right-click the code file in Solution Explorer to open a shortcut menu that gives you both the View Code and View Designer options. You'll learn more about the Code Editor in Chapter 2.

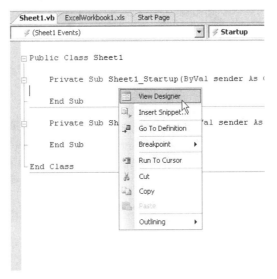

Figure 1.6. *Switching to the designer from the Code Editor*

Code Files in VSTO

When you create a new VSTO solution, Visual Studio creates a number of files. For example, if you create a Word document solution in Visual Studio, you will see the files represented as nodes in Solution Explorer, as shown in Figure 1.7. These files are stored in the location you indicate in the New Project dialog box. In this book, all examples should be saved at the root of your system drive, in a subdirectory named Samples. For example, if your root drive is C:\, you would save the projects in the C:\Samples directory.

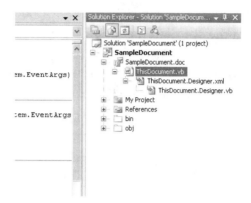

Figure 1.7. *Solution files displayed in Solution Explorer when Show All Files is selected*

You will typically write your code in the ThisDocument.vb source file. This file contains the ThisDocument class, which has two event handlers (ThisDocument_Startup and ThisDocument_Shutdown). You can open this file in Notepad to view its contents. Figure 1.8 shows the contents of a ThisDocument code file when you first create a Word solution using VSTO.

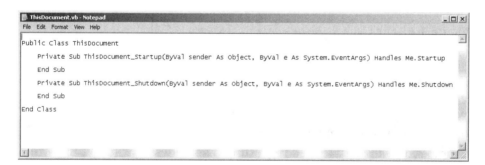

Figure 1.8. *Viewing ThisDocument.vb in Notepad*

Of course, you would not add your code to this file using Notepad, although you could if you wanted to. The ThisDocument.vb file is available to you inside Visual Studio. You can right-click this file in Solution Explorer and select View Code, as shown in Figure 1.9.

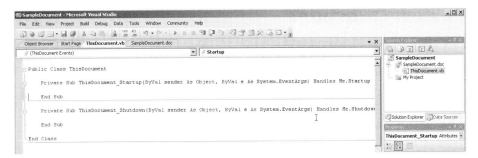

Figure 1.9. *Viewing ThisDocument.vb in Visual Studio*

Here you have all the rich features of the Visual Studio IDE, including IntelliSense and debugging tools to make your coding tasks easier. There are some additional files behind ThisDocument.vb, which holds the code that VSTO automatically generates. The files are ThisDocument.Designer.xml and ThisDocument.Designer.vb. You'll learn more about these files in Chapter 2.

Summary

We started this chapter with a brief introduction to VSTO, and you discovered why you might choose to create an Office solution using VSTO versus using VBA. Next, we looked at the features of VSTO, including the extended Office objects in Word and Excel, support for Windows Forms controls on documents, and support for creating Outlook add-ins. We also described features such as caching data, creating smart tags, and customizing task panes.

Next, we took a closer look at the VSTO project system for creating VSTO solutions in Visual Studio. You learned about VSTO's support for document-level and application-level customizations and reviewed the available VSTO project templates. You learned how VSTO integrates with Visual Studio, with the Word or Excel application being hosted inside Visual Studio. Finally, you learned about the add-ins you can create with VSTO 2005 SE.

Review Questions

1. What are host items and host controls?

2. What is the difference between an application-level customization and a document-level customization?

3. How do Word and Excel integrate with Visual Studio?

4. Are all Windows Forms controls and host controls available on the Toolbox? If not, which type of controls are not supported and why?

5. Name three reasons you might choose to create an Office solution using VBA instead of VSTO.

6. How does a Word template project differ from a Word document project?

7. Name one way that a VSTO add-in project differs from a VSTO 2005 SE add-in project.

2

The Programming Environment

*If debugging is the art of removing bugs, then
programming must be the art of inserting them.*
—ANONYMOUS

Topics Covered in This Chapter

Introduction to the Visual Studio IDE

Viewing IDE Windows

Tools for Writing Code

Building and Running Code

Debugging Your Code

Locating and Using Help

Summary

Review Questions

Introduction to the Visual Studio IDE

The Visual Studio integrated development environment (IDE) consists of
tools to help you create and edit code when developing VSTO and VSTO
2005 SE customizations. If you've ever written any VBA code or even
recorded a macro and then tweaked it to perform a specific task, then
you are already familiar with the VBA development environment, known
as the Visual Basic Editor (VBE).

You might also have experience using the typical editing and debugging
tools, such as setting breakpoints or using IntelliSense. For example,

IntelliSense in VBA makes it easier to write code by displaying a listing of constants, methods, and properties whenever you type a period (.) after typing an object name.

Visual Studio 2005 offers a much richer set of code editing and debugging tools. These tools help you write code quickly, help ensure that there are no compile-time errors, and help you locate and fix run-time errors that might exist in your code.

Environment Settings

When you Install VSTO, you are asked to specify a setting to apply to the Visual Studio 2005 IDE. These settings customize the IDE and include general development settings, Visual Basic settings, and Visual C# settings. The Visual Studio user interface can differ depending on the settings you choose.

In this book, the screen shots reflect the Visual Basic settings. If you have chosen a different setting, your IDE may look different. You can customize your environment settings by clicking Import and Export Settings on the Tools menu. You can export your current settings, import settings from a file, or reset all settings to the default collection of settings.

If you want to change your settings to the Visual Basic profile, first click Reset All Settings and then click Next on the Import and Export Settings Wizard, as shown in Figure 2.1.

Here you can save your current settings or overwrite the existing settings. Make your choice, and then click Next. In the next page of the wizard, select Visual Basic Development Settings, and then click Finish, as shown in Figure 2.2.

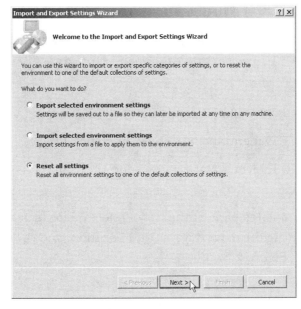

Figure 2.1. *Import and Export Settings Wizard*

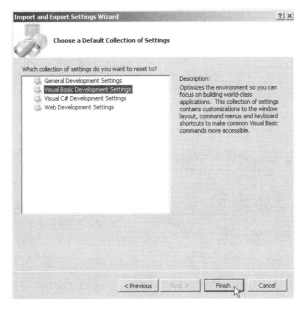

Figure 2.2. *Selecting Visual Basic development settings*

Creating a Visual Studio Tools for Office Project

Before diving into the various windows in the Visual Studio IDE, let's first create a VSTO project and examine the integrated development environment.

1. Open Visual Studio.

2. Click the File menu, point to New, and click Project.

3. In the New Project dialog box, expand the Visual Basic node and click Office.

4. In the Templates pane of the New Project dialog, select Excel Workbook, leaving the default Name and Location, and then click OK, as shown in Figure 2.3.

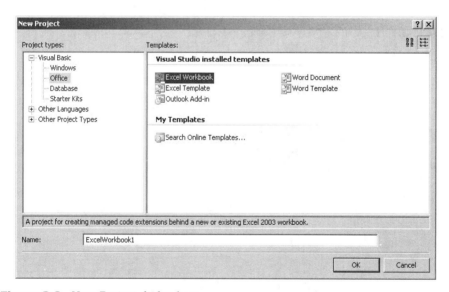

Figure 2.3. *New Project dialog box*

5. In the Visual Studio Project Wizard, select Create a New Document, as shown in Figure 2.4, and then click OK.

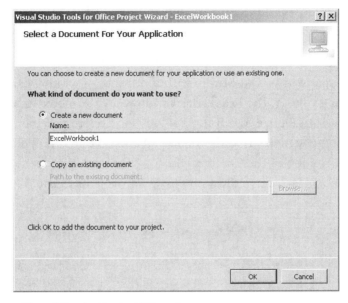

Figure 2.4. *Visual Studio Project Wizard*

Granting Access to the VBA Project System

The very first time you create a VSTO project for Word and Excel, VSTO displays a dialog box informing you that the project must have access to the Visual Basic for Applications project system, as shown in Figure 2.5. You must click OK to create a VSTO project. If you click Cancel, the project will not be created.

Figure 2.5. *Allowing access to the Visual Basic for Applications project system*

This dialog box appears only the first time you create a Word project and the first time you create an Excel project using VSTO. VSTO does not actually use Visual Basic for Applications, but it requires access to the VBA project system in order to support controls on the document.

After you have granted access to the VBA project system, the Excel workbook opens in Visual Studio with a number of windows open, such as Solution Explorer, the Properties window, and Toolbox, similar to the screen shown in Figure 2.6. If the Toolbox isn't open, you can open it by clicking the View menu and then clicking Toolbox. If you click the push-pin icon at the top of the Toolbox, the Toolbox remains open. This makes it easier for you to drag and drop controls onto the document.

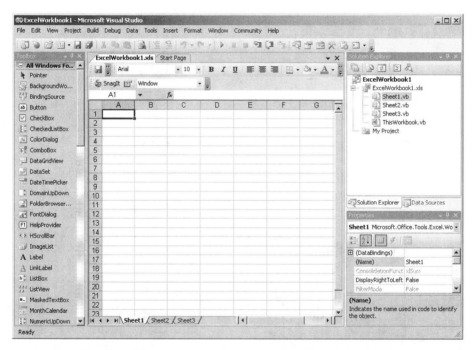

Figure 2.6. *Excel workbook open as the designer in Visual Studio*

Menus and Toolbars

Most of the Office 2003 menus and toolbars available in Word or Excel are available in Visual Studio. For example, in an Excel workbook solution you will notice that the designer (Excel) contains the toolbars. You can show and hide the toolbars by right-clicking the toolbar and clicking a toolbar on the context menu, as shown in Figure 2.7.

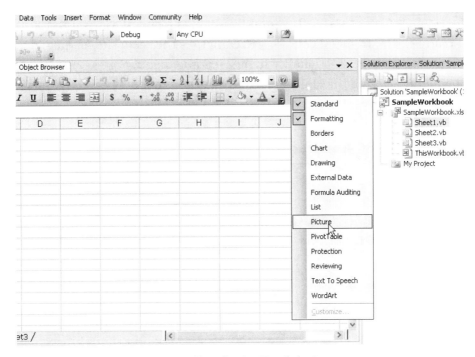

Figure 2.7. *Selecting a new toolbar for the Excel designer*

These toolbar buttons work exactly as they would if you were using the application outside Visual Studio. However, VSTO disables some of these toolbar commands, including the command to customize the toolbar itself. Notice that the Customize menu item is grayed out in Figure 2.7. If you want to customize a toolbar in VSTO, you have to write code.

Notice also that there are no menu items directly above the toolbars for the Excel designer. The same is true for the Word designer. Instead, VSTO merges the menus and menu items with the Visual Studio menus. VSTO organizes these menus and menu items so that the ones particular to Word or Excel are available only when the Word or Excel designer has focus. If you move focus to an area of Visual Studio outside the designer, only the Visual Studio menu items are available.

For example, if you select an Excel worksheet so that it has focus, you will see menus that are specific to Excel, such as the Insert menu. The Insert menu is not visible if Visual Studio has focus. If a menu in Excel already exists in Visual Studio, VSTO merges the menu items, placing the Excel-specific functionality in a cascading menu. Figure 2.8 shows the menu merging that takes place in the Data menu when Excel has focus, and Figure 2.9 shows the Data menu when Visual Studio has focus.

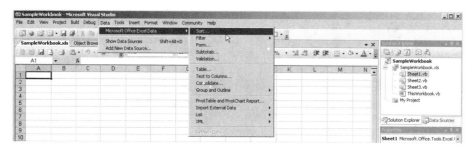

Figure 2.8. *Selecting an Excel command in the Data menu*

Figure 2.9. *Selecting a Visual Studio command in the Data menu*

This menu merging can take a little getting used to. If you can't find a command in the menu, remember that the document designer must have focus for you to view the Word or Excel menu items. First select the document or worksheet, and then you should be able to locate the command.

Because there is no design surface for add-in solutions, no menu merging takes place. You have access only to the code view in the Visual Studio editor, and thus only the Visual Studio menus and toolbars are available when you create an add-in.

Viewing IDE Windows

The Visual Studio IDE makes a number of windows available. These windows provide tools to help you design your application, write and debug code, and navigate your solution in Visual Studio. In this section we look at some of these windows, including Solution Explorer, the Properties window, Object Browser, and Project Properties.

Code View

The windows that are visible may vary according to your settings, but you can view any of the windows by selecting it in the View menu in Visual Studio. There are many ways you can change to code view. One way is to select Code from the View menu. Another way is to right-click the code file in Solution Explorer and then click View Code. A third way is to right-click the document or worksheet and select View Code, as shown in Figure 2.10.

This action changes the view in Visual Studio so that you are now view-ing the code in the Sheet1.vb class. Two methods are visible: Sheet1_Startup and Sheet1_Shutdown. You can add code to the Startup method, which handles the Startup event.

1. As shown in Figure 2.11, add the following code to the Startup method: `MsgBox("Hello world!")`

   When you build and run the project, this code will run as soon as initialization of the document is complete.

Figure 2.10. *Changing to code view*

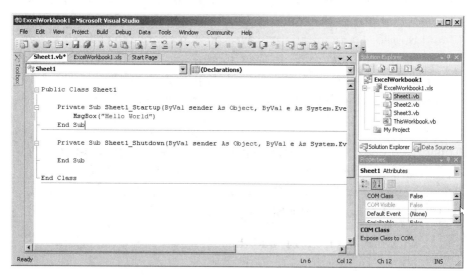

Figure 2.11. *Adding code to the Startup event handler of Sheet1*

> ❖**Note** Although you can display a message box in Visual Basic
> using MsgBox("Hello world") as you can with VBA, you can also
> use MessageBox.Show("Hello world").

2. Press F5 to run the code. When the Excel workbook opens, a mes-
    sage box displays the text "Hello world!"

3. Close the Excel workbook.

Now that you're familiar with creating a simple solution, we can take a
closer look at the various features of VSTO and the Visual Studio IDE.
First, we describe the features you're probably already familiar with
from your days of writing VBA code in the VBE, pointing out any differences and enhancements. These include Solution Explorer, Object
Browser, the Properties window, IntelliSense, and various debugging
windows. Then you will learn about Visual Studio 2005 features that you
might be less familiar with because similar tools do not exist in the VBE.

Exploring Solution Explorer

Visual Studio projects are displayed and managed in a window called
Solution Explorer. Solution Explorer acts as a container for all the items
in your solution. For example, the solution might contain multiple
projects, and each project might contain multiple items such as code
files, Windows forms, or resources.

When you create a VSTO solution, Visual Studio automatically creates
a project for the solution, along with a default set of associated items.
For example, when you create an Excel workbook solution, Visual
Studio automatically adds to your solution a class for a workbook and
classes for each worksheet in the default Excel workbook. Visual
Studio also adds any references that are required by VSTO. For example, a reference is automatically added to the Excel namespace
(Microsoft.Office.Interop.Excel) when you create an Excel workbook
or template project.

Solution Explorer in Visual Studio is similar to Project Explorer in the VBE, in that Solution Explorer displays a hierarchical view of the items in your project. Solution Explorer gives you access to all the projects and project items in your solution and enables you to navigate quickly to a particular file. You can also alternate between designer view and code view by using Solution Explorer. As described earlier, you can right-click a worksheet in Solution Explorer and select View Code from the shortcut menu to display the associated code file. If Solution Explorer is not visible, you can access it by clicking the View menu and then selecting Solution Explorer.

Visual Studio provides an alternative mechanism to Solution Explorer for navigating through the files in your project. After a file has been opened in code view, Visual Studio adds the file to Visual Studio as a tabbed window, as shown in Figure 2.12. You can then navigate to a particular file by clicking the appropriate tab. To close a tabbed window, right-click a tab and then click Close. You can use these code tabs in conjunction with Solution Explorer to help manage your project.

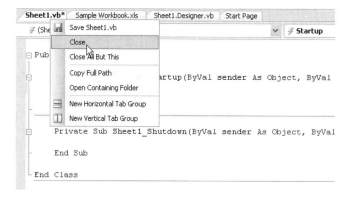

Figure 2.12. *Tabbed windows in Visual Studio*

In Solution Explorer, an Excel workbook solution is at the top of the hierarchical tree and contains a project node. The project node contains the Workbook.xls file, which contains four default code files—Sheet1.vb,

Sheet2.vb, Sheet3.vb, and ThisWorkbook.vb—as shown earlier in Figure 2.11. It is in these code files that you will write the majority of your code when you customize an Excel application.

Note that the number of sheets that are created can vary if you've changed your Excel options to specify a larger or smaller number of sheets to be created in a new blank workbook. You can rename these worksheets in two ways. The first way is within the Excel application, where you right-click the tab at the bottom of the worksheet and click Rename. This action renames only the sheet name that is visible to the end user; it doesn't change the programmatic name. Figure 2.13 shows how Sheet1 was changed to MyWorksheet in the Excel tab, but the name in Solution Explorer is Sheet1.vb (MyWorksheet). If you look at the Properties window, the programmatic name is still Sheet1. When you refer to this worksheet in code, you still must refer to the programmatic name of Sheet1.

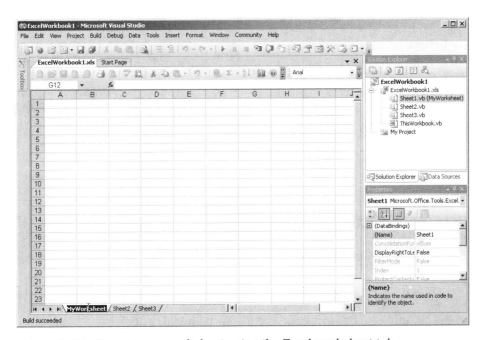

Figure 2.13. *Renaming a worksheet using the Excel worksheet tab*

Similarly, if you use the second technique—renaming the worksheet in the Properties window—only the programmatic name of the worksheet is changed, and it doesn't affect the display name of the worksheet.

Although this might seem strange at first, it's actually a good thing. After you've deployed your solutions to end users, they are free to change the names of the worksheets; but such a change would not cause your code to fail, because the programmatic name of the sheet remains unchanged. If you want to change the display name, file name, and programmatic name so that they are all the same, you can do this by renaming the tab, changing the Name property of the worksheet, and changing the File Name property of the code file, as shown in Figure 2.14.

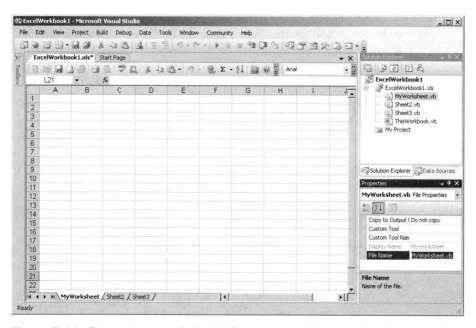

Figure 2.14. *Renaming a worksheet's file name, display name, and programmatic name*

There is only one default code file for Word and Outlook solutions. The default code file in Word is ThisDocument.vb, and the default code file in Outlook is ThisApplication.vb. You'll notice that there is also a My

Project node within the project. The My Project folder gives you access to the properties for the active project and contains information about any project resources.

There are additional (hidden) code files behind each of the class files, and these files are visible only when you click Show All Files in Solution Explorer. Figure 2.15 shows a VSTO Excel solution in Solution Explorer that displays only the default code files (left) and an Excel solution that displays all the code files (right).

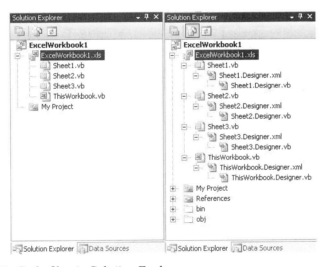

Figure 2.15. *Code files in Solution Explorer*

The additional files listed under each class have the same name as the class but a different extension. For example, Sheet1.vb contains a Sheet1.Designer.xml file and a Sheet1.Designer.vb file. There is a ".Designer.xml" and a ".Designer.vb" file for each workbook and worksheet in the project. The .Designer.xml files are read-only and provide information about programmable objects on the worksheet or in the workbook; these files should not be modified. The Designer.vb files contain auto-generated code.

In VBA, lots of code runs automatically behind the scenes; you concern yourself only with the code that you personally write. In Visual Basic 2005, this auto-generated code is exposed through these hidden files. The idea is that the code you write is separate from the code that gets automatically generated. For example, the initialization code that is generated when you add a button to a document need not be mixed in with the code that you write to handle the button's Click event handler.

Looking at the code in these files can be a great learning tool, but you should not modify it in any way. This is because these code files get regenerated, and any changes you've made will likely get overwritten. For example, if you want to write code to customize Sheet1, you should add the code to the Sheet1.vb source file; you should not modify the Sheet1.Designer.vb source file, because this code will get overwritten when the file is regenerated.

Table 2.1 describes the nodes displayed in Solution Explorer for a Word solution named SampleDocument.

Table 2.1. *Solution Nodes Displayed in Solution Explorer*

Node	Description
Solution 'Sample Document'	The top-level node that represents the solution. A solution is a file used by Visual Studio to manage one or more related projects. In this example, the solution is named SampleDocument. This corresponds to the SampleDocument.sln file saved in the C:\Samples directory.
SampleDocument	The project. In this example, the project is also named SampleDocument. This corresponds to the SampleDocument.vbproj file saved in the C:\Samples directory.
SampleDocument.doc	The Word document that you are customizing.

(continues)

Table 2.1. *Solution Nodes Displayed in Solution Explorer (Continued)*

Node	Description
ThisDocument.vb	The code file that corresponds to the ThisDocument.vb file saved in the C:\Samples directory.
ThisDocument.Designer.xml	An XML file that contains information about controls that are added to the document. This file is visible only when Show All Files is clicked in the toolbar in Solution Explorer. You should not edit this file.
ThisDocument.Designer.vb	The code file that contains the auto-generated code created by the designer. This corresponds to the ThisDocument.Designer.vb file saved in C:\Samples. This file is visible only when Show All Files is clicked in the toolbar in Solution Explorer. You should not edit this file.
MyProject	Contains project settings, such as resources for the solution.
References	Contains references to other managed assemblies or COM type libraries. This file is visible only when Show All Files is clicked in the toolbar in Solution Explorer.
Bin	Contains the compiled solution assembly generated from the code-behind files, which contain your customizations. Also contains related files, such as the Word document that uses the customizations in the compiled assembly. This file is visible only when Show All Files is clicked in the toolbar in Solution Explorer.
Obj	Contains the files that Visual Studio uses to link and create the binary output for a project. This file is visible only when Show All Files is clicked in the toolbar in Solution Explorer.

Similar files are created for Excel and Outlook solutions. For Outlook solutions, the ThisApplication.vb node contains a ThisApplication.Designer.xml file and a ThisApplication.Designer.vb file. In an Excel solution, there is a ThisWorkbook.vb and three worksheet files (Sheet1.vb, Sheet2.vb, and Sheet3.vb). There is a corresponding .Designer.xml and .Designer.vb for each of these files in Excel projects. In VSTO 2005 SE add-ins, a ThisAddin.vb node contains a ThisAddin.Designer.xml file and a ThisAddin.Designer.vb file.

Project Items

The kinds of items available within a VBA project differ from those available in a Visual Studio project. There are basically three types of items you can add to a VBA project: user forms, modules, and class modules. You can also choose to insert an existing file into your project or add references to other assemblies.

Visual Studio offers a number of project items. You can add numerous kinds of items—such as Windows forms, bitmap files, datasets, XML files, and classes—to a project in Visual Studio, as illustrated in the Add New Item dialog box in Figure 2.16. To add a new item to your project, right-click the solution node in Solution Explorer, point to Add, and then click New Item.

In the Add New Item dialog box, you can select the desired item from the Templates list, provide a name for it, and then click Add to insert the item into your project.

Properties Window

Both Visual Studio and the VBE have a Properties window. This window, which displays the properties of the currently selected item in your project, enables you to modify the properties during application design. However, some of the property values do not change until the project is actually running. For example, if you set the Visible property of a Win-

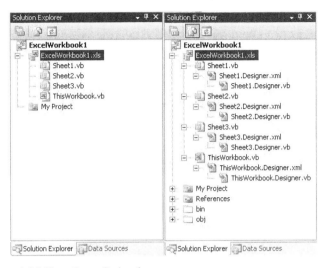

Figure 2.16. *Add New Item dialog box*

dows Form control to False, the control becomes invisible only when the application is running; but if you set the control's Text property, the resulting text can be viewed immediately because it is displayed at design time as well as at run time. Also, some properties cannot be changed at design time, and they are displayed as grayed-out entries. These properties are either informational and cannot be set (read-only) or can be changed only at run time.

When you create a VSTO solution, such as a workbook project, you'll notice that the Properties window displays and makes available the properties of the workbook or any of the worksheets that were created. You get the same behavior in the Excel VBE, but there are some differences. First, you are viewing the properties of two different objects. In the VBE, you are viewing properties of an Excel Worksheet object, and in VSTO, you are viewing properties of a Microsoft.Office.*Tools*.Excel.Worksheet. Because a VSTO worksheet has additional functionality, you'll see additional properties on a VSTO worksheet that are not found on a native worksheet object. For example, notice that there is a DataBindings property, because you can bind data directly to a VSTO worksheet.

If you click the Events button (the lightening bolt) in the Properties window in Visual Studio, it displays all the events that are available for a VSTO worksheet.

Another difference is that many of the properties available in the VBE are not equally available in Visual Studio (and vice versa). One reason is that many of the properties that are available in the VBE are filtered in Visual Studio. Also, Visual Studio displays some read-only properties that are not available in the VBE. Figure 2.17 shows the Properties window for Sheet1 in the VBE and in Visual Studio.

Figure 2.17. *Properties window for Sheet1 in the VBE (left) and in Visual Studio (right)*

Browsing the Object Browser

The Visual Studio IDE has an Object Browser similar to the one you find in the VBE. You can use the Object Browser to view all the methods, properties, and events of a particular object, as shown in Figure 2.18.

For example, you can use the Object Browser to learn about all the extended objects in VSTO. The Object Browser displays all available

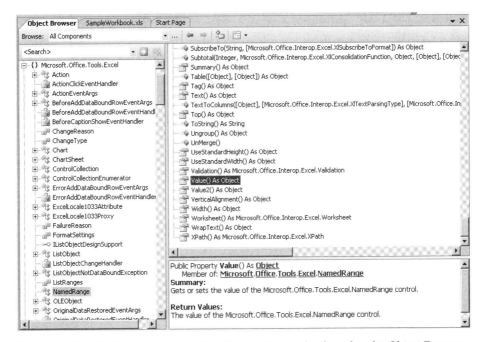

Figure 2.18. *The Value property of the NamedRange displayed in the Object Browser*

objects in your project in the Objects pane on the left. You can expand each object to display additional information, such as its properties, methods, events, and constants. This information appears in the Members pane on the upper-right side.

To open the Object Browser, click the View menu and then click Object Browser. If you want to change the browsing scope of the objects you're viewing, you can use the Browse drop-down menu. For example, if you click the drop-down box and select My Solution, only the namespaces pertinent to your current solution—including all components referenced in your solution—will be visible in the Object Browser. You can also search for objects in the Object Browser by using the Search menu, or you can change the view of the objects, such as displaying only namespaces, base types, derived types, or public members.

When you select an object in the Objects pane, Visual Studio displays its members in the Member pane and displays information about the object in the Description pane in the lower-right portion of the browser. Let's say that you want to see all the properties, methods, and events of a NamedRange. You select the NamedRange object under the Microsoft.Office.Tools.Excel namespace, and all its members are displayed in the Members pane. When you select a particular member, such as Value, the Description pane displays additional information, including a summary and a return value for the property, as shown in Figure 2.18. You can get additional information about the types or members by selecting an object and pressing F1. This action opens a document in Help that pertains to the object under your cursor.

As you browse through the objects in your solution, notice that there are two namespaces listed for Word, for Excel, and for Outlook. In a Word solution, you'll find the Microsoft.Office.*Interop*.Word namespace, which represents the primary interop assembly for Word. There's also a Microsoft.Office.*Tools*.Word namespace, which contains all the VSTO enhanced objects.

In Excel, you'll find a Microsoft.Office.*Interop*.Excel namespace and a corresponding Microsoft.Office.*Tools*.Excel namespace. Similarly, in Outlook, there is a Microsoft.Office.*Interop*.Outlook namespace and a corresponding Microsoft.Office.*Tools*.Outlook namespace.

It's important to note this, because when you want to look up a particular member of an object, you'll want to make sure that you are viewing the member in the appropriate namespace. For example, the members of a Bookmark in Microsoft.Office.*Tools*.Word are different from the members of a Bookmark in Microsoft.Office.*Interop*.Word. You will learn more about these differences in Chapter 6, Customizing Word with VSTO.

Project Properties

You can set various properties for your project using the Project Designer. To open the Project Designer, select <ProjectName> Properties from the Project menu. Or you can double-click the MyProject node in Solution Explorer, as shown in Figure 2.19.

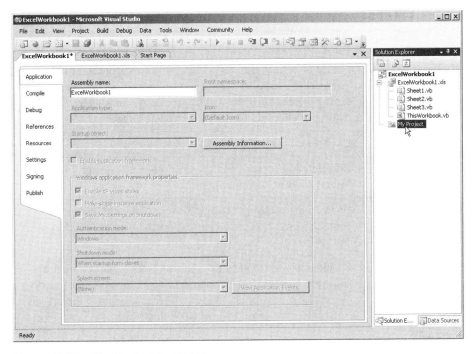

Figure 2.19. *The Project Designer*

Several pages are available in the Project Designer. You can navigate to each page by clicking the appropriate tab on the left side of the window. Table 2.2 briefly describes each page.

Table 2.2. *Project Files Output During Build*

Page	Description
Application	Used to set the application settings for your project, such as the name and version of the assembly.
Compile	Enables you to set parameters for compilation of your project.

(continues)

Table 2.2. *Project Files Output During Build (Continued)*

Page	Description
Debug	Provides debugging properties for your project, such as any actions to take when the application starts, various start options, and the ability to enable debuggers for unmanaged code and SQL Server debugging.
References	Used to manage references in your project.
Resources	Enables you to add and remove resources, such as images, icons, and strings.
Settings	Used to set custom application-specific settings for the project. You can scope the settings to the application or the user.
Signing	Provides a way to sign application and deployment manifests with an Authenticode certificate, as well as to strong-name the assembly. Deployment manifests are described in Chapter 11, Security and Deployment.
Publish	Provides deployment configuration settings. Deployment is described in Chapter 11, Security and Deployment.

Viewing Other Visual Studio Windows

When customizing Office solutions, you will likely often use two additional windows in Visual Studio: the Toolbox and the Data Sources window.

The Toolbox

One of the first things you'll notice when you create a Word or Excel solution is that you open the application in Visual Studio. The Word or Excel document is actually available in your solution as a designer that you can add controls to, in much the same way you would add controls to a Windows form to create a Windows application.

The Toolbox lists all the Windows Forms controls that are available to your solution. The type and number of controls shown on the Toolbox depend on what item in your project has focus. When a Windows form or user control is open in the designer, the controls on the Toolbox are in the System.Windows.Forms namespace. When a Word document or Excel worksheet is open in the designer, the controls on the Toolbox are found in the Microsoft.Office.Tools.Excel.Controls namespace (for Excel controls) or the Microsoft.Office.Tools.Word.Controls namespace (for Word controls). The Toolbox also contains some host controls, such as a Bookmark, NamedRange, and ListObject (see Figure 2.20).

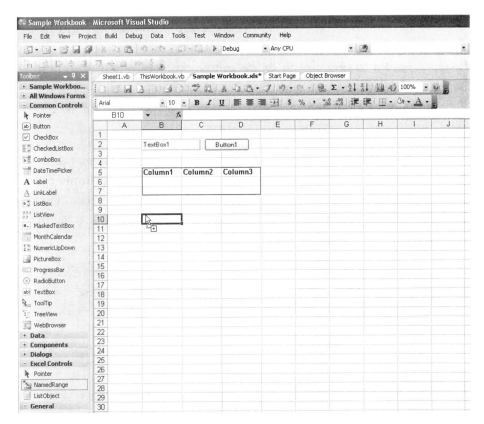

Figure 2.20. *Dragging a control from the Toolbox to the worksheet designer*

The way you add a control to a Windows form, an actions pane control, or a document is similar to the way you add controls to a UserForm in

VBA. You simply drag the control from the Toolbox to an area on the form, actions pane control, or document. If the Toolbox is not open, you can find it in the View menu. Clicking the pushpin icon in the upper-right portion of the Toolbox will keep the Toolbox open as you drag and drop controls to your document.

The Data Sources Window

The Data Sources window is a new feature in Visual Studio 2005 that helps you create or open data connections and bind data to controls in your solution. For example, you can add a Windows form to your solution and bind a combo box on the form to a data source. In the Data Sources window, you can select the desired control and drag it to a Windows form. Visual Studio adds a data-bound control to the Windows form and displays the data when the form is launched.

You can also drag items from the Data Sources window directly to a Word document or Excel worksheet. You can select from a number of controls, including Windows Forms controls and host controls. Figure 2.21 shows the Data Sources window with a connection to the Northwind database in Microsoft Access.

Recall from Chapter 1 that host controls are extended Office objects, such as bookmarks or ranges. Binding data to controls is described more thoroughly in Chapters 6 and 7. To view the Data Sources window, click Show Data Sources on the Data menu.

Tools for Writing Code

A number of tools in the Visual Studio IDE make writing code easier than ever before. In addition to the IntelliSense features of Visual Studio, smart tags detect and mark errors as you type your code, providing error correction options. You can also insert preinstalled code snippets.

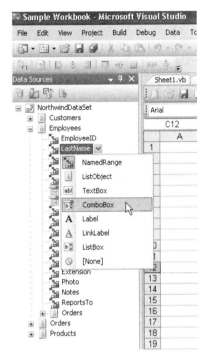

Figure 2.21. *Selecting the control to be added when users drag this data value to a document*

Using IntelliSense

IntelliSense lets you write code quickly by providing information and word completion as you type. IntelliSense is also useful for flagging problems in your code. For example, if you don't see the member of an object that you would expect to see in the List Members list, your code might contain a typographical or other error. Identifying these types of errors as you type code is very useful, because it makes it easy to fix problem code before it has been compiled.

The IntelliSense features of Visual Studio are much richer than those in the VBE. The type of IntelliSense available in Visual Studio includes the following:

- List members

- Parameter Info

- Quick Info

- Complete word

- Code checking, smart tags

- IntelliSense code snippets

List Members

Visual Studio makes it easy for you to explore all the members of an object without having to search through the Object Browser. You can access this information directly in the Code Editor as you type your code. When you type the name of a type or namespace followed by a period (.), Visual Studio displays a list of all the members available for the type or namespace. This feature, also available in the VBE, is known as List Properties/Methods.

In Visual Studio, you can insert an item from the list into your code file by double-clicking the member and pressing TAB or ENTER. A tool tip, known as Quick Info, also appears and displays the declaration of the member. Figure 2.22 shows the members of an ActionsPane displayed in a list, as well as Quick Info for the currently selected item in the list.

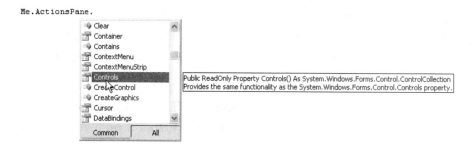

Figure 2.22. *Quick Info for a list member*

Notice the two tabs at the bottom of the list. The Common tab displays the most commonly used members, and the All tab provides a complete list of available methods, properties, and events.

Parameter Info

When you type the name of a property or method and then type an open parenthesis (the "(" key), the Visual Studio IDE displays the necessary parameters, indicating optional ones. This works in the same way as it does in VBA; square brackets ([ ]) surrounding the parameter indicates that the parameter is optional and can be excluded. You also see a description of each parameter, as shown in Figure 2.23. As you type additional parameters, the description is updated.

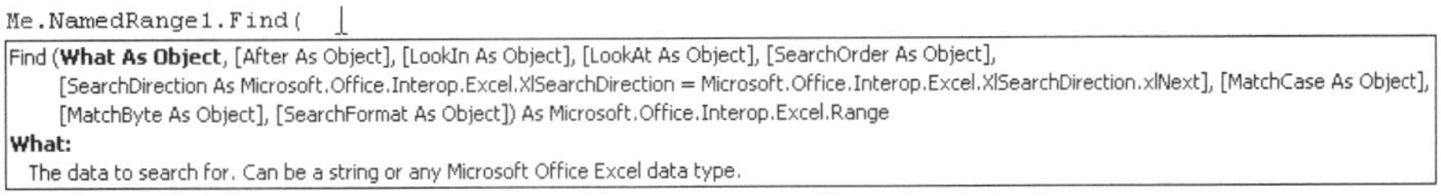

```
Me.NamedRange1.Find( |
Find (What As Object, [After As Object], [LookIn As Object], [LookAt As Object], [SearchOrder As Object],
      [SearchDirection As Microsoft.Office.Interop.Excel.XlSearchDirection = Microsoft.Office.Interop.Excel.XlSearchDirection.xlNext], [MatchCase As Object],
      [MatchByte As Object], [SearchFormat As Object]) As Microsoft.Office.Interop.Excel.Range
What:
   The data to search for. Can be a string or any Microsoft Office Excel data type.
```

Figure 2.23. *Parameter Info for the Find method of an Excel NamedRange*

This rich IntelliSense provides summaries of types, members, and parameters inside IntelliSense tool tips in the Code Editor and in the Object Browser for types or members that exist in the Microsoft.Office.Tools.Excel and Microsoft.Office.Tools.Word namespaces. If you want to have the same type of IntelliSense (with the addition of the summary description) for Microsoft.Office.Tools.Outlook or for the primary interop assemblies (Microsoft.Office.Interop.Word, Microsoft.Office.Interop.Excel, and Microsoft.Office.Interop.Outlook), you must install the IntelliSense XML Files for Visual Studio Tools for Office Developers XML files. To download and install these files, search for "VSTO IntelliSense" on the Microsoft Download Center at http://www.microsoft.com/downloads. Without these IntelliSense XML files, you still get IntelliSense capabilities such as list members and Parameter Info, but you will not have the additional summary descriptions.

Quick Info

A feature in Visual Studio's IntelliSense that is not available in VBA is Quick Info. When you hold the mouse cursor over an identifier, Visual Studio displays a Quick Info tip, which shows the declaration of the identifier. Each time the cursor is moved to a new section of the code, the tool tip displays updated Quick Info about the target identifier. Notice in Figure 2.24 that the tool tip is updated when the cursor position is moved in the code from ActionsPane to Add to DateTimePicker.

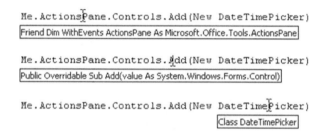

Figure 2.24. *Quick Info displayed when a control is added to the actions pane*

Complete Word

If you're not a very fast typist or you are not sure of the exact member name, then you will probably enjoy the Complete Word feature in Visual Studio. This feature is not available in VBA. When you start typing a word in the Visual Studio Code Editor, you can press ALT+right arrow or CTRL+spacebar, and Visual Studio will automatically complete the word (provided you have typed enough characters that it can be recognized). If several choices are associated with the characters you have typed, Visual Studio provides a drop-down list from which you can choose the correct word. Visual Studio also supports auto-completion of various keywords, such as Option (to turn on Option Strict or Option Explicit) and auto-completion of enumerations.

Many of these IntelliSense options are on by default, but you can modify the settings. For example, in the Options dialog box, shown in

Figure 2.25, you can set statement completion options such as Auto List Members and Parameter Information. To display the Options dialog box, click the Tools menu and then click Options. Expand the Text Editor node, and then select the General tab under the All Languages node. Next, clear the Auto List Members check box or the Parameter Information check box to disable these features. If you want to apply these changes only for Visual Basic, you can optionally change these settings in the General tab under the Basic node.

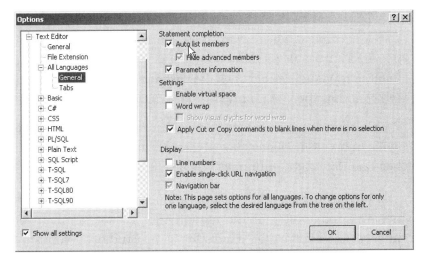

Figure 2.25. *Statement completion options for Text Editor*

Auto-Correct Smart Tags

In the same way that Word places squiggles under errors in grammar or spelling, Visual Studio uses squiggles to indicate errors in code. When a word in your code is marked with a squiggle, you can view more information by holding your mouse cursor over the word to display a tool tip, or you can view the information in the Error List window in Visual Studio. If multiple errors exist, you can click the entry in the error list to move directly to the problem code.

The squiggles come in a variety of colors; each represents a different kind of error or potential problem.

- Red squiggles indicate that your code contains a syntax error. After you correct the syntax error, the squiggle disappears.

- Blue squiggles indicate that your code contains semantic errors. For example, if you misspell the name of a class, the class name will have a blue squiggle under it until you've fixed the error. Visual Studio even provides smart tags with suggestions for fixing the code, as shown earlier in Figure 2.23.

- Green squiggles indicate warnings. For example, if you've declared a variable in your code but have not made any assignment to it, Visual Studio flags the variable with a green squiggle to indicate that there is an unused variable.

- Purple squiggles indicate new errors in code that you've written while in break mode (discussed later in this chapter under the heading Edit and Continue).

When you hold your mouse cursor over a blue-squiggled word, a smart tag panel gives you additional information and presents a way to fix the error quickly. These smart tag panels in Visual Studio are very similar to the smart tags in Word and Excel. They provide an action that you can perform on the erroneous text. When you click the smart tag panel, you can open the Error Correction Options window to select from a list of correction options. In Figure 2.26, the Error Correction Options window displays information about why the error occurred and provides a way to fix it. In this example, you can click the Change 'Strin' to 'String' link and the code is fixed in the Code Editor.

Figure 2.26. *Error Correction Options window*

IntelliSense Code Snippets

One of the nice features of Visual Studio 2005 is the ability to use IntelliSense code snippets. These are XML files that enable you to insert a *shell* procedure into your code and then "fill in the blanks" to make the code snippet specific to your application. They are called IntelliSense code snippets because they are available as you type code directly in the Visual Studio Code Editor, just as other IntelliSense features are available when you type a period after an object name.

You can access IntelliSense code snippets by typing the shortcut name of the code snippet and pressing the TAB key, or by right-clicking the Code Editor and selecting Insert Snippet. Visual Studio ships with a number of IntelliSense code snippets for VSTO, and they are organized by language and category. If you have created a VSTO project for Visual Basic, then when you use the Insert Snippet feature, only the code snippets written in Visual Basic are visible. When you select Insert Snippet from the shortcut menu, a number of folders become visible, as shown in Figure 2.27.

Figure 2.27. *IntelliSense code snippets folders for Visual Basic*

You can then navigate through the folders to the desired snippet. Figure 2.28 shows the code snippets available in the Excel Controls folder under Office Development.

In addition to preinstalled IntelliSense code snippets for VSTO, Visual Studio ships with a number of code snippets for common coding patterns.

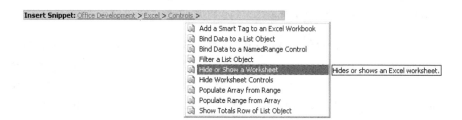

Figure 2.28. *IntelliSense code snippets in the Office Development | Excel | Controls folder*

These snippets include conditionals and loops (such as a Do While loop), exception handling (such as Try Catch statements), and properties, procedures, and type declarations. If a code snippet has an assigned shortcut, you can type the shortcut name and press the TAB key to insert the code snippet into the Code Editor. The code snippet in Figure 2.29 appears in the Code Editor after you type *Property* followed by pressing the TAB key.

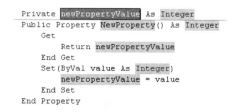

Figure 2.29. *IntelliSense code snippet creating a property*

Visual Studio creates placeholders and highlights each of the items that can be replaced in the code snippet. You can tab from placeholder to placeholder. If you hold your cursor over a placeholder, Visual Studio displays a tool tip that gives you additional information about how to replace the contents of the placeholder. You can learn how to create your own custom XML code snippets in Appendix A.

Edit and Continue

Edit and continue refers to the ability to make changes to code while in break mode and then to resume stepping through the code. A VBA developer would expect to have this feature because it was available in VBA and Visual Basic 6. If you have gone from VBA or Visual Basic 6 to programming with Visual Basic .NET, you will have noticed that this feature was not available before Visual Basic 2005. You'll be equally happy that it is available again in Visual Basic 2005. Typically you can modify any line of code with success, but some modifications are too complex for the Visual Studio Code Editor, and you must rebuild the project.

Building and Running Code

When you build an Office solution in VSTO, the code is compiled, assemblies are created, and the project is output to the \bin directory of your project's location. Several files associated with the project are saved to the output directory, as described in Table 2.3. When an Outlook solution is built, registry entries that are necessary to load the add-in are created on the development computer.

Table 2.3. *Project Files Output During Build*

Word and Excel Projects	Outlook Projects
The project assembly and dependent assemblies that have their Copy Local property set to True (see the Properties window when the project is selected). This property indicates that the assembly can be copied to the output directory.	The project assembly and dependent assemblies that have their Copy Local property set to True. This property indicates that the assembly can be copied to the output directory.

(continues)

Table 2.3. *Project Files Output During Build (Continued)*

Word and Excel Projects	Outlook Projects
The application manifest, which is embedded in the document or workbook. An application manifest is an XML file that contains assembly location information.	The application manifest, which is an external XML file that contains assembly location information.
A program database file (PDB file), which stores information needed when you debug your application.	A program database file (PDB file), which stores information needed when you debug your application.
A copy of the project document or workbook.	

To build a VSTO solution, click Build Solution on the Build menu. If you want to run the solution, either press F5 or click Start Debugging on the Debug menu. This action is similar to clicking Run Sub/User Form to run a VBA solution in the VBE. Because you chose Visual Basic environment settings, Visual Studio automatically determines whether to create a Debug or Release version of your application. For example, you should create a Release version before releasing your solution, but you should create a Debug version while you're coding.

When you select options in the Build menu, Visual Studio automatically creates a Release version; when you select Start from the Debug menu, Visual Studio creates a Debug version of the application. When you start debugging, Visual Studio builds the solution and runs the code if no build errors are encountered. Any build errors that occur are displayed in the Error List window. You can also start the application without using the debugger by pressing CTRL+F5 or by opening the Excel or Word document directly. In either case, the code will run, but you will not be able to debug any errors. This is nice way to test the end user's experience of working with your VSTO solution.

Whenever you build a VSTO project, Visual Studio grants full trust by default (referring to a new .NET security layer known as code access security) to the project assemblies using URL evidence (the directory in which you are running the code). If you move your project to a new location and rebuild it, the permissions for the original location are removed, and new permissions are granted. This means that as long as you are developing your solution, the solution will be granted the permissions needed to run the code on your development machine. But if you move the document or assembly to another folder on your computer without first compiling the code, you will most likely get a security error or a "cannot load assembly" error. If you deploy the solution, you need to set security permissions on the end user's machine, or else the .NET Framework will prevent execution of the code. In Chapter 11 you will learn more about security and deployment.

You can remove the built files from the output directory by clicking Clean Solution on the Build menu. Whenever you run the Rebuild command, Visual Studio first removes the files from the output directory and then rebuilds the solutions. When you click Clean Solution in an add-in, the add-in is removed from the registry and no longer loads when the application is opened.

Debugging Your Code

It has been said that the best measure of good programmers is how well they can debug their code. Visual Studio ships with a number of tools that help you find and fix coding errors. Understanding how and when to use these tools is key to successful debugging. A similar version of some of these tools is available in the VBE, but there is no comparison to the rich features of Visual Studio. In this section, we describe some of the debugging tools you're probably familiar with from using VBA, pointing out any differences or enhancements, and discuss the additional debugging tools that are part of Visual Studio.

When you're ready to debug your application, the first step is to set some debugging options. The first is Break When Exceptions Cross AppDomain or Managed/Native Boundaries (Managed Only). You'll find this option in the Options dialog box under the Debugging tab. An *application domain* is a special environment within which your .NET assembly runs. Unless otherwise specified, managed code runs in the default domain. A VSTO solution assembly runs in a separate application domain that is isolated from the default application domain.

As a result, exceptions thrown in event handlers are often ignored, and code execution continues without displaying the exception—or it simply fails without any warning or explanation—because exceptions don't cross the boundary between these application domains. However, if you select the Break When Exceptions Cross check box, the code enters break mode and the exceptions are displayed when the solution is run from Visual Studio. You can open this dialog box by selecting Options from the Tools menu. You will learn more about application domains in Chapter 3.

The second option you should set is in the Exceptions dialog box (click Exceptions on the Debug menu). Select Common Language Runtime Exception, and select both the Thrown check box and the User-Unhandled check box. When a common language runtime exception is thrown, it will break into the debugger even if you've written code to handle the exception, such as enclosing the code in a Try Catch statement. The Options and Exceptions dialog boxes are shown in Figure 2.30. You can set additional options in these dialog boxes, such as choosing Edit and Continue or Just-in-Time debugging.

When you're debugging Excel solutions, another option you might consider is to temporarily set the ExcelLocale1033 attribute setting to False. By default, this attribute is set to True, and it ensures that the data passed to the Excel object model is formatted as English (United States) regardless of the locale currently set for the computer. This is the same behavior you get when you create solutions using VBA.

For VSTO to duplicate this behavior, it creates a thin wrapper for each object (called a *transparent proxy*) that tells Excel that the locale is English (United States). Unfortunately, when you are debugging Excel

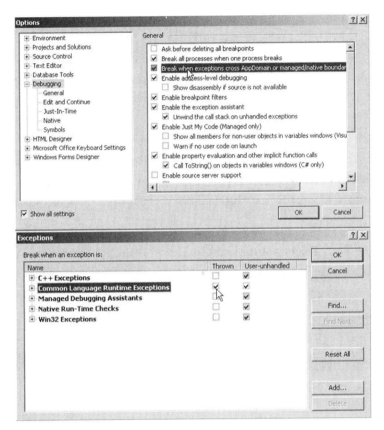

Figure 2.30. *VSTO debugging options*

solutions, these objects are of type _TransparentProxy, and you cannot obtain any additional information about an object (such as the values of its members) because the wrapper isn't transparent to the debugger. Figure 2.31 shows an Excel Range object in the debugger when the ExcelLocale1033 attribute is set to True.

```
Dim myRange As Excel.Range = Me.Range("A1")
```
myRange {System.Runtime.Remoting.Proxies._TransparentProxy}
Children could not be evaluated

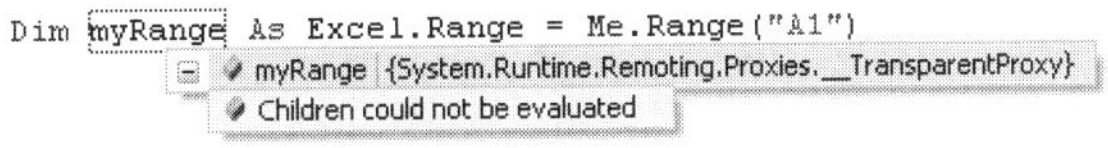

Figure 2.31. *Excel object types when the ExcelLocale1033 attribute is set to True*

You can change the setting for the ExcelLocale1033 attribute in the AssemblyInfo.vb file, which is located in the My Project folder of the directory where you saved your project. You can access this file in Solution Explorer if you click Show All Files on the Solution Explorer toolbar. The attribute is set as follows:

```
<Assembly: ExcelLocale1033(True)>
```

Figure 2.32 shows the ExcelLocale1033 attribute being changed to False in the AssemblyInfo.vb file. Figure 2.33 shows an Excel Range object in the debugger when the ExcelLocale1033 attribute is set to False.

Setting the ExcelLocale1033 attribute to False is useful when you are debugging your Excel solutions, but you should be sure to reset this attribute to True before you deploy these solutions. Otherwise, your

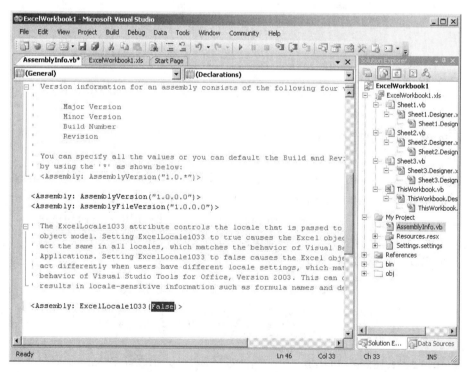

Figure 2.32. *Setting the ExcelLocale1033 attribute to False in AssemblyInfo.vb*

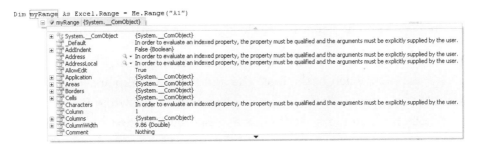

Figure 2.33. *Excel object types when the ExcelLocale1033 attribute is set to False*

code might not behave as expected if you run it on a computer with different Windows regional settings. You'll learn more about the Excel locale issue in Chapter 7.

Setting Breakpoints

A *breakpoint* is a setting that you can add to a line of code to temporarily pause execution at that line. Whenever code execution is halted because of a breakpoint, the code is said to be in *break mode.* The purpose of a breakpoint in Visual Studio is identical to that in VBA; however, as described later in this chapter, enhancements have been made to breakpoints in Visual Studio. Typically, you set breakpoints to pause code execution so that you can check the value of a variable or check for logic errors by stepping through the code one line at a time.

You can add a breakpoint to an executable line of code by selecting Toggle Breakpoint from the Debug menu. You can also add a breakpoint by clicking the area to the left of a line of code. Keep in mind that breakpoints cannot be added to just any line of code. You cannot add breakpoints to lines that contain only code comments or blank spaces.

A number of debugging windows become available only when your application is in break mode. These windows, located in the Debug menu, include the Watch window, the Locals window, and the Call

Stack window. You can also access these windows by right-clicking a line of code and choosing the window from the shortcut menu.

When you add a breakpoint, the line of code is highlighted and a red circle appears to the left of the line. The additional breakpoint features in Visual Studio are available in a shortcut menu, as shown in Figure 2.34. To access these options, right-click a breakpoint in the Code Editor.

Figure 2.34. *The options for a breakpoint*

The breakpoint options enable you to specify conditions for a breakpoint, edit its location, or assign a custom action (known as *setting a trace point*). Let's look at each option.

Location

Use this option to specify the line and character for which you want to break execution of the code.

Condition

Adding a condition to a breakpoint instructs the debugger to break only if a particular condition is met. For example, you can add a condition that checks whether an expression is true before the code breaks. This feature is nice if you're checking code within a loop; you don't have to break each time the line is hit, but rather only when the specified condition is met.

Hit Count

Use this option to track the number of times a breakpoint is hit. You can change the default behavior so that the code enters break mode only if the breakpoint is hit *n* number of times. This feature is also nice if you're checking code within a loop, because you can specify a certain number of times the line can be hit before the application enters break mode.

Filter

Use this option to add a filter to a breakpoint so that it breaks only when encountered in a particular thread or process.

When Hit

Use this option to specify custom actions to run when a breakpoint is hit, such as running a macro or printing a message. It's a great way to trace all the code that got executed up to a certain point, because you can print a message to the Debug window whenever the breakpoint is hit. You can use this feature to trace the sequence of execution of a particular block of code.

The Breakpoints Window

The Breakpoints window lets you see all the breakpoints in your application in one place. You can easily disable and enable breakpoints using the check boxes next to each breakpoint in the window. To view the Breakpoints window, click the Debug menu, point to Windows, and click Breakpoints. Figure 2.35 shows the Breakpoints window, with the current breakpoint displayed in bold.

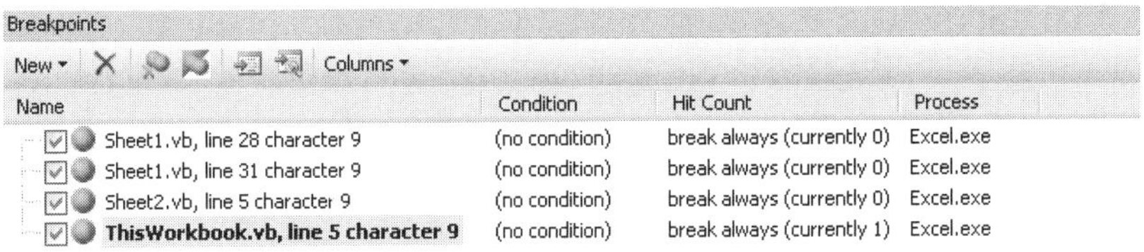

Figure 2.35. *The Breakpoints window*

Stepping Into, Over, and Out of Code

When your application enters break mode, you can locate errors by stepping through the code and evaluating one line at a time. The Debug menu contains three options for stepping through code: stepping into, stepping over, and stepping out. You can use additional commands to change the execution of your application in break mode as you step through your code.

Stepping Into

Stepping into code means that the Visual Studio debugger executes a line of code, and if that line contains a call to another function, the debugger moves to the first line of the function being called. You should use this command when you want to step through all lines of code, including any calls to functions that you have defined in your code. The debugger doesn't step into code for which there is no source code.

Stepping Over

Stepping over code means that the Visual Studio debugger executes a line of code, and if that line contains a call to another function, the debugger executes the entire function, moving to the first line after the function call. You should use this command if you want to avoid stepping into function calls when you know the problem doesn't occur in the function.

Stepping Out

Stepping out of code means that the Visual Studio debugger executes the remainder of the current function and returns to the calling procedure. You should use this command if you have stepped into a function and want to return to the calling procedure without stepping through the rest of the function.

Other Execution Change Commands

In addition to stepping into, over, and out of code, you can use other commands to change execution within your application. One option is Run To Cursor. To run this command, right-click a line of code that exists after the current breakpoint, and then select Run To Cursor in the shortcut menu. This command executes all code that exists between the breakpoint and the target line of code. The debugger then stops at the target line. It literally runs all the code up to the cursor location.

Another option is Set Next Statement. Again, you can call this command by right-clicking a line of code and then selecting Set Next Statement in the shortcut menu. This time, the code that exists between the breakpoint and the target line of code is ignored, and only the target line is executed. This command is useful for skipping identified errors in your code without having to restart execution.

Just My Code

Just My Code debugging, a new feature in Visual Studio 2005, provides a way to have the debugger step into only the code you've written. Visual Studio 2005 will step over automatically generated code and code from referenced assemblies so that you can look only for your own coding errors.

Earlier in this chapter, you learned about some of the hidden files behind the classes that contain auto-generated code. The code is stored in a separate file as a way to separate this auto-generated code from the code you write. Enabling the Just My Code setting ensures that as you step through your code, the debugger executes the code in these hidden files without stepping into any of the auto-generated code. This works because the generated code is marked with an attribute that indicates that it should not be considered as belonging to "Just My Code."

However, if you're interested in learning about the code in these hidden files, you can disable the Just My Code setting and step through calls into these code files. To disable Just My Code, click the General tab of the Debugging node in the Options dialog box and clear the Enable Just My Code (Managed Code) check box. Again, keep in mind that you should not modify code in these hidden files because regeneration of the files can overwrite any changes you've made.

The Exception Assistant

An *exception* is an error that occurs when your application is running. The Exception Assistant is a new feature that provides information whenever an unhandled exception occurs at run time. The Exception Assistant displays the location of the coding error and shows tips on how to resolve the issue.

To disable the Exception Assistant, select the General tab of the Debugging node in the Options dialog box, and then clear the Enable the Exception Assistant check box. After you disable this option, the exception information is displayed in a message box instead. For an example of the Exception Assistant, see Figure 2.36.

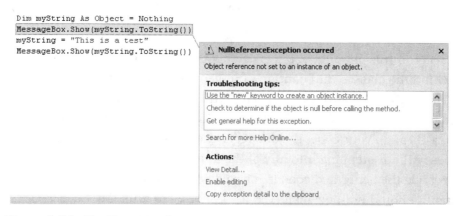

Figure 2.36. *The Exception Assistant*

Trying Out the Debugging Tools

It's one thing to read about the tools in Visual Studio that help you debug your applications, but it's quite another thing to actually try them out on some code. The following sections demonstrate some of the techniques for debugging a simple code example.

Setting Debugger Options

First, you set some options in Visual Studio so that the debugger does not stop on all exceptions.

1. Click Debug in the Solution Configurations list box on the Standard toolbar.

2. On the Tools menu, click Options to open the Options dialog box.

3. Expand the Debugging node, clear the Break When Exceptions Cross AppDomain or Managed/Native Boundaries (Managed Only) check box, and click OK.

4. On the Debug menu, click Exceptions to open the Exceptions dialog box.

5. Clear the Thrown and User-unhandled check boxes next to the Common Language Runtime Exception node, and then click OK to close the dialog box.

Writing Code in an Excel Workbook

In this section, you will create a new Excel workbook and add code that contains errors. (The user interface might differ depending on your Visual Studio development settings. The examples in this book assume that you have chosen the Visual Basic development setting.)

1. Create a directory at the root of the C:\ drive, and name it Samples. This is the directory where you can store all the VSTO solutions described in this book.

2. Open Visual Studio 2005.

3. On the File menu, point to New and then click Project.

4. In the Project Types pane, expand the Visual Basic node and select Office.

5. Select an Excel workbook in the Templates pane, leaving the default name (ExcelWorkbook1 if this is your first Excel project), and then click OK to create a new workbook project.

6. In the Visual Studio Tools for Office Project Wizard, select Create a New Document and then click OK.

7. Right-click the project in Solution Explorer, and click View Code.

8. Create a BeforeDoubleClick event handler by selecting Sheet1 Events in the Class Name drop-down and then selecting BeforeDoubleClick in the Method Name drop-down.

9. Add the code in Listing 2.1 to the BeforeDoubleClick event handler of Sheet1.

Listing 2.1. *Code that raises an exception*

```
Private Sub Sheet1_BeforeDoubleClick(ByVal Target As _
    Microsoft.Office.Interop.Excel.Range, _
    ByRef Cancel As Boolean) Handles Me.BeforeDoubleClick

    Dim myString As Object = Nothing
    MsgBox(myString.ToString)
    myString = "This is a test"
    MsgBox(myString.ToString)

End Sub
```

10. Save the solution to the Samples directory at the root of the C:\ drive.

11. Run the code by pressing F5.

The code is built and the application opens. When you double-click Sheet1, the exception that should occur when you try to convert a null variable to a string is swallowed by the debugger, and no error is displayed in a message box. By default, Visual Studio does not display errors that are thrown by Microsoft Office 2003 applications. This is why it's important to set the debugging options correctly before you start debugging your application.

Resetting Debugger Options

Now you can go back into the debugging options and set the debugger options to stop on all exceptions.

1. On the Tools menu, click Options to open the Options dialog box.

2. Expand the Debugging node, select the Break When Exceptions Cross AppDomain or Managed/Native Boundaries (Managed Only) check box, and click OK.

3. On the Debug menu, click Exceptions to open the Exceptions dialog box.

4. Select the Thrown and User-unhandled check boxes next to the Common Language Runtime Exception node, and then click OK to close the dialog box.

5. Press F5 to run the code, and double-click Sheet1.

This time the solution opens, the application enters break mode, and the Exception Assistant displays the expected NullReferenceException, offering troubleshooting tips to resolve the error.

Toggle Breakpoints

Now we look at how you can set breakpoints and use the execution change commands as you step through your code.

1. In the Code Editor, select the second line of code.

2. On the Debug menu, click Toggle Breakpoint. This sets a break-point in the line of code that we know causes an error.

3. Press F5 to run the solution code. The application halts at the line of code that contains the breakpoint before that line is executed. If you were to right-click the next line and click Run To Cursor, the debugger would encounter the exception and display the Exception Assistant.

4. Right-click the line of code beneath the breakpoint, and click Set Next Statement in the shortcut menu.

The debugger moves to the next line of code without executing the line that causes the exception. This feature enables you to continue step-ping through your code without having to rebuild and rerun the appli-cation. At this point, you can stop debugging and close the application.

Using Debugging Windows

Several windows in Visual Studio offer features that help you locate and fix errors in your code. In this section you will look at the windows that are always available in the IDE, and then at the windows that are avail-able only when the application is in break mode.

Command Window

The Command window can be used to execute commands directly in the Visual Studio IDE. To display the Command window, click the View menu, point to Other Windows, and then click Command Window. This window is available whether or not you are in break mode. For example, if you want to view the value of a variable, you can type the following code into the Command window and press the ENTER key:

```
Debug.Print myVariable
```

Visual Studio has a number of shortcuts, known as *aliases,* that you can use to enter a command into the Command window. When you use an alias, you can type

```
? myVariable
```

in the Command window instead of typing

```
Debug.Print myVariable
```

and get the same results. To view a complete list of the aliases available, type the command

```
>alias
```

in the Command window and press the ENTER key.

You can create your own aliases for use in the Command window by typing the following commands and then pressing the ENTER key. Be sure to replace <aliasName> with the name you want to assign to the command, and replace <commandName> with the name of the command.

```
>alias <aliasName> <commandName>
```

To delete the alias, type the following command and then press the ENTER key.

```
>alias <aliasName> /delete
```

Output Window

The Output window displays status information in the Visual Studio IDE. When you build a solution, information about its success is displayed in the Output window as shown in Figure 2.37. If the build fails, an Error List window is displayed. To display the Output window, click Output on the View menu. Also, the Output window automatically opens whenever you build a VSTO solution.

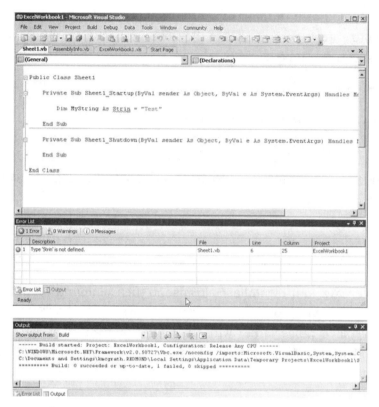

Figure 2.37. *The Output window*

The following windows are available only when the application is in break mode. To open these windows, click the Debug menu and then select Windows.

Call Stack Window

The *call stack* is a list of all procedures that have executed. The Call Stack window displays the name of every function or procedure that is currently in the stack. The top of the stack is always the current point of execution. To display the Call Stack window, click the Debug menu, point to Windows, and then click Call Stack.

By default, Visual Studio hides nonuser code. This hidden code is represented by the text [<External Code>]. To view this code, right-click the window and select Show External Code. (This is identical to clearing the Just My Code setting.) In this way, you can view any code that resides in the hidden code files by double-clicking a line of code in the stack (see Figure 2.38).

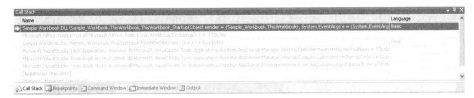

Figure 2.38. *The Call Stack window with Show External Code selected*

Watch Window

Use the Watch window to add code variables that you want to monitor. You can add multiple variables to this window. The Watch window shows you the value of a variable in real time. As you step through code, changes made to the value of the variables are automatically updated in the Watch window, as shown in Figure 2.39.

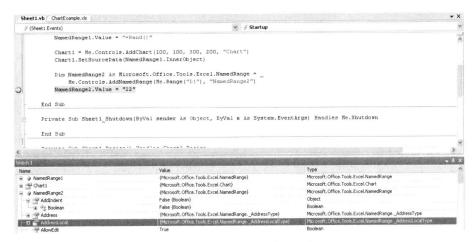

Figure 2.39. *Evaluating variables in the Watch window*

QuickWatch Window

The QuickWatch window works in the same way as the Watch window except that you can add only one variable to the QuickWatch window. When you are in break mode, you right-click a variable in the debugger and select QuickWatch from the context menu. This action displays the variable in the QuickWatch dialog box. If you want to evaluate the values at another time, add the variable or expression to the Watch window. Figure 2.40 shows the value of the NumberFormat property for the variable myRange in the QuickWatch window.

You can also obtain information about a variable by holding your mouse cursor over the variable. A DataTips window displays the value of each member of the variable, as shown earlier in Figure 2.32.

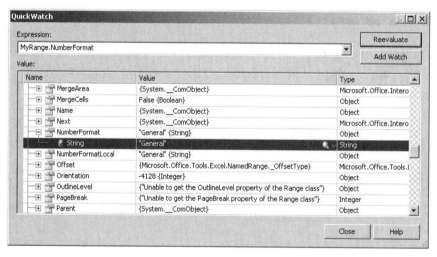

Figure 2.40. *Evaluating a variable in the QuickWatch window*

Autos Window

The Autos window displays any variables that are in use in and around the current line of code. You can display this window when you are in break mode by pointing to Windows on the Debug menu and then clicking Autos. The Autos window is automatically populated with variables by the debugger.

Locals Window

The Locals window works in the same way as the Autos window in that it automatically displays variables and their values. The main difference is that the Locals window displays only those variables that exist in the method you're currently debugging. You can open this window by pointing to Windows on the Debug menu when you are in break mode.

Immediate Window

The Immediate window is used to run commands immediately. To display the Immediate window, enter break mode, point to Windows on the Debug menu, and then click Immediate. For example, typing

```
? myString
```

in the Immediate window returns Nothing if a value has not been assigned.

The advantage of using the Immediate window over the Autos window is that you can type formulas into the Immediate window. For example, you cannot type

```
myString = "test string"
```

in the Autos window (you can type only the value of myString), but using this formula in the Immediate window works just fine.

Keep in mind that the Immediate window, Watch window, Locals window, and Autos window are not just informative. You can change the values from within these windows. You can test your code in the middle of execution by changing a variable to an expected value and continue running your code. It simulates what would happen if the code had the expected value to begin with. In this way, you can continue debugging your code without having to stop execution and rerun the code.

Locating and Using Help

Thousands of topics are included in the Help system in Visual Studio. The types of Help collections that are available to you depends on the applications you've installed. You can get help for a specific object by selecting the object in the IDE and pressing F1. Help is presented in a window called Microsoft Document Explorer. You can also access Help by clicking the Help menu and selecting one of the following options:

- How Do I
- Search
- Contents
- Index
- Help Favorites
- Index Results
- Dynamic Help

If you want to access Help for Word and Excel, you can locate it on a cascading menu when focus is on the designer (document). Figure 2.41 shows the Microsoft Office Word Help menu item, which reveals various Microsoft Office Word Help options.

Table of Contents

The Contents page provides a table of contents (TOC) in a hierarchical view that links to the topics in the Help system. Using the TOC gives you a good overview of the content that is available in the VSTO Help

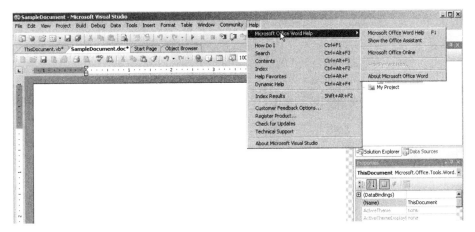

Figure 2.41. *Help available in a Word project*

collection. To find Help on VSTO through the TOC, you expand the following nodes: Development Tools and Languages | Visual Studio | Visual Studio Tools for Office.

The contents are organized into actionable categories, such as Getting Started, Upgrading Office Solutions, Creating Office Solutions in Visual Studio, Building and Debugging Office Projects, and Deploying Office Solutions (see Figure 2.42). You can filter the TOC to narrow the scope of topics that appear in the TOC. The filter also affects the items that appear in the Index window. When creating VSTO solutions, you should select the Office Development filter.

The Reference node contains the application programming interface (API) documentation for VSTO. You can also find documentation on the Office primary interop assemblies for Word and Excel, as well as Microsoft Office Core PIA documentation.

Index

You can search for information using keywords on the Index page. The index displays the keywords in alphabetical order. To reduce the

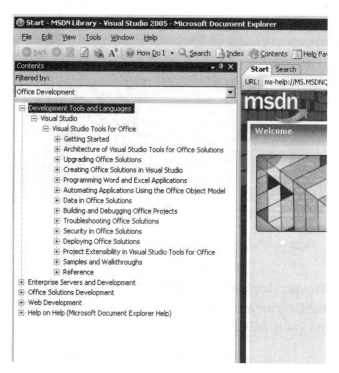

Figure 2.42. *The VSTO Help collection displayed in the TOC*

number of topics that are returned in the Index Results window, set the
Filtered By drop-down to Office Development.

Search

The Search page provides a way to perform a full-text search for infor-
mation that is in the local Help, online on Microsoft Developer Network
(MSDN), and within the Codezone community. You can specify whether
you want to load the Help content from the local Help, online content, or
both. To get the most up-to-date content, you should select Try Online
First, Then Local, as shown in Figure 2.43. With this option set, Visual
Studio will return the latest online content when you perform a search.
You can also scope the search by selecting the Web sites to search for
content in the Codezone Community list box of the Options dialog box.

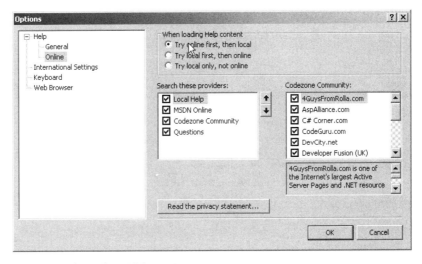

Figure 2.43. *The online Help options*

You can perform full-text searches for information by using the Search page. You can use logical operators—such as AND, OR, and NOT—but wildcard characters (*) are not supported. If you want to reduce the number of search results returned, you can search for an exact phrase by enclosing it in quotation marks. You can also filter your search based on language, technology, and content type.

To help you locate information, the Search page provides a drop-down where you can sort the results. You can select Rank, Source, Title, Locale, or only the Help resources that contain code samples.

How Do I

The How Do I pages provide links to common tasks and conceptual information about VSTO features. You can browse through the various categories of the How Do I pages to locate content. Figure 2.44 shows the subcategories available on the Automating Word Applications How Do I page. You can expand each subcategory by clicking the + sign. In

Figure 2.44, the Bookmarks node is expanded to reveal several topics that describe how to perform tasks related to Bookmark controls.

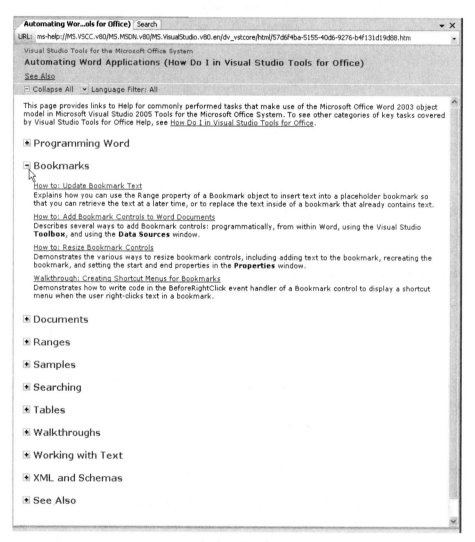

Figure 2.44. *A sample How Do I page*

Dynamic Help

Dynamic Help is a window in Visual Studio that provides links to Help topics related to the code you are currently typing in the Editor. You display the Dynamic Help window by clicking Dynamic Help in the Help menu. Figure 2.45 shows the available Help topics related to worksheets.

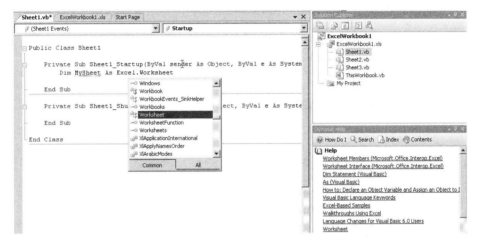

Figure 2.45. *Dynamic Help window*

Summary

We began this chapter with an introduction to the Visual Studio 2005 integrated development environment and compared it to the programming environment in VBA. We took a closer look at the Properties window, Solution Explorer, Object Browser, and IntelliSense features, explaining how to locate and insert IntelliSense code snippets into your code. Next, you learned about what happens when you build a VSTO solution, including which project files are copied to the output folder. Then you discovered various debugging windows and learned debugging techniques such as setting breakpoints and stepping through your code to evaluate one line at a time, and you saw how this technique can help you quickly locate errors in your code. Finally, we looked at the Help system and described how to locate VSTO-related topics in Visual Studio.

Review Questions

1. How does Solution Explorer in Visual Studio differ from Project Explorer in Visual Basic Editor?

2. What is the purpose of the hidden code files behind each of the class files in a Word or Excel project?

3. What kind of file is used to create an IntelliSense code snippet, and what is the file extension?

4. Name two additional features of breakpoints in Visual Studio.

5. What is Just My Code debugging?

6. Which execution change command enables you to skip over code (without running it) while in break mode?

7. Why is it important to break on common language runtime exceptions when you debug your code in VSTO?

3

Introduction to Managed Code

*Technology is dominated by two types of people: those
who understand what they do not manage, and those
who manage what they do not understand.*
—PUTT'S LAW

Topics Covered in This Chapter

What Is Managed Code?

Introduction to Object-Oriented Programming

Exploring the .NET Framework

VSTO and Managed Code

Summary

Review Questions

What Is Managed Code?

Code that runs within the .NET Framework is considered *managed
code.* This includes applications written in languages such as Visual C#
and Visual Basic 2005. Code that is not managed by the .NET Framework is typically referred to as *unmanaged code.* This includes applications written in programming languages such as C++, Visual Basic 6.0,
and VBA.

All Office solutions created using VSTO are written in managed code.
VSTO supports both Visual Basic 2005 and Visual C#; however, we refer
only to Visual Basic 2005 in text and in code examples in this book

because we believe it is easier to transition from VBA to Visual Basic 2005. Keep in mind that there is much to learn about the .NET Framework and managed code; this chapter only scratches the surface.

Following are some benefits of using managed code:

- **Improved security.** Often, security permissions are enabled or disabled by end users or determined by the identity of the user who is attempting to run code. However, code managed by the .NET Framework uses the security model code access security (CAS), which is based on the code's identity and location.

- **Automatic resource management.** Code managed by the .NET Framework eliminates common programming errors such as memory leaks and memory corruption. To eliminate memory leaks, the .NET Framework releases all memory used by the program when it closes.

- **Verification of type safety.** The .NET Framework ensures that code is type safe before it is run. A programming language that is type safe prevents operations from being performed that are not appropriate for that type.

- **Code reuse.** The .NET Framework improves productivity by providing a class library that gives you thousands of classes you can use in your code. You can also create your own custom class library.

- **Language interoperability.** Applications that use managed code can be written in multiple languages that are supported by the .NET Framework. For VSTO, this includes Visual Basic and Visual C#.

- **Partial classes.** Visual Basic 2005 supports the use of partial classes, thereby separating designer-generated code from your own code. The partial classes are merged into one unified class when the code is compiled.

For VBA developers moving to managed code, an additional advantage is the ability to use all the coding and debugging tools in the Visual Studio IDE and the ability to design solutions using a true object-oriented programming language.

Introduction to Object-Oriented Programming

Object-oriented programming is a type of programming that relates coding constructs to *objects.* The objects that are created in code can have similar characteristics to objects in the real world. You define *properties* for an object to define its characteristics. For example, light bulbs might have a color property. The *value* of this property might differ for each individual light bulb; some might be white, and others yellow.

You define *methods* for an object to describe the actions it can take. Using our light bulb example, the methods might be TurnOn, AdjustBrightness, and TurnOff. You can define *event handlers* for an object so that certain actions are performed when a particular *event* on the object occurs. For example, if a BeforeTurnOff event is raised, it would enable you to first decrease the brightness of the light bulb before turning it off. You also define the type of data the object can contain and any logic that is required to manipulate the data.

Understanding Classes and Objects

Classes contain methods, events, and properties that enable access to data. These methods, events, and properties of a class are known as its *members.* In VBA, you use *procedural programming,* writing most of your code within a code module (although classes are available in VBA). In object-oriented programming, most, if not all, of your code is contained within classes.

A class is often described as being a sort of cookie cutter or blueprint for an object. You can also think of a class as a template for an object.

Think about how you would use a Word template. You can add boiler-plate text and special formatting (styles) to the template. Then when a document is created based on that template, the new document contains the same characteristics that were applied to the template. The document has access to all the styles defined in the template, but an end user can make additional changes to the document and apply styles to different sections of the document. In this same way, a class contains the base functionality of an object, and yet you can later change properties of each object to make them different. Although a class contains a base set of functionality such as methods, properties, and events, these class members can be used, and the data associated with the object can be accessed, only when you've created an *instance* of the class. An object is an instance of a class, and the process is known as *instantiation*.

You learned in Chapter 1 about the extended objects that VSTO provides for Word and Excel. One of these is a NamedRange. A NamedRange is actually a class, and each time you add one to the worksheet, you are creating an instance of that class, or a NamedRange object. VSTO generates a unique name for each instance by appending an incremental number to the end of the class name: NamedRange1, NamedRange2, and so on. If you want to provide a different name, you can make the change in the Properties window. If you also change the value of the properties of NamedRange1—such as setting a specific font or adding a border—then the appearance of NamedRange1 will differ from that of NamedRange2. Even though each NamedRange is unique, the two of them share the same characteristics (properties) because both of them were created from the same NamedRange class.

When you create a VSTO application using Visual Basic 2005, you have numerous objects to work with. There are objects such as Windows Forms and controls, and there are Word, Excel, and Outlook objects such as documents, list objects, and e-mail items. Additionally, the .NET Framework contains a class library that you can use to create objects in your code.

You use the New keyword to create an instance of a class. In the case of a NamedRange, VSTO automatically creates the instance of the class in the auto-generated code of the worksheet's hidden partial class whenever you add a NamedRange (or any other control) to the worksheet. When you create your own class, you can store data privately; to do that, you create variables, known as *private member variables,* to store data. Then you create public properties so that the data can be accessed by other methods outside the class. This gives you complete control over the access to this data.

Creating Properties

To create a property, you add a Property statement. Private member variables are accessible only from outside the class when the Get and Set property procedures are accessed. These private member variables are also known as *fields.* The Get property procedure returns the value of the field, and the Set property procedure enables you to assign a value to the field. You can create a property in Visual Basic by typing the Property statement, such as the following, and then pressing the ENTER key.

```
Property Text() as String
```

Visual Basic automatically creates the Get and Set statements for you, as the code example in Listing 3.1 shows.

Listing 3.1. *Creating a property*

```
Property Text() As String
    Get

    End Get
    Set(ByVal value As String)

    End Set
End Property
```

Notice that the value field is created for you as a parameter of the Set property procedure. To assign the value to the member variable in the Set property procedure, you must create a member variable and write code. You must also write code to return the member variable in the Get property procedure. You can create a read-only property by using the ReadOnly keyword before the property. In the case of a read-only property, you need only provide a Get property procedure.

So far, the Text property you created lets you set and get a value for the Text property. You cannot use these properties or store any data in the class until you have actually created an instance of the class (an object). Each object that you create can hold a different value for the Text property.

Creating Classes

In this section you will create a simple Sentence class in a Word solution. As in Chapter 1, you will save the VSTO solutions that are described in this book in the Samples directory at the root of the C:\ drive.

1. Open Visual Studio 2005.

2. On the File menu, point to New and then click Project.

3. In the New Project dialog box, select Word Document in the Templates pane.

4. Name the solution SampleDocument, and set the location to C:\Samples.

5. In the Visual Studio Tools for Office Project Wizard, select Create a New Document, and then click OK.

6. In Solution Explorer, right-click the solution node, point to Add, and select New Item.

7. In the New Item dialog box, select Class, name the class Sentence.vb, and click Add.

Visual Studio creates the Sentence class and then opens the class file in code view.

8. Add the code in Listing 3.2 to the Sentence class.

Listing 3.2. *Creating a property named Text for the Sentence class*

```
Public Class Sentence
    Private TextValue as String
    Property Text() As String
        Get
            Return TextValue
        End Get
        Set (ByVal value As String)
           TextValue = value
        End Set
    End Property
End Class
```

The variable TextValue is a private member variable. You can retrieve and set its value only by using the public Text property.

Instantiating Objects

Now that you have a Sentence class, you will create two instances of the class, assigning a different value to the Text property of each class. Finally, you'll retrieve the value of the Text property for each Sentence object and insert it into your document. Follow these steps:

1. In Solution Explorer, right-click ThisDocument.vb and select View Code.

2. The Code Editor opens, and two default event handlers are visible. The first is the Startup event handler, and the second is the Shutdown event handler for the document.

3. Add the code in Listing 3.3 to the Startup event handler of ThisDocument.

The code concatenates the text in Sentence1 and Sentence2 and then uses the InsertAfter method to insert the text into the first paragraph of the document. Because the code is added to the ThisDocument class, the Me keyword is used to represent the VSTO document (Microsoft.Office.Tools.Document, which wraps the native Document class).

Listing 3.3. *Creating two Sentence objects*

```
Dim Sentence1 As New Sentence()
Dim Sentence2 As New Sentence()
Sentence1.Text = "This is my first sentence. "
Sentence2.Text = "This is my second sentence. "
Me.Paragraphs(1).Range.InsertAfter( _
    Sentence1.Text & Sentence2.Text)
```

4. Press F5 to run the solution.

    When the solution runs and the Word document is created, the Startup event handler is raised and two instances of the Sentence class are created. The code then assigns a different string to each Sentence object. Finally, the value of each Sentence object is retrieved and inserted into the first paragraph of the document, as shown in Figure 3.1.

Figure 3.1. *Text inserted into the document using the Sentence class*

5. Stop execution of the solution code by clicking Stop Debugging on the Debug menu, and then close the solution.

Creating and Calling Constructors

As you saw in the example in Listing 3.3, you use the New keyword to create an instance of a class. The New keyword calls the constructor of the class. A *class constructor* describes how to initialize the properties and methods of the class. Every class has a default constructor that is automatically generated for you as a method called Sub New.

You can override this default constructor by adding your own procedure named Sub New. Constructors can take parameters and can also be overloaded so that you can create an instance of the class in several ways. *Overloading* means that there are multiple versions of the same method, each with different parameters. Visual Basic 2005 enables you to create constructors that take one or more parameters so that you can pass data when you create an instance of the class. To overload the constructor, you add multiple Sub New methods that take different parameters.

1. Add the constructors in Listing 3.4 to your Sentence class.

Listing 3.4. *Adding two constructors to a class*

```
Public Sub New()
    TextValue = "Hello World! "
End Sub

Public Sub New(ByVal myText as String)
    TextValue = myText
End Sub
```

The first constructor overrides the default parameterless constructor and assigns the text "Hello World" to the member variable, TextValue. If you instantiate the class without passing any text, "Hello World" will be the value of the Sentence class. The second constructor takes a string as a parameter and assigns the string to the member variable.

2. Replace the code in the Startup event handler of ThisDocument
    with the code in Listing 3.5.

Listing 3.5. *Passing parameters to a constructor*

```
Dim Sentence1 As New Sentence()
Dim Sentence2 As New Sentence("This is my second sentence.")
Me.Paragraphs(1).Range.InsertAfter( _
    Sentence1.Text & Sentence2.Text)
```

Notice that when you type the open parenthesis after the word
Sentence, IntelliSense lists the overloaded methods and displays
the required parameter (myText As String) in method 2 of 2, as
shown in Figure 3.2.

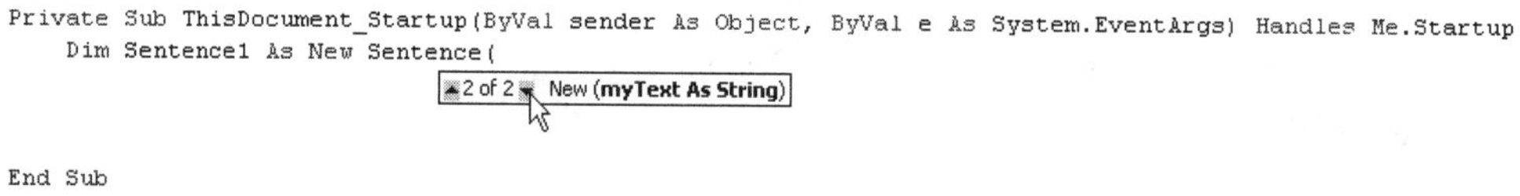

```
Private Sub ThisDocument_Startup(ByVal sender As Object, ByVal e As System.EventArgs) Handles Me.Startup
    Dim Sentence1 As New Sentence(
                            ▲ 2 of 2 ▼  New (myText As String)

End Sub
```

Figure 3.2. *IntelliSense displays a parameter required by the constructor of the
Sentence class.*

3. Press F5 to run the solution.

This time, when the solution runs, the value to be assigned to
Sentence2 is passed to the constructor of the Sentence class when the
class is instantiated. Although you could assign a value to the Text
property of Sentence2 after it's instantiated (as shown in Listing 3.7),
this example (Listing 3.5) uses the default value "Hello World!"

Adding Methods

You can also add methods to your class to perform an operation on the
data. If you want the method to be accessible from the instance of the
class, you must declare the method as a public method; to make it

accessible from instances of the class in the same assembly, declare it as Friend. Private methods are available only to other members within the class.

1. Add the method in Listing 3.6 to your Sentence class. This method calls the ToUpper method of a String, which is provided by the .NET Framework.

Listing 3.6. *Creating a public method for a class*

```
Public Sub UpperCase()
    TextValue = TextValue.ToUpper()
End Sub
```

2. Replace the code in the Startup event handler of ThisDocument with the code in Listing 3.7 so that the UpperCase method is called only on Sentence1.

Listing 3.7. *Calling the UpperCase method of the Sentence class*

```
Dim Sentence1 as New Sentence()
Dim Sentence2 As New Sentence("This is my first sentence.")
Sentence1.Text = "This is my first sentence. "
Sentence1.UpperCase()
Me.Paragraphs(1).Range.InsertAfter( _
    Sentence1.Text & Sentence2.Text)
```

3. Press F5 to run the solution.

When the solution runs, the code in Listing 3.6 passes text to the constructor for the second object, but it uses the default (parameterless) constructor for the first object and then reassigns a value to the Text property of Sentence1. After the call to the UpperCase method on the first object, the first sentence that is inserted into the document appears in uppercase, and the second sentence appears in sentence case, as shown in Figure 3.3.

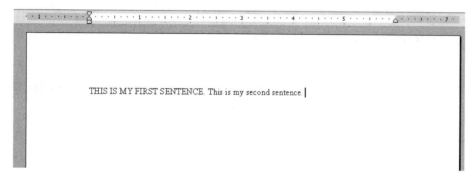

Figure 3.3. *Text inserted into the document using the Sentence class*

Adding Events

You can add events to your class to indicate that objects created from this class can raise the events you've added.

1. Add the code in Listing 3.8 to your Sentence class. This code adds an event statement and replaces the UpperCase method.

Listing 3.8. *Creating an event for a class*

```
Public Event CaseChanged()

Public Sub UpperCase()

    TextValue = TextValue.ToUpper()
    RaiseEvent CaseChanged()

End Sub
```

2. Replace the code in the Startup event handler of ThisDocument with the code in Listing 3.9 so that a message box is shown when the event is raised.

   You can create an event handler for the CaseChanged event by declaring the variables for the Sentence objects with the WithEvents keyword, as shown in Listing 3.9. This code also adds a method that handles the OnChanged event for the Sentence1 and

Sentence2 classes. Notice that the Sentence_ChangeCase method lists both Sentence1.CaseChanged and Sentence2.CaseChanged in the Handles clause.

Listing 3.9. *Displaying a message box when an event is raised*

```
WithEvents Sentence1 as New Sentence()
WithEvents Sentence2 As New Sentence( _
    "This is my first sentence.")

Private Sub ThisDocument_Startup(ByVal sender As Object, _
    ByVal e As System.EventArgs) Handles Me.Startup

    Sentence1.Text = "This is my first sentence. "
    Sentence1.UpperCase()
    Me.Paragraphs(1).Range.InsertAfter( _
        Sentence1.Text & Sentence2.Text)

End Sub

Sub Sentence_CaseChange() Handles Sentence1.CaseChanged, _
    Sentence2.CaseChanged

    MsgBox("Case changed.")

End Sub
```

   3. Press F5 to run the code.

Only one message box is displayed because only Sentence1 called the UpperCase method, which raised the CaseChange event. If you add code to call UpperCase on Sentence2, the event will be raised on both objects, and therefore two messages will be displayed.

Partial Classes

Partial classes are a new feature in .NET Framework 2.0 and are supported in Visual Basic 2005. The Partial keyword enables you to split a class into separate source files. You can also define partial structures and interfaces.

You learned in Chapter 2 that there is a hidden code file behind the ThisDocument.vb file in Word solutions (and behind ThisWorkbook.vb, Sheet1.vb, Sheet2.vb, and Sheet3.vb in Excel solutions). These code files are partial classes. VSTO uses partial classes as a way to separate auto-generated code from the code that you write so that you can concentrate on your own code. Partial classes are also used in Windows Forms to store auto-generated code when you add controls to a Windows Form.

Figure 3.4 shows the partial class named MyForm, which contains the code that is generated whenever you add a control to the form. This code is stored in the MyForm.Designer.vb file; in contrast, the code you

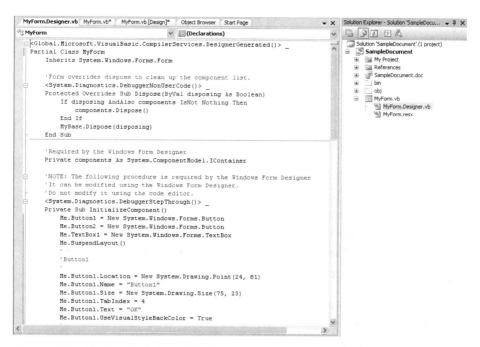

Figure 3.4. *Partial class for a Windows Form named MyForm, where auto-generated code is stored*

write to set properties or handle the events of the control should be written in MyForm.vb, as shown in Figure 3.5.

Notice that the class definition for MyForm.Designer.vb is Partial Class MyForm. The class definition for MyForm.vb does not contain the Partial keyword. Instead, it is simply Public Class MyForm.

Figure 3.5. *Partial class for a Windows Form named MyForm, where developer-written code is stored*

The Partial keyword is not needed for the main class definition; it is needed only for any additional class definitions that share the same class name. When you compile the code, Visual Basic automatically merges the code from the partial classes with the code for the main class.

Another way you might use partial classes is to divide a programming task between two developers. If each developer writes code in a separate class file, you can then add each class to the main project and Visual Studio will automatically merge the classes during the build process as if they were a single class file.

Generic Classes

Generic classes are a new feature in the .NET Framework and are supported in Visual Basic 2005. A *generic class* is a single class that provides functionality for different data types, without the need to write a separate class definition for each data type. You can also define generic methods, structures, and interfaces.

A generic class uses type parameters as placeholders for the data types. The code example in Listing 3.10 shows the declaration of a generic class using *t* to represent the type parameter. You can specify more than one parameter by separating the parameters with commas. When you want to instantiate the class, you must specify the data type, rather than the type parameter, in the declaration, as shown in Listing 3.10.

Listing 3.10. *Creating a Generic class*

```
Public Class MySampleClass(Of t)

    ' Implementation code for the class goes here.

End Class


Sub CreateGenericClasses()

    Dim myStringClass As New mySampleClass(Of String)
    Dim myIntegerClass As New mySampleClass(Of Integer)

End Sub
```

In the System.Collections.Generic namespace, the .NET Framework provides a number of generic collection classes that correspond to existing (nongeneric) collection classes. For example, you can use a Dictionary class to specify the data type for a key-value pair (rather than use a Hashtable), and a List is the generic class that corresponds to an ArrayList.

Interfaces

Like classes, *interfaces* define properties, methods, and events of an object. Unlike classes, interfaces do not provide any implementation, and you cannot create an instance of an interface. A class can implement one or more interfaces.

Any class that implements an interface must implement all the members of the interface as they are defined. An interface should not change after it has been deployed in your solution, because any such change could possibly break existing code.

You declare interfaces using the Interface statement. For example, the code in Listing 3.11 defines an interface that must be implemented with a method that takes an Integer argument and returns an Integer. When you implement this interface in a class, the data type for the arguments and the return value of the method must match those of the method defined (in this case, Integer). You can implement this interface within a class by using the Implements keyword, as shown in Listing 3.11.

Listing 3.11. *Creating and implementing an interface*

```
Public Interface ISampleInterface
    Function SampleFunction(ByVal Count As Integer) As Integer
End Interface


Public Class SampleClass
    Implements ISampleInterface

    Function SampleFunction(ByVal Count As Integer) As Integer _
        Implements ISampleInterface.SampleFunction

        ' Add code to perform the function here.
    End Function

End Class
```

Code Modules

Code modules in Visual Basic work in the same way as they do in VBA. A *code module* is a container for global methods and properties that can be used by other parts of your application. Unlike classes, you do not need to create a new instance of a module in order to call the methods.

Nor do you need to fully qualify your call unless the same method exists in multiple modules. To fully qualify the method name you would use moduleName.methodName().

Modules are a simple way to create code that can be accessed from anywhere in your application, but in general it is better to use classes and object-oriented techniques. In the next section you will learn about the benefits of object-oriented programming.

Object Orientation

To be considered a true object-oriented language, a language should support the following features:

- Encapsulation
- Inheritance
- Polymorphism

All these features were available in VBA except inheritance. This is one reason many people never considered VBA a true object-oriented programming language. This isn't to say, however, that Visual Basic 2005 is merely VBA plus inheritance. Many more capabilities and enhancements have been made to Visual Basic 2005.

In this section we look at these encapsulation, inheritance, and polymorphism requirements of object-oriented programming.

Encapsulation

Encapsulation enables you to control the access to data within a class. For example, suppose your class has a number of methods that work on some data. Code that calls into the instantiated class (the object) need not know how a particular operation functions. To perform an action, the calling code need know only that the functionality exists and that it needs to call it. By not allowing direct external access to those methods and by hiding the logic used in the class, you are following the principle of encapsulation.

You can hide the implementation of your class by using access modifiers that prevent code outside the class from modifying data within the class or calling its methods. For example, you can use the Private keyword with a property or method that you don't want outside code to access. However, if you want to manipulate data from outside the class, you must provide public properties or methods. This was illustrated in the Sentence class you created earlier in this chapter. The Text property of the Sentence class had a Get property procedure and a Set property procedure that enabled you to write code to assign values to and retrieve values from the property. The actual data, however, was stored in a private member variable that was not directly accessible from outside the class.

The value of this feature becomes clearer if we add logic along with setting the internal value, such as checking the spelling of the sentence. The developer who sets the text property doesn't have to know *how* the Sentence object is checking the spelling, only that it *does* check the spelling when it sets the value.

Inheritance

Using *inheritance*, you can create a class that is based on an existing class, giving your new class all the behavior and functionality of the existing class. The class that you inherit from is known as the *base class*, and the class that is inheriting the functionality is known as the *derived class.* You can extend the functionality of the derived class by adding properties or methods that did not exist in the base class, or you can override inherited properties or methods so that they behave differently in the derived class.

Visual Basic 2005 supports inheritance, although it doesn't support multiple inheritance. A derived class can have only one base class.

Using inheritance, you can reuse existing code that performs most of the functionality you require. You modify only a portion of the code to meet your needs, instead of having to reinvent the wheel. Whenever you need functionality in your application, you should look at the .NET Framework class library to see whether the functionality exists or whether you can inherit the base functionality from one of the classes. For example, if you want to extend an existing Textbox control, you can create a new class that derives from the Windows Forms Textbox control, as shown in Listing 3.12.

Listing 3.12. *Inheriting from an existing Windows Forms control*

```
Public Class MyTextBox

    Inherits System.Windows.Forms.TextBox

    ' Add code to override existing TextBox functionality.

End Class
```

Polymorphism

Polymorphism is the ability to create identically named methods or properties within a number of derived classes that perform different functions. You can implement polymorphism by using interfaces or inheritance. For inheritance-based polymorphism, you override methods in a base class with new implementations of the methods in the derived class. For interface-based polymorphism, you implement an interface differently in multiple classes. You saw an example of this when you created multiple constructors for your Sentence class.

Exploring the .NET Framework

The .NET Framework is made up of the common language runtime and a set of code libraries called the Framework Class Library. This framework is a platform for building .NET applications such as Windows applications, Web-based applications, and VSTO customizations. Before delving into the common language runtime, we briefly cover three concepts that are important to programming in managed code: assemblies, namespaces, and application domains.

Assemblies

An *assembly* is a collection of classes and functionality that is stored as an executable file (.exe) or a library (.dll). When you compile a .NET language such as Visual Basic 2005, your code is not compiled directly into machine language, or binary code. Instead, it is compiled into an assembly-like language known as Intermediate Language (IL). No matter which language you use (Visual Basic 2005 or C#) to create a VSTO solution, the build process compiles the code into IL. The assembly contains both IL and metadata that describes each class and its members, along with information about the assembly itself, such as the assembly name, version, and any dependencies it has.

Assemblies can be private or shared. A *private* assembly normally contains code that is intended to be used by only one application. These assemblies can reside in the same folder as the application that uses them, or in a subfolder of the application. For example, when you create and build a VSTO solution, the compiled code is saved in a subfolder of your solution.

Shared assemblies, on the other hand, are designed to be shared among many applications. Because any software can access these assemblies, they should be stored in a special directory known as the *global assembly cache* (GAC). An example of a shared assembly is an Office primary interop assembly (PIA) described later in this chapter.

Namespaces

Namespaces help you organize the objects in an assembly, such as classes, interfaces, structures, enumerations, and other namespaces.

Using namespaces helps you avoid problems such as naming collisions or conflicts within your code. For example, let's say you have a class named Math that contains functionality to add or subtract the value of Excel ranges. You could add a reference to an assembly that contains a class also named Math but having different functionality. When you run your application, there would be no way for the .NET Framework to distinguish between your Math class and the referenced Math class.

Creating namespaces for your classes gives you another level of naming that helps disambiguate your classes. In the same way that using people's last names can help distinguish them from others who share the same first name, using a namespace along with a class name (also known as *fully qualifying* a class) helps the .NET Framework runtime distinguish one class from a like-named class. Often a company name is used as an alias of a namespace, so, for example, MyCompany.Employees can be easily distinguished from YourCompany.Employees.

To fully qualify the name of an object, you simply prefix the object with the namespace. For example, the Button class that you add to a Word document is in the Microsoft.Office.Tools.Word.Controls namespace and is referenced as Microsoft.Office.Tools.Word.Controls.Button. In contrast, the Button class you add to a Windows Form is in the System.Windows.Forms namespace and is referenced as System.Windows.Forms.Button.

You can include a namespace in your project by using the Imports statement, and you can optionally provide an alias to be used in place of the namespace. For example, you could add the following line to the top of your code file:

```
Imports Microsoft.Office.Tools.Word
```

Or, to disambiguate this namespace from the Microsoft.Office.Interop.Word namespace, you might use an alias:

```
Imports Tools = Microsoft.Office.Tools.Word
```

In this way, you can refer to an object within that namespace by using the alias. So instead of declaring myBookmark as a Microsoft.Office.Tools.Word.Bookmark, you could declare it as a Tools.Bookmark.

Application Domains

Application domains give the .NET Framework a way to isolate applications that are running in the same process. For example, if you're running multiple add-ins for your application and if one of them needs to be reloaded, you would want to ensure that the other add-ins are not affected. Loading the add-ins into a separate application domain guarantees this isolation. You can run several application domains in a single process and achieve the same level of isolation that exists when you run the applications in separate processes.

You can also set security permissions on an application domain. For example, when an application domain is created for a VSTO solution, the VSTO runtime sets policy for the application domain so that it does not trust the My Computer Zone. This practice ensures that the code in the My Computer Zone has been granted trust explicitly rather than allowing all code to run by default. You'll learn more about security in Chapter 11, Security and Deployment.

Common Language Runtime

The *common language runtime* is a runtime environment that supports multiple .NET Framework programming languages, such as Visual Basic 2005 and Visual C#. The common language runtime manages your code and provides compilation services, exception handling services, reflection services, memory management services, and a security mechanism for running secure code.

Compilation

At run time, the common language runtime compiles IL code into machine code (binary) that is specific to the hardware and operating system the code is currently running on. The common language runtime compiler is known as the Just-In-Time (JIT) compiler because it doesn't go through and compile all the code in the assembly at one time but rather compiles code only as it is being called. If the same method is called again while the solution is running, the common language runtime runs the binary that is already in memory rather than rerun it through JIT compilation. One benefit of this arrangement is that only the code that needs to be run is compiled, saving time and memory compared with compiling it all at once.

Additionally, the common language runtime can read the metadata of the IL stored in the assembly and can verify that the code is type safe before attempting to access memory locations. Note also that the verification process can be skipped if security policy is set to do so.

Exception Handling

The common language runtime provides an exception notification service so that it's easy to determine that an error has occurred. The .NET Framework provides a number of exception classes that describe the most common types of exceptions. With managed code, you should use structured exception handling—such as Try Catch Finally (Try Catch) statements—to check whether an exception is thrown within your code and handle the exception accordingly. Rather than use the method of error handling used in VBA code (On Error GoTo statements), you should instead favor the more robust exception handling of a Try Catch statement.

A Try Catch statement is made up of a Try block, a Catch block, and an End Try statement. You add the code that can possibly cause an exception in the Try block as a way to "try out" the code. Then you "catch" any exceptions that are thrown by handling the exception in the Catch block.

If needed, you can break out of a Try Catch statement by using the Exit Try keyword. The Finally block is always executed, whether or not an error is raised and handled.

You end a Try Catch statement with End Try. For example, the code in Listing 3.13 shows how you can check whether a folder exists. The code sets a folder named Personnel as the current Outlook folder in a Try block and displays an error in the Catch block if an exception is raised. An exception is raised if inbox.Folders does not contain an entry for "Personnel." Note, however, that it is better to specify the type of exception in the Catch statement (if it is known) than to catch all exceptions as in this example.

Listing 3.13. *Try Catch statement*

```
Try
    Me.ActiveExplorer().CurrentFolder = inBox.Folders( _
        "Personnel")
Catch Ex As Exception
    MsgBox(Ex.Message)
End Try
```

Reflection

Using *reflection*, you can discover which types exist in an assembly at run time, as well as examine its methods, properties and events, and attributes. *Attributes* are metadata tags that you can apply to your code. The common language runtime uses classes within the .NET Framework class library that are part of the System.Reflection namespace to programmatically inspect an assembly.

The .NET Framework 2.0 SDK contains a tool named ILDASM that uses reflection to display all the types and members of an assembly. You can also view the assembly's IL. There are other tools that use reflection on an assembly that do not ship with the .NET Framework, such as .NET Reflector.

Garbage Collection

The common language runtime provides automatic memory management known as garbage collection. *Garbage collection* is a process of releasing memory used to store an object or object reference when it is no longer being used. The garbage collector examines variables and objects and checks whether there are any existing references. If the objects are not being referenced, they are not destroyed; rather, they are flagged for garbage collection. The .NET Framework determines the time frame in which the garbage collection actually occurs.

The garbage collector reclaims any memory that is no longer being used. The garbage collector functionality is exposed through the GC class. At times, you should mark an object as being eligible for garbage collection (for example, setting the object variable to Nothing); at other times, you might want to force a garbage collection to free up memory (for example, calling GC.Collect()). Under normal circumstances you shouldn't force garbage collection.

Security

The common language runtime offers *code-based* security, in which permissions are based on the identity of the code, rather than *role-based* security, which is based on the identity, or role, of the user trying to run the code. This security model is known as code access security (CAS), and the security policy set determines what the code can do and how much the code is trusted. Security is covered in more detail in Chapter 11.

Common Language Specification

For code to interact with objects implemented in any language, the objects must expose common features to the common language runtime. The Common Language Specification (CLS) defines the rules that must be adhered to. For example, it specifies that arrays must have a lower bound of zero.

The *common type system,* which defines how types are declared and used, is defined in the CLS. The common type system ensures that objects written in different languages can interact. All types derive from System.Object, and they are typically classified into value types and reference types.

Value Types and Reference Types

There are two main categories of types that are managed by the common language runtime: value types and reference types. The difference between them is that *reference types,* such as objects, are stored on a portion of memory in the computer called the *heap,* whereas *value types,* such as numeric data types, are stored on another portion of memory called the *stack.*

Value types include structures, the numeric data types (Byte, Short, Integer, Long, Single, Double), enumerations, Boolean, Char, and Date. Reference types include classes, delegates, arrays, and Strings, and they can be accessed only through a reference to their location. When you create a variable for a value type without assigning it a value, the type is automatically initialized to a default value.

Table 3.1 lists some common data types, shows how they map to the System namespace in the .NET class library, and lists their default values. When you create a reference type variable, however, its value defaults to Nothing.

Table 3.1. *Default Value for Data Types*

Data Type	Namespace Map	Default Value
Byte	System.Byte	0
Short	System.Int16	0
Integer	System.Int32	0
Long	System.Int64	0

(continues)

Table 3.1. *Default Value for Data Types (Continued)*

Data Type	Namespace Map	Default Value
Single	System.Single	0
Double	System.Double	0
Decimal	System.Decimal	0D
Boolean	System.Boolean	False
Date	System.DateTime	01/01/0001 12:00:00AM
String	System.String	Nothing

.NET Framework Class Library

As the name suggests, the .NET Framework class library is a library of classes that contains popular functionality for use in your code. For example, an XMLReader class in the System.XML namespace gives you quick access to XML data. Instead of writing your own classes or functionality, you can use any of the thousands of classes and interfaces— such as Windows Forms controls and input/output (IO) functions—that are included in the .NET Framework class library. You can also derive your own classes from classes in the .NET Framework. When you're working with the Framework class library, it's important to understand that these classes are organized within the context of namespaces.

The .NET Framework class library is organized into hierarchical namespaces according to their functionality. This arrangement makes it easier to locate functionality within the library and provides a way to disambiguate class names. A number of namespaces are automatically imported, or referenced, when you create a project in Visual Studio. For example, in a Windows Forms application, you do not need to fully qualify the Button class as Microsoft.Windows.Forms.Button, because the Microsoft.Windows.Forms namespace is automatically imported into your project. Instead, you can refer to the Button class directly. When you're using Visual Studio Tools for Office, however, there is a Button class in Excel and Word that differs from the Windows Forms Button class. In this case, you must fully qualify any references to the VSTO Button. The code example in Listing 3.14 illustrates.

Listing 3.14. *Fully qualifying an object*

```
' Declare a variable for a Windows Forms button.
Dim myButton As Button

' Declare a variable for a button to be used on a Word document.
Dim myWordButton As Microsoft.Office.Tools.Word.Button
```

In Visual Basic, you can use an Imports statement at the top of your code file to include a namespace in your project. In this way, you do not have to type the fully qualified namespace every time you reference the classes within that namespace. You can also create an alias for the namespace, as shown in Listing 3.15.

Listing 3.15. *Creating an alias for a namespace*

```
Imports Tools = Microsoft.Office.Tools.Word

Sub Test()
    ' Declare a variable for a Windows Forms button.
    Dim myButton As Button

    ' Declare a variable for a button to be used on a
    ' Word document.
    Dim MyWordButton As Tools.Button
End Sub
```

Table 3.2 lists some of the popular namespaces in the .NET Framework class library that you might use in your VSTO solutions.

To use a .NET Framework class in your code, you must first set a reference to the assembly that contains the class. To set a reference, you click Add Reference from the Project menu. When the Add Reference dialog box appears, you select the component name from the .NET tab

Table 3.2. *Popular Namespaces in the .NET Framework Class Library*

Namespace	Description
System	Contains the base data types, such as String, Boolean, and Object. This namespace is automatically included in your project, so you need not qualify any of the types in this namespace. Most languages, including Visual Basic 2005, define their own data types, which typically map to the types in this namespace. This is one reason for some of the language changes (data type changes) between VBA and Visual Basic 2005. For example, a Short in Visual Basic 2005 is equivalent to an Integer in VBA, and the Variant data type in VBA is no longer supported. These types were updated in Visual Basic 2005 to conform to the types in the System namespace.
	In addition to providing the base data types, the System namespace has classes such as exception classes and the Math class (for computations).
System.Collections	Contains classes and interfaces used to define collections of objects, such as the ArrayList, CollectionBase, and SortedList classes. This namespace is typically used to create collection classes and also contains many generic collection classes.
System.Data	Contains the classes for ADO.NET. You need references to this namespace when creating data binding in VSTO objects. Defined types in this namespace include the IDbConnection interface, IDataAdapter interface, and DataSet class.
System.IO	Contains the classes for reading and writing files synchronously or asynchronously. Objects defined in this namespace include the File, Directory, and Stream classes.

(continues)

Table 3.2. *Popular Namespaces in the .NET Framework Class Library (Continued)*

Namespace	Description
System.Text	Contains the StringBuilder class and supports various String manipulation functions, such as insert or remove text and others. You do not need to create a new String object, which the concatenation operator (&) implicitly does, in order to modify a string.
System.Windows.Forms	Contains a number of control classes that can be added to a form to create rich GUI applications. The controls include DateTimePicker, Textbox, Button, and ListBox.
System.Xml	Used for processing XML. This namespace includes a reader for parsing XML and classes such as XmlDocument and XmlNode.

and then click OK to add the reference and close the dialog box. Figure 3.6 shows the Add Reference dialog box in Visual Studio. You can also set references to component object model (COM) type libraries or browse to a particular assembly on your system. All references to your project

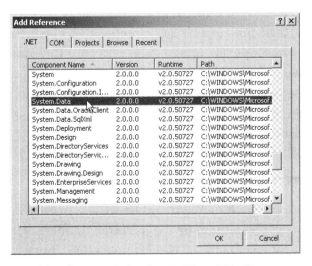

Figure 3.6. *The Add Reference dialog box in Visual Studio*

are displayed in the References node in Solution Explorer. You might have to click Show All Files to view the references.

After setting the reference, you can add an Imports statement at the top of your code file so that you don't have to fully qualify an object in the namespace. You can optionally create an alias for the namespace as was shown in Listing 3.15. Some namespaces, such as the System namespace, are automatically included in your solution; therefore, it is not necessary to add a reference or create an alias for these namespaces.

VSTO and Managed Code

When you create VBA solutions for Word and Excel, your code typically is stored in the document or in an attached or global template. To access code in a template separate from your solution, you set a reference from your document to the template.

However, when you create VSTO solutions, your code is stored in an assembly. You can set references in your project to other assemblies, such as .NET Framework assemblies and interop assemblies, but you cannot set a reference to other VSTO solution assemblies. Only one VSTO solution assembly can be associated with a document or workbook. However, multiple documents can reference the same solution assembly. This is the case when you create multiple documents based on a VSTO-customized template. Note that because Outlook solutions are application-level, you can load multiple add-ins into Outlook. The same is true for add-ins created with VSTO 2005 SE.

Primary Interop Assemblies

Office applications, such as Word and Excel, are written in unmanaged code. For your VSTO solution (managed code) to interoperate with the unmanaged COM objects in the Office application, it must use an *interoperability assembly.* Visual Studio can create an interoperability assembly for you when you set a reference to a COM type library, but generating an interoperability assembly in this way is not recommended. Instead, you should use the official interoperability assembly that is provided by the publisher of the type library. This is known as the *primary interop assembly* (PIA). If the PIAs are installed on your computer and you set a reference to the type library, Visual Studio automatically loads the PIA instead of generating a new interop assembly.

Microsoft provides PIAs for its Office applications. The name of the Excel PIA is Microsoft.Office.Interop.Excel.dll. Word and Outlook follow the same naming convention for their PIAs: Microsoft.Office.Interop.Word.dll and Microsoft.Office.Interop.Outlook.dll.

The PIAs get installed in your computer's GAC when you run a complete installation of Office 2003. Whenever you create a new VSTO solution, Visual Studio automatically adds to your solution a reference to the appropriate Office PIA and any of its dependent assemblies. You can view the contents of the GAC by opening the Windows\assembly directory of your root drive. Figure 3.7 shows the Microsoft PIAs.

The namespace for these PIAs is determined by the name of the assembly. VSTO automatically creates an alias for these namespaces, as shown in Table 3.3.

If the PIAs have not been correctly installed on your development machine because a complete installation of Office 2003 was not performed, you can run a reinstall or repair of Office 2003, assuming that .NET Framework 1.1 or later is already installed on your computer. Alternatively, you can use Add or Remove Features in the Maintenance Mode Options section of the Microsoft Office 2003 Setup, and click Next (see Figure 3.8). For information on redistributing the PIAs when you deploy your solutions, see Chapter 11.

On the next page of the Setup wizard, select Choose Advanced Customization of Applications, and then click Next.

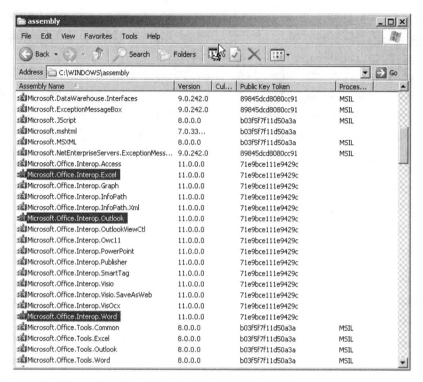

Figure 3.7. *Microsoft Office PIAs displayed in the GAC*

Table 3.3. *Excel, Word, and Outlook PIAs, Namespaces, and Aliases*

PIA	Namespace	Alias
Microsoft.Office.Interop.Excel.dll	Microsoft.Office.Interop.Excel	Excel
Microsoft.Office.Interop.Word.dll	Microsoft.Office.Interop.Word	Word
Microsoft.Office.Interop.Outlook.dll	Microsoft.Office.Interop.Outlook	Outlook

Set each of the following components to Run from My Computer. See
Figure 3.9 for an example.

- Microsoft Office Excel | .NET Programmability Support

- Microsoft Office Outlook | .NET Programmability Support

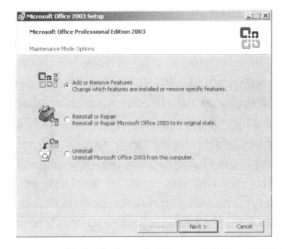

Figure 3.8. *Maintenance Mode Options in Microsoft Office 2003 Setup*

- Microsoft Office Word | .NET Programmability Support

- Office Tools | Microsoft Forms 2.0 .NET Programmability Support

- Office Tools | Smart Tag .NET Programmability Support

- Office Tools | Microsoft Graph, .NET Programmability Support

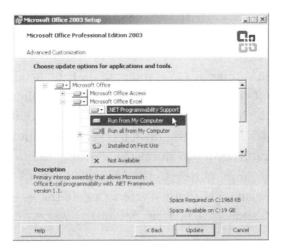

Figure 3.9. *Advanced Customization in Microsoft Office 2003 Setup*

Solution Assemblies

As you learned earlier in this chapter, an assembly is a collection of classes and functionality that is stored as an executable file (.exe) or a library (.dll). When you build a VSTO solution, the code is compiled and stored in a single assembly (DLL file) located in the \bin\debug (or \bin\release) directory of your solution. The assembly isn't stored inside the document, but the document does include an application manifest, which contains information about the name and location of the assembly. There are two manifests: an *application manifest* (which is stored in the document via an embedded control called the Runtime Storage Control) and a *deployment manifest,* which is located in the same directory where the assembly is deployed.

Even though you can associate a VSTO solution assembly only with a particular document (you can have only one solution assembly associated with a document), your solution assembly can reference other assemblies. For example, to add a common group of user controls to the actions pane, you can save a library of user controls in an assembly and then reference that assembly from multiple VSTO solutions.

How do you determine which VSTO assembly is associated with a particular document? You look at the document properties. You can view the document properties of a Word document or Excel workbook by clicking Properties in the File menu. A VSTO-enabled document has two custom document properties that indicate that the document is a VSTO solution. The first custom property is named _AssemblyName. If the value of _AssemblyName is an asterisk (*), it means that the document has an associated VSTO customization (assembly). The second custom property, _AssemblyLocation, stores the globally unique identifier (GUID) of the Runtime Storage Control (which contains the application manifest and information about where to locate the associated assembly). Figure 3.10 shows the custom document properties of a Word solution.

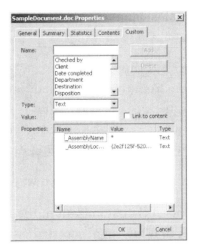

Figure 3.10. *Custom document properties of a Word solution*

Adding Customization to Existing Documents

You can attach an existing solution assembly to an uncustomized document or worksheet in one of two ways. The first is to add the _AssemblyName property with a value of asterisk (*), add the _AssemblyLocation custom property with the location of the deployment manifest as its value, and then save, close, and reopen the document. The second approach involves using the AddCustomization method of the ServerDocument class. These techniques are described in more detail in Chapter 13, Advanced Topics in VSTO 2005.

Running VSTO Solutions

For a VSTO solution to run, the assemblies must have full trust permissions. On the development machine, full trust is automatically granted to your solution's assembly and any referenced assemblies whenever you build the project. The evidence used for this trust is based on location (the URL of the assembly). When you deploy your solution, you need to grant full trust to the document and the assembly by using a strong name or by digitally signing the assembly. This procedure is discussed in greater detail in Chapter 11.

As a developer, you can run your customization by pressing F5 or by clicking Start Debugging from the Debug menu in Visual Studio. You can also open the document or workbook that is stored in the /debug/ bin directory of the location in which you saved your solution, or press Ctrl+F5 to run the solution without debugging it.

An end user can run a solution in one of two ways.

1. To run a document-level customization, the user opens the document or workbook that has an associated customization assembly. Alternatively, the user can create a new document or workbook that is based on a template that has an associated customization assembly.

2. To run an application-level customization (add-in), users have two options. They can open the application, which contains instructions to load an add-in when the application starts. Or they can manually enable the add-in in the COM Add-ins dialog box of the application.

Summary

We began this chapter with an introduction to managed code and object-oriented programming. You looked at classes and learned how you can instantiate a class to create an object and then create properties, methods, and events for your class. You then learned how to create partial classes, generic classes, and interfaces. Next, you looked at the .NET Framework and learned that the common language runtime provides a framework for running managed code that includes compilation services, exception handling, reflection, and memory management. We looked at some common namespaces in the .NET Framework class library. Finally, we put this all together by looking at how a VSTO solution uses primary interop assemblies and how solution assemblies are created and run.

Review Questions

1. How do objects differ from classes?

2. What is the default constructor of any class in Visual Basic 2005? How can you override and overload a constructor?

3. How do Windows Forms and VSTO use partial classes in their programming models?

4. Define the three features that an object-oriented language must support.

5. What is IL? Why is it important to .NET programming?

6. Name three services provided by the common language runtime.

4

Moving from VBA to VSTO and Visual Basic 2005

The great thing in this world is not so much where you stand, as in what direction you are moving.
—OLIVER WENDELL HOLMES

Topics Covered in This Chapter

Moving to Visual Basic 2005

New Features of Visual Basic 2005

Language Differences of VBA and Visual Basic 2005

UserForms Versus Windows Forms

Summary

Review Questions

Moving to Visual Basic 2005

VSTO 2005 supports two programming languages: Visual C# and Visual Basic 2005. If you're planning to move from VBA to managed code, it might not make a difference which language you choose, and it might even be in your best interest to learn both. However, developers who are familiar with C++ would probably find it easier to learn C#, because there are many similarities between the languages. For example, C++ and Visual C# share a similar syntax. Similarly, VBA developers might find it easier to move to Visual Basic 2005.

It's challenging enough to learn to use a new integrated development environment, debugging tools, the .NET Framework class libraries, the .NET Framework security model, and object-oriented programming concepts without having to learn a completely different programming language. Additionally, if you migrate your existing VBA solutions to VSTO and plan to use any migration tools, such as the Visual Basic Migration Wizard, these tools would most likely convert the VBA code directly to Visual Basic 2005. You would have to take additional steps to then convert the code into Visual C#. For more information about migrating VBA solutions to VSTO, see Chapter 12.

For these reasons, we believe it makes sense to make the move from VBA to Visual Basic 2005 rather than to Visual C#. Once you are more familiar with programming Office applications using VSTO, you can transfer those skills if you decide to program with C#.

Although there are many similarities between VBA and Visual Basic 2005, there are several differences. These differences range from language changes such as data types and array bounds to new features of Visual Basic 2005, such as the My objects and IntelliSense code snippets. You also must learn about the differences between ActiveX controls and Windows Forms controls. In this chapter we describe these differences and introduce you to some of the new features in Visual Basic 2005.

New Features of Visual Basic 2005

Many new features in Visual Basic 2005 help increase your productivity. Some of these features are enhancements to the IDE, such as improved IntelliSense capabilities, the ability to use preinstalled code snippets, and debugger enhancements such as Edit and Continue, the Exception Assistant, and Just My Code. (These new IDE features are described in Chapter 2.) Other new features include the .NET Framework enhancements that are supported by Visual Basic 2005 (such as partial classes and generics) and enhancements to Visual Basic 2005 (such as the new My objects and the ability to create IntelliSense code snippets).

The My Objects

The new My objects give you easy access to application, system, and user information without having to search through the .NET Framework class libraries to locate equivalent functionality. Instead, if you type My followed by a period, IntelliSense displays all the members of the My objects that are available to VSTO solutions. Table 4.1 describes these objects as well as those that are not available.

Table 4.1. *The My Objects in Visual Basic 2005*

My Object	Description
My.Application	Enables you to access information about the application. For example, you can change the culture of your application to English (US) by using My.Application.ChangeCulture("en-US").
My.Computer	Enables you to set properties for computer components such as the file system and the Clipboard. For example, you can clear the Clipboard by using My.Computer.Clipboard.Clear(). You can also retrieve information about the computer, such as its name or operating system.
My.Resources	Provides read-only access to resources in your application. For example, you can retrieve a string resource by referencing the name of the string. If you have a string resource named ControlName, using My.Resources.ControlName retrieves the value of the string.
My.Settings	Provides access to application settings. For example, you can reset the application settings to their default values by using My.Settings.Reset().

(continues)

Table 4.1. *The My Objects in Visual Basic 2005 (Continued)*

My Object	Description
My.User	Gives you access to information about the current user. For example, you can check the name of the current user by using My.User.Name.
My.WebServices	Provides an instance of every Web service that is currently referenced in the project. You can call a function within a Web service by using My.WebServices.
My.Forms	Not available in VSTO projects.
My.Log	Not available in VSTO projects.
My.Request	Not available in VSTO projects.
My.Response	Not available in VSTO projects.

One example of using a My object is to access the name of the current user. Note, however, that VSTO does not set My.User by default. You must first call InitializeWithWindowsUser. The code in Listing 4.1 displays the current user in a message box.

Listing 4.1. *Displaying the user's login name in a message box*

```
My.User.InitializeWithWindowsUser()

MsgBox(CStr(My.User.Name))
```

In this section you will create a simple Word application that demonstrates some of the My object features.

1. On the File menu, point to New and then click Project.

2. Select a Word document in the Templates pane, leaving all the default settings in the New Project dialog box. Click OK to create a new document project.

3. In the Visual Studio Tools for Office Project Wizard, select Create a New Document, and then click OK.

4. Drag a combo box and list box from the Toolbox to the document, and resize the controls so that it looks similar to the document shown in Figure 4.1.

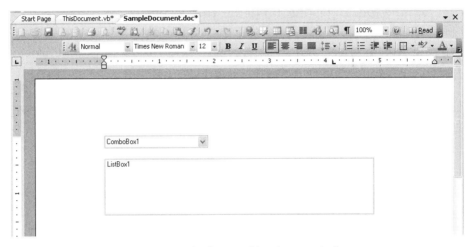

Figure 4.1. *Document with combo box and list box controls*

5. In Solution Explorer, right-click ThisDocument.vb and select View Code.

   The Code Editor opens and displays two default event handlers: Startup and Shutdown.

6. Replace the code in the Startup event handler with the code in Listing 4.2. This code adds entries to the combo box when the document first opens.

Listing 4.2. *Adding entries to the combo box*

```
Private Sub ThisDocument_Startup(ByVal sender As Object, _
    ByVal e As System.EventArgs) Handles Me.Startup

    With Me.ComboBox1.Items
        .Add("Ports")
        .Add("Drives")
```

```
    .Add("Loaded Assemblies")
End With

End Sub
```

7. Add the code in Listing 4.3 to the ThisDocument class. This code uses the My objects to populate the list box with information about the system drives and ports, along with the assemblies that are loaded when the application is running.

Listing 4.3. *Using the My objects to obtain system information*

```
Private Sub ComboBox1_SelectedValueChanged(ByVal sender _
    As Object, ByVal e As System.EventArgs) Handles _
    ComboBox1.SelectedValueChanged

    Select Case ComboBox1.SelectedItem
        Case "Loaded Assemblies"
            Dim i As Integer = 0
            Dim TotalAssemblies = My.Application.Info. _
                LoadedAssemblies.Count
            Me.ListBox1.Items.Clear()
            For i = 0 To TotalAssemblies - 1
                Me.ListBox1.Items.Add(CStr(My.Application.Info. _
                    LoadedAssemblies(i).FullName))
            Next
        Case "Drives"
            Dim i As Integer = 0
            Dim TotalDrives = My.Computer.FileSystem.Drives.Count
            Me.ListBox1.Items.Clear()

            For i = 0 To TotalDrives - 1
                Me.ListBox1.Items.Add(CStr(My.Computer. _
                    FileSystem.Drives(i).Name))
            Next
        Case "Ports"
            Dim i As Integer = 0
            Dim TotalPorts = My.Computer.Ports. _
                SerialPortNames.Count
            Me.ListBox1.Items.Clear()
```

```
              For i = 0 To TotalPorts - 1
                  Me.ListBox1.Items.Add(CStr(My.Computer. _
                      Ports.SerialPortNames(i)))
              Next
          End Select
      End Sub
```

8. Run the code by pressing F5.

The code is built and the Word application opens. When you select Ports in the combo box, the list box displays the name of the ports on your system. When you select Drives, the list box displays all the available drives. The Loaded Assemblies option displays all the assemblies that the application has loaded on your system, as shown in Figure 4.2.

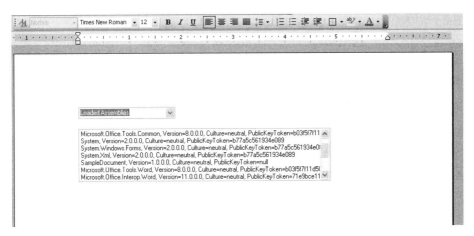

Figure 4.2. *Displaying the assemblies loaded by the application*

IntelliSense Code Snippets

IntelliSense code snippets are a new .NET Framework feature supported by Visual Basic 2005. The IntelliSense code snippets are saved in XML files and become available in the Visual Studio IDE when you right-click the Code Editor and select Insert Snippet.

Visual Studio comes with a number of preinstalled snippets. When you select a code snippet to insert, an entire code block is inserted into the Code Editor. You can then customize the code for your application. For example, you can change the highlighted variable names to names you have defined in your application. Chapter 2 describes the default code snippets and the additional snippets you can download from www.microsoft.com.

You can insert an IntelliSense code snippet into the Code Editor in a number of ways. You can right-click the Code Editor, select Insert Snippet, and then navigate through the folders to the desired snippet. Or you can type the snippet's shortcut name and press the TAB key.

Another technique is to type the first few letters of the shortcut name, followed by a question mark (?), and then press the TAB key. A list of all the shortcuts that begin with the letters you typed appears in a drop-down list, and you can select the appropriate snippet. In addition to numerous preinstalled Visual Basic 2005 and VSTO code snippets that ship with Visual Studio, you can search for additional code snippets on the Internet, and you can create your own code snippets.

You create your own IntelliSense code snippets by creating an XML file that has a .snippet extension. You might find it useful to create these snippets to store frequently used functions as a type of function library for your projects. Instead of having to manually type the code or use the Toolbox as temporary storage for code snippets, you can create IntelliSense code snippets and then quickly add complete procedures to your code. It's similar to storing autotext entries as you do in Word, but here, you insert them into the Code Editor. If you're interested in creating your own XML code snippets, you can find a description of how to manually create a simple code snippet in Appendix A.

Statements

Two new statements in Visual Basic 2005 make coding tasks easier: the Continue statement and the Using statement.

Continue Statement

You can use the Continue statement in a Do loop, a For loop, or a While loop to transfer execution to the next iteration within the loop. Listing 4.4 shows how to use a Continue statement to identify the number of styles in use in a Word document.

Listing 4.4. *Using a Continue statement in a For loop*

```
Sub CountStyles()

    Dim styleCount As Integer = 0

    For Each currentStyle As Word.Style In Me.Styles
        If currentStyle.InUse = False Then Continue For
        styleCount += 1
    Next

    MsgBox("Total styles: " & Me.Styles.Count & vbCrLf & _
        "Styles available: " & styleCount)

End Sub
```

In this code example, you use the += operator to add a value to a numeric variable and then assign the result to the variable. Using VBA, you type this:

```
styleCount = styleCount + 1
```

Using Visual Basic 2005, you can type the following to get identical functionality:

```
styleCount += 1
```

Using Statement

You can use a Using statement to ensure that unmanaged resources are disposed of properly. Recall from Chapter 3 that you do not need to track and manage the memory resources for your application because the garbage collector reclaims any memory that is no longer being used. However, if you want to ensure that unmanaged resources are properly disposed of, or if you are using a managed resource that uses a lot of memory, you can use a Using block to ensure that the resource is disposed of whenever the block is exited.

In the Using block, you specify the resources that you want to manage. You use the End Using statement to indicate that you are no longer using the resource and that the system can dispose of any resources that were controlled by the Using block. Listing 4.5 shows how to use the Using statement with a SQL database. You should always close a SQLConnection by calling Close or Dispose, but when you declare the connection within a Using statement, it ensures that the Dispose method is called for you. The example assumes that the string Connection is a valid connection string.

Listing 4.5. *A Using block manages a resource.*

```
Sub SampleCode(ByVal Connection As String)

    Using sqlConnection As New System.Data.SqlClient. _
        SqlConnection(Connection)

        'Add code to open connection and work with data.

    End Using

End Sub
```

Operators

Visual Basic 2005 introduces a new IsNot operator. Also, there are two logical operators introduced in an earlier version of Visual Basic .NET that you might not be familiar with: the AndAlso and OrElse operators.

IsNot Operator

The IsNot operator lets you compare two object references. This operator returns False if both objects refer to the same object; otherwise, it returns True. This is equivalent to using Not with the Is operator, but it makes your code easier to read. In Listing 4.6, both If statements behave in the same way, but the If statement that uses the IsNot operator is much easier to read.

Listing 4.6. *Comparing the Is and IsNot operators*

```
Dim explorer As Outlook.Explorer = Me.ActiveExplorer()

If Not explorer Is Nothing Then
    'Add code to customize the active explorer.
End If

If explorer IsNot Nothing Then
    'Add code to customize the active explorer.
End If
```

AndAlso Operator

The AndAlso operator is used to evaluate two expressions but evaluates the second expression only if the first expression is True. For example, if you want to access a property of a Bookmark object only if the bookmark exists (thus avoiding an error), you can use the AndAlso statement, as shown in Listing 4.7. This technique is often referred to as *short circuiting.*

Listing 4.7. *Using the AndAlso operator*

```
If Bookmark1 IsNot Nothing AndAlso Bookmark1.Bold Then
    MsgBox("The bookmark text is bold")
End If
```

OrElse Operator

The OrElse operator is used to evaluate two expressions but evaluates the second expression only if the first expression is False. The code in Listing 4.8 checks whether the text in a bookmark named Bookmark1 has italic formatting. If it doesn't, it then checks whether the bookmark has bold formatting. If either of these expressions is true, a message box is displayed.

Listing 4.8. *Using the AndAlso operator*

```
If Bookmark1.Italic OrElse Bookmark1.Bold Then
    MsgBox("The bookmark text has formatting")
End If
```

Language Differences of VBA and Visual Basic 2005

Visual Basic 2005 is an object-oriented programming language that supports encapsulation, inheritance, interfaces, and overloading. Additionally, many language differences exist between VBA and Visual Basic 2005.

Data Types

To comply with the common language specifications, data types in languages supported by the .NET Framework must map to the types in the System namespace. For example, an Integer maps to System.Int32, and a Long maps to System.Int64. Because of these requirements, some data types in Visual Basic 2005 differ from those in VBA. When you write your code, you can use either the Visual Basic aliases for the data type (Integer, Long, etc.) or the .NET Framework data types (System.Int32, System.Int64, etc.). However, the aliases provided for Visual Basic are much easier to read and remember.

Data Type Differences

In VBA an integer is 16 bits, which is equivalent to a Short in Visual Basic 2005. A Long is 32 bits in VBA, which is equivalent to an Integer in Visual Basic 2005.

The Currency data type is not supported in Visual Basic 2005. Instead, you can use the Decimal data type. Decimal is more accurate than the Currency data type. Decimal is a 128-bit fixed-point data type that can hold up to 28 digits to the right of the decimal point. You can force the data type of a literal value to Decimal by adding a *D* to the end of the literal value. For example, 23445937D is forced to be interpreted as a Decimal. Without the *D*, the literal value is interpreted as a Long.

The Variant data type is not supported in Visual Basic 2005. When you copy VBA code into the Visual Basic 2005 Code Editor, if that code either declares a variable as a Variant or does not specify the data type, it is automatically converted to the Object type. Instead of declaring a variable as an Object, you should specify its data type to avoid late binding of the object. *Late binding* means that the type of the object is not known until run time. Early binding gives you the added bonus of having access to all the IntelliSense features of Visual Studio at design time.

A Date in Visual Basic 2005 maps to a System.DateTime type in the .NET Framework. In VBA, the Date data type is stored as a floating-point number. To convert between a Double and a Date data type in Visual Basic 2005, you should use the Date's ToOADate and FromOADate methods. Listing 4.9 demonstrates the conversion of a date stored in an Excel range to a Date. The example assumes that cell A1 contains a valid date.

Listing 4.9. *Using the FromOADate method*

```
Sub GetDate()
    Dim myDate As Date = Date.FromOADate( _
        Globals.Sheet1.Range("A1").Value2
    MsgBox(CStr(myDate))

End Sub
```

When the GetDate method runs, the message box displays the date in cell A1. If you rewrite the code to declare myDate as a Double and assign it the value of cell A1, the message box displays the value as a double rather than in date format.

Table 4.2 shows the mapping between data types in Visual Basic 2005, VBA, and the .NET Framework.

Table 4.2. *Data Types in VBA, Visual Basic 2005, and the .NET Framework*

VBA	**Visual Basic 2005**	**.NET Framework**
Integer	Short	System.Int16
Long	Integer	System.Int32
Currency	Decimal	System.Decimal
Variant	Object	System.Object
Date (stored as double)	Date	System.DateTime

Strings Are Objects

In Visual Basic 2005, a String is an object that has its own members, which you can use to manipulate the String. For example, if you start typing the code in Listing 4.10, when you type the period after AuthorName, IntelliSense displays all the methods and properties available for a String, as shown in Figure 4.3.

Listing 4.10. *Methods for a String*

```
Dim AuthorName As String = "Kathleen McGrath"
Dim Names() As String = AuthorName.Split(" ")
MsgBox("First Name: " & Names(0) & vbCrLf & _
    "Last Name: " & Names(1))
```

You can convert data types to strings using the CStr function, but many types can be converted to a String by using the ToString() method. For

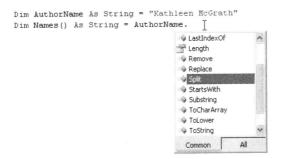

Figure 4.3. *Calling the Split method on a String*

example, if you want to display an integer in a message box and you have Option Strict turned on, you must first convert the Integer to a String. Replace the code in the ThisDocument class of a Word document solution with the code in Listing 4.11, and then run the code.

Listing 4.11. *Displaying an Integer in a message box*

```
Option Strict On
Public Class ThisDocument

    Private Sub ThisDocument_Startup(ByVal sender As Object, _
        ByVal e As System.EventArgs) Handles Me.Startup

        Dim ParagraphCount As Integer = Me.Paragraphs.Count
        MsgBox(ParagraphCount)

    End Sub

    Private Sub ThisDocument_Shutdown(ByVal sender As Object, _
        ByVal e As System.EventArgs) Handles Me.Shutdown

    End Sub

End Class
```

When you run the code in Listing 4.11, a build error occurs indicating that Option Strict On disallows implicit conversions from Integer to

String. You can do one of two things. The first is to turn off Option Strict. Keep in mind that in addition to ensuring that you explicitly convert numeric types and strings, Option Strict restricts data type conversion that could result in data loss and generates errors when objects are late bound. Turning Option Strict on can help reduce errors in your code.

The second option is to explicitly convert the Integer to a String. You do this by using the CStr function or by calling the ToString() method on the integer. Change the line of code that reads MsgBox (ParagraphCount) to MsgBox (ParagraphCount.ToString()), and press F5. This time the message box displays the total number of paragraphs in the document.

String Functions

It is important to note that the string handling functions for bytes and double-bytes in VBA are not supported in Visual Basic 2005. Visual Basic 2005 strings are in Unicode, and conversion of Strings to double-byte character sets is no longer needed. Table 4.3 lists the VBA functions that are no longer supported and their equivalent Visual Basic 2005 functions (found in the Microsoft.VisualBasic namespace).

Table 4.3. *Unsupported VBA Functions and the Equivalent Visual Basic 2005 Functions*

VBA	Visual Basic 2005 Equivalent
AscB	Asc
ChrB, ChrB$	Chr
InstrB	Instr
LeftB, LeftB$	Left
LenB	Len
MidB, MidB$	Mid
RightB, RightB$	Right

Fixed-Length Strings

Fixed-length strings have a specific length that is specified when the variable is declared. When you assign text that is longer than the specified length, the text gets truncated. Although it is possible to declare fixed-length strings in VBA, they are not supported in Visual Basic 2005.

Arrays Are Zero-Based

Visual Basic 2005 arrays cannot have a lower bound other than zero (0). You cannot set the lower bound to 1, as you can when you use VBA. If you want to initialize the array at the time you declare it, you can place curly brackets ({ }) around all the elements you want to add. You'll notice later in Listing 4.12 that to display the first element of the array (apples), you must reference the element 0.

Even though arrays and collections are zero-based in managed code, keep in mind that when you write code against the Office object models, many of the collections are 1-based instead of 0-based. For example, if you tried to access the first bookmark in the Bookmarks collection using the following code example, a run-time error would occur:

```
MsgBox(CStr(Me.Bookmarks(0).Name))
```

Methods

There are a few differences between methods that are created in VBA and methods that are created in Visual Basic 2005. For example, you must use parentheses in method calls when you pass parameters to a method in Visual Basic 2005. This differs from the behavior in VBA, where parentheses are sometimes, but not always, required.

Parameters

By default, parameters are passed by reference in VBA. In Visual Basic 2005, they are passed by value. If you create a method in Visual Basic

2005 that takes parameters and if you do not specify whether the parameter must be passed by reference or by value, Visual Basic 2005 automatically inserts the ByVal keyword into the Code Editor.

Method Overloading

Optional parameters are still supported in Visual Basic 2005. You will use them often when you call methods on the Office object models, because many of the methods in Word and Excel accept optional parameters. However, there is another way to provide methods that can take a variety of parameters in Visual Basic 2005. This feature is known as *method overloading.*

In Visual Basic 2005, you can create multiple methods that have the same name but differ only in the type or number of arguments. Each additional method defined is an overload of the method. For example, the code example in Figure 4.4 shows a Print method with three overloads. The first overload prints the document to a file; therefore, it contains some arguments specific to printing to a file, such as Append and OutputFileName. These arguments don't make sense in the second overload, which does not allow a document to be printed to a file. The third overload doesn't accept any arguments and instead prints the document with all the default arguments.

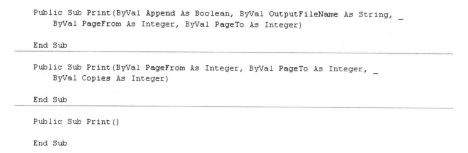

```
Public Sub Print(ByVal Append As Boolean, ByVal OutputFileName As String, _
    ByVal PageFrom As Integer, ByVal PageTo As Integer)

End Sub

Public Sub Print(ByVal PageFrom As Integer, ByVal PageTo As Integer, _
    ByVal Copies As Integer)

End Sub

Public Sub Print()

End Sub
```

Figure 4.4. *Providing overloaded methods*

Variable Declaration and Scope

When you declare a variable within a Visual Basic 2005 class, the variable is available only within that instance of the class and cannot be accessed by another instance. If you declare the variable as Shared, it is available to all instances of the class. In VBA, variables declared within a code block, such as a loop, are available locally to the entire procedure, but variables in Visual Basic 2005 are available only within the code block itself. If you declare a variable within a looping structure, the variable is not available outside the loop.

As in VBA, you declare a variable in Visual Basic 2005 using the Dim statement and specify a data type for the variable. If you do not specify a data type in VBA, the variable is automatically created as the type Variant. The Variant data type is no longer supported in Visual Basic 2005. Instead, an unspecified variable is created as an Object.

As a best practice, you should always explicitly type any variables that you declare. This is to avoid late binding to variables. Although late binding is supported in Visual Basic 2005, early-bound variables aid in code readability, and enable IntelliSense on the object. Figure 4.5 shows the differences in IntelliSense capabilities when a variable's data type is not specified versus when it is specified.

In VBA, if you declare more than one variable within a statement, you must specify the type for each variable or else it defaults to the Variant type. In Visual Basic 2005, you can declare multiple variables as the same type. Table 4.4 shows the difference in multiple variable declarations between VBA and Visual Basic 2005.

Array variables should not be declared using the New keyword (As New). In VBA, you can automatically initialize array members by declaring the array with the New keyword. This keyword is not supported for arrays in Visual Basic 2005. Instead, you must explicitly initialize the members of an array, as shown in Listing 4.12.

Figure 4.5. *Late binding to variables (top) versus early binding*

Table 4.4. *Variable Declaration in VBA and Visual Basic 2005*

Declaration	VBA	Visual Basic 2005
Dim iCount, iTotal As Integer	iCount is Variant, iTotal is Integer.	Both iCount and iTotal are Integers.
Dim iCount	iCount is a Variant data type.	iCount is an Object data type.

Listing 4.12. *Initializing an array*

```
Dim Fruit() As String = {"apples", "oranges", "bananas", "pears"}
MsgBox(Fruit(0))
```

Default Properties

Default properties are supported in Visual Basic 2005 only if the properties take arguments. For example, the Label control in VBA has a property called Caption that is the default property; this means that you can assign a value to this control directly, without specifying the property name. In Visual Basic 2005, you must specify the property when assigning values to properties. For example, you would have to type Label1.Text = "OK" to assign the OK string to the label. Typing Label1 = "OK" would cause an error.

An example of a default property that takes an argument is the Item property. You do not need to explicitly specify the Item property because it takes an index as a parameter. For example, you can reference a bookmark using Me.Bookmarks(1) instead of specifying the Item property using Me.Bookmarks.Item(1).

Because of this change, you no longer need to use the Set keyword when assigning an object to a variable. The Set keyword was used to differentiate between the assignment of an object and the assignment of a value to a default property of the object. Removing the support for default properties removes the ambiguity of assignment.

Enumerations

You must fully qualify enumeration constants in Visual Basic 2005. You might be accustomed to using a constant, such as xlUnderlineStyleSingle, when you assign an underline style to an Excel worksheet cell. In Visual Basic 2005, you must fully qualify the enumeration by typing Excel.XlUnderlineStyle.xlUnderlineStyleSingle, as shown in Listing 4.13. Note that Excel is an alias for the Microsoft.Office.Interop.Excel namespace.

Listing 4.13. *Fully qualifying enumeration constants*

```
' VBA
Dim myRange As Excel.Range
myRange = Range("A1")
myRange.Font.Underline = xlUnderlineStyleSingle

' Visual Basic 2005
Dim myRange As Excel.Range
MyRange.Font.Underline = Excel.XlUnderlineStyle _
    .xlUnderlineStyleSingle
```

Exception Handling

Using VBA, you typically handle errors by using an On Error statement that specifies the location of the error handling code. When an error is encountered, execution moves to the previous On Error statement in the subroutine, which then moves execution to the location specified. The On Error statement can specify three things:

- The code execution should move to a particular line or label (On Error GoTo xErrorHandler).

- The code execution should move to the next statement in the code where the error occurred (On Error Resume Next).

- The error handling should be disabled within the procedure (On Error GoTo 0).

Visual Basic 2005 supports the On Error statement, but you should consider using structured error handling. Structured error handling in Visual Basic 2005 translates to the Try Catch Finally (Try Catch) statements (see Listing 4.14). These statements enable you to catch errors that are thrown at run time and handle the errors gracefully so that the application doesn't just crash unexpectedly. You can write code to handle specific exceptions that you know might occur in your code, or you can catch unspecified exceptions in a general Catch block.

Listing 4.14. *Try Catch statement*

```
Try
    ' Code that might cause an exception.

Catch ex As Exception
    ' Code to handle the exception.

Finally
    ' Additional code to run whether or not exception occurs.
End Try
```

Visual Basic 2005 has the Try Catch statement available as a code snippet. Three statements are available, and each snippet has a corresponding shortcut that you can expand by typing the shortcut name and then pressing the TAB key.

- Try Catch EndTry, which has the shortcut TryC
- Try Catch Finally EndTry, which has the shortcut TryCF
- Try Finally EndTry, which has the shortcut TryF

To add a Try Catch statement using a code snippet shortcut, type TryCF in the Code Editor, and then press the TAB key. Notice that the variable ApplicationException in the Catch statement is automatically highlighted. You should change this variable to the type of exception that you expect. For example, you can change it to a NullReferenceException if it is possible that a variable has not yet been assigned a value, as shown in Listing 4.15. You can have more than one Catch block to handle different types of exceptions.

You add the code that might cause an error to the Try block. If an error occurs, execution moves to the Catch block, which should contain the code that handles the error. Code execution then moves to the first statement after the End Try statement. If the optional Finally statement is present before the End Try statement, the code execution always moves to the Finally block. Code within a Finally block runs after the errors are handled and runs even if an error is not encountered. Often, developers add cleanup code, such as closing a database connection, to the Finally block.

Listing 4.15. *Catching a NullReferenceException*

```
Dim myString As Object = Nothing

Try

    MsgBox(myString.ToString())
```

```
Catch ex As NullReferenceException

    MsgBox(ex.Message)

End Try
```

If code in a method encounters an error and if a Catch block for the type of exception thrown cannot be located, the exception is passed up to the calling method. This continues until the top of the call stack is reached. If a Catch block is still not found, the default exception handler runs. The Message property of the exception contains information about the cause of the error, and you can display this information to end users in a message box. You can even provide a link to a Help topic that contains additional information.

If you plan to upgrade existing VBA code to Visual Basic 2005, keep in mind that you cannot combine the VBA-style error handling with structured error handling within the same methods. Doing so will cause a compiler error, as shown in Figure 4.6.

```
On Error Resume Next
Method cannot contain both a 'Try' statement and an 'On Error' or 'Resume' statement.
Try
        MessageBox.Show(myString.ToString())
Catch ex As NullReferenceException
        MessageBox.Show(ex.Message)
End Try
```

Figure 4.6. *Error when using a Try statement with an On Error statement*

UserForms Versus Windows Forms

When you use VBA to create an Office solution, you can design a user interface to display a dialog box. To do so, you add a UserForm to your project and then add controls to the UserForm. These controls are

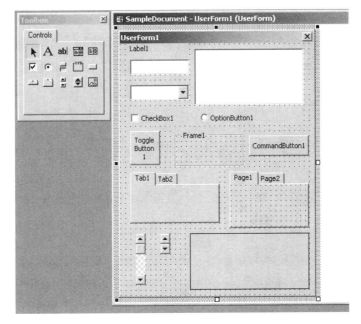

Figure 4.7. *A UserForm in VBA that contains all the default ActiveX controls*

referred to as ActiveX controls. Whenever the UserForm has focus, the Toolbox, which contains all the default controls, becomes visible. Figure 4.7 shows a UserForm that contains all the default ActiveX controls.

When you use VSTO to create an Office solution, you can design the user interface by designing a Windows Form that can be displayed as a window, as a dialog box, or on a user control that appears in the document or Document Actions task pane. The Toolbox in Visual Studio displays all the Windows Forms controls that are available for a Windows Form. Figure 4.8 shows a Windows Form with all the controls that are displayed on the UserForm in Figure 4.7. The Toolbox in Figure 4.8 also shows some of the controls that can be added to the Windows Form.

Notice that some of the controls that are available for a UserForm are not available on a Windows Form—for example, the Toggle control, the Spin control, and the MultiPage control. Many additional Windows

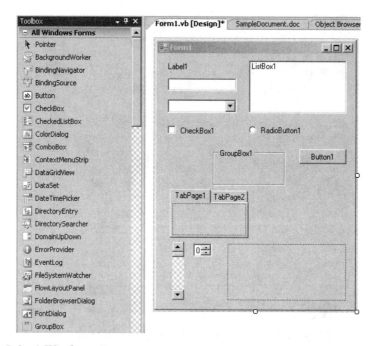

Figure 4.8. *A Windows Form in VSTO with Toolbox displaying a portion of the available controls*

Forms controls that appear on the Toolbox are not displayed in Figure 4.8. These controls are described in Chapter 8.

Comparison of ActiveX Controls to Windows Forms Controls

ActiveX controls differ from the corresponding Windows Forms controls in many ways. For example, the names of some of the controls and their properties, methods, and events are different. The left column in Table 4.5 shows the names of the ActiveX controls, and the right column shows the names of the corresponding Windows Forms controls.

Table 4.6 shows the changes in the names of the properties, methods, and events that are common to many of the controls listed in Table 4.5.

Table 4.5. *ActiveX Controls in VBA and the Corresponding Windows Forms Controls in Visual Basic 2005*

ActiveX Controls (VBA)	Windows Forms Controls (Visual Basic 2005 Controls)
TextBox	TextBox
Label	Label
ComboBox	ComboBox
ListBox	ListBox
CheckBox	CheckBox
OptionButton	RadioButton
ToggleButton	N/A (can use a CheckBox control and set its Appearance property to Button)
CommandButton	Button
TabStrip	TabControl
MultiPage	TabControl
ScrollBar	VScrollBar, HScrollBar
SpinButton	NumericUpDown
ImageControl	N/A (can use a PictureBox control instead)

Table 4.6. *Changes to Common Members of the Windows Forms Controls*

Member	VBA	Visual Basic 2005
Property	Caption	Text
Property	Container	Parent
Property	Height	Height, Size
Property	HWnd	Handle
Property	MousePointer	Cursor
Property	Parent	FindForm method

(continues)

Table 4.6. *Changes to Common Members of the Windows Forms Controls (Continued)*

Member	VBA	Visual Basic 2005
Property	Picture	Image
Property	SelLength	SelectionLength
Property	SelStart	SelectionStart
Property	SelText	SelectedText
Property	ToolTipText	ToolTip component
Property	Width	Width, Size
Method	Move	SetBounds
Method	SetFocus	Focus
Method	ZOrder	BringToFront, SendToBack
Event	DblClick	DoubleClick
Event	GotFocus	Enter
Event	LostFocus	Leave
Event	Validate	Validating

In addition to the differences in the properties, methods, and events, there are differences in the members that are unique to each control. Table 4.7 lists these differences.

Table 4.7. *Members of the ActiveX Controls Compared with Windows Forms Controls*

Control	VBA	Visual Basic 2005
TextBox	Alignment	TextAlign
TextBox	Locked	ReadOnly
TextBox	Change	TextChanged

(continues)

Table 4.7. *Members of the ActiveX Controls Compared with Windows Forms Controls (Continued)*

Control	VBA	Visual Basic 2005
Label	Alignment	TextAlign
Label	BackStyle	BackColor set as transparent
Label	WordWrap	(Automatic)
ComboBox	List	Items
ComboBox	ListCount	Count
ComboBox	ListIndex	SelectedIndex
ComboBox	Locked	DropDownStyle = DropDownList
ComboBox	Style	DropdownStyle
ComboBox	AddItem	Add, AddRange, Insert
ComboBox	RemoveItem	Items.Remove
ComboBox	Change	TextChanged
ComboBox	Click	SelectedIndexChanged
ListBox	Columns	MultiColumn, ColumnWidth
ListBox	List	Items
ListBox	ListColumn	Count
ListBox	ListIndex	SelectedIndex
ListBox	MultiSelect	SelectionMode
ListBox	SelCount	Count
ListBox	Selected	GetSelected, SetSelected
ListBox	AddItem	Add, AddRange, Insert
ListBox	RemoveItem	Remove
ListBox	ItemCheck	N/A (available only on a CheckedListBox)
CheckBox	Alignment	CheckAlign

(continues)

Table 4.7. *Members of the ActiveX Controls Compared with Windows Forms Controls (Continued)*

Control	VBA	Visual Basic 2005
CheckBox	Style	Appearance
CheckBox	Value	CheckState
CheckBox	Click	CheckStateChanged
OptionButton	Alignment	TextAlign
OptionButton	Appearance	FlatStyle
OptionButton	Value	Checked
OptionButton	Click	CheckedChanged
Frame	Appearance	FlatStyle (GroupBox)
Frame	Click	Click (Panel)
CommandButton	Cancel	N/A (use the CancelButton of the Form instead)
CommandButton	Default	N/A (use the AcceptButton of the Form instead)
CommandButton	Value	N/A
ScrollBar	Max	Maximum
ScrollBar	Min	Minimum
ScrollBar	TabIndex	TabIndexChanged
ScrollBar	TabStop	TabStopChanged
ScrollBar	Value	ValueChanged

The following section describes some of the differences between an ActiveX control and the corresponding Windows Forms control.

TextBox versus TextBox

The ActiveX control TextBox provides a way to collect user input. The default property is Value, and the default event is Change. The equivalent Windows Forms control is also named TextBox. The property used to display text in the TextBox control is the Text property, and the default event is TextChanged.

Label versus Label

The ActiveX control Label is used to display information on a Windows Form. The default property is Caption, and the default event is Click. The equivalent Windows Forms control is also named Label. The property used to display text in the Label control is the Text property, and the default event is Click.

In VBA, the WordWrap property is used to determine whether a label wraps. Text wrapping in Visual Basic 2005 is automatic for a Label. The BackStyle property is no longer available for a Label. Instead, you can set the BackColor property to transparent.

ComboBox versus ComboBox

The ActiveX control ComboBox combines the features of a ListBox and a TextBox. The default property is Value, and the default event is Change. You can change the Style property to make the ComboBox appear as a drop-down list. The equivalent Windows Forms control is also named ComboBox. The property used to display text in the ComboBox control is the Text property, and the default event is SelectedIndexChanged.

ListBox versus ListBox

The ActiveX control ListBox displays a list of values that users can select. The default property is Value, and the default event is Click. You can change the ListStyle property to change the appearance of the ListBox so that it displays option buttons or check boxes within the list. The equivalent Windows Forms control is also named ListBox. To add items to a ListBox, you use the Add method. The default event is SelectedIndexChanged. You cannot change the appearance of a ListBox control to display check boxes; instead, you should use the CheckedListBox control.

CheckBox versus CheckBox

The ActiveX control CheckBox enables users to choose between two options (true/false, on/off, yes/no). The default property is Value, and the default event is Click. The equivalent Windows Forms control is also named CheckBox. The property used to display text in the CheckBox control is the Text property. The default event is CheckedChanged, which occurs when the value of the check box changes.

OptionButton versus RadioButton

The ActiveX control OptionButton enables users to choose between mutually exclusive options. The default property is Value, and the default event is Click. The equivalent Windows Forms control is RadioButton. The property used to display text in the RadioButton control is the Text property. The default event is CheckedChanged, which occurs when the value of the radio button changes.

ToggleButton versus CheckBox

The ActiveX control ToggleButton shows whether an item is selected. The default property is Value, and the default event is Click. To create an equivalent Windows Forms control, you can add a CheckBox control and then set the Appearance property of the CheckBox to Button.

Frame versus GroupBox and Panel

The ActiveX control Frame is used to group controls. For example, any OptionButton controls added to a frame are mutually exclusive. The default event is Click.

There are two Windows Forms controls that are similar to the Frame control. The first is the GroupBox control, and the second is the Panel control. The property used to display text in the GroupBox control is the Text property, and the default event is Enter. The default event for the Panel control is Paint. Note that GroupBox and Panel cannot be added directly to a Word document or Excel worksheet at design time. Instead, you can add these controls to a user control and then add the user control to the document or worksheet.

CommandButton versus Button

The ActiveX control CommandButton is used to trigger an event, such as starting or stopping an action. The default property is Value, and the default event is Click. The equivalent Windows Forms control is the Button control. The property used to display text in the Button is the Text property, and the default event is Click.

The Windows Forms Button control does not have a Default or Cancel property. Instead, you can pass the Button control to the CancelButton or AcceptButton property of the Windows Form. The equivalent of setting a CommandButton's Value to True is calling the BeforeClick method of a Button.

TabStrip versus TabControl

The ActiveX control TabStrip is used to group related controls, and it contains a Tabs collection. The default property is SelectedItem, and the default event is Change. The equivalent Windows Forms control is the TabControl, which contains Tab pages. This control is like a combination of a TabStrip and a MultiPage control. The default event is Click.

MultiPage versus TabControl

The ActiveX control MultiPage enables you to combine related information, and it contains a Pages collection. The default property is Value. The default event is Change. There is no equivalent Windows Forms control; however, a TabControl is like a combination of a TabStrip and a MultiPage control.

ScrollBar versus VScrollBar and HScrollBar

The ActiveX control ScrollBar enables you to provide scrolling capabilities to another control. The default property is Value, and the default event is Change. You can create a horizontal or vertical scroll bar by dragging the sizing handles on the UserForm.

There are two Windows Forms controls that are equivalent to the ScrollBar: the VScrollBar (for vertical scrolling) and the HScrollBar (for horizontal scrolling). Most controls have their own scrolling capabilities, but these ScrollBar controls enable you to provide scrolling capabilities for other controls, such as the PictureBox. The default event is Scroll.

SpinButton versus NumericUpDown

The ActiveX control SpinButton enables you to change and update the value of another control. The default property is Value. The default event is Change. There is no equivalent Windows Forms control; however, there is a NumericUpDown control, which can be used to spin through a series of numbers.

ImageControl versus PictureBox

The ActiveX control ImageControl enables you to display pictures. The default event is Click. You can use a PictureBox control to display pictures on a Windows Form. The default event for a PictureBox control is SelectedIndexChanged.

Changes to Control Functionality

In addition to changes in the names of the properties, methods, and events, the functionality of the controls might also differ. For example, Windows Forms controls have a different implementation for handling data access and fonts.

Fonts

Using VBA, you can set the font of a control by setting the font properties directly. In Visual Basic 2005, you must create an instance of a System.Drawing.Font object whenever you want to programmatically set the font property of a control. Listing 4.16 shows how to change the text and font used on a CommandButton in VBA and a Button in Visual Basic 2005. When you create a Font object in Visual Basic 2005, you must choose one of ten overloaded constructors. In Listing 4.16, we pass the font size and style when we instantiate the Font object and then assign it to the Font property of the Button.

Listing 4.16. *Setting the font on a control*

```
' VBA
Private Sub CommandButton1_Click()
    Me.CommandButton1.Caption = "Sample"
    With Me.CommandButton1.Font
        .Name = "Courier New"
        .Size = 8
        .Italic = True
    End With
End Sub


' Visual Basic 2005
Private Sub Button1_Click (ByVal sender As System.Object, _
    ByVal e As System.EventArgs) Handles Button1.Click

    Me.Button1.Text = "Sample"
    Dim myFont as new System.Drawing.Font("Courier New", _
        8, FontStyle.Italic)
    Me.Button1.Font = myFont

End Sub
```

Colors

In VBA, colors are of type Long, and there are eight constants that can be used: vbBlack, vbRed, vbGreen, vbYellow, vbBlue, vbMagenta, vbCyan, and vbWhite. In Visual Studio 2005, colors are of type Color, and there are more than 100 choices. Why set text to blue when you can choose DarkSlateBlue or DeepSkyBlue, as shown in Figure 4.9?

Figure 4.9. *Setting the ForeColor of a Button to DeepSkyBlue*

Controls inherit the colors of their parents (the form) in Visual Basic 2005. Listing 4.17 shows that to set the ForeColor of a CommandButton on a UserForm in VBA, you must set the ForeColor of the control; setting the ForeColor of the UserForm does not affect the color of any of its controls. However, in Visual Basic 2005, if you set the ForeColor property of the Windows Form, all the controls on the form automatically inherit the color setting.

Listing 4.17. *Inheriting ForeColor property settings*

```
' VBA
Private Sub CommandButton1_Click()
    Me.ForeColor = vbBlue
End Sub


' Visual Basic 2005
Private Sub Button1_Click (ByVal sender As System.Object, _
    ByVal e As System.EventArgs) Handles Button1.Click

    Me.ForeColor = Color.Blue

End Sub
```

Using VBA, you can also set the color using the RGB function, where you pass an integer value between 0 and 255 for each color component: red (R), green (G), and blue (B). For example, to set the ForeColor of a control to blue, you can set the property to RGB(0, 0, 255). In Visual Basic 2005, you can assign only a value of type System.Drawing.Color.

You can use the ColorTranslator class to convert an RGB value to a Color structure. Listing 4.18 shows how to set the ForeColor of a CommandButton control using an RGB function in VBA. It also shows how to translate the RGB value to a Color structure in Visual Basic 2005 so that it can be set to the ForeColor property of a Button control.

Listing 4.18. *Using RGB in Visual Basic 2005*

```
' VBA
Private Sub CommandButton1_Click()
    Me.CommandButton1.ForeColor = RGB(0, 0, 255)
End Sub

' Visual Basic 2005
Private Sub Button1_Click (ByVal sender As System.Object, _
    ByVal e As System.EventArgs) Handles Button1.Click

    Dim colorValue as Integer = RGB(0, 0, 255)
    Me.Button1.ForeColor = System.Drawing.ColorTranslator _
        .FromOle(colorValue)

End Sub
```

You can also use the FromArgb method of a Color structure:

```
Me.Button1.ForeColor = System.Drawing.Color.FromArgb(0, 0, 255)
```

Displaying a Form

To display a form in VBA, you call the Show method of the form. You can indicate whether to display the form as modal or modeless by passing vbModal or vbModeless. If you do not pass either parameter, the form shows as modal by default.

In Visual Basic 2005, forms are classes, and you must instantiate the form before you can display it. You call the Show method to display a modeless form, and you call the ShowDialog method to show the form as a modal dialog box. Listing 4.19 demonstrates how to show a modal UserForm using VBA, and a modal Windows Form using Visual Basic 2005. The code is called from the Click event handler of one form, which causes the second form to be displayed.

Listing 4.19. *Displaying a form in VBA versus Visual Basic 2005*

```
' VBA
Private Sub CommandButton1_Click()
    UserForm2.Show (vbModal)
End Sub

' Visual Basic 2005
Private Sub Button1_Click (ByVal sender As System.Object, _
    ByVal e As System.EventArgs) Handles Button1.Click

    Dim myForm As New Form2
    myForm.ShowDialog()

End Sub
```

Size and Location

In VBA, you adjust the size of a control by using the Height and Width properties. The unit of measurement for these properties is twips. In Visual Basic 2005, the Height and Width properties are combined into a single Size property, which is measured in pixels.

When you display a form, you often want to control exactly where it will appear on the screen. In VBA, you set the StartUpPosition property. For example, you can set the StartUpPosition property to Manual and then set the Top property to 0 and the Left property to 0, displaying the form in the upper-left corner of the application.

To manually control the position of a Windows Forms control using
Visual Basic 2005, you use the StartPosition and Location properties.
The location is calculated (in pixels) in relation to the upper-left portion
of the display area. You can instead specify the location by using the
form's Left and Top properties directly. Listing 4.20 shows how to display a UserForm and a Windows Form in the upper-left corner of the
screen.

Listing 4.20. *Setting the location of a UserForm and a Windows Form*

```
' VBA
Private Sub UserForm_Initialize()
    Me.StartUpPosition = Manual
    Me.Left = 0
    Me.Top = 0
End Sub


' Visual Basic 2005
Private Sub Form1_Load(ByVal sender As System.Object, ByVal e _
    As System.EventArgs) Handles MyBase.Load

    Me.StartPosition = FormStartPosition.Manual
    Me.Location = New Point(0, 0)

End Sub
```

You can move the form to a new location by using these properties; or
you can use the Move method in VBA, or the SetBounds method in
Visual Basic 2005. Both of these techniques require that you indicate
the location and size of the form. You can pass the Form's current
height and width, as shown in Listing 4.21.

Listing 4.21. *Changing the location of a UserForm and a Windows Form*

```
' VBA
Private Sub CommandButton1_Click()
    Dim UserFormHeight As Integer
    Dim UserFormWidth As Integer
```

```
    UserFormHeight = Me.Height
    UserFormWidth = Me.Width
    Me.Move 0, 0, UserFormWidth, UserFormHeight
End Sub


' Visual Basic 2005
Private Sub Button1_Click (ByVal sender As System.Object, _
    ByVal e As System.EventArgs) Handles Button1.Click

    Dim formHeight As Integer = Me.Height
    Dim formWidth As Integer = Me.Width
    Me.SetBounds(0, 0, formWidth, formHeight)

End Sub
```

Control Arrays

Control arrays are not supported in Visual Basic 2005; however, you
can implement the same functionality by extending an event handler to
handle multiple controls. Notice in Listing 4.21 that the Button1 Click
event handler has a Handles clause at the end of the statement
(Handles Button1.Click). To implement this event handler for multiple
controls, you can add references to the controls in the Handles clause.
For example, you can indicate that the Click event handler of Button1
should also handle the Click event of Button2, as shown in Listing 4.22.

Listing 4.22. *Handling the events of multiple controls*

```
' Visual Basic 2005
Private Sub Button1_Click (ByVal sender As System.Object, _
    ByVal e As System.EventArgs) Handles Button1.Click, _
    Button2.Click

    Dim formHeight As Integer = Me.Height
    Dim formWidth As Integer = Me.Width
    Me.SetBounds(0, 0, formWidth, formHeight)

End Sub
```

Dynamic Controls

In addition to adding controls to a document or worksheet by dragging them from Toolbox, you can add Windows Forms controls programmatically. The way you add these controls to a document differs from the way you would add them to a Windows Form; VSTO provides a number of helper methods that eases the task of adding these controls to your documents. You will learn more about adding controls to a document in Chapter 8.

Data Binding

You can fill ActiveX controls with data in VBA by using an ActiveX Data Object (ADO). For example, you can fill a ComboBox with data by reading the ADO recordset, adding each row of the recordset to an array and then assigning the array to the List property of the control. Using Visual Basic 2005, you can bind a control directly to a data source using the control's DataBindings property. You can bind to a data source such as a column in a database, or to any structure that contains data, including XML. You can also bind any property of the control to a data source.

Windows Forms controls support either simple data binding or complex data binding. *Simple* data binding enables you to bind one element of data to a control. *Complex* data binding enables you to bind a control to more than one data element, and it is typically supported in controls that display lists of information.

Programmatically, you can data-bind a control using the Add method of the control's DataBindings property, passing three parameters: the property you want to bind the data to, the data source, and the data member. For example, to bind data to a text box, you could use code similar to this:

```
TextBox1.Databindings.Add("Text", ds, data.member)
```

It is much easier to bind data to controls at design time using the Data Sources window and dragging data-bound controls to the document or to a Windows Form. Data binding is covered in more detail in Chapters 6 and 7.

Summary

We started this chapter with a discussion of why you might consider a move from VBA to Visual Basic 2005 and VSTO. Next, we looked at the new features of Visual Basic 2005, and you learned how to use the new My objects and how to use IntelliSense code snippets. We then took a closer look at the language changes between VBA and Visual Basic 2005, including changes to data types, variable declarations, variable scope, and structured error handling. Finally, you learned about the differences between ActiveX controls and the corresponding Windows Forms controls available in Visual Basic 2005.

Review Questions

1. Name two new features of Visual Basic 2005.

2. What is the file format of IntelliSense code snippets?

3. What is the difference between an option button and a radio button?

4. What is the main purpose of a Using statement?

5. Name two data types that are no longer supported in Visual Basic 2005. Which types can be used instead?

6. What is the preferred alternative to declaring optional parameters on a method?

7. What are two advantages of specifying data types for variable declarations?

Part II
Word and Excel

5

Customizing Word and Excel Task Panes

*The mark of good action is that it
appears inevitable in retrospect.*
—Robert Louis Stevenson

Topics Covered in This Chapter

What Is a Task Pane?

Customizing the Document Actions Task Pane

Managing the Actions Pane

Designing Actions Pane Solutions

Creating Context-Sensitive Solutions

Summary

Review Questions

What Is a Task Pane?

To gather user input, Office developers typically display forms to be filled out by end users. There are disadvantages to this approach because it often forces users to attend to the form before they can continue working in the document. The form also obstructs users' view of the contents of the document. In this chapter, you will learn how to customize the Document Actions task pane to provide a rich user interface that is easily accessible, convenient, and dynamic.

If you've ever applied a style to a paragraph in Microsoft Office Word or searched for Help in Microsoft Office Excel, then you're already familiar with *task panes*. Word and Excel can present functionality to users by displaying controls such as text boxes, list boxes, and buttons on the task pane, which organizes related tasks so that users do not have to search through the menus to locate options. These applications have a number of built-in task panes to assist users in performing particular tasks. For example, Word presents a Styles and Formatting task pane where users can define and apply formatting to areas in the document. An Excel user can use the XML Source task pane to apply XML schemas and XML elements to a worksheet.

The task pane is actually a type of toolbar that can be docked along the side of a document. By default, the task pane displays vertically on the right side of the document or worksheet. End users can manually move the task pane so that it docks on the left side, the top, the bottom, or floating anywhere on the screen. To move the task pane, you select the upper-left area of the task pane, near the title, and drag the pane to the desired docking location. Because the task pane is really just a toolbar, you can programmatically access it through the CommandBars collection. For example, to dock the task pane to the bottom of the screen, you can set the Position property of the CommandBar called "Task Pane," as shown in Listing 5.1.

Listing 5.1. *Docking the task pane to the bottom of the screen*

```
Me.CommandBars("Task Pane").Position = _
    Microsoft.Office.Core.MsoBarPosition.msoBarLeft
```

The 2007 Microsoft Office system has an application-level task pane called the custom task pane. You can customize this task pane when you create an add-in using VSTO SE. This is different from the document-level task pane which is only available to a particular document or template. In Chapter 14, you'll learn more about using VSTO 2005 SE to customize the application-level task pane. The remainder of this chapter discusses the document-level task panes that are customizable with VSTO.

Customizing the Document Actions Task Pane

You can customize the task pane in Word and Excel by using Smart Document technology or by using the ActionsPane object in VSTO. After you have customized the task pane, it appears in the list of task panes available and is called the Document Actions task pane. Figure 5.1 shows the Document Actions task pane listed along with the built-in Word task panes. This entry does not appear until after you have written code to customize the task pane, and you cannot change the name of this task pane; it will always be labeled "Document Actions."

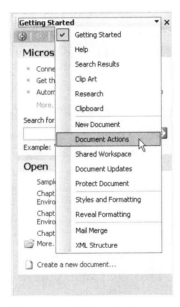

Figure 5.1. *Selecting the Document Actions task pane*

To navigate away from and back to the Document Actions task pane, you select the desired task pane from the drop-down list shown in Figure 5.1.

Using the ActionsPane Object

VSTO provides an ActionsPane object that enables you to customize the task pane with one line of code. You can think of the actions pane as a container for Windows Forms controls. The actions pane sits inside the Document Actions task pane, which is hosted within the Word or Excel task pane. To customize the Document Actions task pane, you simply add controls to the ActionsPane object.

You can add a Windows Forms control directly to the actions pane through code. As soon as you add the control, the Document Actions task pane becomes visible in the application and displays your control. For example, if you want to display a DateTimePicker control on the actions pane, you can write the code in Listing 5.2. This code displays the DateTimePicker control on the task pane as soon as the document opens because the code is written in the Startup event handler of the document.

Listing 5.2. *Adding a control to the actions pane in Word*

```
Private Sub ThisDocument_Startup(ByVal sender As Object, _
    ByVal e As System.EventArgs) Handles Me.Startup

    Me.ActionsPane.Controls.Add(New DateTimePicker)

End Sub
```

If you want to display controls on the actions pane in response to events, you can write code against any event in Word or Excel. For example, you can capture the SelectionChange event of a worksheet and make changes to controls on the actions pane, as you will see later in the "Designing Actions Pane Solutions" section. You can also choose to map XML to your document and show and hide controls on the actions pane according to the user's cursor location, as you will see later in "Creating Context-Sensitive Solutions."

Managing the Actions Pane

Several layers of *containers* make up the actions pane. Figure 5.2 illustrates these layers.

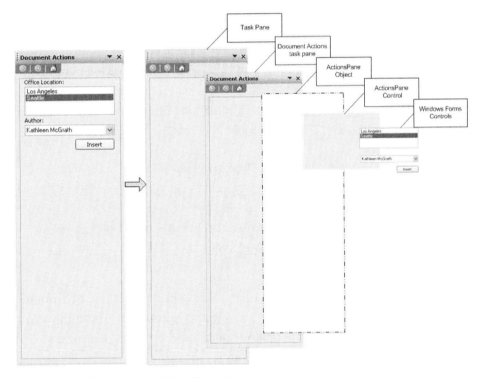

Figure 5.2. *Containers within the actions pane*

The first container is the Office task pane itself. This container holds individual panes, such as the Document Actions task pane. The ActionsPane object is contained by the Document Actions task pane and acts as a container for Windows Forms controls. You can programmatically add Windows Forms controls directly to the ActionsPane, or you can use container controls such as user controls or actions pane controls that can contain multiple Windows Forms controls. Adding controls to an actions pane control in VSTO follows the same process as designing a UserForm in VBA.

Managing the Size and Position of the Actions Pane

To manage the positioning of the actions pane or the controls on it, you must consider which container you're trying to manipulate. If you want to remove a control that you've added to the actions pane, you can access it directly through the ActionsPane object by calling the Remove method, as shown in Listing 5.3. When you remove a control from the task pane, the task pane is still visible even if it displays no other controls. You can check whether the number of controls on the task pane is less than 1 and, if so, hide the task pane. Listing 5.3 shows how to write this code for Excel. In Word, the code would be identical except that you would need to change "ThisWorkbook" to "ThisDocument."

Listing 5.3. *Removing a control from the actions pane in Excel*

```
Me.ActionsPane.Controls.Remove(myControl)

If Globals.ThisWorkbook.ActionsPane.Controls.Count < 1 Then
    Application.CommandBars("Task Pane").Visible = False
End If
```

If you want to display a different task pane, you can access it through its container, the TaskPane object, which is available on the Application object. You can reference the desired task pane by using one of the many task pane enumerations available. For example, to display the Styles and Formatting task pane, set its Visible property to True. Notice that the code in Listing 5.4 uses the fully qualified enumeration Word.WdTaskPanes.wdTaskPaneFormatting instead of just wdTaskPaneFormatting.

Listing 5.4. *Displaying a built-in task pane*

```
Application.TaskPanes(Word.WdTaskPanes.wdTaskPaneFormatting) _
    .Visible = True
```

If you want to change the position of the actions pane so that it docks at the top of the document, you must access the task pane through the CommandBars object, as shown in Listing 5.5.

Listing 5.5. *Docking the task pane*

```
Me.CommandBars("Task Pane").Position = _
    Microsoft.Office.Core.MsoBarPosition.msoBarTop
```

Resizing the ActionsPane object does not change the size of the task pane, and the task pane doesn't automatically resize to fit the width of the controls that you add to it. If you want to resize the task pane, you must set the Width property of the CommandBar object, as shown in Listing 5.6.

Listing 5.6. *Resizing the task pane*

```
Me.ActionsPane.Controls.Add(New MonthCalendar)
Me.CommandBars("Task Pane").Width = 200
```

Showing and Hiding the Actions Pane

The first time you add a control to the actions pane, the pane becomes visible to end users. If you want the actions pane to be visible as soon as the document is opened, you should write code that adds the control to the actions pane in the Startup event handler of the document (or workbook). If you want the actions pane to appear only when a user takes a particular action, you should add the code to the event handler of that action—for example, when the user right-clicks the document. If you do this, make sure that you add code to the Startup event handler of the document or workbook to detach the actions pane (which closes the Document Actions task pane) when the document is opened. If the user hasn't closed the task pane before saving and closing the document, an empty task pane might be visible on the document the next time it is opened. To detach the actions pane, use the following code:

```
ActionsPane.Clear()
```

Adding a control to the Controls collection of the ActionsPane causes it to be visible only the first time it is added. If you subsequently hide the task pane, as was shown in Listing 5.3, the act of adding another control to the Controls collection will not cause it to be visible. Instead, you must specifically show the task pane again the next time you add a control. For example, you must specifically write code to set the Visible property to true:

```
Application.CommandBars("Task Pane").Visible = True
```

Designing Actions Pane Solutions

You cannot drag and drop controls directly on the actions pane because it does not have a design surface. However, you can use a custom user control as your design surface. You can use a user control, or you can use a type of user control provided by VSTO called the actions pane control. This control is identical to a user control; it was made available in the Add New Item dialog box so that developers can discover it more easily.

You can add the actions pane control to your project and then drag and drop all your desired Windows Forms controls to the actions pane control in the same way you drag controls to a UserForm in a VBA project. After you have designed the actions pane control to your liking, you can programmatically add it to the actions pane.

> ❖ **Note** In Word, you access the ActionsPane through the ThisDocument class. In Excel, you access it through the ThisWorkbook class. There is only one actions pane available for the entire workbook.

To add the actions pane control to your solution, right-click the solution in Solution Explorer, point to Add, and click New Item. In the Add New Item dialog box, select Actions Pane Control, and then click Add (see Figure 5.3).

After the actions pane control has been added to your solution, you can drag Windows Forms controls to the actions pane control. Figure 5.4 shows an actions pane control that contains two Label controls.

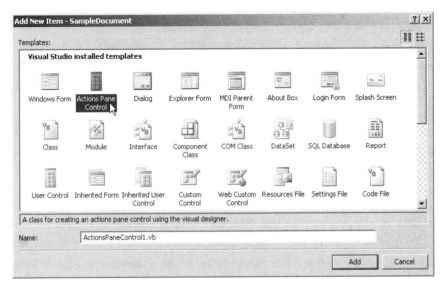

Figure 5.3. *Adding an actions pane control to your solution*

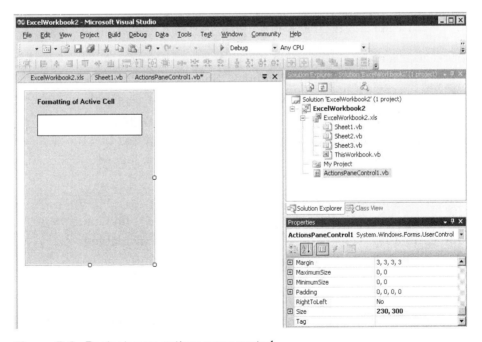

Figure 5.4. *Designing an actions pane control*

Creating an Actions Pane Solution

Usually, you place the code that adds the control to the actions pane in the Startup event handler of either ThisDocument or ThisWorkbook, depending on whether you're working in Word or Excel. This causes the code to add the control to the actions pane so that it is visible when you open the document. You can also add this code to other procedures. For example, you might want to display a control in the Document Actions task pane when a user moves the cursor into a particular area of the document.

You can access objects on the document from the user control on the actions pane by using the Globals class provided by VSTO. For example, if you write code in the Click event handler of a Button on the actions pane so that it adds text to the document, you can access objects in the document, such as the Paragraph object, by typing

```
Globals.ThisDocument.Paragraphs(1).Range.Text = _
    "You clicked the button!"
```

The Globals class gives you access to objects on a worksheet or document from outside the ThisWorkbook, Sheet1, Sheet2, Sheet3, or ThisDocument class. In Excel, Globals gives you access to the workbook or the worksheets, and from there you can access any object on the worksheet. For example, if you want to reference a text box that exists on Sheet2 from the Sheet1 class, you can write the following code:

```
Dim text as String = Globals.Sheet2.TextBox1.Text
```

It is important to understand that the actions pane is document-centric. You cannot have one actions pane that is globally available to every document that you have opened; each document must have a separate actions pane. Because there is only one task pane available for your application, you can display only one actions pane. However, you can display multiple actions pane controls, and you can hide and show controls to simulate various task panes, as discussed in "Creating Context-Sensitive Solutions" later in this chapter.

If you want to display a task pane in multiple documents or show multiple task panes in your solution, you can do so using VSTO 2005 SE and either Office 2003 or Office 2007. In Chapter 14 you'll learn more about creating add-ins for several Office applications using VSTO 2005 SE.

Word has a Styles and Formatting task pane where you can create and apply styles to your document. Excel doesn't have a Styles and Formatting task pane, and the interface for adding these styles is not intuitive. With VSTO, you can create your own custom Styles and Formatting task pane for Excel. The following sections explain how.

Adding an Actions Pane Control

When you design an actions pane control, it can be helpful to resize the control to the width of the task pane so that you can see exactly what the controls will look like when they are visible on the task pane. The actions pane control can be found in the New Items dialog box.

1. Create a new Excel Workbook solution using VSTO.

2. Right-click your Excel solution in Solution Explorer, point to Add, and then click New Item.

3. In the Add New Item dialog box, click Actions Pane Control, and then click Add. See Figure 5.3, presented earlier, for an example.

4. Expand the Size property for the control and set the width to *200*.

    You can add Windows Forms controls to the design surface of the actions pane control by dragging the controls from Toolbox.

5. Add two Label controls, and change the second label to resemble a text box by selecting a white background color, adding a border, and changing the AutoSize property to False (see Figure 5.4).

6. Keep the default name of the label (Label1) for the first label on the control, and change its Text property to *Formatting of Active Cell.*

7. Change the name of the second label to *SelectionFont,* set the TextAlign property to *MiddleCenter,* and clear out any text.

   You should also change the anchor of each of these controls so that the labels resize if the task pane is resized. Set the Anchor property to Top, Left, Right for each label. The code to add this actions pane control to the action pane should be added to the Startup event handler of ThisWorkbook. The variable to reference the control is created at the class level as a public variable so that you can access it from the worksheet using the Globals class.

8. Add the code in Listing 5.7 to the ThisWorkbook class, replacing the existing Startup event handler.

Listing 5.7. *Displaying the actions pane control on the actions pane*

```
Public ActionsControl As New ActionsPaneControl1

Private Sub ThisWorkbook_Startup(ByVal sender As Object, _
    ByVal e As System.EventArgs) Handles Me.Startup

    Me.ActionsPane.Controls.Add(ActionsControl)

End Sub
```

Accessing the Actions Pane from a Document

To determine which text and formatting should appear in the label on the actions pane, write code in the SelectionChange event handler of Sheet1. When the selection in the worksheet changes, apply the formatting of the ActiveCell to the text (the style name) in the label on the actions pane. You can get access to the label by using the Globals class.

1. Add the code in Listing 5.8 to the SelectionChange event handler of Sheet1.

Listing 5.8. *The SelectionChange event handler of Sheet1*

```
Private Sub Sheet1_SelectionChange(ByVal Target As _
    Microsoft.Office.Interop.Excel.Range) Handles _
        Me.SelectionChange

    ' Set a variable to the label on the actions pane control.
    Dim Actions As System.Windows.Forms.Label
    Actions = Globals.ThisWorkbook.ActionsControl.SelectionFont

    ' Retrieve font information from currently selected cell.
    Dim FontName As String = Application.ActiveCell.Font.Name
    Dim FontSize As Short = Application.ActiveCell.Font.Size
    Dim FontBold As Boolean = Application.ActiveCell.Font.Bold
    Dim FontItalic As Boolean = _
        Application.ActiveCell.Font.Italic
    Dim FontAttribute As FontStyle = FontStyle.Regular
    Dim ExcelStyle As Excel.Style = Application.ActiveCell.Style
    Dim StyleName As String = ExcelStyle.Name

    ' Apply Bold, Italic, and Underline styles to label if they
    ' are applied to the active cell.
    If FontBold = True Then
        FontAttribute = FontStyle.Bold
    End If

    If FontItalic = True Then
        FontAttribute = FontStyle.Italic
    End If

    If Application.ActiveCell.Font.Underline = _
        Excel.XlUnderlineStyle.xlUnderlineStyleSingle Then

        FontAttribute = FontStyle.Underline
    End If

    ' Add the Style name and formatting of the active cell to the
    ' label on the actions pane.
    Actions.Text = StyleName
    Actions.Font = New Font(FontName, FontSize, FontAttribute)

End Sub
```

2. Press F5 to run the code.

When you run this code, the custom control you designed is displayed on the actions pane as soon as the document opens. When you move your cursor into a cell, the style name of the currently selected cell (the active cell) is displayed in the label on the actions pane with the formatting from the active cell applied, as shown in Figure 5.5.

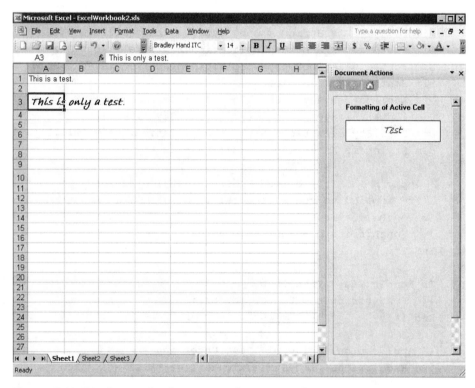

Figure 5.5. *Displaying the formatting of text in a cell on the actions pane*

Accessing the Document from the Actions Pane

In the preceding section, you learned how you can access the actions pane from within the document. This time, you'll learn how to access the document from the actions pane. The code for creating and applying the styles should be written behind the actions pane control. First, you add some Windows Forms controls to the actions pane control to enable your users to apply styles to cells in the worksheet.

1. Add a Label control to ActionsPaneControl1, and change the Text property of the label to *Pick formatting to apply.*

2. Add a ListBox control to ActionsPaneControl1 below the label, leaving the default name of ListBox1.

3. Add the code in Listing 5.9 to ActionsPaneControl1.vb.

    This code fills the ListBox control with the name of all the styles that are currently defined in the workbook. Because you cannot apply different styles to each entry in the list box, we'll format all the text as Times New Roman.

Listing 5.9. *Loading styles from worksheet into ListBox on ActionsPane*

```
Private Sub ActionsPaneControl1_Load(ByVal sender As _
    System.Object, ByVal e As System.EventArgs) _
    Handles MyBase.Load

    ' Add style names from document into the list box.
    Dim CurrentStyle As Excel.Style

    Me.ListBox1.Font = New Font("Times New Roman", 14, _
        FontStyle.Regular)

    For Each CurrentStyle In Globals.ThisWorkbook.Styles
        Me.ListBox1.Items.Add(CurrentStyle.Name)
    Next

End Sub
```

4. Add the code in Listing 5.10 to the MouseClick event handler of the ListBox control to apply the selected style to the active worksheet cell. Then add the ResetStyle code beneath the MouseClick event handler.

Listing 5.10. *Applying selected styles in the actions pane to worksheet cells*

```
Private Sub ListBox1_MouseClick(ByVal sender As Object, _
    ByVal e As System.Windows.Forms.MouseEventArgs) _
    Handles ListBox1.MouseClick

    ' Set the active cell to the style selected in the list
    ' box and then call ResetStyle to assign style name and
    ' formatting to label.
    Globals.ThisWorkbook.Application.ActiveCell.Style = _
        Me.ListBox1.SelectedItem
    ResetStyle()

End Sub

Private Sub ResetStyle()

    ' Retrieve format information from Selected style.
    Dim CurrentStyle As Excel.Style = Globals.ThisWorkbook. _
        Styles(Me.ListBox1.SelectedItem.ToString)
    Dim FontName As String = CurrentStyle.Font.Name
    Dim FontSize As Single = CurrentStyle.Font.Size
    Dim FontBold As Boolean = CurrentStyle.Font.Bold
    Dim FontItalic As Boolean = CurrentStyle.Font.Italic
    Dim FontAttribute As FontStyle = FontStyle.Regular

    If FontBold = True Then
        FontAttribute = FontStyle.Bold
    End If

    If FontItalic = True Then
        FontAttribute = FontStyle.Italic
    End If

    If CurrentStyle.Font.Underline = _
        Excel.XlUnderlineStyle.xlUnderlineStyleSingle Then

        FontAttribute = FontStyle.Underline

    End If
```

```
' Set the text of the label to the style and formatting
' selected in the list box.
Me.SelectionFont.Text = Me.ListBox1.SelectedItem.ToString()
Me.SelectionFont.Font = New Font(FontName, FontSize, _
    FontAttribute)

End Sub
```

5. Press F5 to run the code.

When you run this code, the Document Actions task pane displays your custom actions pane control, as shown in Figure 5.6. Now you can apply the styles listed in the task pane to the active cell in your worksheet by clicking the desired style. Unfortunately, there isn't any way to

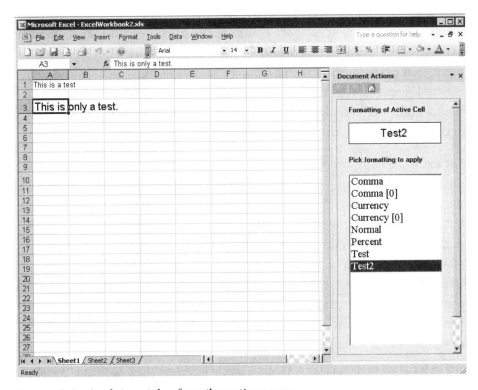

Figure 5.6. *Applying styles from the actions pane*

display the style of each item directly in the list box, but you can view the style in the document and in the label on the task pane.

You might want to consider extending the functionality of your Styles and Formatting task pane for Excel. For example, you might want to add another button labeled "Refresh Styles" to refresh the list of styles that are displayed in the task pane in case new styles were added to the document. In Chapter 14 you will see how to do this when you convert this code to an add-in that customizes the application-level custom task pane in Excel 2007.

Managing Control Order

End users can change the location of the task pane in Word and Excel. The task pane can be docked to the right of the document (the default location) or to the left, top, or bottom of the document. Typically, you want the task pane to be docked so that it doesn't obstruct the document, but because the task pane is a CommandBar, you can also float the task pane on top of the document if you prefer. When you change the location of the task pane in the application, the controls on the actions pane do not automatically reposition themselves.

For example, the controls are stacked from top to bottom by default, and the default position of the task pane is vertical. If you move the task pane so that it is positioned horizontally (docked either at the top or bottom of the document), the controls do not automatically get restacked properly (stacked from left to right). Instead, they remain stacked from top to bottom, and often many of the controls are hidden from view. Of course, this is important only if you have added multiple controls to the actions pane. To see an example, add two new actions pane controls to your solution, and then add a MonthCalendar control to each actions pane control, as shown in Figure 5.7.

Next, add the code in Listing 5.11 to the Startup event handler of ThisWorkbook, and run the code.

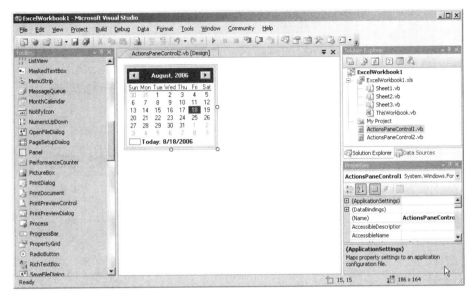

Figure 5.7. *Adding a MonthCalendar control to an actions pane control*

Listing 5.11. *Adding two MonthCalendar controls to the task pane*

```
Private Sub ThisWorkbook_Startup(ByVal sender As Object, _
    ByVal e As System.EventArgs) Handles Me.Startup

    Me.ActionsPane.Controls.Add(New ActionsPaneControl1)
    Me.ActionsPane.Controls.Add(New ActionsPaneControl2)

End Sub
```

This code adds the two actions pane controls (each of which contains a MonthCalendar control) to the actions pane. See Figure 5.8 for an example of how the controls stack when the task pane is docked to the right, and Figure 5.9 for an example of what it looks like when the task pane is docked to the top of the workbook.

When you add multiple controls to the actions pane, they are stacked from top to bottom by default. You can change this behavior by setting the StackOrder property of the ActionsPane. You can assign the following stacking orders to this property: FromLeft, FromTop, FromRight,

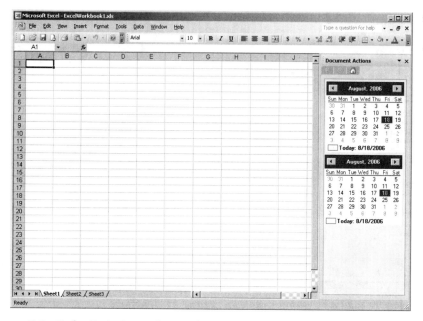

Figure 5.8. *Default stacking of controls when task pane is docked vertically*

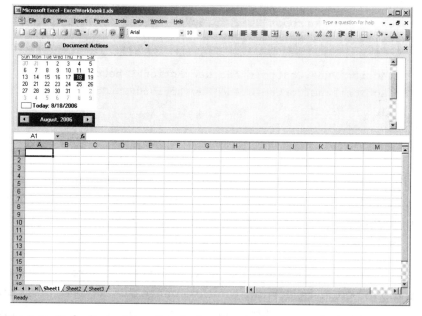

Figure 5.9. *Default stacking of controls when task pane is docked horizontally*

FromBottom, and None. Setting the stacking order to None means that you want to have full control over the position of each of the controls added to the task pane.

You can programmatically determine the stacking order based on the current orientation of the task pane. If you add the code in Listing 5.12 to the ThisWorkbook class and then move the task pane so that it is docked horizontally, the controls correctly stack from left to right; when you return the task pane to a vertical position, the controls correctly stack from top to bottom (see Figure 5.10).

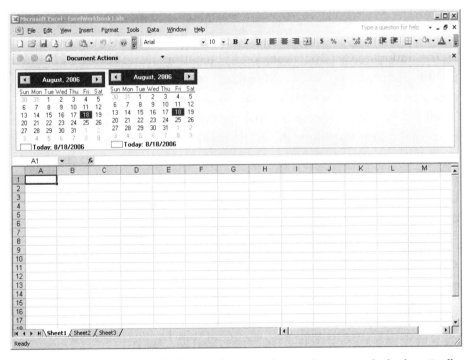

Figure 5.10. *Controls stacked top to bottom when task pane is docked vertically*

Listing 5.12. *Restacking controls on the actions pane based on its orientation*

```
Private Sub ActionsPane_OrientationChanged(ByVal sender As _
    Object, ByVal e As System.EventArgs) Handles _
    ActionsPane.OrientationChanged
```

```
Select Case Me.ActionsPane.Orientation
    Case Orientation.Horizontal
        Me.ActionsPane.StackOrder = _
            Microsoft.Office.Tools.StackStyle.FromLeft
    Case Orientation.Vertical
        Me.ActionsPane.StackOrder = _
            Microsoft.Office.Tools.StackStyle.FromTop
    End Select

End Sub
```

Creating Context-Sensitive Solutions

You can create interactive documents by hiding and showing controls on the actions pane, depending on the location of the cursor in the document. For example, you could respond to the BeforeRightClick event of a Bookmark control on a document by displaying Help content on the actions pane. You might also consider mapping XML to the document so that you can display controls on the document when users move the cursor into an XML mapping, and remove the controls when the cursor moves outside the XML mapping. The following sections describe how to map XML to a letter in Word and write code against the ContextLeave and ContextEnter events to add and remove controls on the actions pane.

Creating an XML Schema

The first step in creating the solution is to create an XML schema that you can attach and map to your Word document. The XML schema in Listing 5.13 represents a letter that contains six elements: Author, Addressee, Salutation, Re, Body, and Closing. Each of these elements is of type String and has its maxOccurs value set to 1. This means that you can map the XML element to the document only one time.

The Addressee node might be a good candidate for a repeating XML schema element because you can address a single letter to more than one person; however, for this example, you can add the name and address for each recipient within the Addressee elements. You can create schemas using Visual Studio, or you can manually add XML elements to a schema file.

Create a schema named Letter.xsd using the XML elements found in Listing 5.13. To create this file manually, type the XML elements into a file in Notepad, and then save the file with the name Letter.xsd.

Listing 5.13. *Letter schema*

```
<?xml version="1.0" encoding="utf-8" ?>
<xs:schema targetNamespace=
    "http://schemas.microsoft.com/vsto/samples"
    elementFormDefault="qualified"
    xmlns="http://schemas.microsoft.com/vsto/samples"
    xmlns:mstns="http://schemas.microsoft.com/vsto/samples"
    xmlns:xs="http://www.w3.org/2001/XMLSchema">

    <xs:element name="Letter" type="LetterType"></xs:element>
    <xs:complexType name="LetterType">
        <xs:all>
            <xs:element name="Address" type="AddressType"
                minOccurs="0" maxOccurs="1" />
            <xs:element name="Content" type="ContentType"
                minOccurs="0" maxOccurs="1" />
        </xs:all>
    </xs:complexType>
    <xs:complexType name="AddressType">
        <xs:sequence>
            <xs:element name="Author" type="xs:string"
                minOccurs="0" maxOccurs="1" />
            <xs:element name="Addressee" type="xs:string"
                minOccurs="0" maxOccurs="1" />
            <xs:element name="Re" type="xs:string" minOccurs="0"
                maxOccurs="1" />
        </xs:sequence>
    </xs:complexType>
```

```
<xs:complexType name="ContentType">
    <xs:sequence>
        <xs:element name="Salutation" type="xs:string"
            minOccurs="0" maxOccurs="1" />
        <xs:element name="Body" type="xs:string"
            minOccurs="0" maxOccurs="1" />
        <xs:element name="Closing" type="xs:string"
            minOccurs="0" maxOccurs="1" />
    </xs:sequence>
</xs:complexType>
</xs:schema>
```

The parent element, AddressType, is a complex type that contains three child elements. The XML is structured in this way so that you can easily determine when the user's cursor location is within a specific context. In this way, you can determine when the cursor is in a general area of the document rather than in a specific element, such as the Author element. The parent element ContentType was created for the same reason. As you will see in the next section, when you map the parent element, the three child elements also become available for mapping.

Mapping XML Elements to Your Document

To base a document on XML, you must attach an XML schema to your document and begin mapping the XML elements.

1. Attach the XML schema to your document by selecting Templates and Add-Ins from the Microsoft Office Word Tools menu.

2. Click Add Schema on the Schema tab, and select the schema you just created in Listing 5.13.

3. Type any text into the Alias field of the Schema Settings dialog box, and click OK.

   You map each element by selecting the desired text in the document and then clicking the element in the XML Structure task pane.

4. Map the Letter node to the entire document.

5. Select the area starting at the company address until right before the Re line, and map the Address node.

6. Select the area of the salutation to the end of the letter, and map the Content node.

7. Map the child nodes of the Address node (Author and Addressee) and child nodes of the Content node (Salutation, Body, and Closing) to appropriate areas within the document.

Your final document should resemble the one in Figure 5.11.

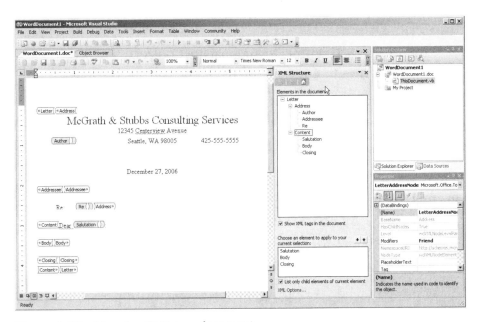

Figure 5.11. *Mapping XML to a document*

Each time you map an element from the XML Structure task pane to the document, a new XMLNode control is added to the Controls collection. You will learn more about XMLNode controls in Chapter 6. For this example, all you need to know is that these XMLNodes have events that you can program against.

The name of each XMLNode control contains the parent schema element name, followed by the schema element name, followed by the word *Node.* For example, the Address node is named LetterAddressNode.

Creating Multiple Actions Pane Controls

To have a dynamic actions pane, you must create multiple controls that you can add and remove according to the user's context in the document. In this section you will create two controls. You can use the default control names for all of the Windows Forms controls that you add to the actions pane controls.

1. Add two actions panes controls to your Word solution, keeping the default names (ActionsPaneControl1 and ActionsPaneControl2).

2. Add three Label controls to ActionsPaneControl1, and set their Text properties to *Author, Addressee,* and *Re,* respectively.

3. Add a Button control to ActionsPaneControl1, and change its Text property to *Insert.*

4. Add a ComboBox control and two TextBox controls to ActionsPaneControl1, as shown in Figure 5.12.

5. Add three Label controls to ActionsPaneControl2, and set their Text properties to *Salutation, Body,* and *Closing,* respectively.

6. Add a Button control to ActionsPaneControl2, and change its Text property to *Insert.*

7. Add two ComboBox controls and two TextBox controls, as shown in Figure 5.12.

Notice that both controls contain an Insert button. Normally, you would display only one button to insert the text of all the controls that appear on the task pane. In this case, you're showing only one control at a

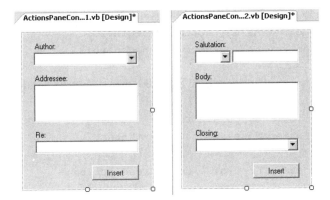

Figure 5.12. *Two actions pane controls*

time, so you need to ensure that there's a way to insert the data from the controls into the document, even if only one of the actions pane controls is visible. You could also create a separate actions pane control that contains the Insert button and handles the insertion of the text from both ActionsPaneControl1 and ActionsPaneControl2, but to keep this example simple, we use two separate Insert buttons.

Showing and Hiding Controls on the Actions Pane

In this section you will write code in the ContextEnter and ContextLeave event handlers of the XMLNodes that are mapped to your document. The *context* is the area between the opening XML tag and its closing tag. This context can include child XML nodes.

The code in Listing 5.14 adds ActionsPaneControl1 to the actions pane when the context of the LetterAddressNode is entered, and shows ActionsPaneControl2 when the context of the LetterContentNode is entered. In addition, the control is removed whenever you exit the context of the XMLNode control. Notice that the variables for the actions pane controls are declared outside the procedure.

Listing 5.14. *Adding and removing controls on the actions pane*

```
Dim AddressControl As New ActionsPaneControl1
Dim ContentControl As New ActionsPaneControl2


Private Sub LetterAddressNode_ContextEnter(ByVal sender _
    As Object, ByVal e As _
    Microsoft.Office.Tools.Word.ContextChangeEventArgs) _
    Handles LetterAddressNode.ContextEnter

    Me.ActionsPane.Controls.Add(AddressControl)

End Sub


Private Sub LetterAddressNode_ContextLeave(ByVal sender _
    As Object, ByVal e As _
    Microsoft.Office.Tools.Word.ContextChangeEventArgs) _
    Handles LetterAddressNode.ContextLeave

    Me.ActionsPane.Controls.Remove(AddressControl)

End Sub


Private Sub LetterContentNode_ContextEnter(ByVal sender _
    As Object, ByVal e As _
    Microsoft.Office.Tools.Word.ContextChangeEventArgs) _
    Handles LetterContentNode.ContextEnter

    Me.ActionsPane.Controls.Add(ContentControl)

End Sub


Private Sub LetterContentNode_ContextLeave(ByVal sender _
    As Object, ByVal e As _
    Microsoft.Office.Tools.Word.ContextChangeEventArgs) _
    Handles LetterContentNode.ContextLeave

    Me.ActionsPane.Controls.Remove(ContentControl)

End Sub
```

Adding Functionality to the Actions Pane Controls

The code in Listing 5.14 shows how to add and remove actions pane controls on the actions pane based on the ContextEnter and ContextLeave events of XMLNodes within the document. Next, you'll learn how to make the controls functional.

You can add code to prepopulate the combo boxes. Typically, you would bind these controls to a data source. However, for the purposes of this example, you will hard-code a few names to populate the Author combo box in the Load event of the actions pane control.

1. Add the code in Listing 5.15 to the Load event handler of ActionsPaneControl1, and the Click event handler of Button1 on ActionsPaneControl1.

   When the Insert button is clicked, the code adds the data from the actions pane control to the document by assigning the value of the Text property of the controls to the Text property of the corresponding XMLNode control. The text in each text box is then removed.

Listing 5.15. *Adding data to actions pane controls*

```
Private Sub ActionsPaneControl1_Load(ByVal sender As _
    System.Object, ByVal e As System.EventArgs) Handles _
    MyBase.Load

    With Me.ComboBox1.Items
        .Add("Kathleen McGrath")
        .Add("Paul Stubbs")
    End With

    Me.ComboBox1.SelectedIndex = 0

End Sub

Private Sub Button1_Click(ByVal sender As System.Object, _
    ByVal e As System.EventArgs) Handles Button1.Click
```

```
' Add the contents of the controls to the document.
With Globals.ThisDocument
    .AddressAuthorNode.Text = Me.ComboBox1.Text
    .AddressAddresseeNode.Text = Me.TextBox1.Text
    .AddressReNode.Text = Me.TextBox2.Text
End With

'Clear data out of the text boxes.
Me.TextBox1.Text = ""
Me.TextBox2.Text = ""

End Sub
```

2. Add the code in Listing 5.16 to the Load event handler of ActionsPaneControl2.

   This code populates the Salutation combo box with titles, and populates the Closing combo box with standard closings when the actions pane is loaded.

Listing 5.16. *Populating controls on the actions pane with text*

```
Private Sub ActionsPaneControl2_Load(ByVal sender As _
    System.Object, ByVal e As System.EventArgs) Handles _
    MyBase.Load

    With Me.ComboBox1.Items
        .Add("Miss ")
        .Add("Mr. ")
        .Add("Mrs. ")
        .Add("Ms. ")
    End With

    With Me.ComboBox2.Items
        .Add("Very truly yours,")
        .Add("Yours truly,")
        .Add("Sincerely,")
    End With

End Sub
```

3. Add the code in Listing 5.17 to the Click event handler of Button1 on ActionsPaneControl2.

    When the Insert button is clicked, the code writes the values of the controls into the document and clears the control content.

Listing 5.17. *Writing values in the actions pane to the document*

```
Private Sub Button1_Click(ByVal sender As System.Object, _
    ByVal e As System.EventArgs) Handles Button1.Click

    With Globals.ThisDocument
        .ContentSalutationNode.Text = Me.ComboBox1.Text & " " _
            & Me.TextBox1.Text
        .ContentBodyNode.Text = Me.TextBox2.Text
        .ContentClosingNode.Text = Me.ComboBox2.Text & vbCrLf _
            & vbCrLf & vbCrLf & .AddressAuthorNode.Text
    End With

    'Clear data out of the controls.
    Me.ComboBox1.Text = ""
    Me.ComboBox2.Text = ""
    Me.TextBox1.Text = ""
    Me.TextBox2.Text = ""

End Sub
```

4. Press F5 to run the code.

Figure 5.13 shows the data from ActionsPaneControl1 already inserted into the document, and ActionsPaneControl2 is visible on the task pane, ready to be filled in.

You might want to consider extending the functionality of your customized task pane. For example, you might want to bind the author list to a data source that contains employee names, or integrate the Outlook address book with the Addressee text box. This technique makes it easy for users to locate and insert the existing information rather than having to type it in a text box.

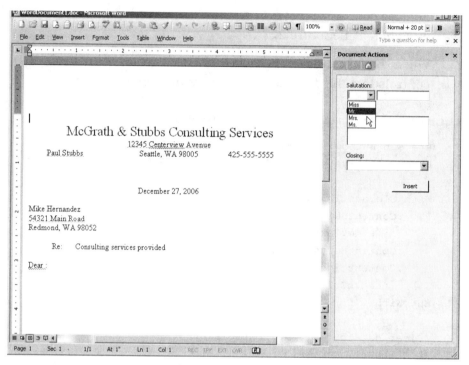

Figure 5.13. *Populating a document with data on the actions pane*

Summary

We started this chapter with a description of the Office task pane and explained that there is one customizable task pane called the Document Actions task pane. You took a closer look at the layers that make up an actions pane and learned how to programmatically dock the task pane to various areas of your document.

You learned how to design an actions pane control, and you created a Styles and Formatting task pane for Excel. In Word, you learned how to map XML to your documents and write code behind the events of the XMLNode controls. This technique lets you display context-sensitive user interface elements on the task pane and hide and show controls according to the location of the user's cursor within the document.

Review Questions

1. What is the difference between an actions pane, a Document Actions task pane, a custom task pane, and an Office task pane?

2. Which class do you use to access an actions pane from a worksheet, or access a control on the document from the actions pane?

3. What is the default stacking order of controls that are added to an actions pane? How do you change the stack order?

4. From which event handler would you write code to change the stack order of multiple controls on an actions pane?

5. From which class do you typically write code to add a control to the actions pane in Word? In Excel?

6

Customizing Word with VSTO

*Whenever you are asked if you can do a job,
tell 'em, "Certainly I can!" Then get busy
and find out how to do it.*
—THEODORE ROOSEVELT

Topics Covered in This Chapter

Programming in Word

Word Host Items and Host Controls

Data Binding to Host Controls on Documents

Programming Against Events

Special Enhancements to the Bookmark

Making Word Documents Smart

Summary

Review Questions

Programming in Word

Word is often used by solution developers for its formatting capabilities.
It is easy to create documents such as reports or letters using Word.
VSTO provides a toolset in Visual Studio that enables you to create
rapid application development (RAD) solutions by displaying the Word
document inside Visual Studio as a designer that you can drag and
drop controls on. These tools make it super easy to customize the task
pane, and they greatly reduce the amount of code (and time) needed to
create a smart tag solution in Word or Excel. VSTO enables you to

create customizations for a specific document (document-level customizations). With the second edition (VSTO 2005 SE), you can create add-ins (application-level customizations). You will learn more about VSTO 2005 SE in Chapter 14. The remainder of this chapter discusses how you can create document-level customizations in Word using VSTO.

You can access all the properties, methods, and events of the Word object model using VSTO (as you can when using VBA). These objects are exposed in VSTO through Word's primary interop assembly (Microsoft.Office.Interop.Word.dll). There are some differences, however, in how you access these objects from VSTO. For example, you are probably used to accessing the Range object directly in VBA. In VSTO, the Range object isn't defined, so you must fully qualify it, as shown in Listing 6.1.

Listing 6.1. *Accessing the Range object in VBA versus VSTO*

```
' VBA
Dim myRange as Range
myRange = ActiveDocument.Range(0, 0)
myRange.Text = "Hello world"

' Visual Basic 2005
Dim myRange As Word.Range
myRange = Me.Range(0, 0)
myRange.Text = "Hello world"
```

Using VBA to customize Word, you have probably made extensive use of the ActiveDocument object to control objects within the currently active document. Because VSTO solutions are document-specific (typically, you are working only with the document that is associated with the code), you can instead use a reference to ThisDocument. If you're writing code within the ThisDocument class, you can access all its members by using the Me keyword. For example, if you wanted to assign text to a particular range in the document, such as the start of the document, you could write Me.Range instead of ActiveDocument.Range, as shown in Listing 6.1. For more information about the differences between VBA and Visual Basic 2005, see Chapter 4.

There are several ways you can use VBA to learn about the methods, properties, and events of Word's object model. You can look at the objects in the Object Browser of the VBE, or you can use IntelliSense within the VBE. These features, along with more advanced features, are also available in Visual Studio when you're creating Word solutions in VSTO. These features are described in more detail in Chapter 2.

VBA also gives you another way to become familiar with the object model: macro recording. The *macro recorder* records actions taken within an application and translates the actions into code. You can use the macro recorder to generate code that you later modify, or to learn about which object you should use to programmatically perform an action. VSTO does not provide this functionality in Visual Studio. However, you can always open Word outside Visual Studio, record a macro, and then translate the resulting code from VBA to Visual Basic 2005.

The VBA code that you generate through macro recording, or code that you write directly in the VBE, can be associated with a button on the toolbar or menu (known as CommandBars) via the Customize menu located in Word's Tools menu. You can click the Macros option and then drag a macro listed in the dialog box to an existing menu or toolbar.

Figure 6.1 shows a macro named BoldItalic in the Customize dialog box. Because code in a VSTO solution is not stored within the document or the template, you cannot associate its code with a CommandBar button in this same way. In fact, you cannot access the Customize dialog box from VSTO. Instead, you must customize toolbars and menus programmatically.

Converting a Recorded VBA Macro to Visual Basic in VSTO

In this section, you will record a simple macro in VBA, but instead of associating the macro with a toolbar button using the Customize dialog box (as shown in Figure 6.1), you'll convert the code to Visual Basic 2005. You can then add the code to the Click event handler of a toolbar button that you'll create programmatically using VSTO.

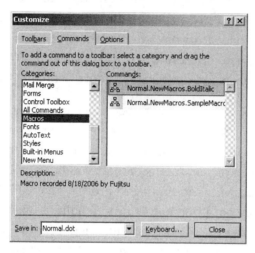

Figure 6.1. *Using the Customize dialog box to associate VBA macros with menu and toolbar items*

Recording a Macro in Word

1. Open a Word 2003 document outside Visual Studio, and type some text in the first paragraph of the document.

2. Select some text within the first paragraph, and then click Tools, point to Macros, and click Record New Macro.

3. In the Record Macro dialog box, type *BoldItalic* in the Macro Name box, and then click OK.

4. On the Formatting toolbar, click the Bold button, and then click the Italic button.

5. On the Stop Recording toolbar, click Stop Recording.

6. Open the VBE by pressing ALT+F11.

Listing 6.2 shows the VBA code you should see in the VBE. Notice that the macro recorder generated the enumeration wdToggle to assign bold and italic formatting to the selection. This means that if the selection is not already bold and italic when the macro is run, it will apply bold and italic; otherwise, it will remove the bold and italic formatting.

Listing 6.2. *Recorded VBA macro*

```
Sub BoldItalic()
'
' Sample Macro
' Macro recorded by Kathleen McGrath
'
    Selection.Font.Bold = wdToggle
    Selection.Font.Italic = wdToggle
End Sub
```

If you open the Customize dialog box, you will see a macro named Project.NewMacro.BoldItalic listed as a command in the Macros categories. At this point you could drag the macro from the dialog box to an area on the toolbar.

We cannot access this dialog box inside Visual Studio while Word is open (and even if we could, the dialog box gives us no way to access VSTO code associated with a Word document or template). This means that you must programmatically add a button to a toolbar and then write code in the button's Click event handler so that it will toggle the formatting. You can access the button's Click event when you create the variable WithEvents, as shown in Listing 6.3.

1. Create a Word document solution using VSTO.

2. In Solution Explorer, right-click ThisDocument, and click View Code.

3. Add the code in Listing 6.3 to the ThisDocument class, replacing the existing Startup event handler.

Listing 6.3. *Creating a toolbar button to toggle bold and italic formatting*

```
Dim commandBar As Office.CommandBar
WithEvents formatButton As Office.CommandBarButton

Private Sub ThisDocument_Startup(ByVal sender As Object, _
    ByVal e As System.EventArgs)Handles Me.Startup

    Me.Application.CustomizationContext = Me.InnerObject

    commandBar = Me.CommandBars("Standard")
    formatButton = CType(commandBar.Controls.Add(1), _
        Office.CommandBarButton)

    With formatButton
        .Caption = "Bold and Italic"
        .Tag = "FormatButton"
        .FaceId = 34
    End With

End Sub

Private Sub formatButton_Click(ByVal Ctrl As _
    Microsoft.Office.Core.CommandBarButton, ByRef CancelDefault _
    As Boolean) Handles formatButton.Click

    Dim Selection As Word.Selection = Me.Application.Selection

    Selection.Font.Bold = Word.WdConstants.wdToggle
    Selection.Font.Italic = Word.WdConstants.wdToggle

End Sub
```

The variables for the CommandBar and CommandBarButton objects are created outside the Startup event handler. This is because we need to access these variables from the method that handles the button's Click event. If we were to declare the variables in the Startup event handler, the variables would go out of scope after the code in the procedure has been run. After the variable is out of scope, it can be garbage collected, and that would prevent the button's Click event handler from firing. We also set the CustomizationContext to ThisDocument (represented by the keyword Me) so that the customization is saved only in the document associated with the code, rather than in the Normal.dot template (the default).

Notice that the code that we added to the button's Click event handler has been revised from the code in the recorded macro. Because the Selection object is available only through the Application object, you need to create a variable for the selection rather than access it directly as you can in VBA. The remainder of the code is identical to what was recorded in VBA except that the wdToggle enumeration must be fully qualified in Visual Basic 2005. When you run this code, a new button is added to the Standard toolbar. Each time the button is clicked, the bold and italic formatting is either applied to or removed from the selected text.

Instead of providing a built-in icon for the button by supplying a FaceID, you can create a custom image and add it to the control. You will learn how to do this in Chapter 8.

Overriding Built-In Commands

It is easy to override a built-in Word command using VBA. To do so, you create a subroutine that has the same name as the built-in command. Each time the user clicks the button for that command on the toolbar or menu or presses a keyboard shortcut, your custom subroutine runs instead of Word's built-in command.

You can't do this in VSTO because of limitations in the Word and Excel architecture. One thing you can do is to create a callback from VBA into your managed code within VSTO. You can use VSTO to replace the built-in button or menu item with your own. Note that you still need to create a callback in VBA to call into your managed code and override Word's built-in keyboard shortcut. You can see an example of how to write a callback for an Excel user-defined function in Chapter 7.

Let's say that you want to replace Word's built-in spell-checking functionality because you have three additional requirements. First, you want to ensure that the spell-check occurs every time the Print button is clicked. (Word's default functionality is to rerun the spell-checker only on new text in the document that hasn't already been checked.)

Second, you want to make sure that the document is saved as soon as the spell-check operation is complete. You can do this by adding a method to your project to ensure that the document will always be rechecked for spelling errors and then calling the Save method on the document after the spell-checking is complete. You can create and add your own button or menu item that is identical to the built-in item; then you hide the built-in item.

Finally, you decide that you don't want to check grammar in the document no matter what options the user has set.

The first step is to create the menu item. Add the code in Listing 6.4 to the ThisApplication class before the code for the Startup method.

Listing 6.4. *Creating a toolbar button to override Word's spell-checking command*

```
Dim MySpellCheckButton As Office.CommandBarButton
Dim MySpellCheckMenuItem As Office.CommandBarButton
Dim ToolsMenu As Office.CommandBar = _
    Application.CommandBars("Tools")
Dim StandardToolbar As Office.CommandBar = _
    Application.CommandBars("Standard")
Const CONTROL_NAME As String = "&Spelling and Grammar..."
Const CAPTION_TEXT As String = "&Spelling..."
Const MENU_TAG As String = "SpellCheck"
Const BUTTON_TAG As String = "CheckSpelling"

Private Sub AddMenuItem()

    Try
            ' If the menu item already exists, remove it, and show
            ' the built-in item.
```

```
    MySpellCheckMenuItem = ToolsMenu.FindControl( _
        Tag:=MENU_TAG)

    If MySpellCheckMenuItem IsNot Nothing Then
        MySpellCheckMenuItem.Delete(True)
        ToolsMenu.Controls(CONTROL_NAME).Visible = True
    End If

Catch Ex As Exception

    MsgBox(Ex.Message)

End Try

' Set the customization context to the document.
Me.Application.CustomizationContext = Me.InnerObject

' Hide the default Spelling and Grammar control.
ToolsMenu.Controls(CONTROL_NAME).Visible = False

' Add the new Spelling item.
MySpellCheckMenuItem = CType(ToolsMenu.Controls.Add( _
    Type:=Office.MsoControlType.msoControlButton, _
    Before:=1, Temporary:=True), _
    Office.CommandBarButton)

With MySpellCheckMenuItem
    .Caption = CAPTION_TEXT
    .Tag = MENU_TAG
    .FaceId = 2
End With

AddHandler MySpellCheckMenuItem.Click, _
    AddressOf SpellCheck

End Sub
```

Next, create the toolbar button, and add it to Word's Standard toolbar by adding the code in Listing 6.5 following the AddMenuItem method.

Listing 6.5. *Creating a menu item to override Word's spell-checking command*

```
Private Sub AddToolbarButton()

    Try
        ' If the button already exists, remove it, and show
        ' the built-in button.
        MySpellCheckButton = StandardToolbar.FindControl( _
            Tag:=BUTTON_TAG)

        If MySpellCheckButton IsNot Nothing Then
            MySpellCheckButton.Delete(True)
            StandardToolbar.Controls(CONTROL_NAME).Visible _
                = True
        End If

    Catch Ex As Exception

        MsgBox(Ex.Message)

    End Try

    ' Set the customization context to the document.
    Me.Application.CustomizationContext = Me.InnerObject

    ' Hide the default Spelling and Grammar control.
    StandardToolbar.Controls(CONTROL_NAME).Visible = False

    ' Add the new Spelling control.
    MySpellCheckButton = CType(StandardToolbar.Controls _
        .Add(Type:=1, Before:=8), Office.CommandBarButton)

    With MySpellCheckButton
        .Caption = CAPTION_TEXT
        .Tag = BUTTON_TAG
        .FaceId = 2
    End With

    AddHandler MySpellCheckButton.Click, _
        AddressOf SpellCheck

End Sub
```

Add the SpellCheck event handler, and add code to the Startup event handler that calls the AddMenuItem and AddToolbarButton methods, as shown in Listing 6.6.

Listing 6.6. *Creating the event handler and calling methods to create menu and toolbar buttons*

```
Private Sub SpellCheck(ByVal ctrl As Office.CommandBarButton, _
    ByRef Cancel As Boolean)

    ' Reset the spell-check options, run spell-check, and
    ' then save the document.
    Application.ResetIgnoreAll()
    Me.SpellingChecked = False
    Me.CheckSpelling()
    Me.Save()

    MsgBox("The spelling check is complete.", _
        MsgBoxStyle.OkOnly, "Microsoft Office Word")

End Sub

Private Sub ThisDocument_Startup(ByVal sender As Object, _
    ByVal e As System.EventArgs) Handles Me.Startup

    ' Create the menu item and toolbar button.
    AddMenuItem()
    AddToolbarButton()

End Sub
```

This code checks for the existence of our custom menu item or toolbar button, and if it finds the item, it deletes it and then re-creates it. In this way, we don't repeatedly add the same button to the toolbar or menu each time the document is opened. The code then hides the built-in commandbar items and creates a Click event handler for both the toolbar button and the menu item. In the event handler, spell-check options are reset so that the entire document will be checked again; the

CheckSpelling method of the document is called, and then changes are saved to the document. To mimic the default functionality, we display a message box to inform users that the document has been spell-checked. This is a necessary visual cue that something actually happened when the user clicked the Spelling button even if no errors occurred in the document.

Creating menu items and buttons is important because it is often the entry point into your code. The Word object model contains many objects that you can manipulate from VSTO, but this chapter does not focus on the existing object model; you can learn more about it by using the Object Browser and IntelliSense within Visual Studio. As mentioned before, you can also learn about Word's object model by using the macro recorder.

VSTO has extended some of the objects in the Word object model. In the remainder of this chapter, we take a closer look at these enhancements and describe how you can use these objects in your Word solutions using VSTO.

Word Host Items and Host Controls

VSTO enhances a number of Word objects by enabling data binding and by exposing events. The VSTO enhancements are in the form of controls that can be added to a container. The container is known as the *host item*, and the controls that the host item contains are called *host controls*.

Host controls are added to host items in much the same way you add a control to a UserForm. For example, in VSTO, the Bookmark host control has events and can be bound to data, and the Document is a host item on which you can add the Bookmark host control (as well as other host controls and Windows Forms controls). Figure 6.2 shows a Bookmark control named Bookmark1, with all its properties listed in the Properties window.

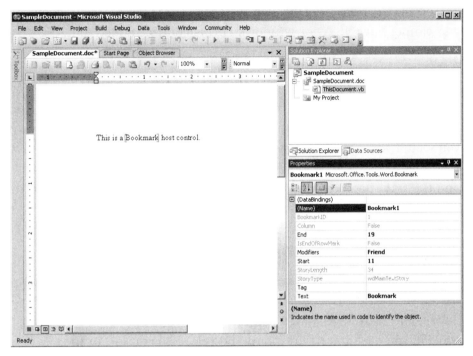

Figure 6.2. *Events of a Bookmark host control*

Host items and host controls wrap the native Office objects; they have the same functionality as the underlying object, but they are enhanced with data binding capabilities and events. The native objects are in the Microsoft.Office.Interop.Word namespace. In this book, we sometimes refer to these objects as Interop objects. The host items and host controls are in the Microsoft.Office.Tools.Word namespace, and we sometimes refer to these objects as VSTO objects or VSTO controls. Three host controls can be added to the host item document: Bookmark, XMLNode, and XMLNodes.

You can add host controls only to a host item. When you create a VSTO solution and choose either a document or a template, it is automatically created as a host item, enabling you to add host controls to the document at design time and at run time. However, if you programmatically add a new document, it will be of the type Microsoft.Office.Interop.Word.Document and cannot have VSTO or Windows Forms controls added to it.

Adding Host Controls to the Document

You can add Word host controls to the document host item in a number of ways. You can always do this through Word's menus, in the same way you would add the native object to the document. VSTO also provides a way to add some host controls: You drag the control from the Toolbox and the Data Sources window onto the document, and you add them programmatically at run time.

Adding Controls at Design Time

There are typically three ways to add host controls to a document at design time. The first is to add the control as if you were adding the native object through Word's menus. For example, to add a Bookmark control, you click the Insert menu and select Bookmark. In the Bookmark's dialog box, you then type the name of the bookmark in the Bookmark Name box and click Add, as shown in Figure 6.3. VSTO automatically creates the bookmark as a VSTO control, complete with data binding capabilities and events that you can program against.

Figure 6.3. *Adding a bookmark to a document using the Insert menu*

You can also add a Bookmark control to the document by using Visual Studio's Toolbox. When you drag the Bookmark control to the document, a dialog box gives you the opportunity to select the text you want to bookmark. Then you click OK to insert the bookmark at that location, as shown in Figure 6.4.

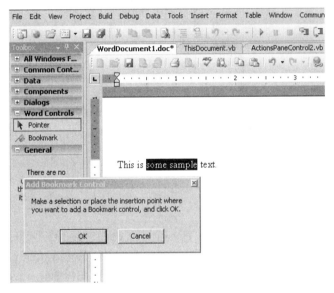

Figure 6.4. *Using the Toolbox to add a bookmark to a document*

When you drag bookmarks from the Toolbox, VSTO automatically names them for you. The name is "Bookmark," with an incremental number appended. For example, the first bookmark you add is named Bookmark1, the second is Bookmark2, and so on. You can change the name of the bookmark in the Properties window after it has been added to the document.

The fact that the Bookmark control is available in the Properties window in Visual Studio is another indication that this VSTO control is a first-class .NET object that you can access directly in code. In the Properties window, you have access to some of the properties, and all the events, of the bookmark. Figure 6.5 shows the events available on a Bookmark control named Bookmark1. To view the events in Visual Studio, select the bookmark either in the document or in the drop-down box in the Properties window, and then click the Events button.

Figure 6.5. *Available properties of a bookmark*

You can also add a data-bound Bookmark control to the document using the Data Sources window. By default, the Bookmark control is available for each field of the table listed in the Data Sources window when the Word document has focus. You select the field in the Data Sources window and drag it to the document, as shown in Figure 6.6. Data binding to controls is described in more detail later in this chapter.

For Word solutions, only the Bookmark control is available on the Toolbox and the Data Sources window. If you want to add an XMLNode or XMLNodes control, you must first attach a schema to the document and then drag the schema elements from the XML Structure task pane to the document. For an example of XML mapping, see Chapter 5.

When you map the XMLNodes control to your document, VSTO automatically creates a host item for each object. Whether the object is added as an XMLNode control or as an XMLNodes control is determined by whether the added element is a repeating schema element (where the

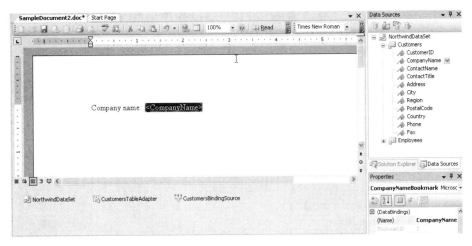

Figure 6.6. *Using the Data Sources window to add a bookmark to a document*

maximum number of occurrences is defined as greater than 1). Repeating schema elements are added as XMLNodes controls. Nonrepeating schema elements are added as XMLNode controls.

In this section you'll create a simple schema and then map it to a Word document.

1. Type the XML in Listing 6.7 into a text file, and name it Sample.xsd. You could also use the XML editor in Visual Studio to create your schema.

Listing 6.7. *Sample schema*

```
<?xml version="1.0" encoding="utf-8" ?>
<xs:schema targetNamespace="http://schemas.samples"
    elementFormDefault="qualified"
    xmlns="http://schemas.samples"
    xmlns:mstns="http://schemas.samples"
    xmlns:xs="http://www.w3.org/2001/XMLSchema">
  <xs:element name="Sample" type="SampleType"></xs:element>
  <xs:complexType name="SampleType">
    <xs:all>
```

```
    <xs:element name="Name" type="NameType" minOccurs="0"
        maxOccurs="1" />
    <xs:element name="Address" type="xs:string" minOccurs="0"
        maxOccurs="1" />
  </xs:all>
</xs:complexType>
<xs:complexType name="NameType">
  <xs:sequence>
   <xs:element name="FirstName" type="xs:string" minOccurs="1"
        maxOccurs="1"/>
    <xs:element name="LastName" type="xs:string" minOccurs="1"
        maxOccurs="1"/>
  </xs:sequence>
</xs:complexType>
</xs:schema>
```

2. On the Tools menu in Visual Studio, point to Microsoft Office Word Tools, and click Templates and Add-ins. If you do not see this menu option, make sure that the document is open in design mode and that the document has focus. Then try to click the menu item again.

3. In the XML Schema tab of the Templates and Add-ins dialog box, click Add Schema.

4. Select the Sample.xsd file that you saved in step 1, type the word *Sample* in the Alias text box, and click OK.

5. In the XML Structure task pane, click Sample to add the sample XMLNode to the document. (Select Apply to Entire Document if requested.)

6. Click inside the Sample node on the document, and then click Name on the XML Structure task pane.

7. Add the text *First Name:* to the document, and then map the FirstName element to the right of the text.

8. Add the text *Last Name:* to the document, and then map the LastName element to the right of the text.

If you click inside the FirstName node on the document and then look at the Properties window in Visual Studio, you will see that an XMLNode control has been created with the name NameFirstNameNode. VSTO automatically names each XMLNode that you add to the document by adding the child name to the parent name and appending the word *Node.* For example, if you click inside the Name node on the document, you'll see that the control's name is SampleNameNode. See the Properties window in Figure 6.7 for an example.

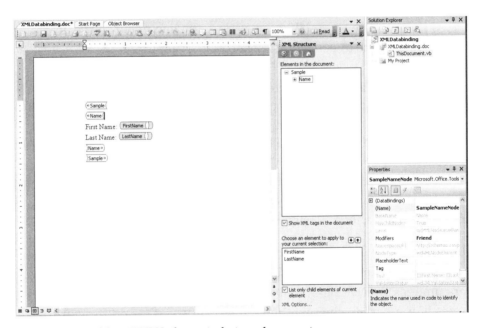

Figure 6.7. *Adding XMLNode controls to a document*

You can continue mapping XMLNode controls to the document so that you also have an Address node within the Sample node. You can uncheck the Show XML Tags in the Document check box to hide the actual nodes in the document. You can also set various options by clicking the XML Options link at the bottom of the XML Structure task pane. For example, you can check the Ignore Mixed Content check box so that you can mix text and XMLNode controls in the document, or you can uncheck the Hide Schema Violations in This Document option to turn off schema validation.

To see how you can write code to respond to an event of the XMLNode, click inside the FirstName node and type your first name. If you double-click the text you just typed, it will take you to the Select event handler of the XMLNode in code view. Add code to display a message box:

```
MsgBox("Hello " & Me.NameFirstNameNode.Text)
```

Press F5 to run the code. When you click the document in the area where your name appears, a message box is displayed.

Adding Controls at Run Time

Most host controls can be added to the Word document at run time. There are two exceptions to this rule, both of them related to XML mapping. VSTO does not provide a way to add XMLNode and XMLNodes controls to the document programmatically. You can add these controls only when you map an XML element to the document using Word's native functionality at design time.

In Chapter 3, you learned that to create an instance of an object you must use the New keyword. This technique is not supported for programmatically creating instances of view controls. Instead, VSTO provides a number of helper methods that enable you to add the controls to the document at run time. These methods are part of the Controls collection, and, in the case of Word, there is only one method available: AddBookmark. The AddBookmark method takes two parameters: the range where you want to add the bookmark, and the name you want to give the bookmark.

The code in Listing 6.8 shows how to add a bookmark to a range of text at run time and then apply bold formatting to the text in the bookmark.

Listing 6.8. *Programmatically adding a bookmark to a range*

```
Dim myBookmark As Microsoft.Office.Tools.Word.Bookmark = _
    Me.Controls.AddBookmark(Me.Paragraphs(1).Range, _
    "myBookmark")
myBookmark.Font.Bold = True
```

When you pass the AddBookmark method a name to give the bookmark, you must make sure that the name is unique. Unlike VBA, where you can programmatically add a bookmark and give it the same name as an existing bookmark (thus moving the bookmark to a new location), you must supply unique names for VSTO bookmarks. If you supply a name that is already in use in the document, you will receive a ControlNameAlreadyExistsException, as shown in Figure 6.8.

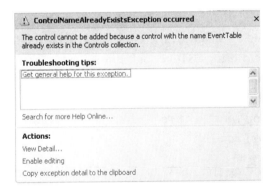

Figure 6.8. *Exception thrown when the bookmark name already exists in the document*

To avoid this error, you should first check to make sure that a like-named bookmark doesn't already exist on the document. You can do that within the Controls collection of the document by using the Contains method, as the code in Listing 6.9 demonstrates.

Listing 6.9. *Checking whether a bookmark already exists before adding it to a range*

```
Dim bookmarkName As String = "EventTable"

If Not Me.Controls.Contains(BookmarkName) Then

    Dim myBookmark As Microsoft.Office.Tools.Word.Bookmark = _
        Me.Controls.AddBookmark(Me.Paragraphs(1).Range, _
        bookmarkName)
    myBookmark.Font.Bold = True

End If
```

Control Persistence

VSTO bookmarks that are added to a document programmatically are not persisted in the document in the way you might expect. After the document is saved and closed, the bookmark is stored in the document, but it does not retain its VSTO capabilities. The bookmark is stored as an Interop bookmark rather than a VSTO bookmark. Any of its data binding capabilities or events are not available the next time you open the document. You must write code to add the bookmark to the Controls collection again.

You do this by adding the VSTO bookmark to the document (using AddBookmark), but this time you pass the Interop bookmark as the location you want the bookmark to appear rather than a specific range. This also means that you can create a VSTO bookmark for an existing Interop bookmark. Listing 6.10 demonstrates how to reconnect an Interop bookmark with VSTO capabilities.

Listing 6.10. *Reconnecting a bookmark with VSTO capabilities*

```
Dim InteropBookmark As Word.Bookmark = Bookmarks.Add( _
    "Bookmark2", Me.Paragraphs(1).Range)
```

```
Dim VSTOBookmark As Microsoft.Office.Tools.Word. _
    Bookmark = Me.Controls.AddBookmark(InteropBookmark, _
    InteropBookmark.Name)

VSTOBookmark.Text = "Sample text"
```

In this case, you can use the same name as an existing bookmark because you are replacing it with a new VSTO bookmark that doesn't already exist in the Controls collection. You'll learn about this, and other bookmark enhancements, later in this chapter.

Accessing a Host Control from an Underlying Interop Object

Each host control has an associated underlying Interop object. You can access this object from the host control by using its InnerObject method. However, there is no way to do the opposite: access a host control from the underlying Interop object. VSTO does not provide a collection for each of the host controls; instead, there is a single Controls collection, which can contain host controls as well as Windows Forms controls.

Although a VSTO Bookmarks collection does not exist, there is an Interop Bookmarks collection (every Bookmark control has an underlying Interop bookmark); therefore, you can loop through all Interop bookmarks in the document just as you can in VBA. An example is shown in Listing 6.11.

Listing 6.11. *The Interop Bookmark collection*

```
For Each bookmark As Microsoft.Office.Interop.Word.Bookmark _
    In Me.Bookmarks

    MsgBox(bookmark.Name.ToString())

Next
```

Unfortunately, you cannot access any VSTO-specific functionality of the
bookmark because they are Interop bookmarks; you do not have access
to the data binding and events that VSTO provides. You cannot use a
For Each statement for VSTO bookmarks because there isn't a VSTO
Bookmarks collection. If you change the code in Listing 6.9 to declare
the bookmark variable as the type Microsoft.Office.Tools.Word.Bookmark,
the code will compile fine, but you will receive an error when you run
the application.

As an alternative, you can use the Controls collection to loop through
each control in the collection and then determine whether it is of the
type you are interested in—in our case, a Bookmark host control. Listing 6.12 loops through all controls in the Controls collection and checks
whether the control is of the type Microsoft.Office.Tools.Word.Bookmark.
If the control is a Bookmark host control, its name is displayed in a
message box. Because you declare myControl as an Object, you must
cast the object back into a Bookmark host control before you can access
its properties, methods, and events.

Listing 6.12. *The Controls collection*

```
Dim myControl as Object

For Each myControl in Me.Controls

    If TypeOf(myControl) Is Microsoft.Office.Tools.Word _
        .Bookmark Then

        Dim VSTOBookmark As Microsoft.Office.Tools.Word. _
            Bookmark = CType((myControl), _
            Microsoft.Office.Tools.Word.Bookmark)

        MsgBox(VSTOBookmark.Name.ToString())

    End If

Next
```

This might seem like a lot of work to do each time you want to access a VSTO host control from the underlying Interop object. Instead, you could create a helper function for each host control so that you can obtain the corresponding host control whenever you have accessed the Interop object, as shown in Listing 6.13. You could create a class that contains all the helper functions and then add this class to each VSTO Word solution that you create. This function, and any other helper functions you create, can then be called from your code as needed.

Listing 6.13. *Helper function for Bookmark host control*

```
Private Function GetBookmarkHostControl(ByVal _
    InteropBookmark As Word.Bookmark) As _
    Microsoft.Office.Tools.Word.Bookmark

        Dim myControl As Object = Nothing
        Dim VSTOBookmark As Microsoft.Office.Tools.Word _
            .Bookmark = Nothing

        ' Loop through each control in the controls
        ' collection and check whether the current
        ' control is a bookmark.
        For Each myControl In Me.Controls
            If TypeOf (myControl) Is Microsoft.Office. _
                Tools.Word.Bookmark Then

                ' Cast the control into a VSTO Bookmark.
                VSTOBookmark = CType((myControl), _
                    Microsoft.Office.Tools.Word.Bookmark)

                ' If VSTO bookmark has the same name as the
                ' Interop bookmark, return it; otherwise,
                ' release the variable and check the next
                ' control.
                If VSTOBookmark.Name = InteropBookmark.Name Then
                    Exit For
                Else
                    VSTOBookmark = Nothing
                End If
```

```
        End If
    Next

    Return VSTOBookmark

End Function
```

Accessing an Interop Object from a Host Control

Sometimes you may need to access the Interop object associated with a given host control. For example, you might be working with the host controls and want to call a method that specifically requires an Interop object. You can call the InnerObject property of the host control to return its underlying Interop object.

Suppose you are creating a new toolbar and you want to ensure that it is available only when a particular VSTO-enabled document is running and has focus. You can set CustomizationContext to the Document object. CustomizationContext is a function on the Word Application object that tells which document the toolbars, menu bars, and key bindings will be saved in. Because the Application object doesn't know anything about VSTO host items or host controls, it requires that an Interop object be passed to any of its methods; you cannot pass the VSTO object directly.

Listing 6.14 shows how to set CustomizationContext to the Interop document by using InnerObject. If you were to try to set CustomizationContext to the VSTO document (without calling InnerObject), it would raise an InvalidCast exception when you run the solution. To see this in use when creating a button for a toolbar, see the earlier example in Listing 6.3.

Listing 6.14. *Using the InnerObject property of a host control*

```
' Set the CustomizationContext property of a Word application
' to the Interop document.
Me.Application.CustomizationContext = Me.InnerObject
```

```
' If you do not call the InnerObject property of
' ThisDocument, VSTO raises an InvalidCast exception
' with the following code.
Me.Application.CustomizationContext = Me
```

Data Binding to Host Controls on Documents

VSTO enables you to bind data to the host controls. In Word, simple data binding is enabled. In *simple* data binding, you bind a single data element to a property of a control, such as the text property of a Bookmark control. Although you can bind data to an XMLNode control, you cannot do so for an XMLNodes control. This is because XMLNodes is actually a collection of XMLNode controls. Word host controls do not support complex data binding. You will learn more about complex data binding in Chapter 7.

Binding Data to Controls

The easiest way to bind data to a Bookmark control is to use the Data Sources window so that you can add to your document a control that is already bound to data. In this section you'll use the Data Sources window to add a connection to the Northwind database in Microsoft Access. You'll then bind some of the data to a Bookmark control.

1. Create a Word document solution using VSTO.

2. On the Data menu, click Add New Data Source.

3. In the Data Source Configuration Wizard, select Database, and then click Next, as shown in Figure 6.9.

4. Click New Connection to open the Add Connection dialog box.

5. Select Microsoft Access Database File for the data source, and select the Northwind.mdb database on your computer. This assumes that you have Microsoft Access installed on your computer.

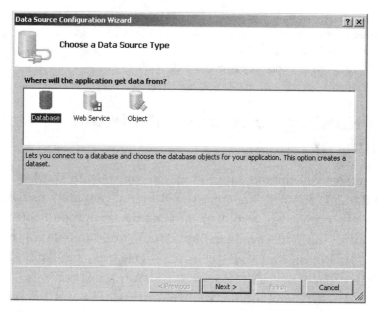

Figure 6.9. *Selecting the data source type in the Data Source Configuration Wizard*

6. For this example, you will not set a password to log on to the database. Click Test Connection, and then click OK to close the Add Connection dialog box (see Figure 6.10).

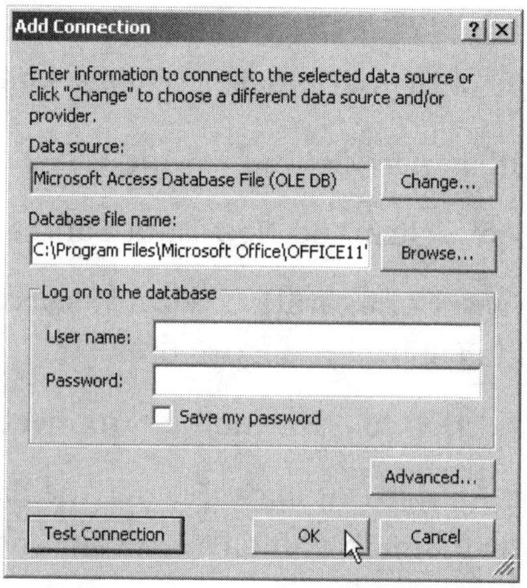

Figure 6.10. *Adding a connection to the Northwind database in Microsoft Access*

7. On the Data Source Configuration Wizard, click Next.

8. When requested, copy the local data file to your project by clicking Yes, as shown in Figure 6.11. This action adds the data file to your project and gives you access to it in Solution Explorer.

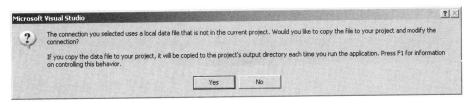

Figure 6.11. *Adding the Northwind data source to the project*

9. Click Next on the Data Source Configuration Wizard using the default connection string.

10. Expand the Tables node, and click the check boxes for the Customers and Employees tables, as shown in Figure 6.12. Then click Finish.

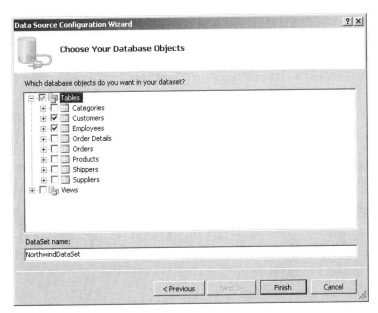

Figure 6.12. *Selecting database objects to use in the dataset*

A new dataset named NorthwindDataSet is added to the Data Sources window. The dataset contains Customers and Employees tables. Next you'll add a data-bound Bookmark control to the document.

1. Expand the Customers table, and click the CompanyName node. Click the arrow next to CompanyName to reveal a drop-down menu, as shown in Figure 6.13.

Figure 6.13. *Types of controls available for a dataset field*

Next, you select the type of control that will be added when you drag the field to the document. Click the drop-down arrow next to the field, and then select the desired control. The default is the Bookmark control, indicated by the flag symbol. We'll use this control type when adding the field to the document.

2. Drag the CompanyName field from the Data Sources window to the document.

The bookmark is added to the document, and the bookmark's name appears between angle brackets in the document. This text will be replaced by the bound data when the solution is run (see Figures 6.14 and 6.15).

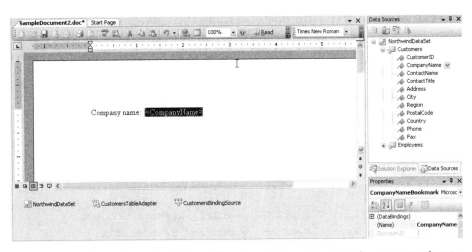

Figure 6.14. *Dragging a data-bound bookmark from the Data Sources window to the document*

Because VSTO controls use ADO.NET for data binding, when you drag the Bookmark control from the Data Sources window, a Dataset, table adapter, and binding source are automatically created and added to the component tray (see Figure 6.14).

3. Press F5 to run the solution. The document displays the first record in the data source for the Company Name field, as shown in Figure 6.15.

Figure 6.15. *Displaying the first record in a data-bound bookmark*

You can add a button to the document and then add code to enable users to move through the records each time the button is clicked. You use the position of the binding source to move from record to record. VSTO automatically created a binding source named CustomersBindingSource when you dragged the bookmark to the document; you can use this binding source to move through the records. Listing 6.15 demonstrates how to write this code.

Listing 6.15. *Moving through records in a dataset that are bound to a Bookmark control*

```
Private Sub Button1_Click(ByVal sender As System.Object, _
    ByVal e As System.EventArgs) Handles Button1.Click

    If Me.CustomersBindingSource.Position < _
        Me.CustomersBindingSource.Count - 1 Then
            Me.CustomersBindingSource.MoveNext()
    Else
        Me.CustomersBindingSource.MoveFirst()
    End If
End Sub
```

If you want to bind data to an XMLNode control, you must do so programmatically, because the XMLNode control is not available through the Data Sources window. If you map the schema described in Listing 6.5 to a Word document, you can add the code in Listing 6.16 to the Startup event handler of ThisDocument. This code binds a data source to the NameFirstNameNode and NameLastNameNode XMLNode controls that are created when you map the FirstName and LastName elements to the document.

Listing 6.16. *Binding data to an XMLNode control*

```
Private Sub ThisDocument_Startup(ByVal sender As Object, _
    ByVal e As System.EventArgs) Handles Me.Startup

    Dim ds As DataSet = New DataSet()
    Dim clientTable As DataTable = ds.Tables.Add("Clients")
```

```
With clientTable
    .Columns.Add("FirstName", GetType(String))
    .Columns.Add("LastName", GetType(String))
    .Rows.Add("Mike", "Hernandez")
    .Rows.Add("Paul", "Stubbs")
    .Rows.Add("Kathleen", "McGrath")
End With

Me.NameFirstNameNode.DataBindings.Add("Text", ds, _
    "Clients.FirstName")
Me.NameLastNameNode.DataBindings.Add("Text", ds, _
    "Clients.LastName")
End Sub
```

Caching Data in the Document

Caching data in the document enables you to access the data when the document is offline or when you want to persist data between sessions or make the data available on the server. An *offline* document is one that is not connected to the network. Data that you bind to controls can be cached in the document by adding the CachedAttribute to a dataset in your solution making it available when the document is offline.

Cached data is stored in the Runtime Storage Control, which is part of every Word and Excel solution created with VSTO. If you have a variable declared as a Dataset within your solution, you can add the following attribute to the left of the declaration to start the data caching:

```
<Microsoft.VisualStudio.Tools.Applications.Runtime.Cached()>
```

Alternatively, in the Properties window you can set the CacheInDocument property of the instance of the dataset to True. Because the dataset instance must be public, you should also change the Modifiers property from Internal to Public.

You can also programmatically add a data object to the document's data cache by calling the StartCaching method on the document and passing the dataset to be cached. You can stop caching the dataset by calling the StopCaching method. Using data caching in documents on a server is described in more detail in Chapter 13.

Programming Against Events

When you create Word solutions, you usually write code that responds to actions that users take within your application. For example, you might add a button to the toolbar that performs an action when the user clicks the button. When you create VBA solutions for Word, it is difficult to write code that responds to user actions—such as selecting text—because most of the objects available in the Word object model do not have events that you can capture.

The enhancements that VSTO adds to host items and host controls expose events on these objects, and you can program against a number of them. Several events are exposed on the Document, and on the Bookmark, XMLNode, and XMLNodes controls. When you create VBA solutions for Word, you cannot write code in response to a user moving the cursor into an area of text that contains a bookmark. With VSTO, this is now possible.

In this section you will look at the events for each of the host controls and the Document host item.

Bookmark Control Events

The following events are available for a Bookmark control in VSTO.

- BeforeDoubleClick

- BeforeRightClick

- BindingContextChanged

- Deselected

- Disposed

- Selected

- SelectionChange

BeforeDoubleClick

The BeforeDoubleClick event handler of a Bookmark control enables you to take action when a user double-clicks text within a bookmark, before the default action for double-clicking the bookmark occurs.

For example, you might show a dialog box when a user double-clicks a table in the document that contains a bookmark. You can first check whether the current selection contains a table and, if it does, display a dialog box that gives information about the table whenever the table is double-clicked. In this section you'll create a small application to demonstrate the BeforeDoubleClick event of a Bookmark control.

1. Create a Word document solution.

2. Add a table to the document, and then add a bookmark named EventTable to the entire table, as shown in Figure 6.16. Notice that the bookmarks are visible on the document in the form of square brackets.

> ❖ **Note** You can also add a separate bookmark to the text "Table" so that you can see that the events pertain only to the bookmark related to the EventTable bookmark.

3. Add a Windows Form to your project by clicking the Project menu and clicking Add Windows Form. Name the form Tables.

4. Add four labels and a Button control to the form.

5. Set the name and value of each control as shown in Table 6.1.

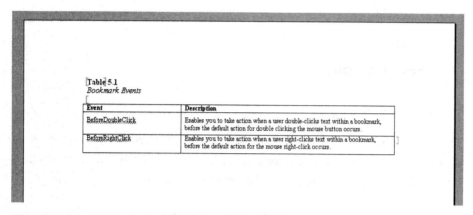

Figure 6.16. *Adding a bookmark to a table*

Table 6.1. *Values for Controls*

Default Label Name	New Label Name	Text Property
Label1	Label1	Total Rows
Label2	TotalRows	0
Label3	Label3	Total Columns
Label4	TotalColumns	0

6. Add a Button control to the form, and change the Name and Text property to *OK*.

 The Windows Form should resemble the form in Figure 6.17.

7. Create an event handler for the DoubleClick event of the Bookmark by selecting EventTable in the Class Name drop-down, and selecting DoubleClick in the Method Name drop-down in Visual Studio.

8. Add the code in Listing 6.17 to the DoubleClick event handler of the TableEvent bookmark. This code checks whether the current selection is within a table and, if it is, displays the Tables form.

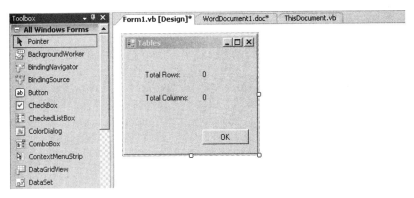

Figure 6.17. *Windows Form to display*

Listing 6.17. *Handling the BeforeDoubleClick event of a Bookmark control*

```
Private Sub EventTable_BeforeDoubleClick(ByVal sender _
    As Object, ByVal e As Microsoft.Office.Tools.Word _
    .ClickEventArgs) Handles EventTable.BeforeDoubleClick

    Dim Selection As Word.Selection = Me.Application.Selection

    If Selection.Information(Word.WdInformation _
        .wdWithInTable) Then
        Dim tableProperties As New Tables
        tableProperties.Show()
        e.Cancel = True
    End If

End Sub
```

9. Right-click the Tables.vb form, and select View Code.

10. Add the code in Listing 6.18 to the Load event handler of the Tables form. This code counts the number of columns and rows in the table and displays the totals in the form.

Listing 6.18. *Adding code to the Load event handler of a Windows Form*

```
Private Sub Tables_Load (ByVal sender As Object, _
    ByVal e As System.EventArgs) Handles MyBase.Load
```

```
Dim myTable As Word.Table = _
    Globals.ThisDocument.EventTable.Tables(1)

Me.TotalColumns.Text = myTable.Columns.Count.ToString()
Me.TotalRows.Text = myTable.Rows.Count.ToString()
```

```
End Sub
```

The Globals class gives you access to objects on the document from outside the Document class. In Listing 6.16, you use the Globals class to access the bookmark that contains the table on the document from within the Windows Form.

11. Add the code in Listing 6.19 to the Click event handler of the OK button to close the form.

Listing 6.19. *Handling the Click event of a button*

```
Private Sub OK_Click (ByVal sender As System.Object, _
    ByVal e As System.EventArgs) Handles OK.Click

    Me.Close()

End Sub
```

12. Press F5 to run the code.

13. When the document opens, double-click the table.

The Windows Form should display the total number of columns and rows in the selected table, as shown in Figure 6.18. You can also try double-clicking an area outside the table to verify that the Windows form is displayed only when the table is double-clicked.

Notice that the event handlers are different from those in VBA. The signature for the Click event handler of a CommandButton differs from the signature for the Click event handler of a Button on a Windows Form, as shown in Listing 6.20.

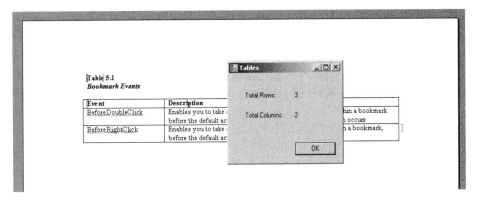

Figure 6.18. *Displaying the total number of rows and columns in the selected table*

Listing 6.20. *Event handlers in VBA versus Visual Basic 2005*

```
' VBA
Private Sub CommandButton1_Click()

End Sub


'Visual Basic 2005
Private Sub Button1_Click(ByVal sender As System.Object, _
    ByVal e As System.EventArgs) Handles Button1.Click

End Sub
```

The event handler for a Button control has two arguments: a *sender* variable of the type System.Object, and an *e* variable of the type System.EventArgs. The sender represents the object that raised the event. The e variable represents the event arguments.

Sometimes there are properties on the event arguments that you can use to perform additional actions. You can see an example of this in Listing 6.17. Here, the code sets the Cancel property to True and cancels the default action for the event (in this case, selecting a word). Try removing the line of code in Listing 6.17 that sets the Cancel property to True (e.Cancel = True), and then rerun the application. This time when you double-click the table, the entire word in the selection is highlighted.

The signature for the method also has a Handles clause. To add events that you want to be handled by this method, separate them with a comma. For example, you could add the following to the end of the method so that the same event handler handles the events for both Button1 and Button2:

```
, Button2.Click
```

This replaces the need for control arrays because you can handle events of multiple controls with one event handler.

BeforeRightClick

The BeforeRightClick event enables you to take action when a user right-clicks text within a bookmark, before the default action for the right-click event occurs. A common example is to display a context menu. You can create your own context menu, or you can add a menu item to the default menu that displays when you right-click a document. In this section you'll create a solution to demonstrate the BeforeRightClick event of a bookmark named Bookmark1.

1. Create a Word document solution.

2. Add a bookmark to text within the document, and name it Bookmark1.

3. Add the code in Listing 6.21 to the top of the ThisDocument class file. This code sets up the variable for the CommandBar button, a CommandBar control, and the string to be assigned to the button's caption. You can assign any string value to the controlCaption variable.

Listing 6.21. *Creating variables for a context menu button*

```
WithEvents newControl As Office.CommandBarButton
Dim myControl As Office.CommandBarControl
Dim controlCaption As String = "New Menu Item"
```

4. Add the code in Listing 6.22 to the BeforeRightClick event handler of the Bookmark.

Listing 6.22. *Adding a control to a context menu*

```
Private Sub Bookmark1_BeforeRightClick(ByVal sender As _
    System.Object, ByVal e As Microsoft.Office.Tools.Word. _
    ClickEventArgs) Handles Bookmark1.BeforeRightClick

    For Each myControl In Application.CommandBars( _
        "Text").Controls
        If myControl.Caption = controlCaption Then
            Application.CommandBars("Text").Controls( _
                controlCaption).Delete()
        End If
    Next

    newControl = Application.CommandBars("Text").Controls.Add
    With newControl
        .BeginGroup = True
        .Style = Office.MsoButtonStyle.msoButtonIconAndCaption
        .Caption = controlCaption
        .FaceId = 1763
        .Tag = controlCaption
    End With
    Me.AttachedTemplate.Saved = True

End Sub
```

The code first loops through all the controls on Word's context menu and checks whether the button was added previously. If it was, the code removes the button before attempting to add another one. Without this code, each time you right-click the bookmark, another button would be added to the context menu.

Next, you add a new control to the Text CommandBar, Word's default context menu. You set various properties to ensure that the button is added to a new group within the menu, to ensure that it can contain both an icon and text, to assign a string to the caption, and to assign a

FaceID for the button. The FaceID property identifies a built-in icon to use. The tag property should be set to a unique value so that Word can determine which button on the context menu was clicked. In this case, you use the same name as the control caption, but instead you could have assigned it a unique value by using a GUID. Next, you need to add a handler for the event.

5. Add the code in Listing 6.23 to the ThisDocument class file.

Listing 6.23. *Creating an event handler for a shortcut menu button*

```
Private Sub ShortcutButtonClick(ByVal ctrl As _
    Office.CommandBarButton, ByRef Cancel As Boolean) _
    Handles newControl.Click

        MsgBox(ctrl.Caption & " was clicked.")

End Sub
```

6. Press F5 to run the code.

When you right-click the bookmark, the event handler adds the button to the context menu, and the menu item becomes available as the final entry in the shortcut menu. When you click the button, a message box displays the name of the clicked control. You can expand this code to handle the right-click event of all bookmarks in the document; you loop through all the bookmarks in the document via the Controls collection (as described earlier in this chapter) and add an event handler for each bookmark.

Because bookmarks can overlap, you should write additional code to ensure that you are handling the event of the correct bookmark. Overlapping bookmarks are described in more detail later in this chapter.

BindingContextChanged

This event is raised when the binding context of the bookmark changes. The BindingContext object manages which data source you are binding to. If the BindingContext changes, it may mean that you are now bound to a different data source. The BindingContextChanged event handler lets you take action when the BindingContext property of a bookmark is changed. The code in Listing 6.24 displays a message when the binding context of a Bookmark control changes.

Listing 6.24. *Displaying a message when the binding context of a bookmark changes*

```
Private Sub Bookmark1_BindingContextChanged(ByVal sender As _
    System.Object, ByVal e As System.EventArgs) Handles _
    Bookmark1.BindingContextChanged

    MsgBox("BindingContext changed")

End Sub
```

Deselected

The Deselected event handler enables you to take action when focus is moved from the bookmark to an area outside the bookmark. For example, you might want to remove a control from the task pane that should only be visible when a table is selected. You could do so by adding code to remove the control in the Deselected event handler.

Disposed

The Disposed event is raised when the bookmark is disposed of. This event typically does not get raised until garbage collection is called to reclaim the memory that held the control.

Selected

The Selected event handler enables you to take action when focus is moved to the bookmark. For example, you might want to display a task pane. In this section, you'll add code to the Selected event handler of the document to display the Styles and Formatting task pane whenever focus moves from outside the bookmark to an area inside the bookmark.

1. Create a Word document solution.

2. Add a bookmark to the document, and name it Bookmark1.

3. Add the code in Listing 6.25 to the Selected event handler of a
   Bookmark control.

Listing 6.25. *Displaying the Styles and Formatting task pane when a bookmark
is selected*

```
Sub Bookmark1_Selected(ByVal sender As Object, ByVal e As _
    Microsoft.Office.Tools.Word.SelectionEventArgs) _
    Handles Bookmark1.Selected

    Application.TaskPanes(Word.WdTaskPanes _
        .wdTaskPaneFormatting).Visible = True
End Sub
```

4. Press F5 to run the code.

5. When the document opens, move your cursor into text that contains the bookmark.

The Styles and Formatting task pane becomes visible (if it isn't already
visible) whenever you move your cursor into the area of the bookmark.

SelectionChange

The SelectionChange event handler enables you to take action when the
selection of a bookmark's content changes. For example, you might
want to display information in the status bar about the characters that
are currently selected. In this section, you'll add code to the Selection-
Change event handler of the bookmark.

1. Create a Word document solution.

2. Add a bookmark to the document, and name it Bookmark1.

3. Add the code in Listing 6.26 to the SelectionChange event handler
   of the Bookmark control.

Listing 6.26. *Displaying the characters in a bookmark up to the current selection*

```
Sub Bookmark1_SelectionChange(ByVal sender As Object, _
    ByVal e As Microsoft.Office.Tools.Word. _
    SelectionEventArgs) Handles Bookmark1.SelectionChange

    Dim mySelection As Word.Selection = Application.Selection
    Dim selectedCharacters As String = mySelection.Text
    Application.StatusBar = "Characters selected: " & _
        selectedCharacters

End Sub
```

4. Press F5 to run the code.

5. Move the mouse cursor into the text of a bookmark, and watch how the status bar displays updated information about which characters are selected as you change the selection within a Bookmark control. Figure 6.19 illustrates.

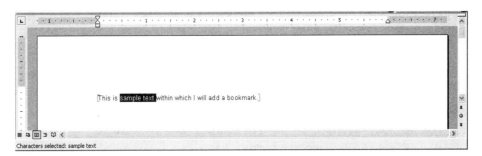

Figure 6.19. *Displaying selected text in the status bar*

XMLNode Control Events

The following events are available for an XMLNode control in VSTO.

- AfterInsert
- BeforeDelete
- BindingContextChanged

- ContextEnter

- ContextLeave

- Deselect

- Disposed

- Select

- ValidationError

AfterInsert

The AfterInsert event handler enables you to take action when a new XMLNode element is added to the document. Because you cannot programmatically add XMLNode controls to your document at run time, it is unlikely that the AfterInsert event will be raised. It will be raised, however, if you delete an XMLNode and then click Undo. When the XMLNode control gets added back into the document, the AfterInsert event is raised. Listing 6.27 displays a message box when the XMLNode is added back into the document after a user undoes the deletion of the control.

Listing 6.27. *Displaying a message when an XMLNode control is restored after deletion*

```
Private Sub NameFirstNameNode_AfterInsert(ByVal sender _
    As Object, ByVal e As Microsoft.Office.Tools.Word. _
    NodeInsertAndDeleteEventArgs) Handles _
    NameFirstNameNode.AfterInsert

    If e.InUndoRedo Then
        Dim deletedControl As Microsoft.Office.Tools _
            .Word.XMLNode = Ctype(sender, _
            Microsoft.Office.Tools.Word.XMLNode)

        MsgBox(deletedControl.BaseName & " was restored")
    End If

End Sub
```

BeforeDelete

The BeforeDelete event handler enables you to take action when an XMLNode control is deleted from the document. Unfortunately, you cannot cancel the deletion. You can, however, warn users that the XMLNode will be deleted and let them undo the action. The code in Listing 6.28 shows how you can warn the user that an XMLNode control named NameFirstNameNode has been deleted from the document.

Listing 6.28. *Displaying a message when an XMLNode control is deleted from a document*

```
Private Sub NameFirstNameNode_BeforeDelete(ByVal sender _
    As Object, ByVal e As Microsoft.Office.Tools.Word. _
    NodeInsertAndDeleteEventArgs) Handles _
    NameFirstNameNode.BeforeDelete

    Dim deletedControl As Microsoft.Office.Tools.Word.XMLNode _
        = Ctype(sender, Microsoft.Office.Tools.Word.XMLNode)

    MsgBox(deletedControl.BaseName & " has been deleted. " _
        & "Click Undo to restore the control.")

End Sub
```

BindingContextChanged

This event is raised when the binding context for the XMLNode changes. The BindingContext object manages which data source you are binding to. If BindingContext changes, it may mean that the control is now bound to a different data source. The BindingContextChanged event enables you to take action when the BindingContext property of an XMLNode control is changed. The code in Listing 6.29 displays a message box.

Listing 6.29. *Displaying a message when the binding context of an XMLNode control changes*

```
Private Sub NameFirstNameNode_BindingContextChanged(ByVal _
    sender As System.Object, ByVal e As _
```

```
Microsoft.Office.Tools.Word. _
NodeInsertAndDeleteEventArgs) Handles _
NameFirstNameNode.BindingContextChanged

    MsgBox("BindingContext changed")

End Sub
```

ContextEnter

The ContextEnter event handler enables you to take action when you enter the context of an XMLNode control. For example, you might want to display a control on the actions pane when a user moves the cursor into the context of an XMLNode control. The context is the entire area that an XMLNode covers (from its starting tag to its ending tag), including any child nodes. Entering the context occurs whenever the cursor moves into this area from outside the area. The ContextEnter event differs from the Selection event of the XMLNode. If you enter the child nodes of the XMLNode, you will still raise the ContextEnter event because child nodes are within the context of their parent nodes. However, if you move from one area within the context of an XMLNode to another area within the same context (for example, from one child node to another child node), the ContextEnter event is not raised. Listing 6.30 demonstrates.

Listing 6.30. *Adding a MonthCalendar control to the actions pane when the context of an XMLNode is entered*

```
Dim calendar As Windows.Forms.Control
Private Sub SampleNameNode_ContextEnter(ByVal sender As _
    Object, ByVal e As Microsoft.Office.Tools.Word _
    .ContextChangeEventArgs) Handles _
    SampleNameNode.ContextEnter

    Calendar = New MonthCalendar
    Me.ActionsPane.Controls.Add(calendar)

End Sub
```

When you move your cursor into the context of the Name node (perhaps by entering any area of the Name node, including the FirstName node or the LastName node), the MonthCalendar control is added to the actions pane.

ContextLeave

The ContextLeave event handler enables you to take action when you leave the context of an XMLNode control. Perhaps you might like to remove the control that was added to the actions pane when the context was entered as soon as you leave the context of the XMLNode control. This is shown in Listing 6.31.

Listing 6.31. *Removing the MonthCalendar control from the actions pane when you exit the context of an XMLNode*

```
Private Sub SampleNameNode_ContextLeave(ByVal sender As _
    Object, ByVal e As Microsoft.Office.Tools.Word _
    .ContextChangeEventArgs) Handles _
    SampleNameNode.ContextLeave

    Me.ActionsPane.Controls.Remove(calendar)

End Sub
```

Deselect

The Deselect event handler enables you to take action when the user deselects the XMLNode. The Deselect event differs from the ContextLeave event in that Deselect is raised only for the XMLNode that is deselected, and not for the parent XMLNode. Listing 6.32 hides the XMLNodes in the document when the XMLNode is deselected.

Listing 6.32. *Hiding the XMLNode markup in the document when text in an XMLNode control is deselected*

```
Private Sub NameFirstNameNode_Deselect(ByVal sender As _
    Object, ByVal e As Microsoft.Office.Tools.Word _
```

```
    .ContextChangeEventArgs) Handles _
    NameFirstNameNode.Deselect

    Me.ActiveWindow.View.ShowXMLMarkup = False

End Sub
```

Disposed

The Disposed event is raised when the XMLNode control is disposed of. This event typically does not get raised until garbage collection is called to reclaim the memory that held the control.

Select

The Select event handler enables you to take action when the user selects an area within an XMLNode. The Select event differs from the ContextEnter event in that Select is raised only for the XMLNode that is selected, and not for the parent XMLNode. Listing 6.33 displays the XMLNodes in the document when the XMLNode is selected.

Listing 6.33. *Showing the XMLNode markup in the document when text in an XMLNode control is selected*

```
Private Sub NameFirstNameNode_Select(ByVal sender As _
    Object, ByVal e As Microsoft.Office.Tools.Word _
    .ContextChangeEventArgs) Handles _
    NameFirstNameNode.Select

    Me.ActiveWindow.View.ShowXMLMarkup = True

End Sub
```

ValidationError

The ValidationError event enables you to take action when a validation error within an XMLNode occurs. A validation error can occur if the data entered into the XMLNode does not conform to the XML schema.

For example, if the schema requires a number and you enter a string, the ValidationError event is raised. Listing 6.34 displays the validation error text in a message box when ValidationError is raised on an XMLNode control named NameFirstNameNode.

Listing 6.34. *Displaying a message box when a validation error occurs within an XMLNode control*

```
Private Sub NameFirstNameNode_ValidationError(ByVal sender _
    As Object, ByVal e As System.EventArgs) Handles _
    NameFirstNameNode.ValidationError

    Dim invalidXML As Microsoft.Office.Tools.Word.XMLNode _
        = CType(sender, Microsoft.Office.Tools.Word.XMLNode)

    MsgBox(invalidXML.ValidationErrorText.ToString())

End Sub
```

For an example of how you can use the events of XMLNode controls to display and hide controls on the actions pane, see Chapter 5.

XMLNodes Control Events

The events of the XMLNodes controls are identical to the events of the XMLNode control, with the exception of the BindingContextChanged event. XMLNodes is a collection of XMLNode objects. BindingContextChanged is not available on an XMLNodes control because data binding is not supported on this control. Because the remaining events are identical to those of the XMLNode control, they are not described here. For examples of these events, see the section of this chapter titled "XMLNode Control Events."

Document Events

Following are the events that are available for a Document object in VSTO. Some of these events are available on the document in VBA and are exposed in the primary interop assembly (PIA), others were added from the Application object, and still others are specific to VSTO. Notice that some of the event names have been changed. For example, the Close event is renamed CloseEvent, because there is both a Close method and a Close event on the Document object. To avoid collisions, VSTO has changed the names of the events where needed.

- ActivateEvent
- BeforeClose
- BeforeDoubleClick
- BeforePrint
- BeforeRightClick
- BeforeSave
- BindingContextChanged
- CloseEvent
- Deactivate
- Disposed
- MailMergeAfterMerge
- MailMergeBeforeMerge
- MailMergeBeforeRecordMerge
- MailMergeDataSourceLoad
- MailMergeWizardSendToCustom
- MailMergeWizardStateChange
- New
- Open
- SelectionChange
- Shutdown

- Startup

- SyncEvent

- WindowSize

- XMLAfterInsert

- XMLBeforeDelete

ActivateEvent

The ActivateEvent event handler enables you to take action when the document is activated. For example, you might want to ensure that the Shared Workspace task pane is always visible whenever your VSTO solution is activated, as the code in Listing 6.35 demonstrates.

Listing 6.35. *Displaying the Shared Workspace task pane whenever a document is activated*

```
Private Sub ThisDocument_ActivateEvent(ByVal sender As _
    Object, ByVal e As Microsoft.Office.Tools.Word _
    .WindowEventArgs) Handles Me.ActivateEvent

    Application.TaskPanes(Word.WdTaskPanes. _
        wdTaskPaneSharedWorkspace). Visible = True

End Sub
```

BeforeClose

The BeforeClose event handler enables you to take action before the document closes. For example, you can programmatically cache data in the document before you close it. The code in Listing 6.36 assumes that you have a dataset named ds.

Listing 6.36. *Caching data in a document before it closes*

```
Private Sub ThisDocument_BeforeClose(ByVal sender As Object, _
    ByVal e As System.ComponentModel.CancelEventArgs) _
    Handles Me.BeforeClose
```

```
If Not (Me.IsCached("ds")) Then
   Me.StartCaching("ds")
End If
Me.Save()
```

```
End Sub
```

BeforeDoubleClick

The BeforeDoubleClick event handler enables you to take action when a user double-clicks the document. For a code example, see Listing 6.17, which shows the BeforeDoubleClick event of a Bookmark control. If you add code to the BeforeDoubleClick event handler of both the Document and the Bookmark, both events are raised when a user double-clicks the Bookmark control. If you do not want both events to be handled, you must write code to determine which object has raised the event, and then handle the appropriate event.

BeforePrint

The BeforePrint event handler enables you to take action in the document before printing it. For example, you might want to hide a graphic in the document if you plan to use preprinted letterhead. The code in Listing 6.37 sets the style of the graphic to hidden, displays the print dialog so that the user can print the document, and then sets the Hidden property of the style to False. Finally, it sets the Cancel property to True so that the document is not printed again. This code example assumes that the document contains a graphic with a style named *Graphic* applied.

Listing 6.37. *Hiding a graphic before sending a document to print*

```
Private Sub ThisDocument_BeforePrint(ByVal sender As Object, _
   ByVal e As System.ComponentModel.CancelEventArgs) _
   Handles Me.BeforePrint
```

```
   Me.Styles("Graphic").Font.Hidden = True
   Application.Dialogs(Word.WdWordDialog.wdDialogFilePrint) _
      .Show()
   Me.Styles("Graphic").Font.Hidden = False
   e.Cancel = True

End Sub
```

BeforeRightClick

The BeforeRightClick event handler enables you to take action when a user right-clicks the document. For example, you can add a menu item to the default context menu whenever the document is right-clicked. For a code example, see Listing 6.22, which shows how to add an item to the context menu when a user right-clicks a Bookmark control. If you add code to the BeforeRightClick event handler of both the Document and the Bookmark, both events are raised when a user double-clicks the Bookmark control. If you do not want both events to be handled, you must write code to determine which object has raised the event, and then handle the appropriate event.

BeforeSave

This event is raised when the document is saved. The BeforeSave event handler enables you to take action when a user saves the document. For example, you might want to ensure that Track Changes is turned on whenever the document is saved, as shown in Listing 6.38.

Listing 6.38. *Ensuring that Track Changes is turned on each time a document is saved*

```
Private Sub ThisDocument_BeforeSave(ByVal sender As Object, _
   ByVal e As Microsoft.Office.Tools.Word.SaveEventArgs) _
   Handles Me.BeforeSave

   Me.TrackRevisions = True

End Sub
```

BindingContextChanged

This event is raised when the binding context of the document changes. The BindingContext object manages which data source you are binding to. If BindingContext changes, it may mean that the document is now bound to a different data source.

CloseEvent

The CloseEvent event handler enables you to take action when the document is closed. However, it is recommended that you use the Shutdown event if you want to ensure that the code in the event handler is run. This is because the user can cancel the actual closing of the document when the CloseEvent event is raised.

Deactivate

The Deactivate event handler enables you to take action when the document becomes deactivated. For example, you might want to save the document when the solution becomes deactivated, as Listing 6.39 demonstrates.

Listing 6.39. *Saving a document whenever it becomes deactivated*

```
Private Sub ThisDocument_Deactivate(ByVal sender As Object, _
    ByVal e As Microsoft.Office.Tools.Word.WindowEventArgs) _
    Handles Me.Deactivate

    If Me.Saved = False Then
        Me.Save()
    End If

End Sub
```

Disposed

The Disposed event is raised when the document is disposed of.

MailMergeAfterMerge

This event handler enables you to take action after all records have been merged. The mail merge events work in the same way that they do in VBA.

MailMergeBeforeMerge

This event handler enables you to take action before merging records in a mail merge.

MailMergeBeforeRecordMerge

This event handler enables you to take action before merging the individual records.

MailMergeDataSourceLoad

This event handler enables you to take action after the data source to be used in the mail merge is loaded.

MailMergeWizardSendToCustom

This event handler enables you to take action when a user clicks the Custom button in the wizard.

MailMergeWizardStateChange

This event handler enables you to take action as the user moves to a new step in the wizard.

New

The New event handler enables you to take action when a new document is created from a template. This event handler is called only once: when a document based on the VSTO template is created. For example, you might want to add a new menu only when the document is first created from a template, rather than each time the document is opened.

Open

The Open event handler enables you to take action when the document is opened. This event handler is called each time the document is opened. The Open event is not raised when a new document based on a template is created. If you want code to always run, you need to add it to both the New and the Open events.

SelectionChange

The SelectionChange event handler enables you to take action when the selection in the document changes. You can see an example of this event on the Bookmark control in Listing 6.26.

Shutdown

The Shutdown event handler enables you to take action when the document closes. For example, you can do additional cleanup. Keep in mind that the document might be in the process of closing when this event is raised.

Startup

This event is raised when the document is opened, or when a document based on the template is created. Because this event is raised every time a document is opened, if you have code that you want to run only the first time the document is created, you should write it in the New event handler of the template. Code that you want to run whenever the document is opened can be written in the Startup or the Open event handler.

SyncEvent

This event is raised when the document is synchronized with a copy of itself that resides on a server.

WindowSize

The WindowSize event handler enables you to take action when the user resizes the window.

XMLAfterInsert

The XMLAfterInsert event handler enables you to take action when an XML element is inserted into the document. See Listing 6.27 for an example of this event on an XMLNode control.

XMLBeforeDelete

The XMLBeforeDelete event handler enables you to take action when an XML element is deleted from the document. For example, you might want to warn the user that an XML element has been deleted. Listing 6.40 demonstrates.

Listing 6.40. *Warning users that an XML element has been deleted from a document*

```
Private Sub NameFirstNameNode_ValidationError(ByVal sender _
    As Object, ByVal e As System.EventArgs) Handles _
    NameFirstNameNode.ValidationError

    Dim invalidXML As Microsoft.Office.Tools.Word.XMLNode _
        = CType(sender, Microsoft.Office.Tools.Word.XMLNode)

    MsgBox(invalidXML.ValidationErrorText.ToString())

End Sub
```

Special Enhancements to the Bookmark

In addition to enabling data binding and providing events, VSTO adds some additional special enhancements to the Bookmark control. VSTO combines an Interop bookmark with an Interop range, and therefore you will find many more properties and methods on a VSTO bookmark than can be found on an Interop bookmark. If you take a look in the Object Browser, you can see the differences. The right pane of Figure 6.20 shows all the members of the Interop bookmark.

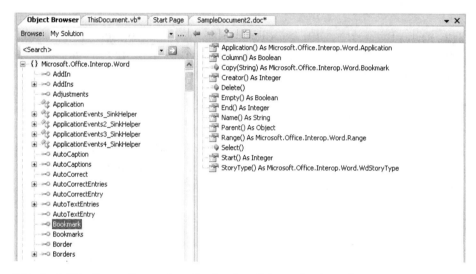

Figure 6.20. *Properties and methods of an Interop bookmark*

The right pane of Figure 6.21 shows all the members of the VSTO bookmark that can fit on the screen. Notice that the window can be scrolled, because there are many more methods, properties, and events on a VSTO bookmark. Take some time to scroll through all the members to familiarize yourself with them.

One important change concerns the Text property. Because the Bookmark and the Range objects are combined, the Text property is available directly as a member of the Bookmark control, rather than through the Range object. In other words, you can assign text to the bookmark using the following code:

```
Bookmark1.Text = "sample"
```

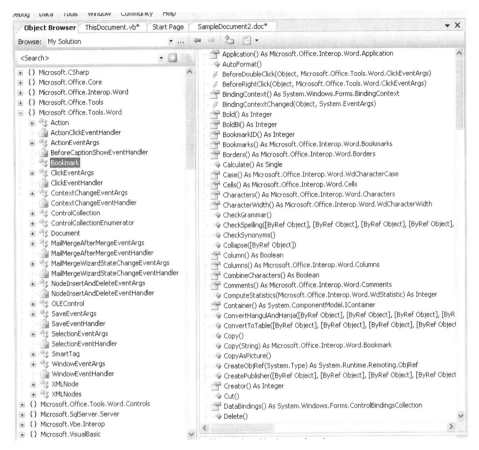

Figure 6.21. *Properties, methods, and events of a VSTO bookmark*

This is as opposed to the code you would have to write for an Interop bookmark:

```
Bookmarks("Bookmark1").Range.Text = "sample"
```

What is interesting about the Text property of a VSTO bookmark is that the text you assign to this property does not delete the bookmark. When you use VBA to assign text to the bookmark, you must first set a range on the bookmark so that when you assign text (and as a result delete the bookmark), you can easily add the bookmark back to the document at the range that was set. This is still the case if you access the Text property from the Range of a Bookmark control (Bookmark1.Range.Text). However, if you assign text directly to the Text property of the Bookmark control (Bookmark1.Text), the text is assigned and the bookmark remains intact, as you would expect.

Although bookmarks in general are still fragile—it is easy for an end user to delete a bookmark, and no event is raised when it happens—VSTO does help increase a bookmark's stability by ensuring that it is not deleted when you make an assignment.

Overlapping Bookmarks

Bookmarks can overlap. For example, text in a document can be shared between bookmarks. Figure 6.22 shows two overlapping bookmarks. The first one is displayed within light gray brackets, and the second one is displayed within black brackets.

[This is some sample [text to show] how bookmarks] can overlap.

Figure 6.22. *Overlapping bookmarks*

In this example, Bookmark1 contains the text "This is some sample text to show," Bookmark2 contains "text to show how bookmarks," and the text in the overlap of the bookmarks is "text to show."

When you write code to handle a bookmark event, you need to make sure that you are handling the event of the correct bookmark. For example, if you have code that handles the double-click event of all the bookmarks in your document, and if a user double-clicks on the word *show*, which bookmark's event should be handled? By default, each bookmark would raise this event and the shared event handler would be called twice.

You can write code to check for overlapping bookmarks and determine which one should handle the event. One approach is to check whether the current selection contains more than one bookmark by checking the Count property of the bookmark (Me.Application.Selection.Bookmarks.Count). If it is greater than 1, you then check which bookmark is closer to the selection and handle only its event.

Assignment also behaves differently in overlapping bookmarks. If you assign new text to Bookmark1, such as "This is text," what would you expect the text of Bookmark1, Bookmark2, and the overlap to be? Using VSTO, Bookmark1 would contain the new text you assigned ("This is text"), and Bookmark2 would contain only the text that did not appear in the original Bookmark1 ("how bookmarks"). The bookmarks would no longer overlap. You should keep this in mind when you assign text to bookmarks. It might be a good idea to check whether there are any overlapping bookmarks before you assign new text to a bookmark.

Making Word Documents Smart

VSTO enables you to create smart tags in your Word solutions. For example, if a user types a company name in the document, you can add code that will recognize the name and add an action. Figure 6.23 shows an example of a built-in smart tag that recognizes names in your document. When the term has been recognized as a smart tag, it is marked with a dotted underline. Then when you hover over the name, a dropdown list appears, where you can click to choose the desired action.

You can create your own smart tags and actions using VSTO. These smart tags differ from those you create outside VSTO in that VSTO smart tags are specific to a particular document rather than to any document that is opened. You will learn more about smart tags in Chapter 9.

If you're familiar with smart documents, you'll definitely want to learn more about VSTO's implementation of the ISmartDocument interface

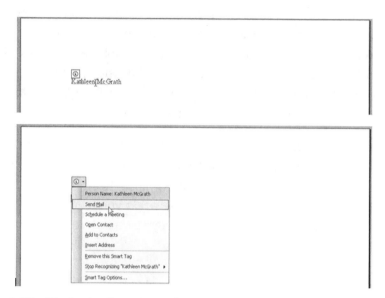

Figure 6.23. *Displaying the actions for a smart tag*

through the ActionsPane object. The ActionsPane object enables you to customize the Document Actions task pane in Word and Excel using only a few lines of code. By adding a single control to the Controls collection of the actions pane, you can create and display the Document Actions task pane and then show and hide controls in response to actions that users take within the document. Earlier in this chapter you saw an example of how to add and remove such a control (Listings 6.30 and 6.31). Chapter 5 describes how to customize the document-level task pane, and Chapter 14 describes how to customize the application-level task pane through an add-in.

Summary

We started this chapter with an overview of the host items and host controls available in Word, and we looked at Visual Studio tools that you can use to learn more about the Word object model. You saw an example of using the macro recorder to generate VBA code on a Word document that is outside Visual Studio, and you learned how to convert the code to Visual Basic 2005 for use in a VSTO solution.

We then took a closer look at how to add host controls to a document host item, both at design time and at run time. Next, you learned about the data binding capabilities of Word host controls, and you saw how you can use the Data Sources window to add data-bound Bookmark controls to a document. We then looked at all the events that are available for each host control and examined some code examples. We also looked at some of the special features that VSTO adds to the Bookmark host control, and we ended with pointers to the chapters that discuss the creation of smart tags and actions pane solutions.

Review Questions

1. What is the difference between a host item and a host control?

2. What are the two main features that VSTO adds to native objects to make them host controls?

3. Which feature in Visual Studio can you use to add a data-bound bookmark to a document?

4. What happens to a dynamically created Bookmark control when the document is saved and closed?

5. How can you override Word's built-in commands?

6. Name one benefit of combining the Range object with the Bookmark object to create a VSTO Bookmark control.

7. How do you add Bookmark controls and XMLNode controls to a document at run time?

7

Customizing Excel with VSTO

Change is not made without inconvenience,
even from worse to better.
—RICHARD HOOKER

Topics Covered in This Chapter

Programming in Excel

Excel Host Items and Host Controls

Data Binding to Host Controls on Worksheets

Programming Against Events

Making Excel Smarter

Summary

Review Questions

Programming in Excel

Many solutions developers use Microsoft Excel as a development platform because of its rich environment. You can take advantage of Excel's
powerful calculation engine, charting capabilities, customizable task
panes, and extensive object model. VSTO enables rapid application
development of Excel solutions by enhancing many of Excel's objects,
enabling quick development of smart tags and customized actions
panes, supporting Windows Forms controls on the worksheet, and providing a robust programming environment: Visual Studio.

Excel solutions created with VSTO are document-level, and this means
that the customization is available only within the document that the

code is associated with. The second edition of VSTO (VSTO 2005 SE) enables you to create application-level add-ins for Excel. You'll learn about the features of VSTO 2005 SE in Chapter 14. The remainder of this chapter describes document-level customizations of Excel using VSTO.

In the same way that you access the objects in the Excel object model using VBA, you can access these objects using VSTO. However, because these objects are exposed through Excel's primary interop assembly (Microsoft.Office.Interop.Excel.dll), there are some differences in the way you reference them. For example, using VBA, you can access the Range object directly. Using VSTO, you must fully qualify the Range object using Excel.Range.

Listing 7.1 shows the difference between using VBA and Visual Basic 2005 to add a formula to a range of cells in Excel. The VSTO code assumes that you're writing the code in the Sheet1 class, and it uses the Me keyword to represent the Sheet1 class. This technique gives you access to all the objects on the worksheet.

Listing 7.1. *Accessing a Range using VBA versus using VSTO*

```
' VBA
Dim myRange As Range
Set myRange = Worksheets("Sheet1").Range("A1:B4")
myRange.Formula = "=RAND()"


' Visual Basic 2005
Dim myRange As Excel.Range
myRange = Me.Range("A1:B4")
myRange.Formula = "=RAND()"
```

Many VBA objects return a Variant data type, which translates to an Object data type in Visual Basic 2005. Often, you must cast the object to the specific data type to view all its methods, properties, and events using the IntelliSense features in Visual Basic 2005. Other differences include the need to fully qualify the data type for variables, and improved error handling. For example, Listing 7.2 shows VBA code that can be used to add random values to a selected range of cells. This example uses Excel's Input box to enable users to select the range.

Listing 7.2. *Using VBA to add values to selected cells*

```
' VBA
Sub AddText()

    Dim SelectedRange

    On Error GoTo CancelButton

    Set SelectedRange = Application.InputBox( _
        Prompt:="Select the cell or cells to " & _
        "add random values.", _
        Title:="Random Values", _
        Default:=Selection.Address, Type:=8)

    SelectedRange.Value = "=Rand()"
    SelectedRange.BorderAround xlDashDotDot, xlMedium, _
        xlColorIndexAutomatic

CancelButton:
    ' User canceled dialog box.

End Sub
```

To make the code work correctly in VSTO, you need to do the following:

- Use a Try Catch statement for handling errors instead of using an On Error GoTo statement. Although the latter type of error handling still works in VSTO, it is better to use Try Catch statements in managed code.

- Remove the Set statement, because it is not supported in Visual Basic 2005.

- Specify the data type for the declaration of the variable SelectedRange. You can put the declaration and assignment in the same statement.

- Qualify the Selection property with the Application object. To access the Address property of the returned Range object, you must cast the Selection to a Range.

- Add parentheses to the BorderAround method in order to pass parameters.

- Fully qualify the enumerations that are passed to the BorderAround method.

Listing 7.3 shows what this code would look like in Visual Basic 2005. To learn more about some of the language differences between VBA and Visual Basic 2005, see Chapter 4.

Listing 7.3. *Using Visual Basic 2005 to add values to selected cells in a VSTO solution*

```
Sub AddText()

Try
    Dim SelectedRange As Excel.Range = _
        Application.InputBox(Prompt:= _
        "Select the cell or cells to add random values.", _
        Title:="Random Values", Default:=CType(Application. _
        Selection, Excel.Range).Address, Type:=8)

    SelectedRange.Value = "=Rand()"
    SelectedRange.BorderAround(Excel.XlLineStyle.xlDashDotDot, _
        Excel.XlBorderWeight.xlMedium, _
        Excel.XlColorIndex.xlColorIndexAutomatic)

Catch ex As InvalidCastException

    ' Inputbox returned a Boolean (user canceled dialog box).

End Try

End Sub
```

When you press F5 to run this code, an Excel Input box appears and lets you select a range of cells. As you select cells on the worksheet, the range appears in the Random Values dialog box, as shown in Figure 7.1.

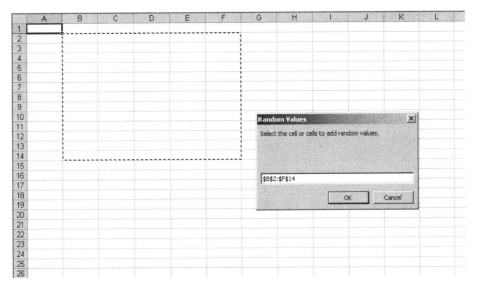

Figure 7.1. *Selecting the range of cells to hold the random values*

When you click OK on the Input box, the random values are added to the selected cells, and a border is added around the range, as shown in Figure 7.2.

Learning About Excel's Object Model

There are several ways you can learn about the Excel object model when you are using VBA. You can look at the objects in the Object Browser of the VBE, and you can use IntelliSense within the VBE. These features are also available, and provide advanced functionality, in Visual Studio when you're creating Excel solutions with VSTO. These features are described in more detail in Chapter 2.

	A	B	C	D	E	F	G	H	I	J	K	L
1												
2		0.089355	0.614723	0.412126	0.912456	0.322105						
3		0.456611	0.786065	0.84896	0.654744	0.523477						
4		0.529421	0.214047	0.54975	0.660675	0.266845						
5		0.009248	0.86176	0.175186	0.08546	0.186239						
6		0.705358	0.108769	0.773245	0.397568	0.207001						
7		0.181593	0.059798	0.396014	0.815809	0.722472						
8		0.763253	0.291315	0.374153	0.42196	0.899609						
9		0.948311	0.550086	0.220959	0.272415	0.952837						
10		0.956239	0.330842	0.083615	0.94928	0.635006						
11		0.545702	0.657662	0.679747	0.536605	0.908891						
12		0.71056	0.308503	0.282483	0.245556	0.370111						
13		0.980105	0.408517	0.506376	0.3975	0.348314						
14		0.29129	0.609579	0.288032	0.253533	0.199606						
15												
16												
17												
18												
19												
20												
21												
22												
23												
24												
25												
26												

Figure 7.2. *Random values are added to the selected range, and a border is applied*

As shown in Listing 7.3, there are some things you should keep in mind when learning to write Visual Basic 2005 code. For example, if you're not seeing a list of methods and properties when you type a period after an object name (one of the features of IntelliSense), you can check whether the variable you created for the object has an explicit type defined. Similarly, the returned value of an object is an Object type; you can cast that object to the correct data type and then see whether the IntelliSense functionality is available.

VBA developers often use VBA's macro recording feature as a tool for learning about the Office object model. As discussed in Chapter 6, the macro recorder records actions taken within an application and translates the actions into code. You can use the macro recorder to generate code that you later modify, or to learn about which objects you should use to programmatically perform an action. Macro recording is not available in VSTO. However, you can always open Excel outside Visual Studio, record a macro, and then translate the resulting code from VBA to Visual Basic 2005.

Often, VBA developers associate code that is generated through macro recording, or code that was written directly in the VBE, with a button on the toolbar or menu (known as command bars) by using the Customize menu located in Excel's Tools menu. After you've added a custom button to the toolbar, you right-click the button and then select Assign Macro from the shortcut menu. Next, you select the desired macro and click OK. The button's context menu also has options for changing the face (or icon) on the button. Figure 7.3 shows a macro named BoldItalic in the Assign Macro dialog box.

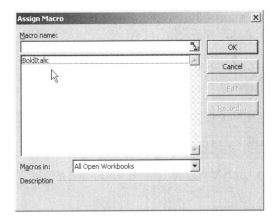

Figure 7.3. *Assigning a VBA macro to a toolbar button*

Because code in a VSTO solution is stored in an assembly rather than in the workbook or the template, you cannot associate VSTO code with a command bar button in this same way. In fact, you cannot access the Customize menu item from VSTO. Instead, you must customize toolbars and menus programmatically.

Converting a Recorded VBA Macro to Visual Basic in VSTO

In this section, you will record a simple macro in VBA and then convert the code to Visual Basic 2005. This example is similar to the one in

Chapter 6 in that you will record a macro that sets the selection to bold and italic. However, there isn't any toggle enumeration available in Excel that is similar to Word's wdToggle enumeration. Using Excel, you must write additional code to apply and remove the bold and italic formatting.

1. Open an Excel workbook outside Visual Studio, and type some text in cells A2 through B3.

2. Select the text within range A2:B3, and then click Tools, point to Macros, and click Record New Macro.

3. In the Record Macro dialog box, type *BoldItalic* in the Macro Name box, and then click OK.

4. On the Formatting toolbar, click the Bold button, and then click the Italic button.

5. On the Stop Recording toolbar, click Stop Recording.

6. Open the VBE by pressing ALT+F11.

Listing 7.4 shows the VBA code you should see in the VBE.

Listing 7.4. *Using the VBA macro recorder in Excel*

```
' VBA

Sub BoldItalic()
'
' BoldItalic Macro
' Macro recorded by Kathleen McGrath
'
    Selection.Font.Bold = True
    Selection.Font.Italic = True

End Sub
```

Unlike Word's macro recorder, the Excel macro recorder sets the Bold and Italic property of the selection to True rather than to an enumeration. If you want to toggle the formatting, you need to modify the code.

Additionally, to bring this code into Visual Basic 2005, you must ~~fully~~ qualify the Selection object because you cannot access it directly. In Listing 7.5, you create a variable named Selection and set it to Application.Selection. If there is mixed formatting, bold and italic are applied to the entire range.

Listing 7.5. *Modifying a recorded macro in Excel to work in VSTO*

```
' Visual Basic 2005

Sub BoldItalic()

    Dim Selection As Excel.Range = Me.Application.Selection

    If Selection.Font.Bold = True And _
        Selection.Font.Italic = True Then

        Selection.Font.Bold = False
        Selection.Font.Italic = False
    Else

        Selection.Font.Bold = True
        Selection.Font.Italic = True
    End If

End Sub
```

If you want to associate this code with a toolbar button, you must write additional code to programmatically add the button to the toolbar. Then you can call the BoldItalic method in the button's Click event handler. For more information about adding buttons to toolbars and menus, see Chapter 8.

Writing Callbacks from VBA into VSTO Code

Typically you should not mix VBA code and VSTO code in your project, but there are some features in Excel that must use VBA because they are not available directly in VSTO. Creating user defined functions

(UDFs) is one such area. In this case, you can create a callback in a VBA module that calls into the managed code of your VSTO solution. To do this, you must first create a public class that has an attribute called ComVisible that is set to True, as shown in Listing 7.6. You can also use this technique when migrating your existing VBA solutions to VSTO. For more information about migrating your VBA solutions, see Chapter 12.

Listing 7.6. *Creating a public class to represent the code for your UDF*

```
<System.Runtime.InteropServices.ComVisible(True)> _
Public Class ManagedUDFs

    Public Function ComputerName() As Object
        Try
            Return My.Computer.Name.ToString()
        Catch ex As Exception
            Return "An error has occurred"
        End Try
    End Function

    Public Function OS() As Object
        Try
            Return My.Computer.Info.OSFullName.ToString()
        Catch ex As Exception
            Return "An error has occurred"
        End Try
    End Function
End Class
```

Next, you must add code to the Startup event handler of ThisWorkbook to register the callback, as shown in Listing 7.7.

Listing 7.7. *Registering a callback when a workbook is opened*

```
Private Sub ThisWorkbook_Startup(ByVal sender As Object, _
    ByVal e As System.EventArgs) Handles Me.Startup

    Me.Application.Run("RegisterCallback", New ManagedUDFs)

End Sub
```

Now you can compile, save, and close the VSTO solution. Next, you will add some VBA code to the workbook. Open the workbook associated with the VSTO solution outside Visual Studio, and make sure that the workbook you open is not the one that is in the \bin directory. Open the VBE by pressing ALT+F11. Right-click the project, point to Insert, and then click Module. Add the code in Listing 7.8. to Module1.

Listing 7.8. *Calling managed code from VBA*

```
Public ManagedUDFs As Object

Public Sub RegisterCallback(callback As Object)
    Set ManagedUDFs = callback
End Sub

Public Function ComputerName() As String
    ComputerName = ManagedUDFs.ComputerName()
End Function

Public Function OS() As String
    OS = ManagedUDFs.OS()
End Function
```

Now you can save and close the workbook. Open the VSTO solution, and press F5 to run the code to call the UDF. Place your cursor inside a cell, and type

```
=ComputerName()
```

Then press the ENTER key. Move your cursor to a new cell and type

```
=OS()
```

Then press the ENTER key. Your computer name and operating system should appear in the worksheet. As you can see, you can access the code for your UDFs by calling into the managed code from VBA.

Overriding Excel Commands

Using VBA, it is easy to override a built-in Excel command. All you need to do is to change the OnAction property of an existing button to point to a procedure that has your modification. Of course, you need to do this for the button as well as the menu item. Listing 7.9 shows how you might override the Save button in Excel using VBA.

Listing 7.9. *Overriding the Save button in Excel with VBA*

```
Sub OverrideButton()

    Dim myNewCommand As Office.CommandBarButton
    Set myNewCommand = CommandBars("Standard").Controls(3)
    myNewCommand.OnAction = "FileSave"

End Sub


Sub FileSave()

    MsgBox ("Cannot save document.")

End Sub
```

You cannot do this in VSTO because the OnAction property can point only to an Excel macro, and not to a method in your VSTO code. You could create callbacks into your VSTO code from VBA, as shown earlier in this chapter. An alternative is to use VSTO to write code that replaces the existing built-in button or toolbar with your own. For an example, see Chapter 6. Although the example shows you how to replace menu items and toolbar buttons in Word, the same principle applies to Excel.

There are many objects in the Excel object model that you can manipulate from VSTO. However, this chapter does not focus on the existing object model. In the remainder of this chapter, we take a closer look at the VSTO enhancements to some Excel objects and explain how you can use these enhancements in your Excel solutions using VSTO.

Excel Host Items and Host Controls

VSTO enhances a number of objects in the Excel object model, such as the ability to bind data to an object and to expose the object's events. These objects are defined as host items and host controls. Recall that host items are containers for host controls in the same way that a UserForm is a container for an ActiveX control. You add the host controls to the host item.

Excel has three types of host items: Workbook, Worksheet, and Chartsheet. There is one Workbook host item and a separate Worksheet host item for each worksheet in the workbook. These host items wrap the native Excel workbook, worksheet, and chartsheet, which are in the Microsoft.Office.Interop.Excel namespace.

As we did with Microsoft.Office.Interop.Word, here we refer to objects in the Microsoft.Office.Interop.Excel namespace as Interop objects. The host items and host controls are in the Microsoft.Office.Tools.Excel namespace, and we sometimes refer to objects in this namespace as VSTO objects. Host items and host controls wrap the native Office objects and have the same functionality as the underlying Interop objects, but they have additional functionality such as enabling data binding and exposing events.

Host Items

Excel has three kinds of host items, and their behaviors differ. Only worksheet host items can contain host controls. You cannot add a host control to a workbook or a chartsheet. The workbook acts as a component tray for components that you want to make available to all worksheets in the workbook. Each worksheet also has its own component tray, but the worksheet itself can contain host controls (or Windows Forms controls). Chartsheets are also considered host items, but they cannot contain any type of control.

Host Controls

Several host controls can be added to the worksheet: Chart, ListObject, NamedRange, and XMLMappedRange. Each of these host controls has an underlying Interop object, but these host controls differ from the Interop object because they expose events and have data binding capabilities.

You may be wondering why you would want to use host controls in your Excel solutions and what advantages you gain by using a host control instead of the underlying Interop object. The most obvious benefit is that you can access these objects directly, without traversing the Office object model. This is because these objects are available in your code as first-class .NET objects. Additionally, binding data to an element in your worksheet, such as a cell, is now extremely easy; you use a NamedRange control on the worksheet cell and then bind the data to the NamedRange control. You can also program against events of the host controls. In most cases, the underlying Excel Interop object does not expose any events or has only a limited number of them. Using VSTO, you can now easily respond to users as they move to different areas within a worksheet.

In the next section, you will learn how to add host controls to the worksheet at design time and run time, how to bind data to the host control, and how to cache data in your document for offline use when you are not connected to the network.

Adding Host Controls to the Worksheet

You can add Excel host controls to the worksheet in a number of ways at design time. You can always add a host control to the worksheet through Excel's menus, in the same way you add a native object to a worksheet. For example, when you have Excel open inside Visual Studio and you add a chart to the worksheet using Excel's menus, VSTO automatically creates the chart as a host control. You can also add some of the host controls by dragging the control from the Toolbox or Data

Sources window onto the worksheet. Additionally, host controls can be added to the worksheet programmatically at run time.

Adding Controls at Design Time

There are three ways to add host controls to a worksheet in Excel. The first is to use Excel's native features. For example, you can add a NamedRange control to the worksheet by typing the name of the range in the Name box and pressing ENTER, as shown in Figure 7.4.

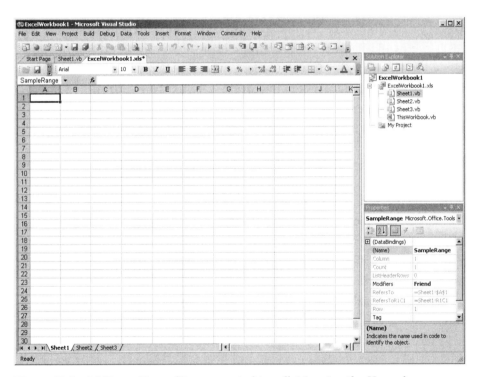

Figure 7.4. *Adding a NamedRange control to cell A1 using the Name box*

Notice that the NamedRange called SampleRange is created in cell A1 when the user types *SampleRange* in the Name box (located next to the formula bar) and presses ENTER, and that the control is shown in the

Properties window in Visual Studio with the same name: SampleRange. Other properties and events of this NamedRange control are also available in the Properties window.

Alternatively, you can add a host control to the worksheet through Excel's menus. For example, you can add a ListObject control to the document by pointing to Microsoft Office Excel Data in the Data menu, pointing to List, and then clicking Create List. VSTO automatically creates the host control and names it List1, incrementing the number for each list that is created.

When you switch to code view, you will see that both SampleRange and List1 are available in the Class Name drop-down of Visual Studio, as shown in Figure 7.5. After the object is selected, you can access all the methods available for the control in the Method Name drop-down and automatically create an event handler when you select an event from the drop-down list.

VSTO adds some of the host controls to the Toolbox so that you can drag a control from the Toolbox directly to your worksheet, in the same way you can drag a control from the Toolbox to a UserForm. When the worksheet has focus, the NamedRange control and the ListObject control are available in the Excel Controls tab of the Toolbox, as shown in Figure 7.6. You can then drag these controls from the Toolbox to an area on the worksheet. When you do that, VSTO provides a dialog box where you can select the cells you want to include in the list or named range; when you click OK, the control is added to the range you selected.

VSTO provides names for the controls when they're added. For example, a NamedRange control is automatically named NamedRange followed by an incremental number (NamedRange1, NamedRange2, etc.). A ListObject control is named List followed by an incremental number (List1, List2, etc.). You can rename these controls by changing the control's Name property in Visual Studio's Properties window.

Figure 7.5. *Host controls displayed in the Class Name drop-down in code view*

You can add data-bound ListObject or NamedRange controls to a worksheet by dragging the control from the Data Sources window to the worksheet. By default, a NamedRange control is available for each field of the table listed in the Data Sources window when the Excel worksheet has focus. You select the field in the Data Sources window and drag it to the worksheet, as shown in Figure 7.7. If you were to drag the entire Customers table to the worksheet, VSTO would create a data-bound ListObject control having a column for every field in the Customers table. You will learn more about data binding later in this chapter.

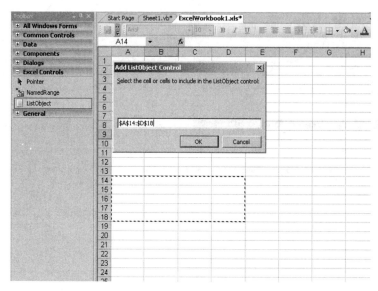

Figure 7.6. *Adding a ListObject control to a worksheet using the Toolbox*

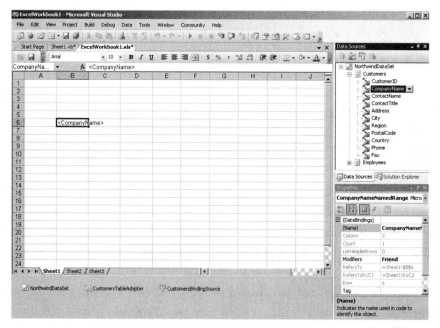

Figure 7.7. *Adding a NamedRange control to a worksheet using the Data Sources window*

For Excel solutions, only the NamedRange and ListObject controls are available on the Toolbox and the Data Sources window. If you want to add a Chart or XMLMapped Range control at design time, you must use Excel's native functionality.

To add a Chart control to the worksheet, you select Chart from the Insert menu and then follow the instructions in the Chart Wizard for each page (see Figure 7.8).

Page 1: Select the type of chart you want to add.

Page 2: Select the range of data that you want to include in the chart.

Page 3: Apply formatting to the chart.

Page 4: Supply a location for the chart.

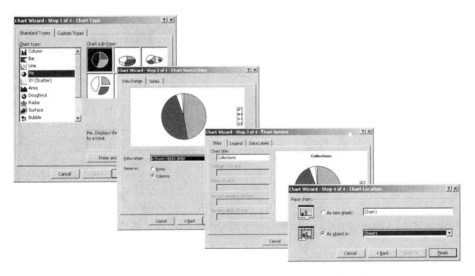

Figure 7.8. *Adding a Chart control to a worksheet using the Chart Wizard*

When you add the chart to the document, VSTO automatically creates the chart as a VSTO control, complete with events and the ability to bind data to the control. If you select the chart and open the Properties window as shown in Figure 7.9, you will see that VSTO automatically names the chart (in our example, it is named chart_2), and you can access all the other available properties and events for the Chart control.

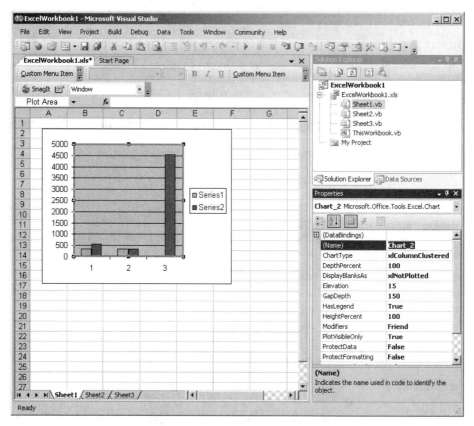

Figure 7.9. *Viewing the properties of a Chart control in the Properties window*

You can add XMLMappedRange controls to the worksheet by mapping XML elements to cells within the worksheet. In this section you will create a schema (using the same simple schema that we used in the Word example in Chapter 5) and map it to an Excel worksheet.

1. Type the XML in Listing 7.10 into a text file, and name it Sample.xsd. (Alternatively, you can use Visual Studio to create the schema.)

Listing 7.10. *Sample schema*

```xml
<?xml version="1.0" encoding="utf-8" ?>
<xs:schema targetNamespace="http://schemas.samples"
    elementFormDefault="qualified"
    xmlns="http://schemas.samples"
    xmlns:mstns="http://schemas.samples"
    xmlns:xs="http://www.w3.org/2001/XMLSchema">
  <xs:element name="Sample" type="SampleType"></xs:element>
  <xs:complexType name="SampleType">
    <xs:all>
      <xs:element name="Name" type="NameType" minOccurs="0"
          maxOccurs="1" />
      <xs:element name="Address" type="xs:string" minOccurs="0"
          maxOccurs="1" />
    </xs:all>
  </xs:complexType>
  <xs:complexType name="NameType">
    <xs:sequence>
      <xs:element name="FirstName" type="xs:string" minOccurs="1"
          maxOccurs="1"/>
      <xs:element name="LastName" type="xs:string" minOccurs="1"
          maxOccurs="1"/>
    </xs:sequence>
  </xs:complexType>
</xs:schema>
```

2. On the Data menu, point to Microsoft Office Excel Data, point to XML, and click XML Source.

3. In the XML Source task pane, click XML Maps.

4. In the XML Maps dialog box, click Add. Navigate to the Sample.xsd schema you created in step 1, and then click OK.

   VSTO automatically adds the schema to the project and makes it visible in Solution Explorer. You can view the schema in the schema designer by double-clicking the schema in Solution Explorer, as shown in Figure 7.10.

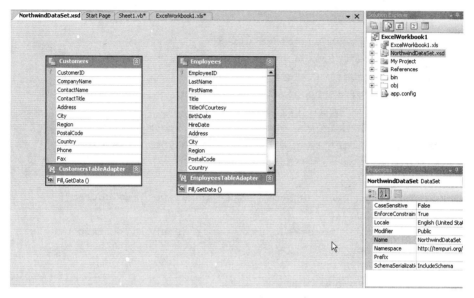

Figure 7.10. *Viewing the generated dataset in class view*

The elements of the schema are also visible in the XML Source task pane in Excel. This task pane automatically opens when a schema is attached to the workbook. You can manually open this task pane by selecting Task Pane from the View menu. When the task pane is open, you can select XML Source in the drop-down, as shown in Figure 7.11.

You can drag the XML elements to the worksheet to create XMLMappedRange controls or ListObject controls. When you map an XML element to the worksheet, VSTO automatically creates an XMLMappedRange for each element you add. As with Word, you can map XML to Excel only by using Excel's native functionality. XMLMappedRange controls are not available in the Toolbox nor in the Data Sources window. If you map a single XML element to the worksheet, it results in the creation of an XMLMappedRange. If you map a data range that includes multiple rows and columns, VSTO creates a ListObject that contains all the fields.

Figure 7.11. *Showing the XML Source task pane*

5. Drag ns1:FirstName from the XML Source task pane to a cell in Excel, as shown in Figure 7.12

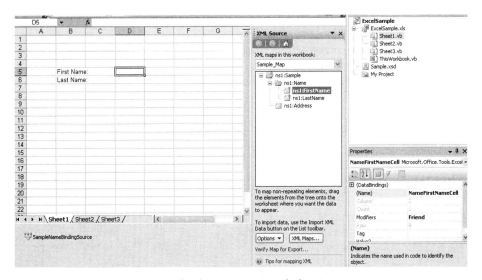

Figure 7.12. *Mapping a single element to a worksheet*

Notice that when the XMLMappedRange is selected, the Properties window displays all its properties and that the name is ParentNode name + ChildNode name + *Cell.* For example, if you click inside the XMLMappedRange on the worksheet, you'll see that the control's name is NameFirstNameCell. See the Properties window in Figure 7.12 for an example. If you click the Events button on the Properties window, all the events available on an XMLMappedRange also would be visible.

Removing Host Controls

Removing controls from a worksheet is usually straightforward. As with most controls, you can select the host control on the worksheet and then press the DELETE key. In the case of NamedRange controls, this isn't possible. Pressing DELETE deletes the contents of the control but not the control itself. Instead, you must use Excel's Define Name dialog box.

To delete the control, right-click the NamedRange and click Managed Named Ranges. In the Define Name dialog box, select the NamedRange you want to delete, and then click Delete, as shown in Figure 7.13.

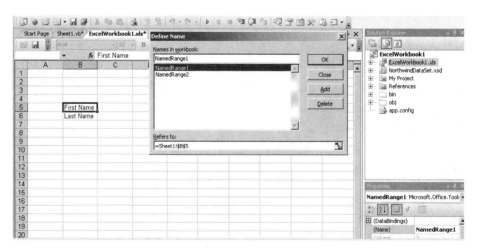

Figure 7.13. *Deleting a NamedRange control*

Adding Host Controls at Run Time

Most host controls can be added to the document at run time. The exception to this rule is related to XML mapping. As you learned earlier, you can add XML-mapped elements only by using the XML Structure task pane. To programmatically add other host controls, such as a ListObject or NamedRange, you must use helper methods provided by VSTO. If you programmatically add a list object, chart, or range object in the same way you add it in VBA, it is created as an Interop object and not a VSTO object. For example, the code in Listing 7.11 adds a list to Sheet1 using the Add method of the ListObjects collection. This is an Interop list, not a VSTO list.

Listing 7.11. *Programmatically adding an Interop ListObject to Excel*

```
Private Sub Sheet1_Startup(ByVal sender As Object, ByVal e As _
    System.EventArgs) Handles Me.Startup

    ' Create an Interop ListObject.
    Dim InteropList As Microsoft.Office.Interop.Excel. _
        ListObject = Me.ListObjects.Add( _
        Excel.XlListObjectSourceType.xlSrcRange, _
        Me.Range("A1", "C3"))
End Sub
```

If you write additional code to access the methods and properties of the InteropList you created, you will notice that none of the data binding methods or properties is available in IntelliSense. This is because an Interop list object is added to the worksheet and it does not have the data binding capabilities (or events) that are found on a ListObject control. Figure 7.14 shows the IntelliSense list, where you don't see data binding properties such as the BindingContent property on the list object.

VSTO provides helper methods that enable you to programmatically add host controls to a worksheet. You cannot instantiate a host control using the New keyword; instead, you must use the VSTO helper methods.

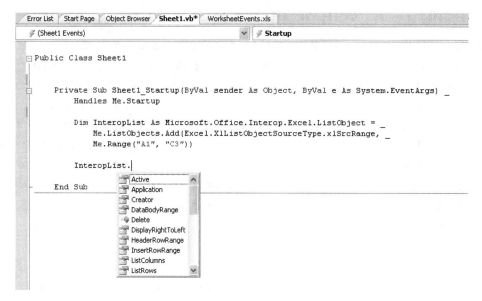

Figure 7.14. *Viewing IntelliSense of an InteropList object*

For Excel, there are three helper methods: AddNamedRange, AddListObject, and AddChart. When you add a ListObject control programmatically, the helper methods have two parameters. The first parameter is the range where you want to add the control, and the second parameter is the name you want to give the control. Listing 7.12 shows you how to add a ListObject control to Sheet1 using the AddListObject helper method.

Listing 7.12. *Programmatically adding a ListObject control to Excel*

```
Private Sub Sheet1_Startup(ByVal sender As Object, ByVal e As _
    System.EventArgs) Handles Me.Startup

    Dim VSTOList As Microsoft.Office.Tools.Excel.ListObject = _
        Me.Controls.AddListObject(Me.Range("A1", "C3"), _
        "VSTOList")

End Sub
```

This time, when you access IntelliSense, you will see properties specific to data that is bound to the control. These properties exist only for a VSTO ListObject control. See Figure 7.15 for the IntelliSense list.

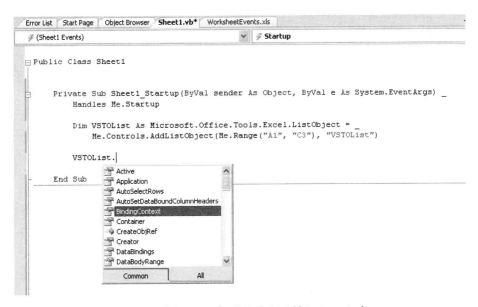

Figure 7.15. *Viewing IntelliSense of a VSTO ListObject control*

Programmatically adding a NamedRange control to the worksheet works in the same way as the ListObject; you use a helper method and pass the desired range and name. The code in Listing 7.13 shows you how to add a NamedRange control to a cell on Sheet1 of a workbook created with VSTO and then add data to the NamedRange.

Listing 7.13. *Programmatically adding a NamedRange to a cell*

```
Dim myNamedRange As Microsoft.Office.Tools.Excel.NamedRange _
    = Me.Controls.AddNamedRange(Me.Range("A1:B4"), _
    "myNamedRange")
myNamedRange.Formula = "=RAND()"
```

When you programmatically add a Chart control to a worksheet, you will see that the AddChart method is overloaded. The first overload requires a range parameter and a name parameter, just as the AddNamedRange and AddListObject methods required. The second overload enables you to add the chart to a specific location and specify its size. You pass in the left and top positions, width and height of the chart, and the name you want to give the control. This helps you to have more control over the exact positioning of the chart.

If you wanted to use the data in the NamedRange to programmatically create a chart, you could do so as the code in Listing 7.14 illustrates.

Listing 7.14. *Programmatically adding a Chart to the worksheet*

```
Dim myNamedRange As Microsoft.Office.Tools.Excel.NamedRange = _
    Me.Controls.AddNamedRange(Me.Range("A1:B4"), "myNamedRange")

myNamedRange.Formula = "=RAND()"

Dim myChart As Microsoft.Office.Tools.Excel.Chart = _
    Me.Controls.AddChart(Me.Range("A6:E15"), "myChart")

myChart.SetSourceData(myNamedRange.InnerObject, _
    Excel.XlRowCol.xlColumns)

myChart.ChartType = Excel.XlChartType.xl3DPie
```

In this code example, you use the RAND function to add data to the range of cells specified by the NamedRange control myNamedRange. The RAND function is a random number generator that adds random data to each cell. You then create a Chart control on the worksheet and use the data in the NamedRange to populate the chart. Although your data will differ, the result of pressing F5 to run this code is a worksheet that contains a NamedRange control and a Chart control similar to the example in Figure 7.16.

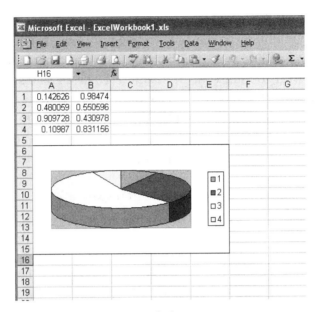

Figure 7.16. *Creating a chart on a worksheet*

Control Persistence

As with programmatically adding a Bookmark control to a Word document, host controls that are added programmatically to an Excel worksheet are not persisted in the worksheet as host controls when you close the workbook. Instead, they are converted to the underlying Excel object (a chart, range, or list), and they no longer have any data binding capabilities or events. You must write additional code to hook up the VSTO enhancements to these objects after the workbook is reopened.

You do this by re-creating the control using the helper method and passing the same control name and the same range of the host control you originally created. This means that you can also turn an existing Interop range into a VSTO NamedRange. Using VSTO, you cannot create an Interop named range at design time; you must do it programmatically, as shown in Listing 7.15. If you create a named range at design time, VSTO automatically creates the named range as a VSTO NamedRange control.

To hook up the VSTO capabilities, you can simply re-create the control when the document opens. For illustrative purposes, you'll create the Interop object first and then use the same range and name to create the NamedRange control. The code in Listing 7.15 first creates an Interop named range at cell A1 and then uses that named range to create a VSTO NamedRange control with the same name and at the same location as those of the Interop named range; you're essentially converting the Interop range into a VSTO NamedRange control.

Listing 7.15. *Reconnecting a range with VSTO capabilities*

```
WithEvents VSTONamedRange As Microsoft.Office.Tools.Excel. _
    NamedRange

Private Sub Sheet1_Startup(ByVal sender As Object, ByVal e _
    As System.EventArgs) Handles Me.Startup

    ' Create an Interop range at cell A1.
    Globals.ThisWorkbook.Names.Add("Range1", ("=Sheet1!$A$1"))
    Dim InteropRange As Excel.Range = Range("Range1")

    ' Create a VSTO NamedRange control using the
    ' Interop named range.
    VSTONamedRange = Me.Controls.AddNamedRange(InteropRange, _
        "Range1")

    VSTONamedRange.Value = "Sample Text"

End Sub

Private Sub VSTONamedRange_BeforeDoubleClick(ByVal Target _
    As Microsoft.Office.Interop.Excel.Range, ByRef Cancel _
    As Boolean) Handles VSTONamedRange.BeforeDoubleClick

    MsgBox("VSTONamedRange was double-clicked.")

End Sub
```

When you press F5 to run this code, you'll notice that a NamedRange called Range1 is created at cell A1. You can determine whether this named range is an Interop named range or a VSTO NamedRange by double-clicking cell A1. A message box appears stating, "VSTONamedRange was double-clicked." You know that this is a VSTO NamedRange control because only VSTO host controls can have associated events. Interop ranges do not expose any events.

Accessing a Host Control from an Underlying Interop Object

You can access the underlying Interop object from a host control by using the control's InnerObject method. However, there is no way to do the opposite: access a host control from the underlying Interop object. VSTO does not provide a collection for each of the host controls; instead, there is a single Controls collection, which can contain host controls as well as Windows Forms controls that are on the worksheet.

Although VSTO does not have a collection of ListObjects, NamedRanges, XMLMappedRanges, and Charts, you can loop through a collection of the underlying Interop objects. Listing 7.16 shows how you can loop through a collection of list objects, just as you can when you use VBA. This code assumes that you have at least one list object on Sheet1 of your workbook.

Listing 7.16. *The Interop ListObject collection*

```
For Each list As Microsoft.Office.Interop.Excel.ListObject _
    In Me.ListObjects

    MsgBox(CStr(list.Name))

Next
```

Because these are Interop list objects, you do not have access to the data binding and events that VSTO provides. You cannot use a For Each statement for a VSTO ListObject collection, because no such collection exists in VSTO. If you change the code in Listing 7.16 to declare the list variable as the type Microsoft.Office.Tools.Excel.ListObject, the code will compile fine, but you will receive an error when you run the solution code.

As an alternative, you can use the Controls collection to loop through each control in the collection and then determine whether the control is of the type you are interested in—in our case, a ListObject host control. Listing 7.17 loops through all the controls in the Controls collection and checks whether the control is of the type Microsoft.Office.Tools.Excel.ListObject. If the control is a ListObject control, its name is displayed in a message box. Because you declare myControl as an Object, you must cast the object back into a ListObject control before you can access its properties, methods, and events.

Listing 7.17. *The Controls collection*

```
Dim myControl As Object

For Each myControl in Me.Controls

    If TypeOf(myControl) Is Microsoft.Office.Tools.Excel. _
        ListObject Then

        Dim VSTOListObject As Microsoft.Office.Tools.Excel. _
            ListObject = CType((myControl), _
            Microsoft.Office.Tools.Excel.ListObject)

        MsgBox(CStr(VSTOListObject.Name))

    End If

Next
```

Instead of calling code like this each time you need to access the host control from the underlying object, you can create a helper function for each host control so that you can obtain the corresponding control whenever you have accessed the Interop object. For an example, see Listing 6.13 in Chapter 6.

Accessing an Interop Object from a Host Control

Sometimes you need to access the Interop object associated with a given host control. For example, you might be working with the host controls and want to call a method that specifically requires an Interop object. You cannot cast a VSTO object into an Interop object, but you can instead call the InnerObject property of the host control to return its underlying Interop object.

For example, if you wanted to write a solution that enables users to add a NamedRange control to the worksheet by clicking a button on the actions pane, you need to identify the active worksheet and then add the NamedRange control to it. The problem is that the ActiveWorksheet property returns an Interop worksheet, and to add a control to a worksheet you must reference a VSTO worksheet. The answer is to use the InnerObject property of a VSTO worksheet to determine whether it is equivalent to the ActiveSheet. The example in Listing 7.18 checks whether the active worksheet is Sheet1 and, if it is, adds a named range to Sheet1. You could expand this code by comparing the ActiveSheet to Sheet2 and Sheet3.

Listing 7.18. *Using the InnerObject property*

```
Dim CurrentRange As Microsoft.Office.Interop.Excel.Range = _
   Application.Selection

Dim NamedRangeCount As Integer = Application.Names.Count


If Globals.ThisWorkbook.ActiveSheet.Equals( _
    Globals.Sheet1.InnerObject) Then
```

```
Globals.Sheet1.Controls.AddNamedRange( _
    CurrentRange, "NamedRange" & NamedRangeCount + 1)
```

```
End If
```

Adding Host Items in Excel

A VSTO solution can contain only one workbook, and the workbook that is created in a VSTO solution is automatically created as a host item. When you add a worksheet or chartsheet to a workbook at design time when Excel is hosted inside Visual Studio, VSTO automatically creates the worksheet or chartsheet as a VSTO object (a host item). VSTO does not provide a way for you to create host controls dynamically. If you add a worksheet to the workbook programmatically by adding a sheet to the Worksheets collection, it is created as an Interop worksheet rather than a worksheet host item. Keep in mind that you will not have any of the VSTO-specific functionality—such as data binding capabilities and additional events—of a worksheet that is added programmatically in this way. You also cannot add a host control or Windows Forms control to an Interop worksheet. Only VSTO worksheets can host these types of controls.

If you look at the code that is generated in the hidden partial class when you add a worksheet to the workbook at design time, you can probably figure out what code is necessary to create the worksheet host item at run time. Because this is not a supported scenario in VSTO, it is not discussed here.

The Excel Locale Issue

When you create Excel solutions with VBA, the Excel object model expects English US formatting regardless of the user's locale settings. VSTO mimics this behavior by creating transparent proxies for the objects that always report that the locale is English US (locale ID 1033). Although the Excel object model expects locale ID 1033, it formats the data according to the user's locale settings when the data is displayed in the worksheet.

The AssemblyInfo.vb file within your Excel solutions contains an attribute called ExcelLocale1033Attribute. The value of this attribute determines whether VSTO creates and uses the transparent proxies and whether or not it behaves in the same way as VBA. By default, this attribute is set to true, causing the Excel object model to always expect locale ID 1033 (the same behavior you get in VBA). If you change this attribute to false, VSTO does not automatically report the locale as English US; instead, the current culture is reported. This can cause errors or unexpected behavior if an English edition of Excel is installed without a Multilingual User Interface (MUI) pack. You typically do not need to change the default setting.

If you must change the default behavior of VSTO by setting the ExcelLocale1033Attribute to false, you must take additional steps to ensure that your code will behave as expected if run on computers with different Windows regional settings. You should also avoid using string literals when you pass parameters or assign values to Excel objects. For example, instead of using a string such as "6/10/07," you should use a System.DateTime object that you can pass to Excel. This is because the String might be interpreted differently in different locales. In one locale, it might be interpreted as June 10, 2007 but interpreted as October 6, 2007 in another locale. If you don't change the default setting for ExcelLocale1033Attribute, there might be some cases where you might want to "unwrap" a particular proxy to access the native PIA object. You can do this by using the Microsoft.Office.Tools.Excel.ExcelLocale1033.Unwrap method of the ExcelLocale1033Proxy class. Be sure to restore the object to its proxied state by calling the Wrap method.

Data Binding to Host Controls on Worksheets

VSTO makes it easy to bind data to host controls. In Excel, you can use simple data binding on NamedRange controls, or complex data binding on ListObject controls. In simple data binding, you bind a single data element to a property of a control, such as the Value property of a NamedRange control. In complex data binding, you bind a control property to more than one data element.

The easiest way to bind data to a NamedRange control is to use the Data Sources window so that you can add a control that is already bound to data in your worksheet. In this section you will use the Data Sources window to add a connection to the Northwind database in Microsoft Access and bind some of its data to a NamedRange control and a ListObject control. Alternatively, you can use the Northwind database in SQL Server.

Creating a Data Source

1. On the Data menu, click Add New Data Source.

2. In the Data Source Configuration Wizard, select Database, and then click Next, as shown in Figure 7.17.

3. Click New Connection to open the Add Connection dialog box.

4. Select Microsoft Access Database File for the data source, and select the Northwind.mdb database on your computer. This assumes that you have Microsoft Access installed.

5. For this example, you will not set a password to log on to the database. Click Test Connection, and then click OK to close the Add Connection dialog box (see Figure 7.18).

6. Click Next on the Data Source Configuration Wizard.

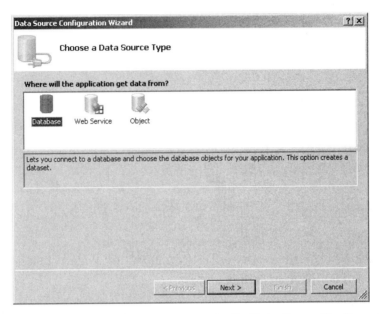

Figure 7.17. *Selecting the data source type in the Data Source Configuration Wizard*

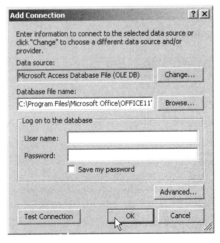

Figure 7.18. *Adding a connection to the Northwind database in Microsoft Access*

7. When prompted to copy the data file to your project, as shown in Figure 7.19, click No. (Clicking Yes adds a copy of the Northwind database to your project, and that is not necessary for this example.)

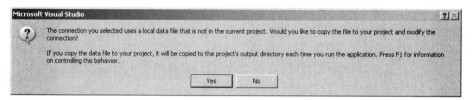

Figure 7.19. *Adding the Northwind data source to the project*

8. Click Next on the Data Source Configuration Wizard using the default connection string.

9. Select the Tables check box, as shown in Figure 7.20, and then click Finish.

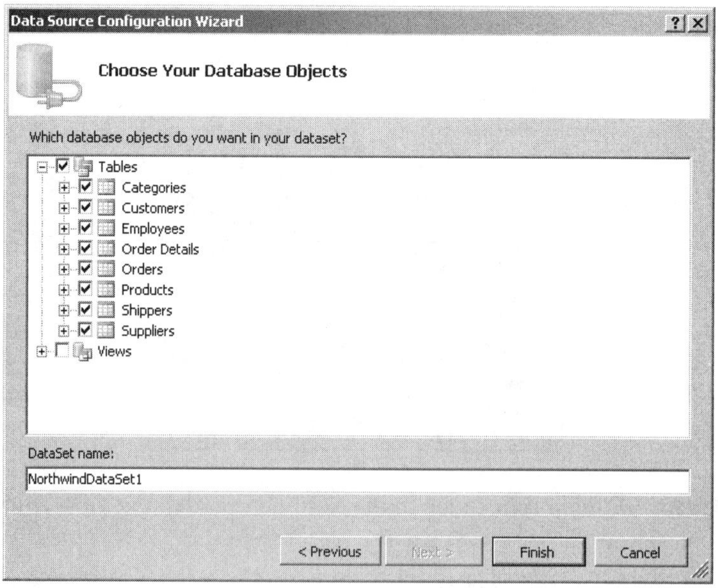

Figure 7.20. *Selecting database objects to use in the dataset*

A new dataset is added to the Data Sources window. NorthwindDataSet contains tables named Customers, Order Details, and Orders. Next you'll add a data-bound NamedRange control to the worksheet.

Adding Data-Bound Controls to the Worksheet

By default, each of the fields in the Customers table in the Data Sources window displays a NamedRange control, indicating the type of control that will be added to the worksheet when you drag the field to it. You can change the type of control by clicking the arrow next to ContactName to reveal a drop-down menu, as shown in Figure 7.21.

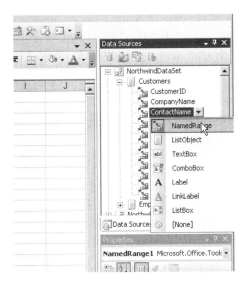

Figure 7.21. *Selecting the type of control to data-bind*

Now you can drag the selected type of control from the Data Sources window to the worksheet. Note that you don't drag the control that is in the drop-down list. Instead, select the desired control in the drop-down and then drag the field (for example, ContactName) to the worksheet. First you add the ContactName field to the worksheet as a data-bound

NamedRange control, and then you add the entire Customers table as a ListObject control and modify its contents.

1. Expand the Customers node in the Data Sources window, and drag the ContactName field to cell A2 on Sheet1 of the workbook so that a NamedRange control is added.

2. From the Data Sources window, drag the entire Customers table to cell A4 on Sheet1 of the workbook so that a ListObject control is added.

3. Right-click the CustomerID field of the ListObject, point to Delete, and then select Column. This action removes the CustomerID column from the ListObject.

4. Remove the following columns from the ListObject as described in step 3: ContactName and ContactTitle. Sheet1 should resemble Figure 7.22.

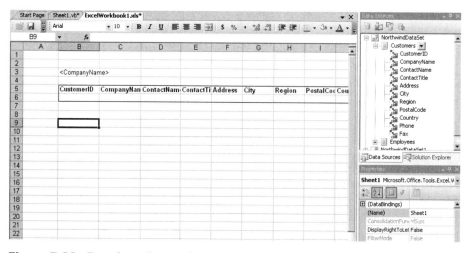

Figure 7.22. *Data-bound controls on a worksheet in Visual Studio*

5. Press F5 to run the code. The worksheet will display data, as shown in Figure 7.23.

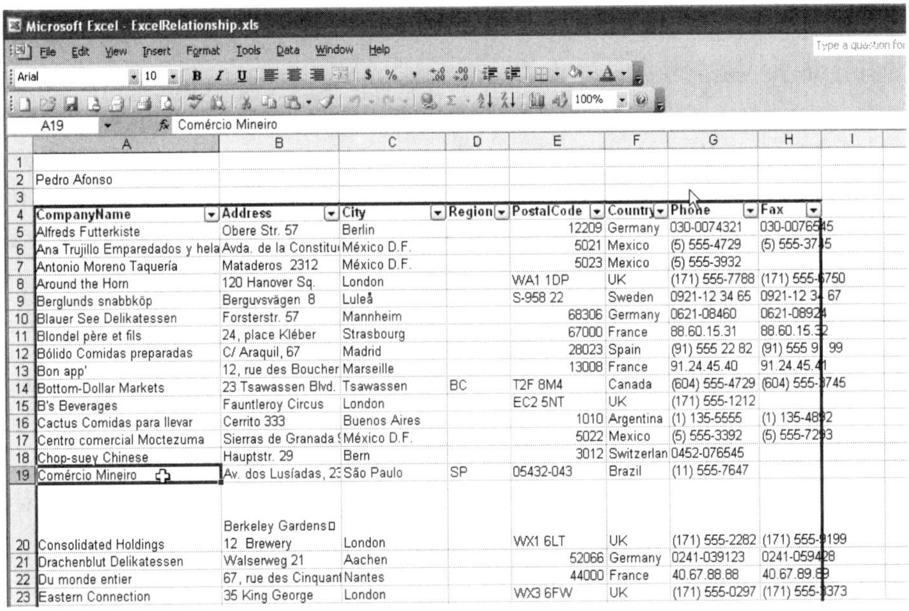

Figure 7.23. *Controls bound to data*

6. Move your cursor from cell A4 to cell A5, and notice that the contact name listed in cell A1 is automatically updated.

Without writing any code, you have bound data to the worksheet by using ListObject and NamedRange controls from the Data Sources window. You can instead bind data to a control programmatically by calling the SetDataBinding method of the control, but it is much easier to drag and drop data-bound controls to your worksheet's surface and let VSTO generate the necessary code for you.

Notice that when you first added the data-bound NamedRange and ListObject controls to the worksheet by dragging them from the Data Sources window, three objects were created and added to the component tray. These objects include a dataset called NorthwindDataSet, a table adapter object called CustomersTableAdapter, and a binding source object called CustomerBindingSource.

The DataSet

When you create the new data source by using the Data Sources Configuration Wizard, a new dataset called NorthwindDataSet is automatically created for you and added to your project. This dataset gets filled with the data in the database that you chose (the Northwind database), but it is then disconnected from the database. The connection to the database is opened only for the time required to fill the dataset, and then it is closed.

The dataset that is created is a *typed* dataset. This means that the various types used in the table are known at design time and you can access information about the dataset through the IntelliSense features. The dataset is stored as a schema in your project. You can examine the schema's design-time view when you right-click NorthwindDataSet.xsd in Solution Explorer and select View Designer. Notice that the designer in Figure 7.24 shows a relationship between the tables, something you'll

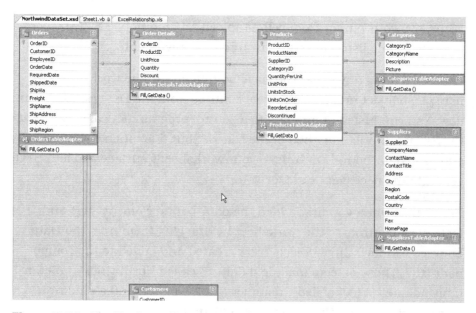

Figure 7.24. *The NorthwindDataSet schema in Visual Studio*

look at again later in this chapter. When you add a control from the Data Sources window to the worksheet, the DataSet is added to the component tray, as shown in Figure 7.25.

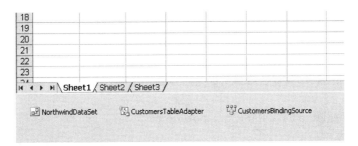

Figure 7.25. *The component tray for data-bound controls on Sheet1*

The BindingSource

The BindingSource control connects the data source to the controls on your document. You can navigate through records in your data source and sort, filter, and update the data through this BindingSource object. The data is not directly bound from the data source to the control. In our example, the NamedRange and ListObject controls are bound to the CustomerBindingSource, which in turn is bound to the NorthwindDataSet. This lets you simultaneously update each control that is bound to the same binding source. For example, when you move your cursor through the company records in the ListObject control, the contact name in the NamedRange control is automatically updated according to the record that is selected in the ListObject control.

Binding the control to the binding source rather than directly to the data source also enables you to set up data-bound controls before the data in the data table is available—for example, if you want to request a user name and password before displaying data in the document. The CustomerBindingSource is added to the component tray, as shown in Figure 7.25.

The TableAdapter

The TableAdapter is an ADO.NET object that enables your application to communicate with a database. The table adapter lets you read to and write from a database. The TableAdapter's Fill method reads the data from the database and populates (fills) the dataset with the data. When the TableAdapter is created, code to fill the dataset with data is automatically added to the Startup event handler of the worksheet that contains the data-bound control, as shown in Listing 7.19.

Listing 7.19. *Automatically filling a dataset*

```
Private Sub Sheet1_Startup(ByVal sender As Object, ByVal e As _
    System.EventArgs) Handles Me.Startup

    'TODO: Delete this line of code to remove the
    'default AutoFill for 'NorthwindDataSet.Customers'.

    If Me.NeedsFill("NorthwindDataSet") Then
        Me.CustomersTableAdapter.Fill( _
          Me.NorthwindDataSet.Customers)
    End If

End Sub
```

You can also use the table adapter to update the database with changes made to data in the data source. To do this, you must call the Update method of the TableAdapter, as shown in Listing 7.20.

Listing 7.20. *Updating a database using a table adapter*

```
Me.CustomersTableAdapter.Update(NorthwindDataSet)
```

For controls that have simple data binding, such as the NamedRange control, you must first write code that updates the data source before calling the Update method of the TableAdapter. You can add this code in the Change event handler of the NamedRange control, as shown in Listing 7.21.

Listing 7.21. *Updating a data source using the WriteValue method*

```
Private Sub ContactNameNamedRange_Change(ByVal Target As _
    Microsoft.Office.Interop.Excel.Range) Handles _
    ContactNameNamedRange.Change

    Me.ContactNameNamedRange.DataBindings( _
        "Value").WriteValue()

End Sub
```

Quickly Bringing Data into a Worksheet

At times you may want to create a solution that displays data from a data source, but you have no intention of updating the data; perhaps you want to use the data binding capabilities of the list object as a way to get data in your document, for the purpose of viewing the data. Because ListObjects have two-way data binding that automatically updates data in the control, you must disconnect the host control from the data source by calling the Disconnect method on the ListObject.

You can add this code to the Startup event handler of the target worksheet. In our example, this is Sheet1 (see Listing 7.22). After you add this code and run the solution, you'll see that the list object contains the company data, but if you move your cursor through the rows of the list object, the NamedRange control that contains the contact information does not get updated. This is because the ListObject is no longer connected to the BindingSource.

Listing 7.22. *Disconnecting a data source from a ListObject*

```
Private Sub Sheet1_Startup(ByVal sender As Object, ByVal e As _
    System.EventArgs) Handles Me.Startup

    'TODO: Delete this line of code to remove the
    'default AutoFill for 'NorthwindDataSet.Customers'.
```

```
    If Me.NeedsFill("NorthwindDataSet") Then
        Me.CustomersTableAdapter.Fill( _
          Me.NorthwindDataSet.Customers)
    End If

    Me.CustomersListObject.Disconnect()

End Sub
```

Working with Related Data

VSTO makes it easy to display related data in a document so that when you scroll through data records in one table, data in related tables is automatically updated. For example, you might want to view the details of product orders placed by a particular company. You can do this by dragging controls from the Data Sources window to your worksheet. In this case, let's use Sheet2.

1. In the Data Sources Window, expand the Suppliers table, and drag a CompanyName NamedRange from the Data Sources window to cell A2 of Sheet2.

   Notice that at the end of the Customers table, there is a Products table; this indicates a relationship between the Products table and the Suppliers table.

2. Drag the entire Products table to cell A5 of Sheet2.

3. Drag a Button control from the Toolbox to cell E2, and change its Text property to Next.

4. Add the code in Listing 7.23 to the Click event handler of Button1.

Listing 7.23. *Moving through records in a dataset*

```
Private Sub Button1_Click(ByVal sender As System.Object, _
    ByVal e As System.EventArgs) Handles Button1.Click

        Me.SuppliersBindingSource.MoveNext()

End Sub
```

Press F5 to run the code. Notice that the product changes along with the supplier's name whenever you click Button1 (see Figure 7.26).

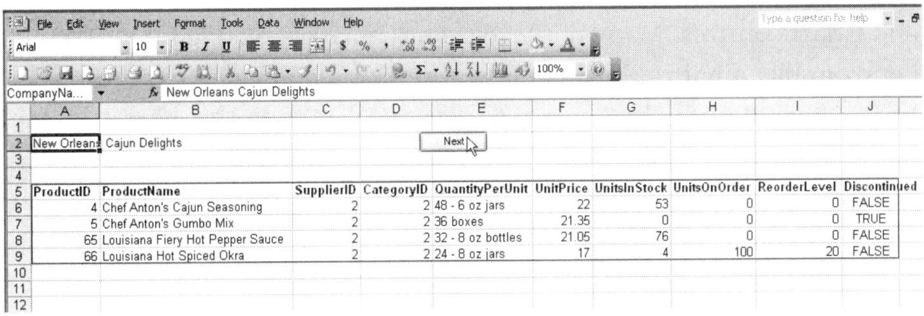

Figure 7.26. *Displaying related data on a worksheet*

Caching Data in the Workbook

A *data cache* is a place where you can store and retrieve data within a document. VSTO allows you to cache data in an Excel workbook. This feature is useful when you bind data to a document and want to let users update the data while they are not connected to a server that contains the database. VBA developers often use a hidden sheet to store data that they don't want to have visible in the document. Now this data can be stored in the data cache. Cached data is stored in a hidden ActiveX control on Sheet1, known as the Runtime Storage Control.

At design time, you can cache data in the document in two ways. The first way is to set the CacheInDocument property of the instance of the dataset to True in the Properties window. The second way is to add an attribute named <Cached> to an object or to the declaration of a variable that contains the data to be cached. At run time, you can call the StartCaching method on the worksheet and pass the dataset to be cached. Chapter 13 has more about using data caching in documents on a server.

Programming Against Events

VSTO lets you program against events of host items and host controls. Events are provided for the NamedRange, ListObject, XMLMappedRange, and Chart controls. Many of these events have been added by VSTO. For example, a native Range object does not have any events, but the VSTO NamedRange object exposes several. You no longer need to listen for an event on the worksheet and then map the event to a particular cell or range of cells on the worksheet; instead, VSTO does this mapping for you by reraising the event on the appropriate host control. VSTO also adds events to the Worksheet and Workbook host items.

In some cases, the name of the event has been changed if a method with the same name already exists. For example, the worksheet has an ActivateEvent event and a Deactivate event. The Activate event has been changed to ActivateEvent because there is an Activate method for a Worksheet object. The Deactivate event is not renamed DeactivateEvent, however, because there is no corresponding Deactivate method.

Because code is typically run in response to a user's action, it is important to be able to write code to respond to events of these host items and host controls. For example, if users right-click a cell, they see a custom context menu in which they can take further action. Or if a new row is added to a data-bound list object and an error occurs, users are told how to fix the error. In this section we look at the events for each of the host controls and host items available in an Excel project.

NamedRange Control Events

Table 7.1 shows the events that are available for a NamedRange control in VSTO.

Table 7.1. *Events of the NamedRange Control*

Event	Description
BeforeDoubleClick	Raised when the NamedRange control is double-clicked. The BeforeDoubleClick event handler enables you to take action when a user double-clicks text within a named range, before the default action for double-clicking the mouse button occurs.
BeforeRightClick	Raised when the NamedRange control is right-clicked. The BeforeRightClick event handler enables you to take action when a user right-clicks text within a named range, before the default action for the mouse right-click occurs.
BindingContextChanged	Raised when the binding context of the named range changes. The BindingContextChanged event handler enables you to take action when the BindingContext property of a named range is changed.
Change	Raised when the contents of the NamedRange are changed programmatically or by an end user. This event is not raised when a recalculation causes the range to change.
Deselected	Raised when a selection within a named range is moved outside the named range.
Disposed	Raised when the NamedRange is disposed of. This typically does not get raised until garbage collection is called to reclaim the memory that held the control.
Selected	Raised when the NamedRange is selected. The Selected event handler enables you to take action when focus is moved to the NamedRange.
SelectionChange	Raised when the selection within a NamedRange changes.

BeforeDoubleClick Event Handler

When you double-click a cell on a worksheet, the default action is to place Excel in edit mode. If you want to replace this action with another one, you can write code in the BeforeDoubleClick event handler.

For example, let's say you want to turn bold formatting on and off whenever a named range is double-clicked. You can add the code in Listing 7.24 to the BeforeDoubleClick event handler of a NamedRange control called NamedRange1. When you run this code, double-click the NamedRange, and then start typing. Then the text you type is appended at the end of the text in NamedRange1. This is because the default action of placing Excel in edit mode still occurs after your code is run.

Listing 7.24. *Turning bold on and off when a NamedRange is double-clicked*

```
Private Sub NamedRange1_BeforeDoubleClick(ByVal Target As _
    Microsoft.Office.Interop.Excel.Range, _
    ByRef Cancel As Boolean) Handles _
    NamedRange1.BeforeDoubleClick

    Me.NamedRange1.Font.Bold = Not CType( _
        Me.NameFirstNameCell.Font.Bold, Boolean)

End Sub
```

Notice that we converted the value returned from Me.NamedRange1.Font.Bold to a Boolean data type because it returns an Object. This is only necessary if you have Option Strict set to True, because the explicit conversion cannot take place. If you want to ensure that the default action does not take place after your code is run, you can add a line of code that sets the Cancel property to True, as shown in Listing 7.25. This time when you double-click the cell, Excel does not enter edit mode and the text in NamedRange1 is replaced by the text you type.

Listing 7.25. *Turning bold on and off then canceling the default action*

```
Private Sub NamedRange1_BeforeDoubleClick(ByVal Target As _
    Microsoft.Office.Interop.Excel.Range, _
```

```
        ByRef Cancel As Boolean) Handles _
        NamedRange1.BeforeDoubleClick

        Me.NamedRange1.Font.Bold = Not CType( _
            Me.NameFirstNameCell.Font.Bold, Boolean)
        Cancel = True

End Sub
```

Selected and Deselected Event Handlers

You can use the Selected and Deselected events of a NamedRange to
perform actions when text within the NamedRange is selected, and
again when it is deselected. For example, suppose you want to show a
control on the actions pane whenever text in a particular named range
has focus and then hide the control when focus is moved away. For this,
you can use the code in Listing 7.26.

Listing 7.26. *Changing the actions pane when text in a NamedRange is selected
and deselected*

```
Dim calendar As New MonthCalendar

Private Sub NamedRange1_Selected(ByVal Target As _
    Microsoft.Office.Interop.Excel.Range) Handles _
    NamedRange1.Selected

    Globals.ThisWorkbook.ActionsPane.Controls.Add(calendar)

End Sub


Private Sub NamedRange1_Deselected(ByVal Target As _
    Microsoft.Office.Interop.Excel.Range) Handles _
    NamedRange1.Deselected

    Globals.ThisWorkbook.ActionsPane.Controls.Remove(calendar)

End Sub
```

SelectionChange Event Handlers

You can use the SelectionChange event of a NamedRange control to perform an action whenever the selection within a particular range changes.

ListObject Control Events

Table 7.2 shows the events that are available for a ListObject control in VSTO.

Table 7.2. *Events of the ListObject Control*

Event	Description
BeforeAddDataBoundRow	Raised when a user attempts to add a new row to a data-bound ListObject. This event is not raised when a new row is programmatically added to the ListObject, only when the user interface is used to add the row.
BeforeDoubleClick	Raised when the ListObject control is double-clicked. The BeforeDoubleClick event handler of a ListObject control enables you to take action when a user double-clicks text within a list, before the default action occurs.
BeforeRightClick	Raised when the ListObject control is right-clicked. The BeforeRightClick event enables you to take action when a user right-clicks text within a list, before the default action occurs.
BindingContextChanged	Raised when the binding context of the ListObject changes. The BindingContextChanged event handler enables you to take action when the BindingContext property of a list is changed.
Change	Raised when the value of a ListObject changes either by user interaction with the ListObject or programmatically. This event is not raised when a recalculation is performed on the ListObject.

(continues)

Table 7.2. *Events of the ListObject Control (Continued)*

Event	Description
DataBindingFailure	Raised when the data binding of a ListObject fails. For example, it is raised if you attempt to drag a data-bound ListObject from the Data Sources window to an area on the worksheet that contains an existing ListObject.
DataMemberChanged	Raised when the value of the DataMemberChange property changes either programmatically or through user action.
DataSourceChanged	Raised when the DataSource property value of the ListObject is changed.
Deselected	Raised when the selection moves from an area inside the ListObject to an area outside the ListObject.
ErrorAddDataBoundRow	Raised when an error occurs when the user tries to add a row to a data-bound ListObject. For example, the error might occur due to a validation violation, such as adding non-unique values to the ListObject.
OriginalDataRestored	Raised when the changed value of the ListObject is restored to its original value when the change causes an error.
Disposed	Raised when the ListObject control is disposed of. This event typically does not get raised until garbage collection is called to reclaim the memory that held the control.
Selected	Raised when the selection moves inside an area of the ListObject from outside the ListObject.
SelectedIndexChanged	Raised when the selected index changes. The selected index is the ordinal position of the currently selected item in the list.
SelectionChange	Raised when the selection within the ListObject changes.

In this section, you'll learn how to use various events of the ListObject. To make it easy for you to test the code, we start with a code example in Listing 7.27 that creates a data-bound list object. This example can be used with each of the ListObject event examples. The example creates a list object named List1 that is bound to a data table called RealtorShowingTable. Users can schedule real estate appointments by adding the MLS number for the property to be viewed, the agent who is showing the property, and the name of the agent's company. The variable for the list object is created "WithEvents" so that you can easily add the event handler for each example.

Listing 7.27. *Creating a data-bound ListObject*

```
Dim RealtorShowingTable As DataTable
WithEvents List1 As Microsoft.Office.Tools.Excel.ListObject

Private Sub Sheet1_Startup(ByVal sender As Object, _
   ByVal e As System.EventArgs) Handles Me.Startup

   RealtorShowingTable = New DataTable("RealtorShowing")

   Dim DateColumn As DataColumn = _
      RealtorShowingTable.Columns.Add("DateScheduled", _
      GetType(Date))

   DateColumn.AllowDBNull = False

   With RealtorShowingTable.Columns
      .Add("MLS Number", GetType(String))
      .Add("Realtor Name", GetType(String))
      .Add("Agency", GetType(String))
   End With

   RealtorShowingTable.Rows.Add("03-05-2007", "123456", _
      "Mike Hernandez", "Mike's Realty")
   RealtorShowingTable.Rows.Add("03-06-2007", "654321", _
      "Mike Hernandez", "Mike's Realty")

   List1 = Me.Controls.AddListObject(Me.Range("A1"), "List1")
```

```
List1.AutoSetDataBoundColumnHeaders = True
List1.SetDataBinding(RealtorShowingTable)

End Sub
```

BeforeAddDataBoundRow Event Handler

The BeforeAddDataBoundRow event can be used to validate data that requires the addition of a new data-bound row to the list object. For example, you might want to check whether the date entered in the Date Scheduled column occurs on or after today's date. The code in Listing 7.28 compares the date entered to today's date and, if it occurs earlier than today, displays a message box and removes the row.

Listing 7.28. *Validating data entered in a ListObject using BeforeAddDataBoundRow*

```
Private Sub List1_BeforeAddDataBoundRow(ByVal sender As Object, _
    ByVal e As Microsoft.Office.Tools.Excel. _
    BeforeAddDataBoundRowEventArgs) _
    Handles List1.BeforeAddDataBoundRow

    Dim row As DataRow = CType(e.Item, DataRowView).Row

    If Not row("DateScheduled") Is Nothing And Not row( _
        "DateScheduled") Is Convert.DBNull Then

        Dim dateEntered As Date = row("DateScheduled")

        If dateEntered < Date.Today Then
            MsgBox("Appointments cannot be scheduled" _
            & " prior to today's date.")
            e.Cancel = True
            Return
        End If
    Else
        MsgBox("You must enter a date.")
        e.Cancel = True
    End If

End Sub
```

BeforeDoubleClick Event Handler

You can write code in the BeforeDoubleClick event handler of the ListObject to add today's date in the selected cell, as shown in Listing 7.29. Setting Cancel to True cancels the default behavior associated with double-clicking the list object.

Listing 7.29. *Adding today's date when a cell in the ListObject is double-clicked*

```
Private Sub List1_BeforeDoubleClick(ByVal Target As _
    Microsoft.Office.Interop.Excel.Range, ByRef Cancel _
        As Boolean) Handles List1.BeforeDoubleClick

    Dim currentRange As Excel.Range = Me.Application.Selection
    currentRange.Value = Today
    Cancel = True

End Sub
```

BeforeRightClick Event Handler

You can use the BeforeRightClick event to perform data validation of the list object. Listing 7.30 uses the same validation code we used in the BeforeAddDataBoundRow, but here it enables you to check the validation before typing all the required information into the remaining columns. Setting Cancel to True cancels the default behavior associated with right-clicking the list object (in this case, displaying the context menu). If a validation fails, a message box is displayed; otherwise, the default behavior associated with right-clicking the list object occurs.

Listing 7.30. *Validating data entered in a ListObject when the list is right-clicked*

```
Private Sub List1_BeforeRightClick(ByVal Target As _
    Microsoft.Office.Interop.Excel.Range, _
    ByRef Cancel As Boolean) Handles List1.BeforeRightClick

    Dim currentRange As Excel.Range = Me.Application.Selection
```

```
If currentRange.Value IsNot Nothing Then
    If CType(currentRange.Columns(1), Excel.Range).Value < _
        Today Then

        MsgBox("Appointments cannot be scheduled" _
            & " prior to today's date.")
        Cancel = True

    End If
End If

End Sub
```

Change Event Handler

The code example in Listing 7.31 resizes the columns in the list object whenever the Change event is raised. In this way, if you type information that does not fit the width of the column, the column automatically resizes to fit the text when you move your cursor to a new cell in the list object.

Listing 7.31. *Resizing the list object whenever data is changed*

```
Private Sub List1_Change(ByVal targetRange As _
    Microsoft.Office.Interop.Excel.Range, ByVal changedRanges _
    As Microsoft.Office.Tools.Excel.ListRanges) Handles _
    List1.Change

    Me.Columns.AutoFit()

End Sub
```

ErrorAddDataBoundRow Event Handler

The code example in Listing 7.32 displays a message if the date field of a data-bound row is left blank. The code that created the list object specified that the date column must not contain a null value, which causes the error.

Listing 7.32. *Capturing an error when a data-bound row cannot be added to a list object*

```
Private Sub List1_ErrorAddDataBoundRow(ByVal sender As Object, _
    ByVal e As Microsoft.Office.Tools.Excel. _
    ErrorAddDataBoundRowEventArgs) Handles _
    List1.ErrorAddDataBoundRow


    Dim currentRange As Excel.Range = Me.Application.Selection

    If CType(currentRange.Columns(1), Excel.Range).Value _
      Is Nothing Then

        MsgBox("Date cannot be empty.")

    End If

End Sub
```

OriginalDataRestored Event Handler

You can use the OriginalDataRestored event handler to take action when data in a ListObject is automatically restored. The code in Listing 7.33 displays a message box to inform the user that the data cannot be deleted or modified. For example, if you run this code and then try to change the heading "Agency" to "Company," the title automatically resets to "Agency" and the message is displayed.

Listing 7.33. *Warning users when a data-bound list object cannot be modified or deleted*

```
Private Sub List1_OriginalDataRestored(ByVal sender As _
    Object, ByVal e As Microsoft.Office.Tools.Excel. _
    OriginalDataRestoredEventArgs) Handles _
    List1.OriginalDataRestored

    MsgBox("Data cannot be deleted or modified.")

End Sub
```

SelectedIndexChanged Event Handler

You can write code in the SelectedIndexChanged event handler to show the value of the currently selected range in a text box on the actions pane, as shown in Listing 7.34.

Listing 7.34. *Displaying the current value of the list object in the actions pane*

```
Dim myTextbox As New TextBox
Private Sub List1_SelectedIndexChanged(ByVal sender As _
    Object, ByVal e As System.EventArgs) Handles _
    List1.SelectedIndexChanged

    Globals.ThisWorkbook.ActionsPane.Controls.Add(myTextbox)
    Dim currentRange As Excel.Range = Me.Application.Selection
    myTextbox.Text = currentRange.Text

End Sub
```

SelectionChange Event Handler

The code in Listing 7.35 shows how you can write code in the Selection-Change event handler of the list object to display the address of the selected range in the status bar.

Listing 7.35. *Displaying the address of a range of cells selected in the list object*

```
Private Sub List1_SelectionChange(ByVal Target As _
    Microsoft.Office.Interop.Excel.Range) _
    Handles List1.SelectionChange

    Dim currentRange As Excel.Range = Me.Application.Selection
    Application.StatusBar = currentRange.Address

End Sub
```

XMLMappedRange Control Events

Table 7.3 shows the events that are available for an XMLMappedRange control in VSTO.

Table 7.3. *Events of the XMLMappedRange Control*

Event	Description
BeforeDoubleClick	Raised when the XMLMappedRange control is double-clicked. The BeforeDoubleClick event handler of an XMLMappedRange control enables you to take action when a user double-clicks text within an XML mapped range, before the default action occurs.
BeforeRightClick	Raised when the XMLMappedRange control is right-clicked. The BeforeRightClick event handler enables you to take action when a user right-clicks text within an XML mapped range, before the default action occurs.
BindingContextChanged	Raised when the binding context of the XMLMappedRange changes. The Binding-ContextChanged event handler enables you to take action when the BindingContext property of an XML mapped range is changed.
Change	Raised when the value of the XMLMapped range changes.
Deselected	Raised when focus within an XMLMappedRange is moved outside the named range.
Disposed	Raised when the XMLMappedRange is disposed of. This typically does not get raised until garbage collection is called to reclaim the memory that held the control.
Selected	Raised when the XMLMappedRange is selected. The Selected event handler enables you to take action when focus is moved to the XMLMappedRange.
SelectionChange	Raised when the selection within an XMLMappedRange changes.

The events available for the XMLMappedRange are identical to the events available on a NamedRange. For code examples, see the section on NamedRange events earlier in this chapter.

Chart Control Events

Table 7.4 shows the events that are available for a Chart control in VSTO.

Table 7.4. *Events of the Chart Control*

Event	Description
Activate	Raised when the chart is activated. The Activate event handler enables you to take action when focus is moved to the Chart control.
BeforeDoubleClick	Raised when the chart is double-clicked before the default action occurs.
BeforeRightClick	Raised when the chart is right-clicked before the default action occurs.
BindingContextChanged	Raised when the binding context of the chart changes.
Calculate	Raised when the data in the chart is changed or new data is set.
Deactivate	Raised when the chart becomes deactivated—for example, when users move the cursor from the chart to another area of the worksheet.
Disposed	Raised when the chart is disposed of. This typically does not get raised until garbage collection is called to reclaim the memory that held the control.
DragOver	Raised when you drag a range of cells over a Chart control.
DragPlot	Raised when you drag a range of cells and drop them onto the Chart control.
MouseDown	Raised when you press the mouse button when the cursor is over a Chart control.
MouseMove	Raised when you move the mouse pointer across the Chart control.

(continues)

Table 7.4. *Events of the Chart Control (Continued)*

Event	Description
MouseUp	Raised when you release the mouse button when the cursor is over a Chart control.
Resize	Raised when the Chart control is resized.
SelectEvent	Raised when the Chart control is selected.
SeriesChange	Raised when data in the Chart control is changed.

In this section, we give examples of how you can use various events of the chart. To make it easy for you to test the code, we start with a code example in Listing 7.36 that creates a chart on Sheet1 of your project. This example can then be used with each of the Chart event examples. The example creates a chart named Chart1 using data that is added to the document via a NamedRange control. The variable for the chart is created With Events in the code-behind file so that you can easily add the event handler for each example.

Listing 7.36. *Creating a chart*

```
WithEvents Chart1 As Microsoft.Office.Tools.Excel.Chart
Private Sub Sheet1_Startup(ByVal sender As Object, _
    ByVal e As System.EventArgs)Handles Me.Startup

    Dim NamedRange1 As Microsoft.Office.Tools.Excel _
        .NamedRange = Me.Controls.AddNamedRange( _
        Me.Range("A1", "C3"), "NamedRange1")
    NamedRange1.Value = "=Rand()"
    Chart1 = Me.Controls.AddChart(100, 100, 300, 200, _
        "Chart")
    Chart1.SetSourceData(NamedRange1.InnerObject)

End Sub
```

DragPlot Event Handler

You can write code in the DragPlot event handler to change the type of chart displayed when a range of cells is selected, dragged from its original position, and then dropped onto the chart, as shown in Listing 7.37.

Listing 7.37. *Using the DragPlot event to change the type of chart.*

```
' Using the DragPlot event to change the type of a chart.
Private Sub Chart_1_DragPlot() Handles Chart_1.DragPlot
    Me.Chart_1.ChartType = Excel.XlChartType.xl3DPieExploded
End Sub
```

MouseDown Event Handler

The code example in Listing 7.38 changes the chart type whenever the mouse button is clicked when the cursor is over the Chart control.

Listing 7.38. *Changing the chart type when the mouse button is clicked over a chart*

```
Private Sub Chart1_MouseDown(ByVal Button As Integer, _
    ByVal Shift As Integer, ByVal x As Integer, _
    ByVal y As Integer) Handles Chart1.MouseDown

    Me.Chart1.ChartType = Excel.XlChartType.xl3DPieExploded

End Sub
```

MouseUp Event Handler

The code example in Listing 7.39 changes the chart type whenever the mouse button is released when the cursor is over the chart control.

Listing 7.39. *Changing the chart type when the mouse button is released over a chart*

```
Private Sub Chart1_MouseUp(ByVal Button As Integer, _
    ByVal Shift As Integer, ByVal x As Integer, _
    ByVal y As Integer) Handles Chart1.MouseUp
```

```
    Me.Chart1.ChartType = Excel.XlChartType.xlColumnClustered

End Sub
```

Resize Event Handler

The code example in Listing 7.40 displays the width of the Chart control whenever it is resized.

Listing 7.40. *Displaying the width of a chart*

```
Private Sub Chart1_Resize() Handles Chart1.Resize

    MsgBox("Chart width: " _
        & CStr(Me.Chart1.PlotArea.Width))
End Sub
```

Worksheet Events

Table 7.5 lists the events that are available for a worksheet in VSTO. Some of these events are available on the worksheet in VBA and exposed in the PIA, others were added from the Application object, and still others are specific to VSTO. Notice that some of the event names have been changed to avoid name collisions.

Table 7.5. *Events of the Worksheet*

Event	Description
ActivateEvent	Raised when the worksheet is activated.
BeforeDoubleClick	Raised when you double-click the worksheet. This event handler enables you to take action when the worksheet is double-clicked, before the default action takes place.
BeforeRightClick	Raised when you right-click the worksheet. This event handler enables you to take action when the worksheet is right-clicked, before the default action takes place.

(continues)

Table 7.5. *Events of the Worksheet (Continued)*

Event	Description
BindingContextChanged	Raised when the binding context of the work-sheet changes.
Calculate	Raised when you recalculate the worksheet.
Change	Raised when a change occurs within the worksheet.
Deactivate	Raised when the worksheet is deactivated.
Disposed	Raised when the worksheet is disposed of. This typically does not get raised until garbage collection is called to reclaim the memory that held the worksheet object.
FollowHyperlink	Raised when you click a hyperlink on the worksheet.
PivotTableUpdate	Raised when you update a pivot table on the worksheet.
SelectionChange	Raised when you move your selection within the worksheet.
Shutdown	Raised when the Worksheet class unloads. You typically add cleanup code to this event handler.
Startup	Raised when the Worksheet class is initialized. You typically add code here to set up the work-sheet when it is created.

ActivateEvent Event Handler

You can write code in the ActivateEvent handler of a worksheet to take action whenever a particular worksheet has focus. For example, you can show only one actions pane per workbook, but you can write code to display various controls on the actions pane that are specific to the visible worksheet. Add the code in Listing 7.41 to the Sheet1 class to see an example.

Listing 7.41. *Showing controls on the actions pane when the ActivateEvent of Sheet1 is raised*

```
Dim Sheet1Control As New MonthCalendar

Private Sub Sheet1_ActivateEvent() Handles Me.ActivateEvent

    Globals.ThisWorkbook.ActionsPane.Controls.Add(Sheet1Control)

    If Globals.ThisWorkbook.ActionsPane.Controls.Count >= 1 Then
        Application.CommandBars("Task Pane").Visible = True
    End If

End Sub

Private Sub Sheet1_Deactivate() Handles Me.Deactivate

    Globals.ThisWorkbook.ActionsPane.Controls.Remove( _
      Sheet1Control)

    If Globals.ThisWorkbook.ActionsPane.Controls.Count < 1 Then
        Application.CommandBars("Task Pane").Visible = False
    End If

End Sub
```

Next, add similar code (Listing 7.42) to the Sheet2 class. In this way, when you give focus to Sheet1, the MonthCalendar control appears on the actions pane, but when you give focus to Sheet2, MonthCalendar is removed and the DateTimePicker control is shown.

Listing 7.42. *Showing particular controls on the actions pane*

```
Dim Sheet2Control As New DateTimePicker

Private Sub Sheet2_ActivateEvent() Handles Me.ActivateEvent

    Globals.ThisWorkbook.ActionsPane.Controls.Add(Sheet2Control)
    If Globals.ThisWorkbook.ActionsPane.Controls.Count >= 1 Then
```

```
        Application.CommandBars("Task Pane").Visible = True
    End If

End Sub

Private Sub Sheet2_Deactivate() Handles Me.Deactivate

  Globals.ThisWorkbook.ActionsPane.Controls.Remove( _
    Sheet2Control)
  If Globals.ThisWorkbook.ActionsPane.Controls.Count < 1 Then
      Application.CommandBars("Task Pane").Visible = False
  End If

End Sub
```

When you run this code, the actions pane is not visible, because even though Sheet1 is visible, the ActivateEvent does not get raised. Either you must activate another sheet and reactivate Sheet1, or you can write additional code in Sheet1's Startup event handler to show the appropriate controls. This example uses a single control on the actions pane, but you can modify it to add multiple controls by designing a user control (or actions pane control) and then adding the user control to the actions pane. See Chapter 5 for more information about the actions pane.

Deactivate Event Handler

In the ActivateEvent example, you learned how to write code to add controls when a worksheet is activated. This example also shows code in the worksheet's Deactivate event handler to remove the control and hide the task pane. See Listing 7.42 for a code example.

FollowHyperlink Event Handler

You can write code in the FollowHyperlink event handler to take action before the event is raised. For example, you can display the link's address in Excel's status bar, as shown in Listing 7.43.

Listing 7.43. *Displaying a hyperlink's URL in the status pane*

```
Private Sub Sheet1_FollowHyperlink(ByVal Target As _
    Microsoft.Office.Interop.Excel.Hyperlink) Handles _
    Me.FollowHyperlink

    Application.StatusBar = "website: " & _
        CStr(Target.Address)

End Sub
```

SelectionChange Event Handler

To capture changes that occur to the selection in a worksheet, you can write code in the SelectionChange event handler.

Startup Event Handler

You write code in the Startup event handler of a worksheet when you want to perform certain actions, such as displaying text or showing controls on the actions pane when the document opens. Because Sheet1 is visible when you first open a document, you typically add this code to the Sheet1 class. Listing 7.44 shows how to add a control to the actions pane when the workbook first opens.

Listing 7.44. *Displaying a control on the actions pane*

```
Dim Sheet1Control As New MonthCalendar
Private Sub Sheet1_Startup(ByVal sender As Object, _
    ByVal e As System.EventArgs) Handles Me.Startup

    Globals.ThisWorkbook.ActionsPane.Controls.Add(Sheet1Control)
    If Globals.ThisWorkbook.ActionsPane.Controls.Count >= 1 Then
        Application.CommandBars("Task Pane").Visible = True
    End If

End Sub
```

Chartsheet Events

Table 7.6 lists the events that are available for a chartsheet in VSTO.

Table 7.6. *Events of a Chartsheet*

Event	Description
ActivateEvent	Raised when the chartsheet is activated.
BeforeDoubleClick	Raised when you double-click the chartsheet. The BeforeDoubleClick event handler enables you to take action when the chartsheet is double-clicked, before the default action takes place.
BeforeRightClick	Raised when you right-click the chartsheet. The BeforeRightClick event handler enables you to take action when the chartsheet is right-clicked, before the default action takes place.
BindingContextChanged	Raised when the binding context of the chartsheet changes.
Calculate	Raised when you recalculate the chartsheet.
Change	Raised when a change occurs within the chartsheet.
Deactivate	Raised when the chartsheet is deactivated.
Disposed	Raised when the chartsheet is disposed of. This typically does not get raised until garbage collection is called to reclaim the memory that held the chartsheet.
MouseDown	Raised when you press the mouse button when the cursor is over a chartsheet.
MouseMove	Raised when you move the mouse pointer across a chartsheet.
MouseUp	Raised when you release the mouse button when the cursor is over a chartsheet.
Resize	Raised when the chartsheet is resized.

(continues)

Table 7.6. *Events of a Chartsheet (Continued)*

Event	Description
SelectEvent	Raised when the chartsheet is selected.
SeriesChange	Raised when a data point on the chartsheet is changed.
Shutdown	Raised when the Chartsheet class unloads.
Startup	Raised when the Chartsheet class is initialized.

The events available for the chartsheet are similar to the events available on a Chart control and on a Worksheet. To see code examples, see the relevant sections earlier in this chapter.

Workbook Events

Table 7.7 lists the events that are available for a workbook in VSTO.

Table 7.7. *Events of a Workbook*

Event	Description
ActivateEvent	Raised when the workbook is activated.
AddinInstall	Raised when the workbook is installed as an add-in. Note that VSTO does not support workbooks that are saved as add-ins (XLA file format).
AddinUninstall	Raised when the workbook is uninstalled as an add-in. Note that VSTO does not support workbooks that are saved as add-ins (XLA file format).
AfterXmlExport	Raised when data is exported to an XML data file.
BeforeClose	Raised when users close the workbook but before it actually closes.

(continues)

Table 7.7. *Events of a Workbook (Continued)*

Event	Description
BeforePrint	Raised when the workbook is sent to print but before it actually prints.
BeforeSave	Raised when users save the workbook but before it is actually saved.
BeforeXmlExport	Raised when data is to be exported to an XML data file but before the export takes place.
BeforeXmlImport	Raised when data is to be imported into Excel but before the import takes place.
BindingContextChanged	Raised when the binding context of the workbook changes.
Deactivate	Raised when the workbook is deactivated.
Disposed	Raised when the workbook is disposed of. This typically does not get raised until garbage collection is called to reclaim the memory that held the workbook.
New	Raised when a new workbook is created from a workbook template.
NewSheet	Raised when a new sheet is added to the workbook.
Open	Raised when the workbook is opened.
PivotTableCloseConnection	Raised when the pivot table closes its connection to a data source.
PivotTableOpenConnection	Raised when the pivot table opens its connection to a data source.
SheetActivate	Raised when a sheet within the workbook is activated.
SheetBeforeDoubleClick	Raised when a worksheet within the workbook is double-clicked.

(continues)

Table 7.7. *Events of a Workbook (Continued)*

Event	Description
SheetBeforeRightClick	Raised when a worksheet within the workbook is right-clicked.
SheetCalculate	Raised when a worksheet within the workbook is calculated.
SheetChange	Raised when any cell is changed on a worksheet within the workbook.
SheetDeactivate	Raised when a worksheet within a workbook is deactivated.
SheetFollowHyperlink	Raised when a hyperlink on a worksheet within the workbook is clicked.
SheetPivotTableUpdate	Raise when a pivot table on a worksheet within the workbook is updated.
SheetSelectionChange	Raised when a selection within a worksheet changes.
Shutdown	Raised when the workbook shuts down.
Startup	Raised when the workbook is initialized.
SyncEvent	Raised when a worksheet on a Document Workspace is synchronized with a copy of the worksheet on a server.
WindowActivate	Raised when a workbook window is activated.
WindowDeactivate	Raised when a workbook window is deactivated.
WindowResize	Raised when a workbook window is resized.

How can you determine when to use events of the worksheet instead of events of a host control? The answer depends on what you're trying to accomplish. If you want to perform an action whenever a user moves the cursor within a worksheet, you might use the worksheet's SelectionChange event. But if you want to take action when the selection changes within a particular range, you're better off writing code in the SelectionChange event handler of a NamedRange control.

BeforeClose Event Handler

You can perform an action before the workbook is closed and cancel the close if necessary. For example, you might want to validate data before closing, or you might want to ensure that the user wants to close the workbook, as shown in Listing 7.45.

Listing 7.45. *Ensuring that the user wants to close the workbook*

```
Private Sub ThisWorkbook_BeforeClose(ByRef Cancel As Boolean) _
    Handles Me.BeforeClose

    Dim Response As Integer = MsgBox("Are you sure you " _
        & "want to close the workbook?", MsgBoxStyle.YesNo, _
        "Workbook Close")

    If Response = vbNo Then
        Cancel = True
    End If

End Sub
```

BeforePrint Event Handler

The BeforePrint event enables you to take action before the document is actually sent to print. Note that the user can cancel the Print dialog, so there is no way to verify that the document actually printed. Listing 7.46 shows how you can require users to view each document in Print Preview before printing the document. This code sets the Cancel property to True because the user can print or cancel printing from within the Print Preview view.

Listing 7.46. *Previewing a document before printing*

```
Private Sub ThisWorkbook_BeforePrint(ByRef Cancel As Boolean) _
    Handles Me.BeforePrint

    Me.PrintPreview()
    Cancel = True

End Sub
```

Deactivate Event Handler

When Excel has focus and then another application receives focus, the Deactivate event of the workbook is raised. You can write code in the Deactivate event handler to take action, such as saving the workbook, as shown in Listing 7.47.

Listing 7.47. *Saving the workbook whenever it is deactivated*

```
Private Sub ThisWorkbook_Deactivate() Handles Me.Deactivate
    Me.Save()
End Sub
```

SheetActivate Event Handler

The SheetActivate event is raised whenever a worksheet in the workbook is activated. Because each of the VSTO worksheets also has an ActivateEvent event, you write code here to capture the event for any of the worksheets. The code in Listing 7.48 displays the name of the active worksheet, along with its code name, in the status bar. To test this code, change the name of a worksheet, and then deactivate and reactivate it.

Listing 7.48. *Displaying the active worksheet in the status bar*

```
Private Sub ThisWorkbook_SheetActivate(ByVal Sh As Object) _
    Handles Me.SheetActivate

    Dim Worksheet As Excel.Worksheet = CType(Sh, Excel.Worksheet)
        Application.StatusBar = "The worksheet " & _
        Worksheet.Name & " (code name " & _
        CStr(Worksheet.CodeName) & ") is active."

End Sub
```

SheetDeactivate Event Handler

The SheetDeactivate event occurs whenever any sheet within the workbook loses focus. You can write code in the Deactivate event handler of the individual worksheet or, if you want to share the code between all worksheets, within the SheetDeactivate event handler of the workbook. The code example in Listing 7.49 asks users whether they want to save the data in a deactivated worksheet.

Listing 7.49. *Saving data when a worksheet is deactivated*

```
Private Sub ThisWorkbook_SheetDeactivate(ByVal Sh As Object) _
    Handles Me.SheetDeactivate

    Dim Result As Integer = MsgBox( _
        "Do you want to save the data in " & _
        CType(Sh, Excel.Worksheet).Name.ToString(), _
        MsgBoxStyle.YesNo, "Save worksheet")

    If Result = vbYes Then
        Me.Save()
    End If

End Sub
```

Startup Event Handler

The Startup event handler of a workbook holds the code that you want to run when the workbook is first opened. For example, in this event handler you often place code to display the actions pane. For an example, see Listing 5.11 in Chapter 5.

Event Order

The order of events on host controls and host items is nondeterministic. This means that you should not rely on the event order within your code. For example, if you have two NamedRange controls on the worksheet, you cannot assume, when you move your cursor from NamedRange1 to NamedRange2, that the Deselected event of NamedRange1 will be raised before the Selected event of NamedRange2.

Making Excel Smarter

It is easier to customize the task pane using VSTO than it is with the traditional smart document technology. You saw several examples of adding controls to the task pane in this chapter (see Listings 7.26 and 7.34). For more about customizing the document-level task pane in Excel, see Chapter 5. For information about customizing the application-level task pane in Excel, see Chapter 14.

Smart tags are available natively in Excel. For example, if you type a date in an Excel worksheet, Excel automatically recognizes the date and creates a smart tag, with a corresponding action. When you click the smart tag, it displays actions such as scheduling a meeting, as shown in Figure 7.27.

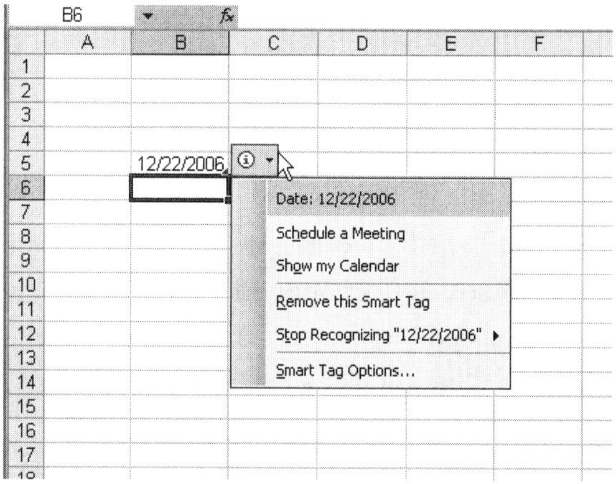

Figure 7.27. *Displaying a smart tag for a date in Excel*

If the smart tag is not visible when you select the date, you might need to turn the option on in Excel. From the Tools menu, select AutoCorrect Options and then click the Date check box. Make sure that the Label Data With Smart Tags check box is selected, and then click OK. Figure 7.28 shows an example. When you retype the date in Excel and press the ENTER key, the smart tag should be visible.

Figure 7.28. *Turning on the smart tag option for a date in Excel*

You can create your own smart tags using VSTO which is much easier than using the ISmartTag interface. Additionally, VSTO smart tags are document-specific rather than application-level smart tags. This makes it easier to tailor your smart tags to a particular document type. For more information about smart tags in Excel, see Chapter 9.

Summary

We started this chapter with a look at how you can learn about the Excel object model. You recorded a simple macro and then learned how to translate the macro to Visual Basic 2005 code in VSTO. You also enhanced this functionality by programmatically adding a button to the toolbar. We next looked at the various host items and host controls available in Excel and explained how to add these controls to worksheets through Excel's native functionality and through VSTO's functionality of dragging controls from the Toolbox to the worksheet.

We then looked at how to bind data to host controls such as list objects and named ranges, and how to cache the data in the document. Finally, we looked at the events available on the host items and host controls and illustrated the use of many of these events through code examples.

Review Questions

1. How many host items are available in Excel? Which of these can contain host controls?

2. Which types of host controls can you create by mapping XML to a worksheet?

3. What is the main difference between the way you can bind data to a ListObject and the way you can bind data to a NamedRange control?

4. How do dynamically created host controls get persisted in the workbook?

5. If you want to use a ListObject to bring data into a document but do not want users to update the data, which method of a ListObject would you use?

8

Controls in Word and Excel

It's a control freak thing. I wouldn't let you understand.
—S.H. UNDERWOOD

Topics Covered in This Chapter

About Controls

Adding Controls to Toolbars and Menus

Using Windows Forms Controls

Adding Controls to a Windows Form

Adding Controls to the Task Pane

Adding Controls to Excel and Word Documents

Summary

Review Questions

About Controls

Controls are typically used as entry points into your code. To perform actions, end users click a button on a toolbar or choose an item in a combo box on a dialog. Using VBA, you can add controls to your Word and Excel solutions in three ways: by adding them to the CommandBar (toolbar or menu); by creating a dialog box and adding ActiveX controls to a UserForm; or by adding these controls to the document. With VSTO, instead of adding ActiveX controls, you can add a variety of Windows Forms controls to a Windows Form, the task pane, or directly on the document. Using VSTO, you must add ActiveX controls to the CommandBar programmatically; you cannot add them at design time.

VSTO extends a number of objects in the Word and Excel object models, such as a Bookmark object, essentially turning them into controls. These controls, called host controls, are described in greater detail in Chapters 6 and 7. In this chapter, we look at the various ways you can customize the user interface in Word and Excel by adding controls to your Word and Excel solutions using VSTO.

Adding Controls to Toolbars and Menus

One of the most common means of allowing users to run code in an application is to add buttons to a toolbar or menu that respond when clicked. In VBA, you can use the Customize menu to associate macro code with a toolbar button; you simply drag the macro to the toolbar. As you learned in Chapters 6 and 7, using VSTO you must programmatically create menus and toolbars and write code in the Click event handlers of the buttons you add. First we look at how you can add a button to an existing toolbar (the Standard toolbar), and then we describe how you can add a custom icon to the button.

Creating Toolbar Buttons

In Chapter 7 (Customizing Excel with VSTO), you learned how to convert a simple VBA macro to Visual Basic 2005 code. In this section we modify that code so that bold formatting toggles on and off in the Click event handler of a button that we add to the Standard toolbar. This code is similar to the code shown in Chapter 6 (Customizing Word with VSTO), but here it is specific to Excel.

We further extend this code example to show you how to add a custom icon to the button. First, you'll write code in the Startup event handler of Sheet1 that adds the control to the toolbar. As shown in Listing 8.1, the code checks to see whether a control with the tag "FormatButton" already exists. If it does, the existing control is deleted before the new one is added. Without this code, a new button would be added to Excel's

Formatting toolbar each time the Startup event handler is called (each time the workbook is opened and Sheet1 is initialized).

Listing 8.1. *Modifying a recorded macro in Excel*

```
' Visual Basic 2005
Dim commandBar As Office.CommandBar
WithEvents formatButton As Office.CommandBarButton

Private Sub Sheet1_Startup(ByVal sender As Object, _
    ByVal e As System.EventArgs) Handles Me.Startup

    Try
        ' If the button already exists, remove it.
        formatButton = Application.CommandBars("Formatting") _
            .FindControl(Tag:="FormatButton")

        If formatButton IsNot Nothing Then

            formatButton.Delete()

        End If

    Catch Ex As Exception

        MsgBox(Ex.Message)

    End Try


    commandBar = Application.CommandBars("Formatting")
    formatButton = CType(commandBar.Controls.Add(1), _
        Office.CommandBarButton)

    With formatButton
        .Caption = "Bold and Italic"
        .Tag = "FormatButton"
        .FaceId = 34
    End With

End Sub
```

You should always set a value in the Tag property of the control so that Excel (or other Office application) can distinguish between multiple controls you've added to the toolbar. Next, in the button's Click event handler you add the code for formatting the selected cells as bold and italic. In this example, the code is handled by the formatButton method. The method takes two parameters: CommandBarButton, which represents the button being clicked; and a Boolean variable that enables you to cancel the button's default action (in the case that you're modifying an existing button). Add the code in Listing 8.2 to the Sheet1 class.

Listing 8.2. *Handling the Click event of a toolbar button in VSTO*

```
' Visual Basic 2005

Private Sub formatButton_Click(ByVal Ctrl As _
    Microsoft.Office.Core.CommandBarButton, ByRef _
    CancelDefault As Boolean) Handles formatButton.Click

    Dim Selection As Object = Me.Application.Selection

    If Selection.Font.Bold = True And _
        Selection.Font.Italic = True Then

        Selection.Font.Bold = False
        Selection.Font.Italic = False

    Else

        Selection.Font.Bold = True
        Selection.Font.Italic = True

    End If

End Sub
```

In this code example, you declare the variables for the CommandBar and CommandBarButton objects outside the Startup event handler.

This is because you must access these variables from the formatButton method. If you were to declare the variables inside the Startup event handler, the variables would fall out of scope after initialization is complete and would become eligible for garbage collection. This would prevent the button's Click event handler from being raised, and that is why you should declare variables for command bar buttons at the class level.

When you run this code, a new button is added to the Formatting toolbar. The graphic that is added to the button (faceID 34) is an ink bottle, as shown in Figure 8.1. Each time you click the button, the bold and italic formatting is either applied to or removed from the selected text, depending on its current state.

Figure 8.1. *Using the faceID property to identify a button graphic*

Extending Code to Add a Custom Graphic to the Toolbar Button

You can extend this code to add a custom graphic rather than the built-in graphic (faceID 34). To do this, you first create two bitmap files. The first bitmap will contain the graphic you want to use. The second bitmap will contain the same graphic, but with a white background and with the entire foreground set to black. This second bitmap, known as a *mask*, indicates which area of the original graphic (the background) should be transparent so that it takes on the color of the toolbar. The first step is to add the bitmap files to your project.

1. Create a bitmap file similar to the one in Figure 8.2, and name it BoldItalic.bmp.

2. Create a second bitmap file with the graphic you just created, but with the entire foreground black and the background white. Name this graphic Mask.bmp.

3. Right-click the solution node in Solution Explorer, and click Properties.

4. On the Resources tab of the Property Pages, click the drop-down arrow next to the Add Resource button, and then click Add Existing File.

5. Navigate to BoldItalic.bmp, and click Open.

6. Add Mask.bmp as a second resource.

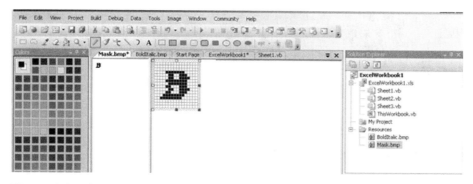

Figure 8.2. *The BoldItalic.bmp and Mask.bmp files in Visual Studio*

Now add code to retrieve this resource. You cannot assign a bitmap file directly to the Picture property of an Office button; instead, you must use an IPictureDisp interface. To convert your bitmap to the correct type, add a class to your project that converts a bitmap to an IPictureDisp.

1. Right-click Sheet1.vb in Solution Explorer, and click Code.

2. Add the class in Listing 8.3 after the Sheet1 class code (after the line End Class). The code in this class converts a bitmap to the type that is required for the Picture property of the button (IPictureDisp).

Listing 8.3. *Adding a class to convert bitmaps to IPictureDisp*

```
' Visual Basic 2005

Public Class BitmapToIPicture
    Inherits System.Windows.Forms.AxHost

    Public Sub New()
        MyBase.New(Nothing)
    End Sub

    Public Shared Function Convert(ByVal _
        Image As System.Drawing.Image) As stdole.IPictureDisp

        Convert = GetIPictureFromPicture(Image)

    End Function

End Class
```

Next, you modify the code in the Startup event handler to add the
BoldItalic bitmap to the button initially, and then add code to the
ButtonClick method to change the button state according to the state
of the formatting. The *state* determines whether the button has a border
and is shaded orange (indicating that the button is pressed). Listing 8.4
shows this new code in bold. Also, notice that the code for setting the
faceID has been commented out because you will use the Picture property instead.

Listing 8.4. *Adding a custom picture to a toolbar button*

```
' Visual Basic 2005
Dim commandBar As Office.CommandBar
WithEvents formatButton As Office.CommandBarButton

Private Sub Sheet1_Startup(ByVal sender As Object, _
    ByVal e As System.EventArgs) Handles Me.Startup

    Try
        ' If the button already exists, remove it.
```

```
    formatButton = Application.CommandBars("Formatting") _
        .FindControl(Tag:="FormatButton")

    If formatButton IsNot Nothing Then

        formatButton.Delete()

     End If

Catch Ex As Exception

    MsgBox(Ex.Message)

End Try


commandBar = Application.CommandBars("Formatting")
formatButton = CType(commandBar.Controls.Add(1), _
    Office.CommandBarButton)

With formatButton
    .Caption = "Bold and Italic"
    .Tag = "FormatButton"
    '.FaceId = 34
    .Picture = BitmapToIPicture.Convert(My.Resources.BoldItalic)
    .Mask = BitmapToIPicture.Convert(My.Resources.Mask)
    .State = Microsoft.Office.Core.MsoButtonState.msoButtonUp
End With


End Sub

Private Sub formatButton_Click(ByVal Ctrl As _
    Microsoft.Office.Core.CommandBarButton, ByRef CancelDefault _
    As Boolean) Handles formatButton.Click

    Dim Selection As Object = Me.Application.Selection
```

```
   If Selection.Font.Bold = True And _
      Selection.Font.Italic = True Then

      formatButton.State = Microsoft.Office.Core _
         .MsoButtonState.msoButtonUp
      Selection.Font.Bold = False
      Selection.Font.Italic = False

   Else

      formatButton.State = Microsoft.Office.Core _
         .MsoButtonState.msoButtonDown
      Selection.Font.Bold = True
      Selection.Font.Italic = True

   End If

End Sub
```

You should also add code to the worksheet's SelectionChange event
handler so that the button's correct state appears when you select text
that is formatted with bold and italic versus when you select text that
does not have this formatting applied. In other words, you want to
mimic the behavior of the built-in italic and bold buttons in Excel.
Right-click Sheet1.vb in Solution Explorer, select View Code, and then
add the code in Listing 8.5.

Listing 8.5. *Changing a custom picture on a toolbar button when the selection
changes*

```
Private Sub Sheet1_SelectionChange(ByVal Target As _
   Microsoft.Office.Interop.Excel.Range) Handles _
      Me.SelectionChange

   If Target.Font.Bold = True And _
      Target.Font.Italic = True Then

      formatButton.State = Microsoft.Office.Core _
         .MsoButtonState.msoButtonDown
```

```
    Else
        formatButton.State = Microsoft.Office.Core _
            .MsoButtonState.msoButtonUp
    End If

End Sub
```

Now when you press F5, a new BoldItalic button with a custom picture (BoldItalic.bmp) is added to the toolbar, and the button's state is updated depending on the formatting that is applied to the selected cells. Figure 8.3 shows the button state when the selected text has bold and italic applied.

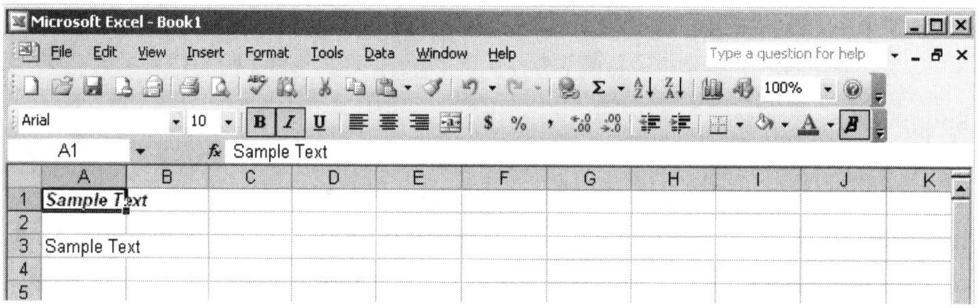

Figure 8.3. *The state of the BoldItalic button is set to msoButtonDown when selected text is bold and italic.*

Figure 8.4 shows the button's state when the selected text does not have bold and italic formatting applied. This behavior matches Excel's default behavior for toggle buttons on the toolbar.

When you run this code and apply bold and italic formatting to a cell, you'll see that the state of the new button matches the state of the standard Bold and Italic buttons; this is the way you can customize any button that you want to act as a toggle button. For buttons that perform only one action (rather than having on and off states), you would not need this code. To see a Word example or to learn how to override a built-in Word command, see Chapter 6.

Figure 8.4. *The state of the BoldItalic button is set to msoButtonUp when selected text is not formatted.*

Creating Menus and Menu Items

Creating a menu item is similar to creating a toolbar button. As with toolbar buttons, using VSTO you must create a menu item programmatically. In this section, you'll create a new menu and then add two menu items to it.

Let's say you want to let your users add a graphic in a first-page header of their document and also let them hide the graphic when it is printed on preprinted letterhead. First, create a new style in your document and name it *Graphic.* You'll apply this style to the graphic that you add. You must create this style for the code example to work, because you will set the style's hidden property to hide the graphic.

You can programmatically add a menu and two menu items to Word when the document opens, and then insert the graphic into the header or print the letterhead (with the graphic hidden) when the appropriate menu item is selected. As shown in Listing 8.6, you first add the variable declarations at the class level of your project (in the ThisDocument class) and then set the customization context to the document in ThisDocument's Startup event handler. Notice that the variables for the CommandBar buttons are declared WithEvents. This gives you access to all the events of the CommandBar button, including the Click event, which allows you to perform an action when the user clicks the button.

Listing 8.6. *Creating variables for a menu*

```
Dim LogoMenu As Office.CommandBarPopup
Private WithEvents CreateLogo As Office.CommandBarButton
Private WithEvents PrintLogo As Office.CommandBarButton
Dim menuBar As Office.CommandBar
Dim LogoStyle As Word.Style = Me.Styles("Graphic")


    Private Sub ThisDocument_Startup(ByVal sender As Object, _
        ByVal e As System.EventArgs) Handles Me.Startup

    Dim controlCount As Integer = 1
    Me.Application.CustomizationContext = Me.InnerObject
    menuBar = Application.CommandBars.ActiveMenuBar
    controlCount = menuBar.Controls.Count - 1
```

You should first check whether the menu already exists. In our case, we delete it and then re-create it. If it doesn't exist you can just create it, as shown in Listing 8.7. You add this code to the Startup event handler after the variable declarations.

Listing 8.7. *Creating a menu and menu items if they don't exist*

```
    Try

        ' If the menu already exists, remove it.
        LogoMenu = Application.CommandBars.ActiveMenuBar _
            .FindControl(Tag:="Logo")

    If LogoMenu IsNot Nothing Then

        LogoMenu.Delete(True)

    End If

    Catch Ex As Exception

        MsgBox(Ex.Message)

    End Try
```

```
If LogoMenu Is Nothing Then
    Dim cmdBarControl As Office.CommandBarPopup = Nothing

    ' Add the new menu.
    LogoMenu = CType(menuBar.Controls.Add( _
        Type:=Office.MsoControlType.msoControlPopup, _
        Before:=controlCount, Temporary:=True), _
        Office.CommandBarPopup)

    LogoMenu.Caption = "&Logo"
    LogoMenu.Tag = "Logo"


    ' Add the menu command.
    CreateLogo = CType(LogoMenu.Controls.Add( _
        Type:=Office.MsoControlType.msoControlButton, _
        Temporary:=True), Office.CommandBarButton)

    With CreateLogo
        .Caption = "&Create"
        .Tag = "CreateLogo"
        .FaceId = 65
    End With

    ' Add the menu command.
    PrintLogo = CType(LogoMenu.Controls.Add( _
        Type:=Office.MsoControlType.msoControlButton, _
        Temporary:=True), Office.CommandBarButton)

    With PrintLogo
        .Caption = "&Print"
        .Tag = "PrintLogo"
        .FaceId = 4
    End With
End If

End Sub
```

Because you created the command bar buttons With Events, you can access all of the button's events in the Code Editor. Select CreateLogo in

the Class Name drop-down, and then select the Click event in the
Method Name drop-down, as shown in Figure 8.5. Next, add the code in
Listing 8.8 to the button's Click event handler. This code uses a clip art
file that is stored in the Program Files directory. If you do not have this
file installed on your computer, you can replace it with a graphic that
you know exists.

Figure 8.5. *Creating an event handler for a command bar button*

Listing 8.8. *Adding code to the Click event handler of each button*

```
Private Sub CreateLogo_Click(ByVal Ctrl As _
    Microsoft.Office.Core.CommandBarButton, _
    ByRef CancelDefault As Boolean) Handles CreateLogo.Click

    Me.PageSetup.DifferentFirstPageHeaderFooter = True
    Me.Sections(1).Headers(Word.WdHeaderFooterIndex _
     .wdHeaderFooterFirstPage).Range.InlineShapes.AddPicture( _
     "C:\Program Files\Microsoft Office\MEDIA\CAGCAT10\" & _
     "j0300840.wmf").Range.Style = Me.Styles(LogoStyle)

End Sub

Private Sub PrintLogo_Click(ByVal Ctrl As _
    Microsoft.Office.Core.CommandBarButton, _
    ByRef CancelDefault As Boolean) Handles PrintLogo.Click

    Me.Styles(LogoStyle).Font.Hidden = True
    Application.Dialogs( _
        Word.WdWordDialog.wdDialogFilePrint).Show()
```

```
Me.Styles(LogoStyle).Font.Hidden = False

End Sub
```

The code in Listing 8.8 changes the font of the inserted graphic so that the font is hidden, thus hiding the graphic. Press F5 to run the code, and then add the logo by clicking Create on the Logo menu. The document will appear as shown in Figure 8.6. Next, select Print from the Logo menu. The document will print without the graphic visible. If you want to test this without actually printing the document, you can make a call to Print Preview.

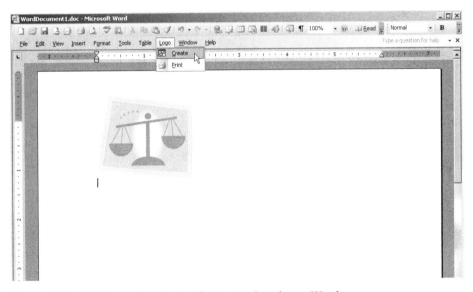

Figure 8.6. *Adding a logo to the first-page header in Word*

Using Windows Forms Controls

A number of Windows Forms controls are available on the Toolbox when a designer has focus in your solution. If your designer is a Windows Form or a user control, you will find the greatest number of controls available on the Toolbox. However, when a Word document or Excel worksheet has focus in Visual Studio, fewer controls are available than for Windows Forms controls.

The controls are grouped into categories within the Toolbox to make it easier to locate a control. For example, when a Windows Form or user control is the designer (it has the focus), the categories are Common Controls, Containers, Menus and Toolbars, Data, Components, Printing, Dialogs, and General, as shown in Figure 8.7.

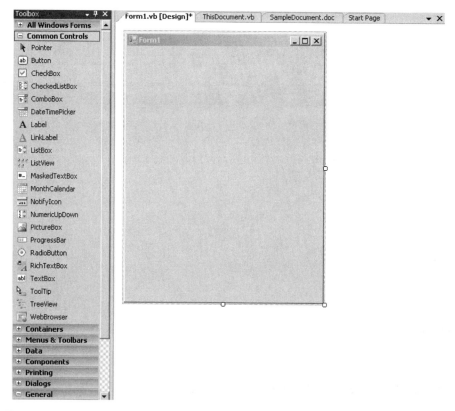

Figure 8.7. *Windows Forms controls available on a Windows Form*

However, when the document is the designer, categories such as Containers, Menus and Toolbars, and Printing do not appear on the toolbar. Figure 8.8 shows the categories of controls available on a document. The Common Controls category is expanded, revealing the most common Windows Forms controls used on a document.

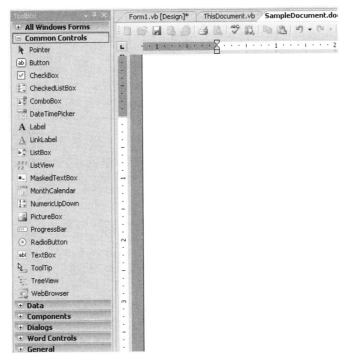

Figure 8.8. *Windows Forms controls available on a Word document*

One reason that these controls are not available on the toolbar is that it doesn't make sense to use controls for printing or adding menus and toolbars to a document; this functionality already exists within the application (you typically add toolbars to the application rather than to the document). As you saw in the preceding section, you can add CommandBar controls to Word's and Excel's menus and toolbars, so there isn't any reason to add this type of control to a document.

Available Windows Forms Controls

In Chapter 4, you looked at some of the differences between the ActiveX controls in VBA and the equivalent Windows Forms controls. Table 8.1 lists all the Windows Forms controls that appear on the Toolbox when a Windows Form has focus and when the document has focus (Design-Time Support in Document). The table includes a short description of each control, but this book does not go into detail about each control's properties and events. We encourage you to explore the VSTO documentation to learn more about the members of these controls.

Table 8.1. *Additional Windows Form Controls*

Control	Description	Design-Time Support in Document
BackgroundWorker	Component that enables you to run an operation in the background (asynchronously) by running it on a separate thread. This is useful when an operation typically takes a long time. The default event handler is DoWork.	Y
BindingNavigator	Component that enables you to navigate through data that is bound to another control. This creates both a UI for the Form and a component on the component tray. The default event handler is RefreshItems.	N

(continues)

Table 8.1. *Additional Windows Form Controls (Continued)*

Control	Description	Design-Time Support in Document
BindingSource	Component that indirectly binds a data source to a control. Instead of binding the control directly to the data source, you bind the control to the BindingSource, which is then bound to the data source. The default event handler is CurrentChanged.	Y
Button	Provides a control that can perform an action when the user clicks it. The default event handler is Click.	Y
CheckBox	Displays an on/off or true/false status. This can also be used to create a ToggleButton if you change the Appearance property to Button. The default event handler is CheckChanged.	Y
CheckedListBox	Displays a list that contains check boxes for each item in the list. The default event handler is SelectedIndexChanged.	Y
ColorDialog	Component that enables you to display a color palette in a dialog box from which users can select a color.	Y
ComboBox	Provides a control with a drop-down arrow from which users can select an item. The default event handler is SelectedIndexChanged.	Y

(continues)

Table 8.1. *Additional Windows Form Controls (Continued)*

Control	Description	Design-Time Support in Document
ContextMenuStrip	Component that provides a context menu (shortcut menu) for another control. This creates both a UI for the form and a component on the component tray. The default event handler is Opening.	N
DataGridView	Provides a grid for displaying data in a table. The default event handler is CellContentClick.	Y
DataSet	Component that enables you to add a typed or untyped dataset to a Windows Form.	Y
DateTimePicker	Provides a drop-down calendar from which users can select a single date and time. The default event handler is ValueChanged.	Y
DirectoryEntry	Component that enables you to access objects within the Active Directory hierarchy.	N
DirectorySearcher	Component that enables you to run queries against an Active Directory hierarchy.	N
DomainUpDown	Combines a text box with a pair of buttons that you can use to navigate up and down a list of items. The default event handler is SelectedItemChanged.	Y
ErrorProvider	Component that displays information to users about validation errors that exist on corresponding controls.	N

(continues)

Table 8.1. *Additional Windows Form Controls (Continued)*

Control	Description	Design-Time Support in Document
EventLog	Component that enables you to read from and write to Windows event logs. The default event handler is EntryWritten.	N
FileSystemWatcher	Component that enables you to capture events when changes occur to a directory or its files. The default event handler is Changed.	N
FlowLayoutPanel	Enables you to create a horizontal or vertical layout flow for the content in the FlowLayoutPanel. The default event handler is Paint.	N
FolderBrowseDialog	Component that displays a dialog box that enables users to browse to a folder or create a new one.	Y
FontDialog	Component that displays a dialog box that contains all fonts that are currently installed on the system. The default event handler is Apply.	Y
GroupBox	Provides a way to group controls and isolate them from other controls on the form. For example, if you want to make option buttons mutually exclusive, you can place them in a GroupBox control. The default event handler is Enter.	N
HelpProvider	Component that associates an application with an HTML Help file.	Y

(continues)

Table 8.1. *Additional Windows Form Controls (Continued)*

Control	Description	Design-Time Support in Document
HScrollBar	Enables horizontal scrolling for another control. Most controls that require scrolling provide this functionality natively. The default event handler for this control is Scroll.	Y
ImageList	Component that displays a list of images that can be used on other controls. Click the Images property to display the Image Collection Editor, where you can add or modify images in the list.	Y
Label	A read-only control for displaying information. This control is typically used to label other controls on the Windows Form or document. The default event handler is Click.	Y
LinkLabel	Enables you to add Web-style links to a Windows Form. The default event handler is LinkClicked.	Y
ListBox	Contains multiple items from which a user can select. The default event handler is SelectedIndexChanged.	Y
ListView	Displays a list of items with associated icons in a hierarchical folder structure similar to the one in the left pane of Windows Explorer. The default event handler is SelectedIndexChanged.	Y

(continues)

Table 8.1. *Additional Windows Form Controls (Continued)*

Control	Description	Design-Time Support in Document
MaskedTextBox	Component that constrains the format of user input. The default event handler is MaskInputRejected.	Y
MenuStrip	Provides a menu system on a Windows Form. This creates both a UI for the form and a component on the component tray. The default event handler is ItemClicked.	N
MessageQueue	Component that provides a way to access a queue on a MessageQueue server.	N
MonthCalendar	Contains a calendar from which users can select a date or range of dates. The default event handler is DateChanged.	Y
NotifyIcon	Component that displays icons in the status bar for background processes that do not have a user interface. The default event handler is MouseDoubleClick.	N
NumericUpDown	Combines a text box with a pair of buttons that you can use to navigate up and down a list of numbers. The default event handler is ValueChanged.	Y
OpenFileDialog	Component that displays a dialog box that enables users to select and open files. The default event handler is FileOK.	Y

(continues)

Table 8.1. *Additional Windows Form Controls (Continued)*

Control	Description	Design-Time Support in Document
PageSetupDialog	Component that displays a dialog box that enables users to set page details for printing.	N
Panel	Provides a way to group other controls and can contain a scroll bar. The default event handler is Paint.	N
PerformanceCounter	Component that collects or publishes performance data.	N
PictureBox	Displays images on a Windows Form or document. The default event handler is Click.	Y
PrintDialog	Component that displays a dialog box where users can select a printer and print a document.	N
PrintDocument	Component that enables users to select print options and then print a document. The default event handler is PrintPage.	N
PrintPreviewControl	Enables you to create your own component for previewing a document.	N
PrintPreviewDialog	Component that displays a dialog box where you can display a document as it will appear when it is printed. The default event handler is Click.	N
Process	Component that gives you access to local and remote processes. The default event handler is Exited.	N

(continues)

Table 8.1. *Additional Windows Form Controls (Continued)*

Control	Description	Design-Time Support in Document
ProgressBar	Displays the progress of an action in a horizontal bar. The default event handler is Click.	Y
PropertyGrid	Displays the properties of another control. The default event handler is Click.	Y
RadioButton	Displays a true/false status. You can make multiple RadioButtons mutually exclusive (only one control in the group can have its value set to True) by adding them to a GroupBox control. For documents, GroupBox controls are not supported, so you must use a custom user control in order to make RadioButton controls on a document mutually exclusive. This control is equivalent to an OptionButton, and the default event handler is CheckChanged.	Y
ReportViewer	Displays reports in a Windows Form. The default event handler is Load.	N
RichTextBox	Displays text in a text box that can contain formatting. The default event handler is TextChanged.	N
SaveFileDialog	Component that displays a dialog box where users can save a file to a particular location. The default event handler is FileOK.	Y

(continues)

Table 8.1. *Additional Windows Form Controls (Continued)*

Control	Description	Design-Time Support in Document
SerialPort	Component that gives you access to serial port data.	N
ServiceController	Component that gives you access to a Windows service, whether it is running or stopped.	N
SplitContainer	Divides a container into two areas that can be resized.	N
Splitter	Enables users to resize a control that is docked. Use SplitContainer instead.	N
StatusStrip	Component that represents a status bar. This creates both a UI for the form and a component on the component tray. The default event handler is ItemClicked.	N
TabControl	Displays controls on different tabs. This control is often used to save screen real estate, and it is handy for use on the actions pane. The default event handler is Click.	N
TableLayoutPanel	Represents a panel that can display its controls in a table format. The default event handler is Paint.	N
TextBox	Collects input from users. The default event handler is TextChanged.	Y
Timer	Component that raises events at regular intervals. The default event handler is Tick.	N

(continues)

Table 8.1. *Additional Windows Form Controls (Continued)*

Control	Description	Design-Time Support in Document
ToolStrip	Component that creates a custom toolbar or menu in a Windows Form. This both creates a UI for the form and adds a component to the component tray. The default event handler is ItemClicked.	N
ToolStripContainer	Provides a panel on each side of a form that contains a ToolStrip control.	N
ToolTip	Component that displays text when a user holds the cursor over other controls. The default event handler is Popup.	Y
TrackBar	Enables navigation through information via a slider that moves in increments. The default event handler is Scroll.	N
TreeView	Displays nodes that are arranged hierarchically and can be expanded and collapsed. The default event handler is AfterSelect.	Y
VScrollBar	Enables vertical scrolling for another control. Most controls that require scrolling provide this functionality natively. The default event handler is Scroll.	Y
WebBrowser	Enables you to host Web pages that have browsing capabilities on a Windows Form. The default event handler is DocumentCompleted.	Y

In addition to visible controls, there are a number of controls known as components. *Components* do not have a user interface; instead, when you drag one to a Windows Form or a document, they appear in an area beneath the visual designer called the component tray. For example, if you drag an ImageList control to your document, it appears in the component tray rather than the document, and you can select the control to set its properties in the Properties window.

You can also add controls to the Toolbox, including third-party controls. For example, if you create a user control and compile your project, the control is added to the Toolbox. You can then drag the user control from the Toolbox to your document. This feature can come in handy when you want to use the functionality of controls that are not available in the Toolbox.

For example, container controls cannot be added to a document at design time because VSTO does not support adding Windows Forms controls within another Windows Form control. This means that you cannot add a control, such as a group box, to the document and then add radio buttons or check boxes to the group box as a way of making the controls mutually exclusive. But you can add the radio buttons to a group box on a user control and then add the user control to the document. For an example of how you can implement this with a custom user control, see the section "Adding Controls to Documents" later in this chapter. First, we look at adding controls to a Windows Form.

Adding Controls to a Windows Form

There are limits to the types of controls you can add to toolbars and menus. Often you might want to provide a user interface where end users can perform multiple tasks, such as selecting an entry from a drop-down list, typing data into a text box, and then clicking a button. Using VBA, you can do this by adding ActiveX controls to a UserForm and then writing code behind the controls. VSTO enables you to use

Windows Forms and a large variety of controls, called Windows Forms controls. In this section, you'll design a Windows Form to collect data from the end user and then add the data to the document.

Using the Logo application we used in the section entitled, "Creating Menus and Menu Items," let's write code to display a Windows Form that enables the end user to select from a variety of logos and insert text to create a letterhead. First, we add a table to the header and then apply formatting. The logo and text will be inserted into these table cells when the user clicks the Insert button on the dialog box.

1. On the View menu, point to Microsoft Office View Word, and click Headers and Footers.

2. On the Header and Footer toolbar, click Page Setup, as shown in Figure 8.9.

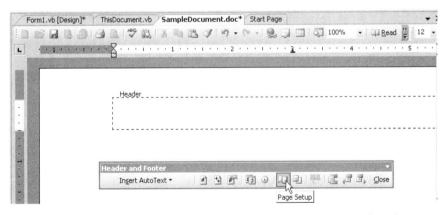

Figure 8.9. *Opening the Page Setup dialog box from within a header*

3. In the Page Setup dialog box, click the Different First Page check box, as shown in Figure 8.10. This setting allows you to add text and graphics to the header for the first page of your document (the first section in your document); the text and graphics don't appear on subsequent pages.

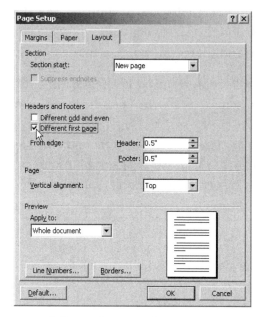

Figure 8.10. *Creating a different first-page header*

4. Add a table with two columns to the header.

5. Format the left table cell to be center aligned, as Times New Roman 8 pt.

6. Format the right table cell to be left aligned, as Times New Roman 36 pt.

7. With your cursor in the right table cell, click the Format menu, and then click Paragraph. In the Indents and Spacing dialog box, set Spacing Before to 12. Your table should resemble the one in Figure 8.11.

Creating a User Control

In this section you'll create a user control and then add Windows Forms controls for selecting graphics and entering text. A user control acts as a container for all the Windows Forms controls that you add to it. You

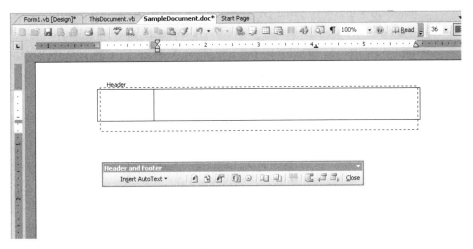

Figure 8.11. *Adding a table to a header*

can then programmatically add the user control to a Windows Form that you'll display when the user clicks the Create button on the Logo menu. Theoretically, you could design a Windows Form simply by adding controls directly to it, but we're choosing to use a user control so that you can see how this control can be reused on the Document Actions task pane in the next section of this chapter. For an example of how to convert a Windows Form to a user control, see Chapter 12.

The first step is to save some graphics to a folder so that you can display them on the Windows Form and also insert the selected graphic into the document header. The next step is to add a user control to your project. Then you'll add a number of controls to the user control.

Adding a User Control to Your Project

1. Right-click the project in Solution Explorer, point to Add, and click User Control.

2. In the Add New Item dialog box, select User Control, leave the default name of UserControl1.vb, and then click OK.

This adds a class to your project called UserControl1.vb. The class has a code view and a design view. By default, the user control appears in Visual Studio in design view. You can then add controls and set their properties in this view.

3. Resize the user control so that its Width is 210, and its Height is 320.

4. Add a Button to the top of the user control, and change the Text property to *Select Graphics*. Then change the Size property to 170, 23.

5. Add a PictureBox control to the document, and change the Size property to 170, 118. Then set the BorderStyle property to FixedSingle. Also change the SizeMode property to StretchImage.

6. Add two LinkLabels above the PictureBox—one to the far left, and one to the far right. Change the Text property of the left LinkLabel control to *Previous*, and change the Text property of the right LinkLabel control to *Next*.

7. Add a TextBox control below the PictureBox, and change the Multiline property to True. Then change its Size property to 170, 62.

8. Add a Button control below the PictureBox control, and change its Text property to *Insert*.

9. Add a FolderBrowserDialog to the form. When you do this, the control is added to the component tray at the bottom of the designer.

Your finished user control should resemble the one in Figure 8.12.

You can add code to the Click event handler of Button1 that displays the File Browser dialog box, creates a collection of file names for each file in the chosen directory that has a .jpg or .bmp extension, and then populates the PictureBox with the first graphic in the collection. Double-click Button1 to change to code view, and place your cursor within the button's Click event handler. Next, add the code in Listing 8.9 to the UserControl1 class. Be sure to add the variable declarations outside the Click event handler.

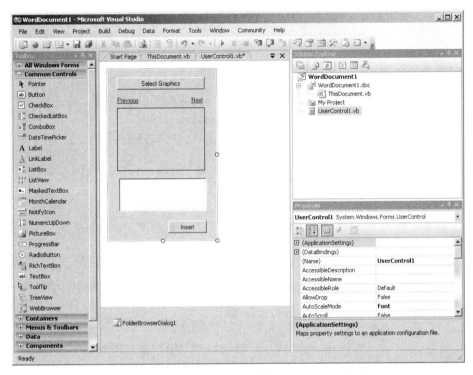

Figure 8.12. *Adding Windows Forms controls to a user control*

Listing 8.9. *Populating a PictureBox control with graphics*

```
Dim FileList As New Collection
Dim current As Integer = 1

Private Sub Button1_Click(ByVal sender As System.Object, _
    ByVal e As System.EventArgs) Handles Button1.Click

    ' Remove any graphics currently in the PictureBox control.
    FileList.Clear()

    Me.FolderBrowserDialog1 = New _
        System.Windows.Forms.FolderBrowserDialog()

    Dim folderName As String
    Dim result As DialogResult = _
        FolderBrowserDialog1.ShowDialog()
```

```
folderName = FolderBrowserDialog1.SelectedPath
Dim sFile As String

If (result = DialogResult.OK) Then

    ' Loop through all files in selected directory and add
    ' graphics to the FileList collection.
    For Each sFile In System.IO.Directory.GetFiles( _
        folderName)
        Dim FileInfo As New System.IO.FileInfo(sFile)

        If FileInfo.Extension = ".bmp" Or _
            FileInfo.Extension = ".jpg" Then

            FileList.Add(FileInfo.FullName, FileInfo.Name)

        End If
    Next

    ' If items exist in FileList collection, add the
    ' first one to the PictureBox control.
    If FileList.Count = 0 Then
        Me.PictureBox1.Image = Nothing
    Else
        Me.PictureBox1.ImageLocation = FileList(current)
    End If

End If

End Sub
```

Next, add code to the Click event handler of the LinkLabel controls, as shown in Listing 8.10. This code checks the location of the current graphic within the FileList collection and moves to (and displays) the next or previous graphic.

Listing 8.10. *Navigating through a FileList collection to change the graphic displayed*

```
Private Sub LinkLabel1_LinkClicked(ByVal sender As _
    System.Object, ByVal e As _
    System.Windows.Forms.LinkLabelLinkClickedEventArgs) _
    Handles LinkLabel1.LinkClicked

    If current > 1 Then
        Me.PictureBox1.ImageLocation = FileList.Item( _
            current - 1)
        current -= 1
    End If

End Sub

Private Sub LinkLabel2_LinkClicked(ByVal sender As _
    System.Object, ByVal e As _
    System.Windows.Forms.LinkLabelLinkClickedEventArgs) _
    Handles LinkLabel2.LinkClicked

    If current < FileList.Count Then
        Me.PictureBox1.ImageLocation = FileList.Item( _
            current + 1)
        current += 1
    End If

End Sub
```

Now you can add code that will insert two things into the header of the Word document whenever the Insert button on the user control is clicked: the selected picture, along with any text that was typed into the text box. Add the code in Listing 8.11 to the button's Click event handler in the UserControl1 class.

Listing 8.11. *Inserting text and a graphic into a document's first-page header*

```
Private Sub Button2_Click(ByVal sender As System.Object, _
    ByVal e As System.EventArgs) Handles Button2.Click
```

```
If Me.PictureBox1.ImageLocation = "" Then
    MsgBox("Please select a graphic to insert.")
    Exit Sub
End If

If Me.TextBox1.Text = "" Then
    MsgBox("Please add text for the header.")
    Exit Sub
End If

Globals.ThisDocument.PageSetup. _
    DifferentFirstPageHeaderFooter = True

Globals.ThisDocument.Sections(1).Headers( _
    Word.WdHeaderFooterIndex.wdHeaderFooterFirstPage). _
    Range.Tables(1).Cell(1, 2).Range.Text = Me.TextBox1.Text

If Globals.ThisDocument.Sections(1).Headers( _
    Word.WdHeaderFooterIndex.wdHeaderFooterFirstPage) _
    .Range.InlineShapes.Count > 0 Then

    Globals.ThisDocument.Sections(1).Headers( _
        Word.WdHeaderFooterIndex.wdHeaderFooterFirstPage) _
        .Range.InlineShapes(1).Delete()
End If

Globals.ThisDocument.Sections(1).Headers( _
    Word.WdHeaderFooterIndex.wdHeaderFooterFirstPage). _
    Range.InlineShapes.AddPicture( _
        Me.PictureBox1.ImageLocation).Range.Style = _
        Globals.ThisDocument.Styles("Graphic")

End Sub
```

Now you can reuse the code for creating the menu items that you
used in Listing 8.7. This time, you'll need to change the code in the
CreateLogo_Click event handler so that it contains the code in Listing
8.12. The CreateLogo_Click event handler is in the ThisDocument class.

Listing 8.12. *Displaying the user control on a Windows Form control when a menu item is clicked*

```
Private Sub CreateLogo_Click(ByVal Ctrl As
    Microsoft.Office.Core.CommandBarButton, ByRef _
    CancelDefault As Boolean) Handles CreateLogo.Click

    Dim myWinForm As New Windows.Forms.Form
    Dim myUserControl As New UserControl1

    With myWinForm
        .Controls.Add(myUserControl)
        .AutoSizeMode = AutoSizeMode.GrowAndShrink
        .AutoSize = True
        .Show()
    End With

End Sub
```

When you press F5 to run the code, you will be presented with a dialog box. You select a folder that contains graphics files (.jpg or .bmp) and then scroll through the graphics by clicking the Previous and Next LinkLabels. Next, you add any desired first-page header text and click Insert. The letterhead will resemble the one in Figure 8.13.

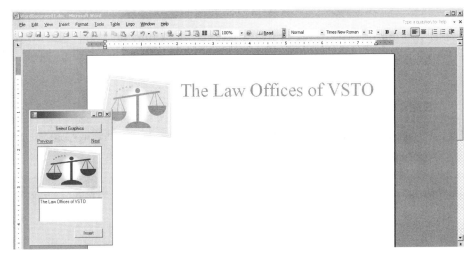

Figure 8.13. *Adding a logo and text to a first-page header*

When you click the Insert button, the logo and text are inserted. If you click the Select Graphics button again, you can change the directory and then load new graphics into the dialog box. In the next section, we show you how easy it is to reuse the user control and corresponding code to display the user interface on the task pane.

Adding Controls to the Task Pane

Adding controls to the task pane is very similar to adding controls to a Windows Form. Using VSTO, you add controls to the ActionsPane object for Word 2003 and Excel 2003 solutions. If you're using VSTO 2005 SE and Office 2007, you can add the controls to the Custom task pane, which is available to any document you have opened. The remainder of this section describes controls on the actions pane, but it is also applicable to the Custom task pane. In Chapter 14 you'll learn more about adding controls to the Custom task pane.

In the preceding section, you added controls to a user control and then added the user control to a Windows Form. Instead, you can add the user control directly to the task pane. In this way, you can provide a user interface that does not take up a lot of space on the document nor hide any of the document's contents.

First, you change the code so that instead of adding the user control to a Windows Form and then displaying the Windows Form, you add the user control to the actions pane.

1. Right-click ThisDocument.vb, and select View Code.

2. Replace the code in the Click event handler of the CreateLogo button with the code in Listing 8.13.

Listing 8.13. *Displaying a user control on the task pane when a menu item is clicked*

```
Private Sub CreateLogo_Click(ByVal Ctrl As _
    Microsoft.Office.Core.CommandBarButton, _
    ByRef CancelDefault As Boolean) Handles CreateLogo.Click
```

```
Dim myUserControl As New UserControl1

If Me.ActionsPane.Controls.Count < 1 Then
    Me.ActionsPane.Controls.Add(myUserControl)
End If

Me.Application.TaskPanes(Word.WdTaskPanes. _
    wdTaskPaneDocumentActions).Visible = True

End Sub
```

This code first checks whether there are any controls on the actions pane before adding the user control. Without the If statement, the controls would be added to the document each time the menu item is clicked. There is also code to set the Visible property of the Document Actions task pane to True. This is needed because the task pane is automatically made visible only the first time you add a control to it. If the end user closes the task pane and then clicks the CreateLogo button again, it would not automatically become visible. Therefore, we add code to make sure the task pane is visible whenever this button is clicked.

Press F5 to run the code. This time the controls are displayed on the Document Actions task pane, and when you add text and a graphic, the header should resemble the document in Figure 8.14.

Any Windows Forms control that can be added to a Windows Form can also be added to the actions pane. You can add the control directly to the Controls collection of the ActionsPane, or, as in this example, you can first add controls to a user control and then add it to the ActionsPane's Control collection. For more about customizing the Document Actions task pane, see Chapter 5.

Now that you know how to display controls on a Windows Form and on the Document Actions task pane, we will take a look at adding controls directly to the document.

Figure 8.14. *Adding a logo and text to the first-page header via the actions pane*

Adding Controls to Excel and Word Documents

In the same way that you add ActiveX controls to a Word document or Excel worksheet and you program against the controls using VBA, you can add Windows Forms controls to your document (or worksheet) with VSTO. To add controls to the document, you drag them from the Toolbox to an area on your document. The controls can be placed anywhere on the document surface except within a header or footer.

You can add controls to your document at design time or at run time. At design time, the document (or worksheet) surface is the designer. Just as you add controls to a UserForm or Windows Form, you drag controls from the Toolbox and drop them directly onto the document designer. To view the Windows Forms controls that can be added to a document at design time, click Toolbox on the View menu in Visual Studio. Figure 8.15 shows the controls available to an Excel worksheet, along with a number of controls that have been added to the worksheet.

The Toolbox contains tabs for various types of controls, such as Common Controls, Components, Excel Controls, and All Windows Forms. This

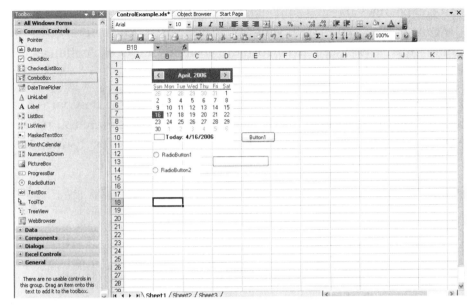

Figure 8.15. *The Toolbox in Visual Studio*

tab design helps you display only those controls that you are interested in instead of having to scroll through all the available Windows Forms controls (and host controls).

Host controls are another type of control that can be added to the document. These controls are described in detail in Chapters 6 and 7; therefore, this chapter focuses on Windows Forms controls that can be added to the document or worksheet.

Windows Forms Controls in Word

By default, VSTO adds Word controls to the document inline with text. This means that the control is placed within the text of a document, and, as the text is repositioned, the control also repositions. For example, if you add text to the beginning of a paragraph that contains an inline control, the control will move with the text, or wrap to the next line, when new text is added.

You can change an inline control into a floating object. This means that the control is placed in a drawing layer that can appear behind or in front of text; it is placed at an absolute position that doesn't change when the text changes.

Figure 8.16 shows five Button controls. Starting with the first paragraph, they are formatted Inline with Text (Button1), Square (Button2), Tight (Button3), Behind Text (Button4), and In Front of text (Button5).

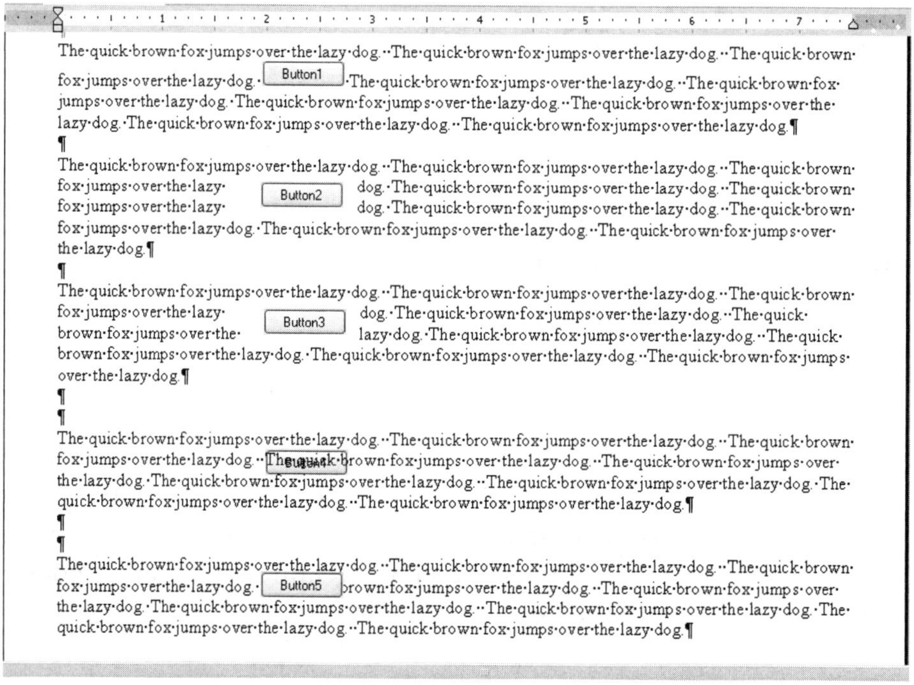

Figure 8.16. *Controls on a Word document with various positioning settings*

Notice that for Button1, the space between the first line of the paragraph and the second line differs from that of the remaining lines. That is because the control is set as Inline with Text, and the bottom of the control is aligned with the bottom of the text. If you were to increase the height of the control, then the space between the first and second lines would also increase.

Button4 is set to appear behind the text, but it appears behind the text only in design view. When you run the application, the button appears in front of the text, enabling users to click it.

If you add text to the beginning of each paragraph, you'll notice that only Button1 moves and always appears between the words *dog* and *The* (it stays inline with the text). For all floating control formats, the control remains stationary and the associated text continues to wrap.

To make a control float within the document, you change the wrapping style of the text so that it has any wrapping style other than In Line with Text.

1. Right-click the control and click Format Control.

2. In the Layout tab of the Format Control dialog box, select Square, as shown in Figure 8.17.

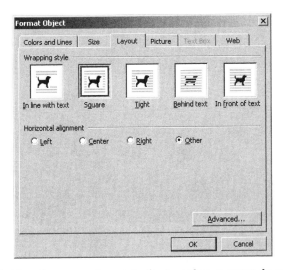

Figure 8.17. *Setting the wrapping style for text that surrounds a control*

3. Select Other in the Horizontal Alignment section, and then click
    OK. You could also set the alignment of the control as Right,
    Center, or Left.

If you click the Advanced button on the Format Control dialog box,
you'll see that there are several other settings you can apply to the
control, such as additional wrapping styles. You'll also find a Picture
Position tab (shown in Figure 8.18), where you can set the control's
horizontal and vertical alignment. In this tab you can also specify
whether the control will move with text and whether it can overlap
another control.

Keep in mind, however, that many of these settings are applicable
only to the design-time view of the control. At run time, controls cannot
overlap and cannot be placed under text in the document. If this Format
Control dialog box looks familiar to you, it is because it is the same
dialog box that you use when formatting pictures that are in your
document.

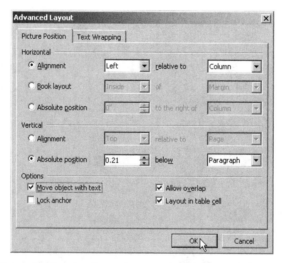

Figure 8.18. *Using the Picture Position tab of the Format Control dialog box*

Windows Forms Controls in Excel

When you add controls to an Excel worksheet, they are added as floating controls. You can move a control to any area of your worksheet, including positioning it between columns or rows, as shown in Figure 8.19. These controls do not automatically resize when you resize a column or row. You can change this behavior by using the Format Control dialog box.

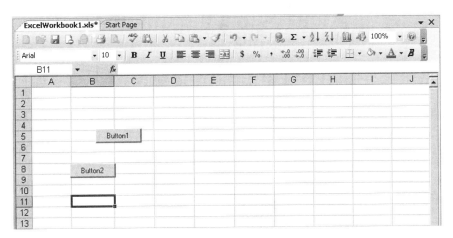

Figure 8.19. *Placing controls on an Excel worksheet*

To make control resize with worksheet cells, you set the Move and Size with Cells option.

1. Right-click the control and click Format Control.

2. On the Properties tab, select the Move and Size with Cells option, as shown in Figure 8.20.

Now when you resize a column, the control also resizes. Figure 8.21 shows Button1, which has resized when column B was resized. Button2 has not resized, because by default it is set to Move but Don't Size with Cells.

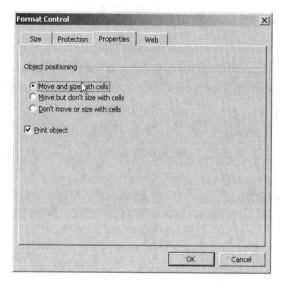

Figure 8.20. *Setting the object positioning properties of a control in Excel*

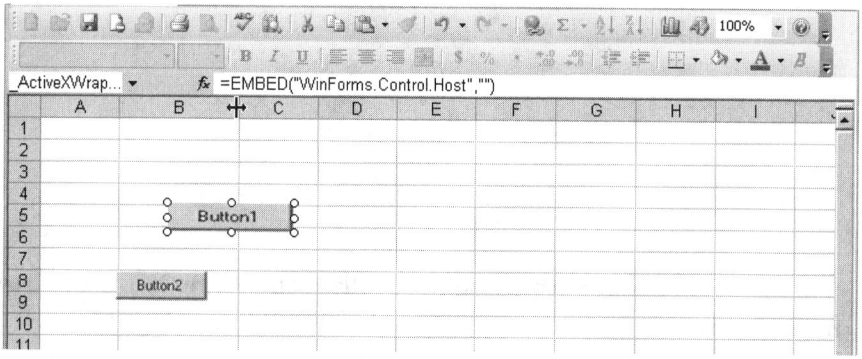

Figure 8.21. *Resizing a column and controls in an Excel worksheet*

Adding Data-Bound Controls

You have the same data binding capabilities on an added control on a document that you have for controls on a Windows Form. In Visual Studio, you can use the Data Sources window to add data-bound controls to your document. First you must create a new data source.

1. On the Data menu, click Add New Data Source. This opens the Data Sources Configuration Wizard.

2. In the Data Sources Configuration Wizard, select Database, and then click Next.

3. Navigate to the Northwind database that comes with Microsoft Access, and then click Next. Depending on where you installed Office, you should be able to find this database in Program Files\Microsoft Office\OFFICE11\Samples.

4. Leave the default settings for saving the connection string, and click Next.

5. Expand the Tables node, select the Products table and the Suppliers table, and then click Finish.

The Data Sources window becomes visible in Visual Studio and contains two tables: Products and Suppliers. When you expand one of these tables, such as the Products table, you will see all the fields available for it. By default, most of these fields appear as NamedRange controls, but if you click the drop-down box to the right of the field name, you can select from a number of other control types, as shown in Figure 8.22.

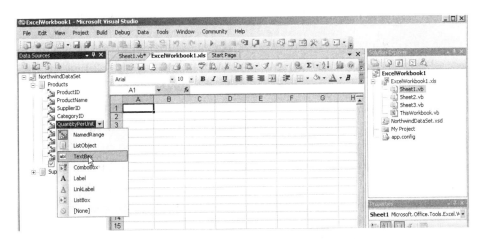

Figure 8.22. *Selecting the type of control to be added to a document*

In the next example, you'll add data-bound controls to the worksheet and see how you can dynamically populate a ListObject and a Chart. First, you add data-bound controls to the worksheet.

1. Expand the Suppliers table in the Data Sources window, and change the CompanyName field to a combo box by clicking the drop-down box next to the CompanyName field and clicking ComboBox.

2. Drag the CompanyName field to cell A2 on Sheet1.

3. Click the drop-down next to the ContactName field, and select Label.

4. Drag the ContactName field to the worksheet below the CompanyName combo box.

5. At the bottom of the Suppliers field, you'll see the Products table. Select that table, and drag it to cell A7. A ListObject is created that contains a column for each field in the Products table.

6. Right-click the ProductID column, point to Delete, and click Column.

7. Using the method described in step 6, delete the following columns of the ListObject: SupplierID, CategoryID, and Discontinued.

You can resize each of the columns in the ListObject so that the headings are visible; to do so, drag the right column boundary to the right, or double-click the right column boundary for each column you want to resize. Note that the worksheet displays a component tray that contains components necessary for data binding. For example, there is a NorthwindDataSet, along with a table adapter and binding source, for each of the tables (Products and Suppliers). These components were added to the project for you when you dragged fields from the table to the worksheet. Your worksheet should resemble the one in Figure 8.23.

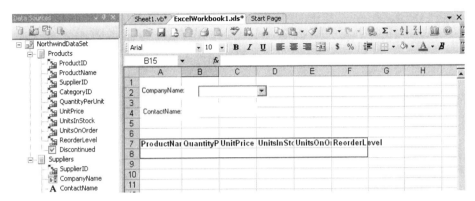

Figure 8.23. *Data-bound controls on a worksheet*

Next, you can create a chart based on the data that will populate the worksheet when the solution is run. This chart will change dynamically as the ListObject data changes. The contents of the ListObject are bound to the Northwind database. Because we created a ListObject from the Products table, which was a child of the Suppliers table, a relationship exists between these two tables. This means that changes made in the CompanyName combo box will cause the data in the ListObject to display the related data for the selected company. Let's create the chart and run the solution to see how this works.

1. Select all the cells in the ListObject, including the header row.

2. On the Insert menu, click Chart. The Chart Wizard will appear.

3. In step 1 of the Chart Wizard, select Column in the Chart Type list box. Select the first chart under Chart Sub-type, and then click Next.

4. In step 2 of the Chart Wizard, select the Series tab. In the Series list box, select Product Name and then click Remove. Then remove QuantityPerUnit and UnitPrice. The Series list box should contain only UnitsInStock, UnitsOnOrder, and ReorderLevel, as shown in Figure 8.24.

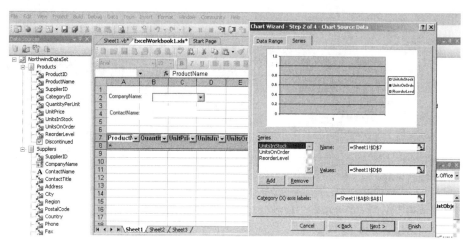

Figure 8.24. *Setting the series data for a chart*

5. Type the following text in the Category (x) Axis Labels text box:

   ```
   =Sheet1!$A$8:$A$13
   ```

   Instead of typing this text, you can select cells A8 through A13 in the ProductName column, as shown in Figure 8.24. You could include additional cells if you know that the data for that column will expand beyond row 13. In our case, each company in the Northwind database has fewer than eight products.

7. Click Finish to complete the wizard and create the chart.

8. Drag the chart to an area below the ListObject, and then resize the chart to the same width as the ListObject.

9. Press F5 to run the code.

10. Click the CompanyName combo box to select a company.

Notice that the data in the ListObject and Chart changes according to the company that is selected in the CompanyName combo box. Figure 8.25 shows the worksheet with controls bound to data in the Northwind database.

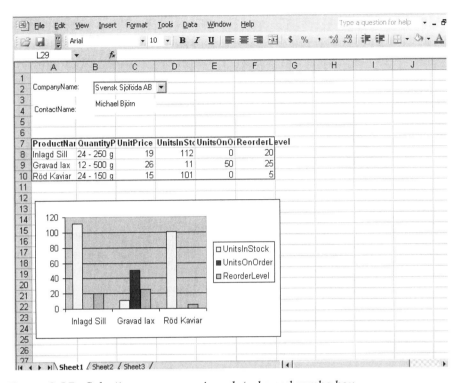

Figure 8.25. *Selecting a company in a data-bound combo box*

Being able to add controls directly to the worksheet or document gives you one more option for presenting a UI to the end user. However, it sometimes might not make sense to put a Windows Form control on a document. You have to assess the purpose of the control and the best way to display the UI. If you want to give users a way to select an item, as we did in our Excel example with the CompanyName combo box, you easily could add this control to the actions pane instead. However, another scenario for using a combo box might be to insert the selected item into the worksheet in place of the control. Choose the type of UI that best meets your needs.

If you print this worksheet, the Windows Forms controls also print. As you saw earlier in this chapter (see Figure 8.20), you can set the control's properties so that the control does not print. Of course, this means that the data in the control will not print. In Word, you cannot set inline controls to be hidden when you print because these controls are *inline shapes.* If you change the format of the control to make it a floating control, it essentially converts the Inline Shape object to a Shape object, which can then be hidden. But remember that the control might not reflow correctly in your document if the text changes and the control is not inline with the text.

One other way around this limitation is to add the control to the document programmatically to assist users in filling out information and then remove the control after the information is received. You'll see an example of this later in the chapter. But first, let's look at how you can add custom controls to a document.

Adding Custom Controls to a Document

At times you'll want to use a third-party control or create your own custom control for use on a document. One way to do this is to create a user control, add some Windows Forms controls to it, and then add the user control to the document.

For example, if you want to make radio buttons mutually exclusive when used on a document, you must use a GroupBox. Unfortunately, GroupBox controls are not supported for use on a document at design time. Instead, you can add the GroupBox control to a user control and then add controls such as RadioButton controls. When you build your project, the user control will be added to the Toolbox. After the user control appears on the Toolbox, you can drag it directly to your document, thus giving you the functionality of the group box. Let's try this on an Excel workbook.

1. Create an Excel workbook project using VSTO.

2. Right-click the Excel solution, point to Add, and then click User Control.

❖**Note** The UI for creating projects might differ depending on the profile you selected when you installed Visual Studio.

3. Keep the default name UserControl1, and click Add.

4. Drag a GroupBox control to the user control, and change the Text property to *Mutually Exclusive*.

5. Drag three RadioButton controls to the GroupBox control, leaving the default names RadioButton1, RadioButton2, and RadioButton3.

6. Build the solution by clicking Build Solution on the Build menu.

7. Right-click Sheet1, and click View Designer.

   The control is added to the Toolbox in the GroupBox Components tab, as shown in Figure 8.26.

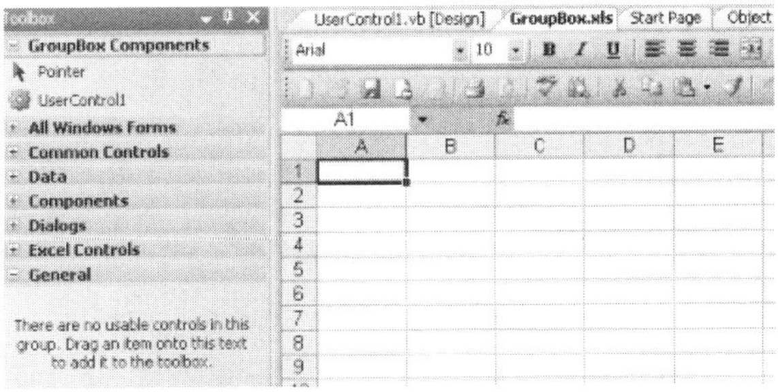

Figure 8.26. *Adding a user control to the Toolbox*

8. Drag UserControl1 to cell A1 of Sheet1.

9. Drag a RadioButton from the Toolbox to cell A9 (or to a cell below UserControl1) on Sheet1, and then add two more RadioButton controls beneath it.

10. Press F5 to run the code.

11. In the Mutually Exclusive GroupBox, click RadioButton1, then RadioButton2, and then RadioButton3.

12. For the controls you added directly to the worksheet, click RadioButton1, then RadioButton2, and then RadioButton3.

Because RadioButton controls that are directly added to the document are not automatically mutually exclusive, all three controls appear to be selected, as shown in Figure 8.27. The RadioButtons that were placed in a GroupBox on a custom user control are mutually exclusive, and only RadioButton3 appears to be selected.

Figure 8.27. *Selecting mutually exclusive RadioButton controls*

Control Type

When you add a Windows Forms control to a document, VSTO creates its version of the Windows Forms control. Instead of the control being in the System.Windows.Forms namespace, it is in the Microsoft.Office.Tools.Word.Controls namespace or the Microsoft.Office.Tools.Excel.Controls namespace, depending on which application you're using.

The document (or worksheet) does not know anything about Windows Forms controls or their behaviors. ActiveX controls are the only thing that documents are aware of. Therefore, the Windows Forms control is not actually placed directly on the document; instead, the control is placed inside an ActiveX control, which in turn is placed on the document.

Actually, there is a third layer of indirection called the ContainerControl. The ActiveX control is hosted on the document and contains the ContainerControl, which contains VSTO's version of the Windows Forms control. But all you and your users see is the Windows Forms control. There is evidence of this, however, in an Excel worksheet. When you add a control, such as a Button, to the worksheet at design time, you'll notice that the formula bar contains the following text, as shown in Figure 8.28:

```
=EMBED("WinForms.Control.Host","")
```

This formula should not be deleted or altered in any way.

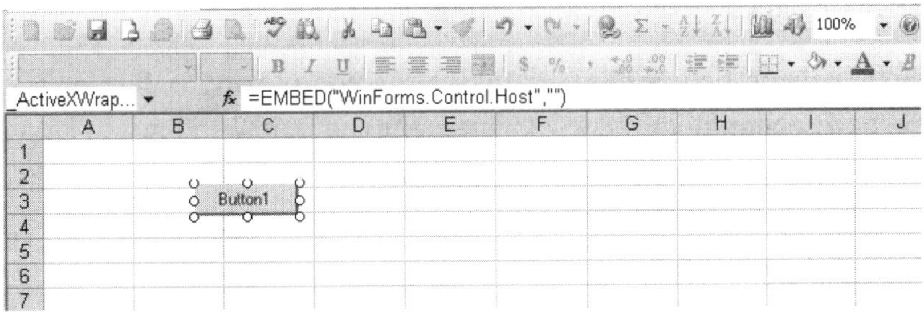

Figure 8.28. *Controls on a worksheet*

Some of the behaviors of the control on a document differ from those of controls on a Windows Form. For example, if you set the positioning properties of the control, they are really being set in relationship to their parent object—the ActiveX control (or ContainerControl)—rather than the document, as you might expect.

One more thing you should keep in mind is that although we've listed the types of Windows Forms controls that are available on the Toolbox when the document is the designer—and some of the controls were removed—this doesn't mean that you cannot add these controls to your document. It just means that you cannot add them to the document surface at design time. VSTO provides a way for you to add these controls to the document at run time by using the AddControl helper method.

Adding Controls at Run Time

Under some circumstances you might want to add controls to a document or worksheet at run time. For example, you might want to give users the ability to select where on the document a control will be added. To do this, you would insert the control at the user's current cursor location. Instead of adding a control by creating a new instance of it, you use a VSTO helper method, such as the AddTextBox method, to add a text box to the document. VSTO helper methods are members of the Controls collection.

These helper methods exist because of the complexity of Windows Forms controls on documents. Remember that the Windows Forms control is not added directly to the document but instead is embedded inside an ActiveX control that is added to the document; as a result, the VSTO helper methods make it easy for you to add controls to the document. These helper methods have overloads so that you can provide a specific range or position where the control will be placed. In Word, controls can be added so that they are either inline with text or floating at a specific position. In Excel, controls can be added to a specific range or floating at a specific position.

In this section, you'll create a simple example that lets users add Windows Forms controls to a document. First, we'll create a user control that supplies some control options and an Insert button that will insert the selected control into the document at the cursor location. This user control will be displayed on the actions pane.

1. Create a Word Template project using VSTO.

2. Right-click the Word solution, point to Add, and then click User Control.

> ❖ **Note** The UI for creating projects might differ depending on the profile you selected when you installed Visual Studio.

3. Keep the default name UserControl1, and click Add.

4. Add a ComboBox control to the user control.

5. Select the ComboBox on the user control, and scroll to the Items property in the Properties window.

6. Click the ellipsis next to (Collection) to open the String Collection Editor. As shown in Figure 8.29, add the following items: ComboBox, DateTimePicker, and TextBox.

Figure 8.29. *Adding items to a combo box in the String Collection Editor*

7. Add a Button control to the user control, and change the Text property to *Insert*.

8. Add the code in Listing 8.14 to the Click event handler of the Button control. Notice that a variable called ControlCounter is declared at the class level (outside the Click event handler of Button1).

Listing 8.14. *Adding selected controls to the current cursor location in a Word document*

```
Dim ControlCounter As Integer = 0

Private Sub Button1_Click(ByVal sender As System.Object, _
    ByVal e As System.EventArgs) Handles Button1.Click

    Dim Selection As Word.Selection = _
        Globals.ThisDocument.Application.Selection

    ' Create a new name for the control
    Dim ControlName As String = "Control" & _
        ControlCounter.ToString()
    ControlCounter += 1

    Select Case Me.ComboBox1.Text
        Case "ComboBox"
            Dim MyComboBox As Microsoft.Office.Tools.Word _
                .Controls.ComboBox = Globals.ThisDocument _
                .Controls.AddComboBox(Selection.Range, _
                100, 50, ControlName)

            With MyComboBox.Items
                .Add("First Item")
                .Add("Second Item")
                .Add("Third Item")
            End With
        Case "DateTimePicker"
            Dim MyDateTimePicker As Microsoft.Office.Tools.Word _
                .Controls.DateTimePicker = Globals.ThisDocument _
```

```
            .Controls.AddDateTimePicker(Selection.Range, _
            100, 25, ControlName)
      Case "TextBox"
         Dim MyButton As Microsoft.Office.Tools.Word.Controls _
            .TextBox = Globals.ThisDocument.Controls _
            .AddTextBox(Selection.Range, 100, 50, ControlName)
   End Select
End Sub
```

Now add the code in Listing 8.15 to the Startup event handler of ThisDocument to add the user control to the actions pane when the document is initialized.

Listing 8.15. *Displaying a custom user control on the actions pane*

```
Dim myUserControl As New UserControl1

Private Sub ThisDocument_Startup(ByVal sender As Object, _
   ByVal e As System.EventArgs) Handles Me.Startup

   Me.ActionsPane.Controls.Add(myUserControl)

End Sub
```

When you press F5 to run this code, the custom user control will be displayed on the Custom Document task pane. Select a control in the combo box, and click Insert to insert the selected control at your current cursor location within the document. Figure 8.30 demonstrates.

You might want to extend this code sample to add functionality. For example, you might want to display additional options on the actions pane when a particular control is selected. If the user selects a combo box, you should provide a UI where the user can add the items that will be displayed in the combo box after it has been added to the document.

You might also want to add a control dynamically to a document when you want to temporarily provide functionality to users. For example, you might want to display a control only when users move the cursor into a

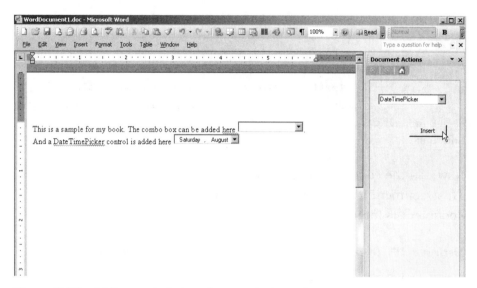

Figure 8.30. *Adding controls to a document at run time*

particular area. After users add or select data in the control, you can add the selected item to the document and remove the control. Here's how.

1. Create an Excel project using VSTO.

2. Add a NamedRange control to cell B2 on Sheet1, and call the control NamedRange1.

3. Add the code in Listing 8.16 to the Sheet1 class.

Listing 8.16. *Displaying a custom user control on the actions pane*

```
Dim myComboBox As Microsoft.Office.Tools.Excel.Controls.ComboBox

Private Sub NamedRange1_Selected(ByVal Target As _
    Microsoft.Office.Interop.Excel.Range) _
    Handles NamedRange1.Selected

    myComboBox = Me.Controls.AddComboBox( _
        NamedRange1.InnerObject, "myComboBox")
```

```
    With myComboBox.Items
        .Add("First Item")
        .Add("Second Item")
        .Add("Third Item")
    End With
End Sub


Private Sub NamedRange1_Deselected(ByVal Target As _
    Microsoft.Office.Interop.Excel.Range) Handles _
    NamedRange1.Deselected

    Me.NamedRange1.Value = myComboBox.SelectedItem
    myComboBox.Delete()

End Sub
```

First, we declared the variable for a Microsoft.Office.Tools.Excel.Controls.ComboBox at the class level of Sheet1. This makes the variable visible to both the Selected and the Deselected event handlers of the named range. In the Selected event handler of NamedRange1, we added code to add a combo box control to the named range, and then we set some strings to be added to the combo box. In the Deselected event handler of NamedRange1, we added code to assign the text selected in the combo box to the named range, and then we deleted the control.

This code, however, resets the combo box each time the named range is selected. Instead, you should add code to insert the current value of the named range into the combo box. Replace the code in the Selected event handler with the code in Listing 8.17. The new code appears in bold font.

Listing 8.17. *Setting the combo box text to the value of NamedRange1*

```
Private Sub NamedRange1_Selected(ByVal Target As _
    Microsoft.Office.Interop.Excel.Range) _
    Handles NamedRange1.Selected
```

```
myComboBox = Me.Controls.AddComboBox( _
    NamedRange1.InnerObject, "myComboBox")

With myComboBox.Items
    .Add("First Item")
    .Add("Second Item")
    .Add("Third Item")
End With

If Me.NamedRange1.Value <> String.Empty Then
    myComboBox.Text = Me.NamedRange1.Value
    Me.NamedRange1.Value = String.Empty
End If

End Sub
```

A number of helper methods are available for adding controls to a document. To see all the controls available, type the following in the Code Editor:

```
Me.Controls.Add
```

IntelliSense will display all the helper methods available, as shown in Figure 8.31.

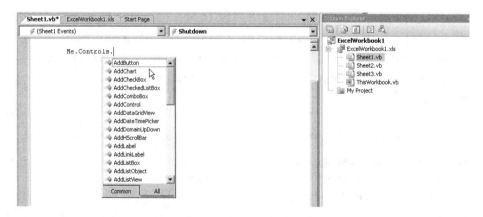

Figure 8.31. *Helper methods for adding Windows Forms controls*

For those controls that do not have a helper method, you can use the generic AddControl method. When you use this method, you are essentially working with two different controls: a custom control that you want to add to the document, and a corresponding OLEControl (or OLEObject in the case of Excel). Together, these two controls make up a VSTO control.

There are complexities in using the AddControl method (which do not exist when you use the specific helper methods, such as AddButton). For example, when you call a method or set a property of the control, you must make sure that you are referencing the correct control. Here's the rule of thumb: For methods and properties that are available on both controls, access these members through the OLEControl (or OLEObject in the case of Excel); otherwise, access the members through the custom control. The code in Listing 8.18 adds the custom user control (see Figure 8.27) to the document at run time.

Listing 8.18. *Dynamically adding a control to a document using AddControl*

```
Private Sub Sheet1_Startup(ByVal sender As Object, _
    ByVal e As System.EventArgs) Handles Me.Startup

    Dim customUserControl As New UserControl1()

    Dim OLEControl As Microsoft.Office.Tools.Excel.OLEObject = _
        Me.Controls.AddControl(customUserControl, 0, 0, 180, _
        80, "OLEControl")

End Sub
```

Functionality of Windows Forms Controls on Documents

The behavior of Windows Forms controls on a document is pretty much the same as the behavior of the same controls on a Windows Form. You can access the same methods and properties of the control, bind data to it, and write code against its events. But there are also some limitations of controls on a Word document or Excel worksheet that do not exist with controls on a Windows Form. Some of the limitations include the inability to zoom a document, tab through controls, and set their positioning properties.

On a Windows Form, there is no reason to change the zoom of a control, and thus this feature is not supported. This contradicts the functionality needed inside a document. If you set the zoom of the document to anything other than 100% (whether you're reducing or increasing the zoom), the VSTO control no longer functions correctly. The representation of the control remains intact and appears larger or smaller, depending on your zoom settings, but you cannot use any of the control's functionality, such as changing a date in a DateTimePicker control or clicking a Button. To regain functionality, you must reset the zoom percentage to 100%. This requirement can present an accessibility issue. If a user increases the zoom to enlarge the characters and thus see the document more clearly, the functionality of the control—and your solution—will not work.

Because the Windows Forms controls are hosted within a Container-Control, you cannot set the control's tab order or even tab from control to control on the document. Neither can you set positioning properties such as Left, Top, Height, or Width.

Whether the Windows Forms controls are added to the document at design time or run time, they are added to the ControlCollection of the document or worksheet. This collection holds Windows Forms controls as well as host controls that are added to the document. Persistence of the dynamic Windows Forms controls differs from the persistence of a dynamic host control on a document.

Dynamic Control Persistence

Windows Forms controls that are created dynamically are persisted in a document in the same way they are persisted on a Windows Form:

They're not persisted at all! Following the model of a Windows application, when the application is closed, any controls that were created at run time are removed from the Form and re-created only the next time the code that created them is run again (when the application opens again). This same model is followed for controls on a document. It doesn't seem to make sense at first, because the behavior of a document is different from that of a Windows application. A user who adds anything to the document expects to see that object or text in the document the next time the document is opened. The user doesn't really have any concept of design time versus run time, and it is important that you take this into account when designing your applications.

If it is important for dynamically created Windows Forms controls to be on the document the next time it is opened, then you must write additional code to re-create the controls. One solution is to cache information about the controls, including their location, and then read the document cache the next time the user opens the document so that you can re-create the controls. In Chapter 12 you'll learn more about caching data in the document.

Summary

We started this chapter with a look at adding buttons to Word and Excel toolbars and menus, and we showed you how to add your own custom graphics to be used on the buttons. Next, you learned about the controls that are available on the Toolbox when a Windows Form is the designer and when a document or worksheet is the designer, and which controls are filtered from use on a document at design time.

We then looked at adding controls to a Windows Form so that you can display a UI in the form of a dialog box, and you saw how you can reuse the controls on the task pane. Finally, we explored the use of controls on a Word document or Excel worksheet, and you learned how to add these controls at design time, bind them to data, and create them dynamically at run time.

Review Questions

1. Why should you create a variable for a CommandBarButton at the class level?

2. How do you add a bitmap to a CommandBarButton?

3. How do you create a mask for your bitmap, and what functionality does the mask provide?

4. What advantages are there in creating a user control when you're designing your solution's UI?

5. What are some reasons you might choose to add controls to a document at run time instead of design time?

6. How do controls that are created dynamically at run time get persisted with a document?

7. How does the AddControl helper method differ from all the other helper methods available for adding Windows Forms controls to a document?

9

Smart Tags in Word and Excel

*Every moment is a golden one for him who
has the vision to recognize it as such.*
—Henry Miller

Topics Covered in This Chapter

What Is a Smart Tag?

Smart tags are a Microsoft Office feature that can be programmed
to recognize certain text and then present users with actions they
can take related to the text. Smart tags implement two interfaces:
ISmartTagRecognizer (the *recognizer*) and ISmartTagAction (the action).

Microsoft Word and Excel include a number of built-in smart tags. For
example, if you type a person's first and last names into a Word document, Word places a red dotted line underneath the name, indicating
that a smart tag has been created for this text, which is recognized as a

417

name. When you move your cursor over the name, a Smart Tag Actions button with an information symbol appears above the name. When the Smart Tag Actions button is selected, a drop-down arrow is revealed. When you click the drop-down arrow, a list appears showing a number of actions associated with the smart tag, such as sending an e-mail or scheduling a meeting, as shown in Figure 9.1.

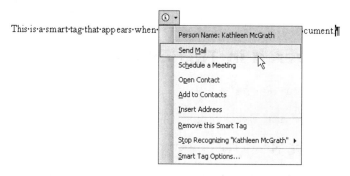

This·is·a·smart·tag·that·appears·when·

| Person Name: Kathleen McGrath |
| Send Mail |
| Schedule a Meeting |
| Open Contact |
| Add to Contacts |
| Insert Address |
| Remove this Smart Tag |
| Stop Recognizing "Kathleen McGrath" ▸ |
| Smart Tag Options... |

Figure 9.1. *Built-in smart tag in Word*

Users can turn off these smart tag options in the AutoCorrect Options dialog box. To open this dialog box, click AutoCorrect Options in the Tools menu. On the Smart Tags tab are two options you should be aware of. The first is the Label Text With Smart Tags check box. When this option is selected, the dotted line will appear under recognized words. The second is the Show Smart Tag Actions Buttons check box. When this check box is selected, recognized words display the Smart Tag Actions button whenever the cursor is above the recognized word. If these options are not selected, the smart tags will not be visible to end users. Figure 9.2 shows these options.

Because these settings can be changed by the end user, you might want to add code to the Startup event handler of ThisDocument, as shown in Listing 9.1. This code ensures that these settings are turned on when you provide smart tags as part of your solution.

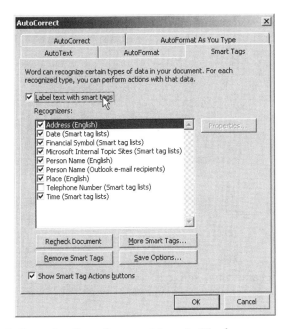

Figure 9.2. *AutoCorrect options for smart tags in Word*

Listing 9.1. *Ensuring that Word smart tag options are turned on at startup*

```
Private Sub ThisDocument_Startup(ByVal sender As Object, _
    ByVal e As System.EventArgs) Handles Me.Startup

    Me.Application.Options.LabelSmartTags = True
    Me.Application.Options.DisplaySmartTagButtons = True

End Sub
```

Rather than change a user's settings (this is not always a good thing to do!), you should probably prompt users to let them know that they need to have these settings turned on to use your solution. You'll see an example in Listing 9.2.

Excel also provides a number of built-in smart tags. For example, text recognized, such as a date in an Excel cell, displays a small triangle in the lower-right corner of the cell. In our example, users can choose an action associated with the recognized date; in this case, they can open the Outlook calendar to the date, as shown in Figure 9.3.

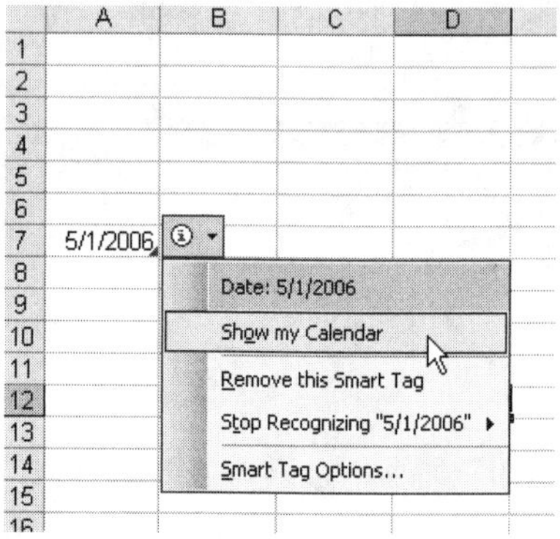

Figure 9.3. *Built-in smart tag in Excel*

In Excel, the smart tag settings are also found in the AutoCorrect options, as shown in Figure 9.4. Selecting the Label Data With Smart Tags check box causes Excel to recognize the term. You can set the

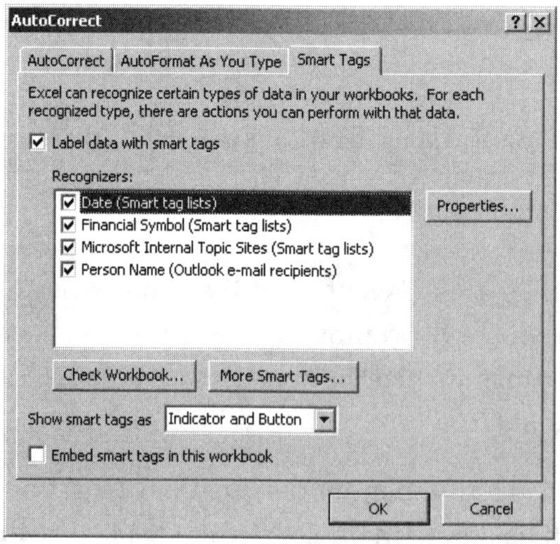

Figure 9.4. *Smart tag options in Excel*

Show Smart Tags As combo box to display any of three combinations: the smart tag indicator (the small triangle) and the Smart Tag Actions button; the button alone; or neither.

Because users can change these options, you should check to see whether these options are set and, if they aren't, let users change these settings, as shown in Listing 9.2. Be sure to restore users' options when the solution is closed.

Listing 9.2. *Ensuring that Excel smart tag options are turned on at startup*

```
Private Sub ThisWorkbook_Startup(ByVal sender As Object, _
    ByVal e As System.EventArgs) Handles Me.Startup

    If Application.AutoCorrect.DisplayAutoCorrectOptions = _
        False Then

        If MsgBox("This document uses smart tags, " _
            & "which are currently disabled. Do you want to " _
            & " enable smart tags?", MsgBoxStyle.YesNo) = _
            MsgBoxResult.Yes Then

            Application.AutoCorrect.DisplayAutoCorrectOptions = _
                True
            Me.SmartTagOptions.DisplaySmartTags = _
                Excel.XlSmartTagDisplayMode.xlIndicatorAndButton

        End If
    End If

End Sub
```

Both Word and Excel have a number of built-in recognizers that you can enable or disable. In addition, you can create your own document-level smart tags with VSTO. These smart tags differ from Office smart tags in that they are available only to the specific document or workbook in which you define them. Although you can create application-level smart tags using a COM or managed shared add-in, VSTO supports only document-level smart tags, and this type of smart tag is the focus of this chapter.

Creating Word and Excel Smart Tags with VSTO

Because VSTO smart tags are available only to the document or workbook in which you add them, you can scope the smart tags to a specific solution rather than create smart tags that might be available to any document that is opened.

VSTO provides two smart tag classes (Microsoft.Office.Tools.Excel.SmartTag and Microsoft.Office.Tools.Word.SmartTag) that enable you to add smart tags to your document or workbook. You enable Word or Excel to recognize certain terms by using these classes to add strings to the Terms property or to add regular expressions to the Expressions property of the smart tag. You'll learn more about regular expressions later in this chapter in "Introduction to Regular Expressions."

When you create a new smart tag, you create an instance of the SmartTag class and pass a unique identifier and a name (caption) for the smart tag. The identifier uses the following constructions: *URI namespace#Tag name.* For example, you might pass the following:

```
"www.aw.com/Sample#SampleSmartTag"
```

Here, the URI namespace is www.aw.com, and the tag name is Sample Smart Tag. To specify actions to be performed on the recognized text, you specify actions in the Actions property of the smart tag instance, and then you add the smart tag instance to the VstoSmartTags collection for the document. Let's look at a simple example.

1. Create an Excel workbook project with VSTO.

2. In Solution Explorer, right-click ThisWorkbook and click View Code.

3. Add the code in Listing 9.3 to the code file after the line Public Class Workbook. This code adds a variable that has events for a Microsoft.Office.Tools.Excel.Action.

Listing 9.3. *Adding a variable for a smart tag action*

```
WithEvents AddControlToActionsPane As _
    Microsoft.Office.Tools.Excel.Action
```

4. Add the code in Listing 9.4 to the Startup event handler of the ThisWorkbook class. This code turns on the smart tag feature, creates a variable named ControlSmartTag for an Excel smart tag, and then adds a number of terms to the smart tag's recognizer. The code then adds an action to the smart tag and adds the smart tag to the workbook.

Listing 9.4. *Creating a smart tag in Excel*

```
Private Sub ThisWorkbook_Startup(ByVal sender As Object, _
    ByVal e As System.EventArgs) Handles Me.Startup

    ' Ensure that smart tags in workbook will be recognized
    ' and displayed.
    Me.Application.AutoCorrect.DisplayAutoCorrectOptions = _
        True
    Me.SmartTagOptions.DisplaySmartTags = _
        Excel.XlSmartTagDisplayMode.xlIndicatorAndButton

    ' Create an instance of a smart tag, passing unique
    ' identifier and caption for the smart tag.
    Dim ControlSmartTag As New Microsoft.Office.Tools.Excel. _
        SmartTag("www.aw.com/Sample#SampleSmartTag", _
        "Control Smart Tag")

    ' Add a number of terms (strings) to be recognized.
    With ControlSmartTag
        .Terms.Add("Button")
        .Terms.Add("ComboBox")
        .Terms.Add("ListBox")
```

```
      .Terms.Add("DateTimePicker")
      .Terms.Add("MonthCalendar")
End With

' Add an action for the recognized term.
AddControlToActionsPane = New Microsoft.Office.Tools _
    .Excel.Action("Add Control to Actions Pane")

ControlSmartTag.Actions = New Microsoft.Office.Tools.Excel _
    .Action() {AddControlToActionsPane}

' Add the smart tag to the VstoSmartTags collection.
Me.VstoSmartTags.Add(ControlSmartTag)

End Sub
```

The terms that we added to the smart tag are control names. The action we'll create for the smart tag will add the selected control to the actions pane. Add code to the Click event handler of the AddControlToActionsPane action, which will add the control to the actions pane, as shown in Listing 9.5. This code should also be added to the ThisWorkbook class.

Listing 9.5. *Adding code to event handlers of the action*

```
Private Sub AddControlToActionsPane_Click( _
    ByVal sender As Object, _
    ByVal e As Microsoft.Office.Tools.Excel.ActionEventArgs) _
    Handles AddControlToActionsPane.Click

    Select Case e.Text
        Case "Button"
            Me.ActionsPane.Controls.Add(New Button)
        Case "ComboBox"
            Me.ActionsPane.Controls.Add(New ComboBox)
        Case "ListBox"
            Me.ActionsPane.Controls.Add(New ListBox)
        Case "DateTimePicker"
            Me.ActionsPane.Controls.Add(New DateTimePicker)
```

```
      Case ("MonthCalendar")
          Me.ActionsPane.Controls.Add(New MonthCalendar)
    End Select

End Sub
```

5. Next, right-click Sheet1 in Solution Explorer, and then click View Designer.

6. Add the following words to cells in Sheet1, as shown in Figure 9.5: Button, ComboBox, ListBox, DateTimePicker, MonthCalendar.

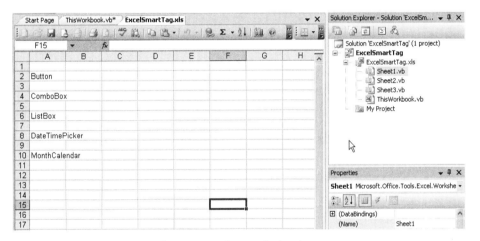

Figure 9.5. *Adding control names to the worksheet*

7. Press F5 to run the code.

When the solution runs, you'll notice that all the cells that contain control names have a smart tag indicator (the little triangle). When you move your cursor above the cell, the Smart Tag Actions button becomes visible. If you select the drop-down arrow on this button, an action called Add Control to Actions Pane appears. When you click the action, the control is added to the actions pane. Figure 9.6 illustrates this with a number of controls added to the actions pane.

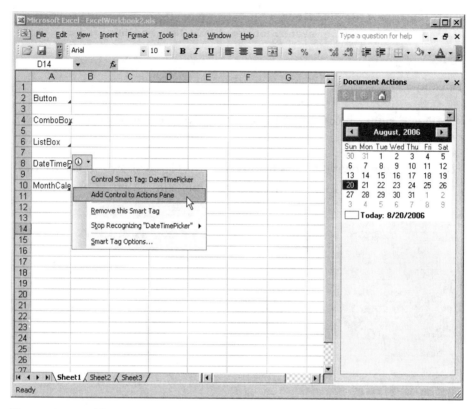

Figure 9.6. *Adding controls to the actions pane via a smart tag*

Understanding Smart Tag Properties

As you saw in the preceding section, there are a number of properties of a smart tag that can be set (or read, in the case of read-only properties). The following properties are available on a smart tag.

Actions Property

The Actions property enables you to get or set a number of smart tag actions. You can create multiple Microsoft.Office.Tools.Excel.Action objects (or Microsoft.Office.Tools.Word.Action objects) by passing an array of actions to the Actions property. In Listing 9.4 you pass an array of actions that contain a single element: the AddControlToActionsPane action.

Caption Property

The Caption property is a read-only property that enables you to retrieve the text that is displayed at the top of the smart tag menu. The Caption property is set when you create the smart tag, and it passes the smart tag's unique namespace identifier and caption. In the example in Listing 9.4, the caption passed is "Control Smart Tag." It is displayed at the top of the Smart Tag menu, followed by the recognized term or expression, as shown in Figure 9.7.

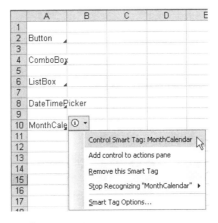

Figure 9.7. *The caption of a smart tag*

Expressions Property

The Expressions property enables you to add a collection of regular expressions to the smart tag. You use the Add method to add regular expressions to the collection. Regular expressions are described later in this chapter.

SmartTagType Property

Using the read-only SmartTagType property, you can retrieve the smart tag's unique namespace identifier. The SmartTagType property is set when you create the smart tag and pass its unique namespace identifier and caption. In the example in Listing 9.4, the unique namespace identifier is

```
"www.aw.com/Sample#SampleSmartTag"
```

Terms Property

The Terms property enables you to add terms (individual words you want recognized) to the smart tag. Note that they must be individual words, because terms cannot contain spaces. In the example in Listing 9.4, the added terms include "ComboBox" but not "combo box." We did this for two reasons: The control name itself does not have a space, and the Terms property recognizes only a single word. If you want to add a phrase to be recognized, you can either create a regular expression or create your own recognizer. Both techniques are discussed later in this chapter.

Taking Action on a Smart Tag

The reason you add a smart tag to a particular term or phrase is to allow users to take further action based on the recognized term. For example, with Word's built-in smart tags, you can send an e-mail addressed to the recognized name, add the name to your contact list, schedule a meeting with the person, and so on.

You can also create multiple actions for the smart tags that you create. You do this by passing an array of actions to the smart tag's Actions property. Because you must pass an array of actions, the maximum number of actions a smart tag can display is predetermined, and you cannot add actions dynamically.

Using the code example in Listing 9.4, let's add another action. First, we add another variable with events for an action. The new code is displayed in bold font in Listing 9.6.

Listing 9.6. *Adding a variable for a smart tag action*

```
WithEvents AddControlToActionsPane As _
    Microsoft.Office.Tools.Excel.Action

WithEvents AddControlToDocument As _
    Microsoft.Office.Tools.Excel.Action
```

Next, add the code in bold font in Listing 9.7 to the Startup event handler of ThisWorkbook. This code creates a new action and passes it to the Actions property of the smart tag as another element in the array of actions.

Listing 9.7. *Creating a smart tag in Excel*

```
Private Sub ThisWorkbook_Startup(ByVal sender As Object, _
    ByVal e As System.EventArgs) Handles Me.Startup

    ' Ensure that smart tags in workbook will be recognized and
    ' displayed.
    Me.Application.AutoCorrect.DisplayAutoCorrectOptions = True
    Me.SmartTagOptions.DisplaySmartTags = _
        Excel.XlSmartTagDisplayMode.xlIndicatorAndButton

    ' Create an instance of a smart tag, passing unique
    ' identifier and caption for the smart tag.
    Dim ControlSmartTag As New Microsoft.Office.Tools.Excel. _
        SmartTag("www.aw.com/Sample#SampleSmartTag", _
        "Control Smart Tag")

    ' Add a number of terms (strings) to be recognized.
    With ControlSmartTag
        .Terms.Add("Button")
        .Terms.Add("ComboBox")
```

```
       .Terms.Add("ListBox")
       .Terms.Add("DateTimePicker")
       .Terms.Add("MonthCalendar")
    End With

    ' Add an action for the recognized term.
    AddControlToActionsPane = New Microsoft.Office.Tools _
        .Excel.Action("Add Control to Actions Pane")

    AddControlToDocument = New Microsoft.Office.Tools.Excel _
        .Action("Add Control to Document")

    ControlSmartTag.Actions = New Microsoft.Office.Tools.Excel _
        .Action() {AddControlToActionsPane, AddControlToDocument}

    ' Add the smart tag to the VstoSmartTags collection.
    Me.VstoSmartTags.Add(ControlSmartTag)

End Sub
```

Then add code to the click event handler of the AddControlToDocument action, as shown in Listing 9.8.

Listing 9.8. *Adding code to event handlers of an action*

```
Private Sub AddControlToActionsPane_Click(ByVal sender As _
    Object, ByVal e As Microsoft.Office.Tools.Excel. _
    ActionEventArgs) Handles AddControlToActionsPane.Click

    Select Case e.Text
        Case "Button"
            Me.ActionsPane.Controls.Add(New Button)
        Case "ComboBox"
            Me.ActionsPane.Controls.Add(New ComboBox)
        Case "ListBox"
            Me.ActionsPane.Controls.Add(New ListBox)
        Case "DateTimePicker"
            Me.ActionsPane.Controls.Add(New DateTimePicker)
```

```
        Case ("MonthCalendar")
            Me.ActionsPane.Controls.Add(New MonthCalendar)
    End Select

End Sub

Private Sub AddControlToDocument_Click(ByVal sender As Object, _
    ByVal e As Microsoft.Office.Tools.Excel.ActionEventArgs) _
    Handles AddControlToDocument.Click

    Select Case e.Text
        Case "Button"
            Globals.Sheet1.Controls.AddButton(e.Range, _
                "Control" & (Globals.Sheet1.Controls.Count + _
                1).ToString)
        Case "ComboBox"
            Globals.Sheet1.Controls.AddComboBox(e.Range, _
                "Control" & (Globals.Sheet1.Controls.Count + _
                1).ToString)
        Case "ListBox"
             Globals.Sheet1.Controls.AddListBox(e.Range, _
                "Control" & (Globals.Sheet1.Controls.Count + _
                1).ToString)
        Case "DateTimePicker"
            Globals.Sheet1.Controls.AddDateTimePicker(e.Range, _
                "Control" & (Globals.Sheet1.Controls.Count + _
                1).ToString)
        Case ("MonthCalendar")
            Globals.Sheet1.Controls.AddMonthCalendar(e.Range, _
                "Control" & (Globals.Sheet1.Controls.Count + _
                1).ToString)
    End Select

    e.Range.Value = ""

End Sub
```

Now when you run this code and the control names are recognized, you are given two actions in the Smart Tag Actions button, as shown in Figure 9.8: adding the control to the action pane, and adding the control to the document in place of the smart tag.

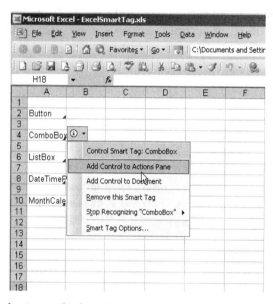

Figure 9.8. *Displaying multiple actions in a smart tag*

Figure 9.9 shows the document with a combo box added to the actions pane, and a month calendar control added to the document.

Suppose you want to change the caption in the Smart Tag Actions button drop-down menu to a cascading menu. To do this, you append a main caption followed by three forward slashes (///) to the action caption. For example, in our smart tag code sample, we have two captions: "Add Control to Actions Pane" and "Add Control to Document." You can change this so that the main caption reads "Add Control" and then the cascading menu contains two items: "to Actions Pane" and "to Document." Change the code in the Startup event handler of ThisWorkbook to match the bold code in Listing 9.9.

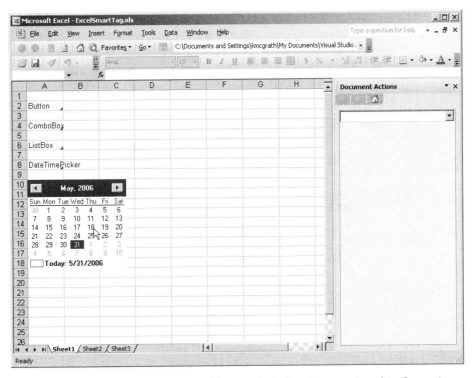

Figure 9.9. *Using a smart tag to add controls to the document and to the actions pane*

Listing 9.9. *Creating a smart tag in Excel*

```
Private Sub ThisWorkbook_Startup(ByVal sender As Object, _
    ByVal e As System.EventArgs) Handles Me.Startup

    ' Ensure that smart tags in workbook will be recognized and
    ' displayed.
    Me.Application.AutoCorrect.DisplayAutoCorrectOptions = True
    Me.SmartTagOptions.DisplaySmartTags = _
        Excel.XlSmartTagDisplayMode.xlIndicatorAndButton

    ' Create an instance of a smart tag, passing unique
    ' identifier and caption for the smart tag.
    Dim ControlSmartTag As New Microsoft.Office.Tools.Excel. _
        SmartTag("www.aw.com/Sample#SampleSmartTag", _
        "Control Smart Tag")
```

```
' Add a number of terms (strings) to be recognized.
With ControlSmartTag
    .Terms.Add("Button")
    .Terms.Add("ComboBox")
    .Terms.Add("ListBox")
    .Terms.Add("DateTimePicker")
    .Terms.Add("MonthCalendar")
End With

' Add an action for the recognized term.
AddControlToActionsPane = New Microsoft.Office.Tools.Excel. _
    Action("Add Control///to Actions Pane")

AddControlToDocument = New Microsoft.Office.Tools.Excel _
    .Action("Add Control///to Document")

ControlSmartTag.Actions = New Microsoft.Office.Tools.Excel _
    .Action() {AddControlToActionsPane, AddControlToDocument}

' Add the smart tag to the VstoSmartTags collection.
Me.VstoSmartTags.Add(ControlSmartTag)

End Sub
```

When you run the code, the Smart Tag Actions button will contain the options shown in Figure 9.10.

Events Available for an Action

The Action object exposes two events. The first is the Click event, where you write the code that handles the event when a user clicks an action on a smart tag. You saw examples of this earlier in this section.

The second event is BeforeCaptionShow. This event enables you to change the caption for an action when the user clicks the Smart Tag Action button, before the menu is shown. For example, you might want to vary the caption title that is shown based on the context of the docu-

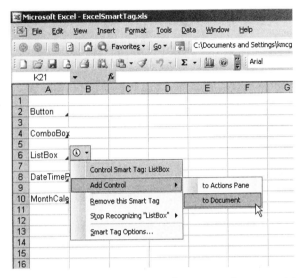

Figure 9.10. *Displaying actions in a cascading menu in a smart tag*

ment. The code in Listing 9.10 displays one caption if the current cursor location is within a Word table; otherwise, it displays a different caption.

Listing 9.10. *Using the Caption property of an Action object*

```
Private Sub ShowTableProperties_BeforeCaptionShow(ByVal sender _
    As Object, ByVal e As Microsoft.Office.Tools. _
        Word.ActionEventArgs) Handles _
        ShowTableProperties.BeforeCaptionShow

    If Globals.ThisDocument.Application.Selection.Information( _
        Word.WdInformation.wdWithInTable) Then

        ShowTableProperties.Caption = "Show Table Properties"
    Else
        ShowTableProperties.Caption = _
            "Show Table Properties (if cursor is within a table)"
    End If

End Sub
```

Introduction to Regular Expressions

Regular expressions are a powerful way of matching patterns of text. In its simplest form, you can use a regular expression to recognize a string of words (a phrase). Regular expressions can also be used to recognize complex text patterns, such as addresses, phone numbers, zip codes, and so on. In this section, we look at how you can use regular expressions with smart tags in Word and Excel.

Using Regular Expressions to Recognize Phrases

As mentioned earlier, you shouldn't add a phrase (multiple words) to the Terms property of a smart tag because the tokens they are matched against contain only one word and thus a match will never be found. One way to have your solution recognize multiple words that are separated by spaces is to add the phrase as a regular expression to the smart tag's Expressions property.

In VSTO, there are several objects, such as SmartTags, ListObjects, and ActionsPanes, that are named by concatenating strings. When used generically, these objects are spelled with a space between words (smart tags, list objects, and actions panes). If you want to create smart tags for each of these spellings, you can use the Terms property for the individual words and use the Expressions property for phrases.

In this section you'll use regular expressions to create a Word customization that recognizes terms and phrases. When the expression is recognized, the smart tag will enable you to perform searches on Windows Live Search for additional information about the recognized text. The search results are displayed in a Web browser control on the actions pane.

Creating the Word Project with VSTO

1. Create a Word document project with VSTO.

2. Right-click the project in Solution Explorer, point to Add, and click New Item.

3. In the New Item dialog box, select Actions Pane Control, and leave the default name ActionsPaneControl1.

4. Drag a WebBrowser control from the Toolbox to the actions pane control, and change the Dock property to Fill.

Creating Smart Tags Using Regular Expressions

1. In Solution Explorer, right-click ThisDocument and click View Code.

2. At the top of the code file, import System.Text.RegularExpressions, and then add three class-level variables for the Action, URL string, and actions pane control, as shown in Listing 9.11.

Listing 9.11. *Adding terms and expressions to a smart tag*

```
Imports System.Text.RegularExpressions

Public Class ThisDocument

    ' Create class-level variables.
    WithEvents LiveSearch As Microsoft.Office.Tools.Word.Action
    Dim url As String
    Dim ap As New ActionsPaneControl1
```

3. In the Startup event handler of ThisDocument, add the code in Listing 9.12. This code creates the smart tag, adds words and phrases to be recognized, adds the action, and changes the position and size of the task pane.

Listing 9.12. *Creating a smart tag with terms and regular expressions*

```
Private Sub ThisDocument_Startup(ByVal sender As Object, _
    ByVal e As System.EventArgs) Handles Me.Startup

    ' Create new smart tag.
    Dim mySmartTag As New Microsoft.Office.Tools.Word.SmartTag( _
        "http://www.sample.com#sample", "sample")
```

```
' Add individual words to be recognized as terms.
mySmartTag.Terms.Add("ActionsPane")
mySmartTag.Terms.Add("SmartTag")
mySmartTag.Terms.Add("ListObject")

' Add phrases to be recognized as regular expressions. The
' \b indicates a word boundary.
mySmartTag.Expressions.Add(New Regex("\bactions pane\b"))
mySmartTag.Expressions.Add(New Regex("\blist object\b"))
mySmartTag.Expressions.Add(New Regex("\bsmart tag\b"))

' Create the action and add it to the smart tag.
LiveSearch = New Microsoft.Office.Tools.Word.Action( _
    "Windows Live Search")
mySmartTag.Actions = New _
    Microsoft.Office.Tools.Word.Action(){LiveSearch}
Me.VstoSmartTags.Add(mySmartTag)

' Change the position of the task pane to dock at the
' top of the document, and set its height and the
' height of the actions pane control.
Me.CommandBars("Task Pane").Position = _
    Microsoft.Office.Core.MsoBarPosition.msoBarTop
Me.CommandBars("Task Pane").Height = 300
ap.Height = 300
End Sub
```

4. In the Click event handler of the LiveSearch action, create the
   search string using the recognized text, and pass it to an
   OpenActionsPane method to display the search results in the
   actions pane, as shown in Listing 9.13.

Listing 9.13. *Passing the URL to the Web browser control on the actions pane*

```
' Set the URL for the WebBrowser and show it on the actions pane.
Private Sub LiveSearch_Click(ByVal sender As Object, ByVal e _
    As Microsoft.Office.Tools.Word.ActionEventArgs) _
    Handles LiveSearch.Click
```

```
    url = "http://search.live.com/results.aspx?q=" & e.Text
    OpenActionsPane(url)

End Sub

' Display the web browser control on the actions pane if it is
' not already visible; then show search results on Live Search.
Private Sub OpenActionsPane(ByVal url As String)

    If Me.ActionsPane.Controls.Count < 1 Then
        Me.ActionsPane.Controls.Add(ap)
        ap.WebBrowser1.Navigate(url)
    Else
        Application.CommandBars("Task Pane").Visible = True
        ap.WebBrowser1.Navigate(url)
    End If

End Sub
```

Running the Project Code

1. Press F5 to run the code.

2. Type the text *The actions pane is cool.* in the document.

3. Hold your cursor over the words *actions pane,* and click the
    Windows Live Search button.

When you click Windows Live Search, the actions pane will open at the
top of the document and display the search results for the words *actions
pane.* If you click the Video tab in Windows Live Search, you should see
a couple of the video demonstrations that we created regarding using
the actions pane. Your document should resemble the one in Figure 9.11.

> ❖**Note**   If the Video tab is not visible on the Windows Live Search
> page, click the drop-down titled More, and then click Video.

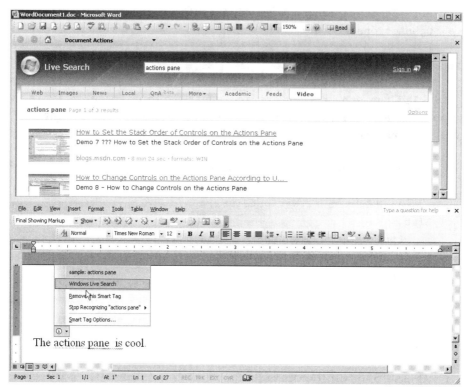

Figure 9.11. *Searching for recognized text on Windows Live Search through use of a smart tag*

Recognizing Patterns of Text

Regular expressions can also be used to search for patterns of text. For example, if you want to search for a text pattern that starts with the letter *s* and ends with the letters *rt* (so that you would find words such as *smart, start, skirt,* and *sport),* you can use a regular expression. The .NET Framework has a number of regular expression classes that can be referenced in the System.Text.RegularExpressions namespace. You can add regular expressions to the list of smart tag expressions by creating an instance of the regular expression and passing a particular pattern.

First, we create a simple smart tag and add the word *smart* as a term to recognize. Later, we convert this to a regular expression and show some of the expressions you can use to recognize text patterns.

1. Add a reference to Microsoft Smart Tags 2.0 Type Library.

2. Right-click ThisDocument, and click View Code.

3. Add the following imports statement to the top of the code file:

   ```
   Import System.Text.RegularExpressions
   ```

4. Add the code in Listing 9.14 to the ThisDocument class. This code creates a smart tag and then adds a term that the smart tag will recognize. Note that this code also replaces the Startup event handler of ThisDocument.

Listing 9.14. *Creating a simple smart tag*

```
WithEvents SampleAction As Microsoft.Office.Tools.Word.Action

Private Sub ThisDocument_Startup(ByVal sender As Object, _
    ByVal e As System.EventArgs) Handles Me.Startup

    Dim MySmartTag As New Microsoft.Office.Tools.Word.SmartTag( _
    "www.aw-bc.com/Demo#RegExExample", "RegEx Example")

    MySmartTag.Terms.Add("smart")
    SampleAction = New Microsoft.Office.Tools.Word.Action( _
        "Perform Action")

    MySmartTag.Actions = _
        New Microsoft.Office.Tools.Word.Action() {SampleAction}

    Me.VstoSmartTags.Add(MySmartTag)

End Sub
```

```
Private Sub SampleAction_Click(ByVal sender As Object, _
    ByVal e As Microsoft.Office.Tools.Word.ActionEventArgs) _
    Handles SampleAction.Click

    MsgBox("Text recognized and action performed.")

End Sub
```

5. In Solution Explorer, right-click ThisDocument and click View Designer.

6. Add the following text to the document: *Starting with Office XP, you can create smart tags that are smarter than you think. Smart tags enable you to start taking action on a recognized term.*

7. Press F5 to run the code.

8. Move your cursor over the word *smart* (it now has a dotted line below it). Click the smart tag drop-down, and then click Perform Action. A message box will appear, as shown in Figure 9.12.

Now let's replace the code that added a single term with code that adds a regular expression to the smart tag's Expressions collection. Revise the code in the Startup event handler of ThisDocument as shown in Listing 9.15. Notice that the code for adding a term has been commented out.

Listing 9.15. *Adding a regular expression to a smart tag*

```
'MySmartTag.Terms.Add("smart")

MySmartTag.Expressions.Add(New Regex("smart"))
```

When you run this code, you don't get quite the same results even though our regular expression is just a series of characters that represent the same word that we passed to the Terms collection earlier. Notice that this time, Word places a dotted line under the characters *smart* in the word *smarter*, as shown in Figure 9.13.

¶
Starting·with·Office·XP,·you·can·create·smart·tags·that·are·smarter·than·you·think.·Smart
tags·enable·you·to·start·taking·action·on·a·recognized·term.¶

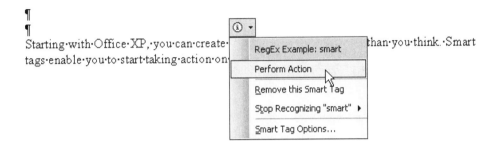

¶
¶
Starting·with·Office·XP,·you·can·create·
tags·enable·you·to·start·taking·action·on·

than·you·think.·Smart

¶
¶
Starting·with·Office·XP,·you·can·create·smart·tags·that·are·smarter·than·you·think.·Smart
tags·enable·you·to·start·taking·action·on·a·recognized·term.¶

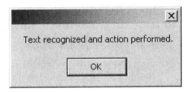

Figure 9.12. *Using a smart tag*

¶
Starting·with·Office·XP,·you·can·create·smart·tags·that·are·smarter·than·you·think.·Smart·
tags·enable·you·to·start·taking·action·on·a·recognized·term.¶

Figure 9.13. *Using a regular expression to create a simple smart tag*

The word *smarter* is recognized because with regular expressions, any
text that matches the pattern is recognized, whether or not it consti-
tutes a whole word. (As you'll see later in this chapter, you can add
expressions that limit recognition to a word boundary.) First, we add an
expression that will satisfy our original goal, which was to recognize any

word that contains any characters between an *s* and *rt*. In Listing 9.16, we change the code that adds the regular expression so that we supply a pattern that recognizes any characters between the *s* and *rt*.

Listing 9.16. *Adding a regular expression to the Expressions collection of a smart tag*

```
MySmartTag.Expressions.Add(New Regex("s+[a-z]+rt"))
```

Using [a-z] indicates that we are looking for a pattern of any characters that fall between *a* and *z*. This time, in addition to the original recognized text, the word *start* is recognized, as shown in Figure 9.14.

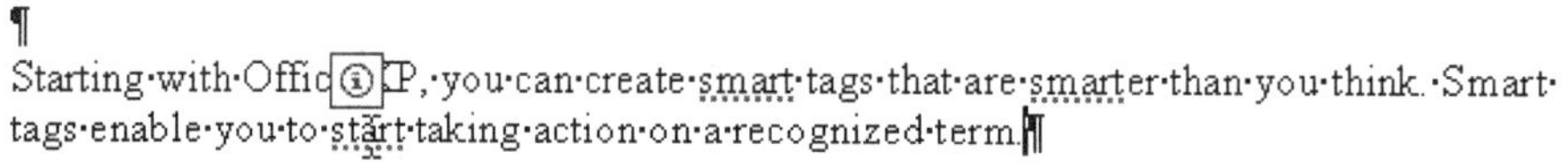

¶
Starting·with·Offic[ⓘ]P,·you·can·create·smart·tags·that·are·smarter·than·you·think. ·Smart·tags·enable·you·to·start·taking·action·on·a·recognized·term.¶

Figure 9.14. *Creating a simple smart tag with an [a-z] regular expression*

You might have noticed that the first word in the sentence (*Starting*) and the first word in the second sentence (*Smart*) were not recognized as smart tags. This is because both of these words start with a capital letter *S*. If you want your regular expression to include uppercase *S* as well as lowercase *s*, you can use the code shown in Listing 9.17. Here, we add a pipe character between the two choices and surround the choices with parentheses: (s|S).

Listing 9.17. *Recognizing lower- and uppercase characters*

```
MySmartTag.Expressions.Add(New Regex("(s|S)+[a-z]+rt"))
```

Now, all instances of words that have any characters between an *s* and *rt* are recognized whether the word starts with a lowercase *s* or an uppercase *S*, as shown in Figure 9.15.

Finally, if you want to change the regular expression so that only words that end in *rt* are recognized (complete words), you can add "\b" to the expression (indicating a word boundary), as shown in Listing 9.18.

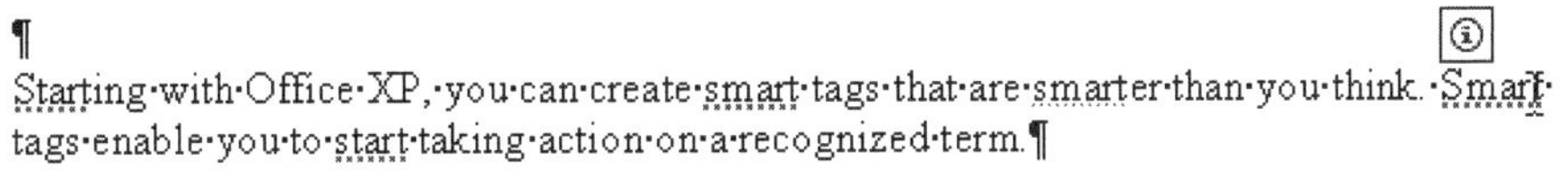

¶
Starting·with·Office·XP,·you·can·create·smart·tags·that·are·smarter·than·you·think.·Smart· tags·enable·you·to·start·taking·action·on·a·recognized·term.¶

Figure 9.15. *Enabling the smart tag to recognize both upper- and lowercase S using (s|S)*

Listing 9.18. *Recognizing word boundaries*

```
MySmartTag.Expressions.Add(New Regex("(s|S)+[a-z]+rt\b"))
```

Now when you run this code, only words that start with *s* or *S* and end with *rt* are recognized, as shown in Figure 9.16.

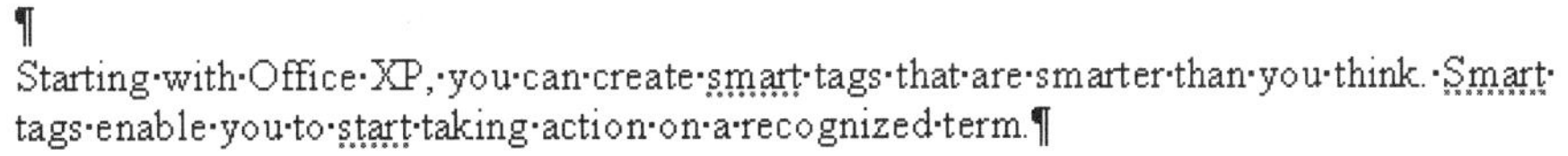

¶
Starting·with·Office·XP,·you·can·create·smart·tags·that·are·smarter·than·you·think.·Smart· tags·enable·you·to·start·taking·action·on·a·recognized·term.¶

Figure 9.16. *Enabling the smart tag to recognize words that start with s or S and end with rt*

You can use regular expressions to create many other patterns. Table 9.1 lists some of the more common expressions.

Table 9.1. *Regular Expressions*

Description	Expression
Match any single character	.
Match zero or more instances of preceding expression	*
Match one or more instances of preceding expression	+
Match any character within a set	[ ]
Match any character not in the set	[^]
Match any alphanumeric character	[a-zA-Z0-9]
Match any alphabetic character	[a-zA-Z]

(continues)

Table 9.1. *Regular Expressions (Continued)*

Description	Expression
Match any numeric character	[0-9]
Match one character or the other, usually within a group	|
Group characters	( )
Escape a character	\
Text boundary	\b
Tab character	\t
Any whitespace character	\s
Decimal digit	\d

This table provides only a very small subset of the characters and matching patterns you can use. We encourage you to become more familiar with regular expressions and the Regex class so that you can enable powerful text recognition in your smart tags. In addition, a number of tools are available for generating regular expressions, eliminating the need to build the expressions by hand. A Web search will reveal numerous tools you might use.

Overriding Smart Tag Recognizers

By default, the smart tag recognizes text if any of the strings in the Terms property (or any of the regular expressions in the Expressions property) matches text in the document. You can override the default recognizer by creating your own smart tag recognizer. If you create your own recognizer, you must write code to (1) parse the text in the document or workbook, (2) locate the terms and regular expressions, and (3) attach the smart tag to the recognized term. This gives you much greater control over which terms will have a smart tag attached. For example, you might want to check for specific conditions before adding the smart tag to the document.

The Recognize method is called by Word or Excel whenever text within the document has changed. Therefore, it's important that when you override this method, you optimize your code to perform well—for example, do not make any unnecessary variable declarations and assignments. Also, you should not make any calls into Word's or Excel's object model from the Recognize method.

To show you how you might override the default recognizer, we look at the example we used in Listing 9.11, rewriting it so that it first checks whether the computer has an Internet connection before adding the smart tag. If a network connection is detected, it loops through tokens in the document to see whether any of them matches the words in the Words collection. Only then does it add the smart tag. The code also changes the caption of the action depending on whether or not the computer is offline.

Note that this code searches for tokens (individual words) by looping through the tokenList passed to the Recognize method. Although you could loop through the text string and parse the text until it matches a phrase or regular expression, we want to present the simplest case in our example.

Creating the Word Project

1. Create a Word solution using VSTO, and name it OffLineSmartTag.

2. Add a reference to the Microsoft Smart Tags 2.0 Type Library (on the COM tab of the Add Reference dialog box).

3. Add an actions pane control to the project, leaving the default name.

4. Add a WebBrowser control to the actions pane control, leaving the default name.

5. Right-click the project name in Solution Explorer, point to Add, and click Class. Name the class OffLine.

6. Replace the code in the OffLine class with the code in Listing 9.19.

Listing 9.19. *Creating a custom smart tag class*

```
Imports Microsoft.Office.Tools.Word
Imports Microsoft.Office.Interop.SmartTag

Public Class OffLine
    Inherits SmartTag

    ' Create variables for the actions, the URL string,
    ' and the actions pane control.
    WithEvents LiveSearch As New Action("Windows Live Search")
    Dim url As String
    Dim ap As New ActionsPaneControl1
    Dim Word As String
    Dim Words As New Collection

    Sub New()

        ' In constructor, create the new smart tag and actions.
        MyBase.New("www.aw.com/Offline#Sample", _
            "Offline Example")
        Actions = New Action() {LiveSearch}

        ' Add words to the Words collection
        With Words
            .Add("ActionsPane")
            .Add("ListObject")
            .Add("SmartTag")
        End With

        ' Change the position of the task pane to dock at
        ' the top of the document, and set its height and
        ' the height of the actions pane control.
        Globals.ThisDocument.CommandBars("Task Pane"). _
            Position = Microsoft.Office.Core. _
            MsoBarPosition.msoBarTop
        Globals.ThisDocument.CommandBars("Task Pane"). _
            Height = 300
        ap.Height = 300

    End Sub
```

```vb
' Override the Recognize method to commit a smart tag.
Protected Overrides Sub Recognize(ByVal text As String, _
    ByVal site As Microsoft.Office.Interop.SmartTag. _
    ISmartTagRecognizerSite, ByVal tokenList As _
    Microsoft.Office.Interop.SmartTag.ISmartTagTokenList)

    ' If the computer is online, add smart tags.
    If My.Computer.Network.IsAvailable Then
        For Each Word In Words
            ' Loop through each term in the tokenList for
            ' a match and add a smart tag if the Network
            ' is available.
            For i As Integer = 1 To tokenList.Count
                Dim token As ISmartTagToken = _
                    tokenList.Item(i)
                If Word = token.Text Then
                    site.CommitSmartTag(Me.SmartTagType, _
                        token.Start, token.Length, Nothing)
                End If
            Next
        Next
    End If

End Sub


' Change the caption to reflect the computer's network
' status.
Private Sub LiveSearch_BeforeCaptionShow( _
    ByVal sender As Object, ByVal e As _
    Microsoft.Office.Tools.Word.ActionEventArgs) _
    Handles LiveSearch.BeforeCaptionShow

    If My.Computer.Network.IsAvailable Then
        LiveSearch.Caption = "Windows Live Search"
    Else
        LiveSearch.Caption = _
            "Windows Live Search is unavailable (Offline)"
    End If
End Sub
```

```
Private Sub LiveSearch_Click(ByVal sender As Object, _
    ByVal e As Microsoft.Office.Tools.Word _
    .ActionEventArgs) Handles LiveSearch.Click

    ' If the computer is online, set the search criteria
    ' and pass URL to the OpenActionsPane method.
    If My.Computer.Network.IsAvailable Then
        url = "http://search.live.com/results.aspx?q=" & _
            e.Text
        OpenActionsPane(url)
    End If

End Sub


' Display the Web browser control on the actions pane if
' it is not already visible; then show search results on
' Windows Live Search.
Private Sub OpenActionsPane(ByVal url As String)

    If Globals.ThisDocument.ActionsPane.Controls.Count _
        < 1 Then
        Globals.ThisDocument.ActionsPane.Controls.Add(ap)
        ap.WebBrowser1.Navigate(url)
    Else
        Globals.ThisDocument.Application.CommandBars( _
            "Task Pane").Visible = True
        ap.WebBrowser1.Navigate(url)
    End If

End Sub

End Class
```

7. Add the code in Listing 9.20 to the Startup event handler of ThisDocument. This code adds to the VstoSmartTags collection the smart tag created in the custom smart tag class.

Listing 9.20. *Adding the smart tag to VstoSmartTags collection*

```
Private Sub ThisDocument_Startup(ByVal sender As Object, _
    ByVal e As System.EventArgs) Handles Me.Startup

    Me.VstoSmartTags.Add(New OffLine)

End Sub
```

Running the Code

1. Press F5 to run the code.

2. On the Tools menu, click AutoCorrect Options and ensure that the Offline Example check box is selected on the Smart Tags tab, as shown in Figure 9.17.

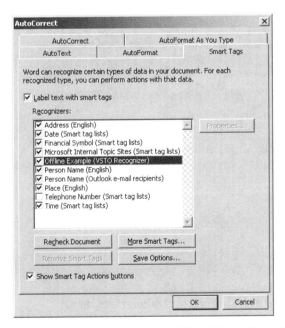

Figure 9.17. *Enabling Word to recognize the Offline Example custom smart tag*

3. With your computer connected to the Internet, add the following text to the document: *This is an example of a SmartTag and an ActionsPane.*

4. The control names should be recognized and marked with a dotted line. When you move your cursor over the term, the Smart Tags Action button should appear, as shown in Figure 9.18.

5. Click the drop-down button and select an action. If the computer is online, the caption will read "Windows Live Search," as shown in Figure 9.18.

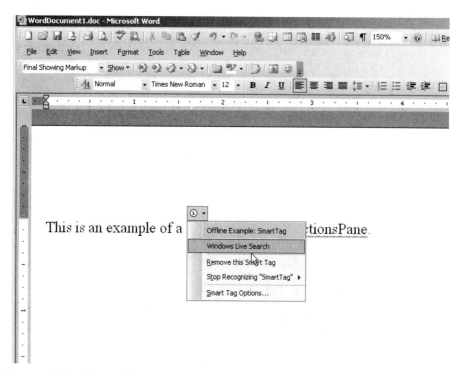

Figure 9.18. *Recognizing terms and adding smart tags*

6. When you click the Windows Live Search action, search results are displayed in the actions pane, as shown in Figure 9.19.

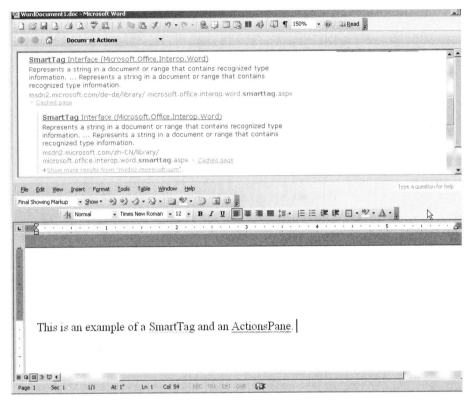

Figure 9.19. *Viewing search results via a smart tag*

Going Offline

Next, we look at the smart tag's behavior when the computer is no longer connected to the Internet. Whenever the Recognize method is called, it first looks to see whether there is a network connection, and it adds the smart tags only if a connection exists.

1. Close the actions pane and take the computer offline (for example, disconnect your computer from the Internet).

2. Add the following text under the first paragraph: *This is an example of a SmartTag and an ActionsPane.* The new text should not contain the dotted line (or smart tag), but the original text still does.

3. Move your cursor over a recognized word in the original text. When you click the drop-down button of the Smart Tags Action button, the caption will read "Windows Live Search is unavailable (Offline)," as shown in Figure 9.20.

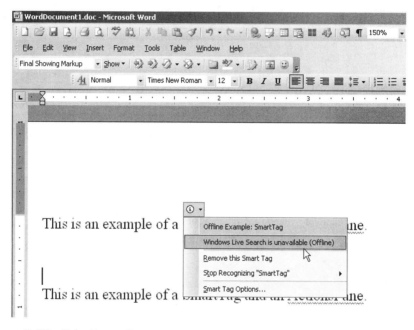

Figure 9.20. *Selecting actions on a custom smart tag*

If the user clicks the action, the Web page is not displayed in the actions pane because the OpenActionsPane method is not called when the computer is offline. If you go back online, the caption should change back to "Windows Live Search," but you'll need to recheck the text before all the matched words appear with smart tags. You can either place your cursor in the paragraph where the smart tag should appear and press the space bar, or call the RecheckSmartTags method on the document. This method calls into the Recognize method that you wrote, so if there is a lot of code or if the document contains a lot of smart tags, it may take a few seconds to complete the recheck. If you want to ensure that the document is rechecked for smart tags each time it is opened, you can call the RecheckSmartTags method in the document's Startup event handler.

Summary

We started this chapter with a description of a smart tag, and we looked at some of Word's and Excel's built-in smart tags. We also looked at the various options you can set to determine whether to display smart tags for recognized text, and we explained how you can programmatically set these options to ensure that your smart tags will be recognized. Then you learned how to create your own smart tags using VSTO, and you saw how easy it is to add individual words to the Terms property of a smart tag and to create actions for the smart tag.

You learned the basics of creating a regular expression and adding it to the Expressions property of the smart tag, and finally, you learned how to create your own smart tag recognizer.

Review Questions

1. Are VSTO smart tags document-level or application-level smart tags?

2. Why can't you add a phrase, such as *actions pane,* to the Terms property of a smart tag?

3. When would you use a regular expression with a smart tag?

4. By default, how can a user determine when a term or phrase has a smart tag associated with it in Word? In Excel?

5. Why might you want to override the recognizer method of a smart tag?

Part III

Outlook and Beyond

10

Creating Add-ins for Outlook with VSTO

I get mail, therefore I am.
—SCOTT ADAMS ("DILBERT")

Topics Covered in This Chapter

Application-Level Customizations Using VSTO

Outlook Object Model Overview

Customizing Menus and Toolbars in Outlook

Debugging Add-ins

Security in Outlook Add-ins Created with VSTO

Summary

Review Questions

Application-Level Customizations Using VSTO

If you have ever customized Outlook by using VBA or by creating a COM add-in, then you know that these customizations are application-level. VSTO supports application-level customization for Outlook through managed add-ins. Because Outlook doesn't have "documents" in the same way that Word and Excel do, it makes sense that the customizations are associated with the entire Outlook application. VSTO provides a type that wraps the Outlook Application object, but it does not add any functionality to the Outlook object model. Instead, VSTO provides a mechanism for loading Outlook add-ins, an add-in project template, a Setup project, and a more stable add-in model.

When you customize Outlook using VBA, your code is added to a VBA project in the Visual Basic Editor. You cannot record macros for Outlook (as you can in Word or Excel); instead, you must write your code directly in a code module in the VBE. You can write your code in the ThisOutlookSession code module, and you can add new code modules to your VBA project.

Using the ThisOutlookSession code module gives you access to a number of application events, where you can create event handlers and write code to handle the events, as shown in Figure 10.1. For example, you might want to write code that is called whenever an e-mail message or meeting request is sent.

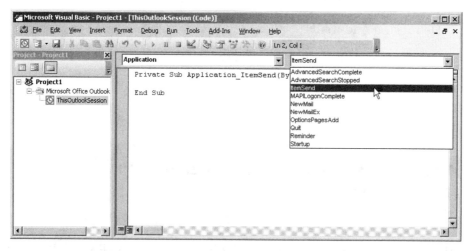

Figure 10.1. *Outlook application events available in the VBE*

Code written in the VBE is available only to the user who created the code, or to users who have imported the code file into their VBA projects. Often, developers instead create COM add-ins. COM add-ins implement the IDTExtensibility2 interface and can be deployed to other computers.

You can create a COM add-in using unmanaged code (Visual Basic 6.0) or managed code (Visual Basic 2005). With Visual Studio, you can create a managed shared add-in using the Shared Add-in project template, but the preferred method for creating Outlook add-ins is to use the VSTO add-in project template. With VSTO 2005 SE, you can create add-ins for several applications in addition to Outlook (see Chapter 14). The remainder of this chapter focuses on Outlook add-ins created with VSTO (not VSTO 2005 SE), but the descriptions of the Outlook object model are applicable to both.

Differences Between Shared Add-ins and VSTO Add-ins

VSTO add-ins differ from other managed add-ins in a number of important ways. VSTO add-ins implement a different interface, and they are loaded into a separate application domain (and thus they can be isolated and loaded and unloaded separately, as explained in Chapter 3). They also help resolve the shutdown issue faced by many add-in developers. Let's look at each of these issues.

Interface Implementation

Shared add-ins implement the IDTExtensibility2 interface. This model is *loosely coupled,* meaning that it can be loaded into multiple hosts (Word, Excel, Outlook, etc.), and the host is determined at run time in the OnConnection method. The OnConnection method is one of five methods available (some of which are seldom used) in add-ins that implement IDTExtensibility2.

VSTO add-ins for Outlook implement an IStartup interface. VSTO add-ins are strongly coupled, and the IStartup interface has only two methods: Startup and Shutdown. Typically, you handle initialization in the Startup event handler, and cleanup is handled in the Shutdown event handler. Figure 10.2 shows the methods that are created when you create a new shared add-in that implements IDTExtensibility2, and the methods that are created when you create a new Outlook add-in that implements IStartup.

Figure 10.2. *Methods in a shared add-in (top) versus a VSTO Outlook add-in*

Loading Add-ins

All managed shared add-ins are loaded into the same application domain. This means that if one add-in crashes it could crash all your add-ins that are running. One workaround for this problem is to create a C++ *shim* (an unmanaged DLL), which enables you to create a separate application domain in which the add-in is loaded. You need to create a separate shim for each add-in you load. This isn't necessary with VSTO add-ins, because they use an add-in loader that acts as a generic shim. Outlook add-ins use a loader provided by VSTO called AddinLoader.dll. Outlook checks the registry for information about the add-in's application manifest and then loads the appropriate add-in from the location specified in the manifest.

The AddinLoader.dll loader starts the common language runtime and the VSTO runtime, and then it loads the assembly for the add-in. The add-in is not loaded into the default application domain; instead, each add-in is loaded into a separate application domain. Because this isolates individual add-ins, it significantly improves the stability of add-ins created with VSTO (misbehaving shared add-ins will not bring down your VSTO add-in).

The Outlook Shutdown Issue

The Outlook shutdown problem occurs when there are unreleased references to Outlook objects in a COM add-in (implementing IDTExtensibility2) when the application is closed. Because there are still references to Outlook objects, the OnDisconnection method never gets called and Outlook doesn't get closed properly. Even though the Outlook user interface might not be visible, Outlook is still running (Outlook.exe is a process still running in the Windows Task Manager).

VSTO helps address this issue by keeping track of the number of Inspectors and Explorers that are opened and closed. When no more windows are open in Outlook, it indicates that Outlook has closed, and VSTO ensures that Outlook is shut down properly. It does this by unloading the application domain in which the add-ins were loaded and releasing any references to COM objects. Note, however, that issues with shutdown might still occur if you are automating Outlook and you create a running instance of Outlook without making it visible or opening any of its windows (the Inspectors and Explorers are never opened, so VSTO cannot track them).

The Outlook Add-in Project Template

When you create an Outlook add-in solution using VSTO, you select the Outlook Add-in Project template in the New Projects dialog box. This project template creates a solution that contains code files, generated code in hidden partial classes, and any necessary references. It also creates a Setup project for your add-in.

In the same way that VSTO provides a thin wrapper around the Document object (ThisDocument) and the Workbook object (ThisWorkbook), VSTO provides a wrapper around the Outlook Application object (ThisApplication). You can write your initialization code in the Startup event handler of ThisApplication and your cleanup code in the Shutdown event handler of ThisApplication. These methods are also available to document and workbook projects, making the development experience consistent across VSTO projects.

VSTO 2005 SE provides templates for creating Outlook add-ins (and add-ins for several other Office applications). Note that the architecture of Outlook add-ins provided in VSTO 2005 SE differs slightly from the model described in this chapter. (Initialization code would be written in ThisAddin.) You can learn more about this add-in model in Chapter 14.

Let's create a new Outlook add-in project so that you can become familiar with the project template and code files.

1. Open Visual Studio.

2. On the File menu, point to New, and click Project. The New Project dialog box appears.

3. Expand the Visual Basic node, and then select the Office node.

4. In the New Project dialog box, select Outlook Add-in and click OK, as shown in Figure 10.3.

   When the solution opens, you'll see two project files in Solution Explorer. The first, OutlookAddin1, contains the ThisApplication.vb file. The second is the Outlook Addin1Setup project.

5. Right-click ThisApplication.vb in Solution Explorer, and click View Code.

Visual Studio opens the ThisApplication class file in code view. This file contains two methods to handle the Startup and Shutdown events, as shown in Figure 10.4.

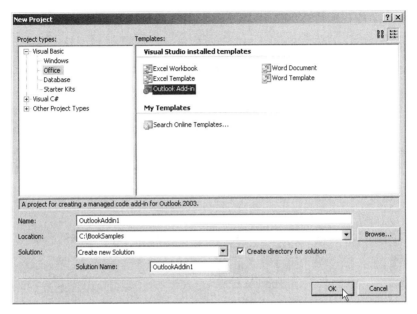

Figure 10.3. *Outlook Add-in project template*

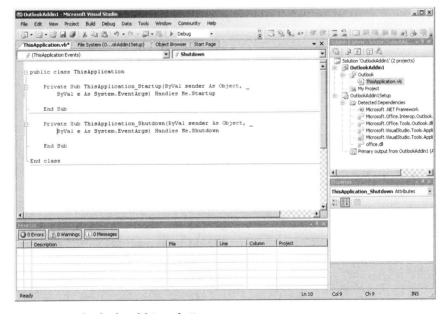

Figure 10.4. *Outlook add-in solution*

Outlook Add-in Project

An Outlook add-in project is created for you whenever you create a new
Outlook add-in solution with VSTO. By default, the project contains one
file, the ThisApplication.vb code file. This file contains the ThisApplication
class, as shown in Figure 10.4. This code file is a partial class where
you will write most of the code for your solution; a corresponding hidden partial class file (ThisApplication.Designer.vb) becomes visible when
you click Show All Files on the Solution Explorer toolbar. Figure 10.5
shows this file and some of the auto-generated code it contains.

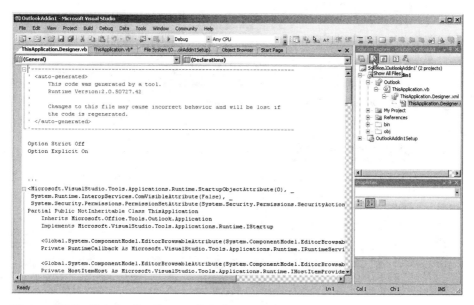

Figure 10.5. *ThisApplication partial class*

You should not make any modifications to this hidden partial class,
because the file is regenerated and your changes will most likely be lost.
You can learn more about these partial classes in Chapter 3.

Outlook Add-in Setup Project

A Setup project is created for you whenever you create a new Outlook add-in solution with VSTO. This Setup project creates a Microsoft Windows Installer (.msi) file that helps you set up requirements when you deploy your Outlook solution. Not all of the prerequisites required to run a VSTO solution are verified. The .msi does, however, verify that the .NET Framework 2.0 is installed and creates the required registry entries.

The main purpose of the .msi is to copy the files, the assemblies, and the manifest to the location where the add-in is deployed. You must take additional steps to verify that the computer in which the add-in is deployed has Microsoft Office 2003 installed. You must also ensure that security policy is set up correctly and verify that the VSTO runtime or Office PIAs are installed on the computer. In Chapter 11 you'll learn more about deploying an Outlook solution.

Converting an Outlook Macro to a VSTO Add-in

In this section you will create a simple VBA macro for Outlook and convert the code to a VSTO add-in. The VBA code is in the ItemSend event handler of the Application object in a VBA project, as shown in Listing 10.1.

Listing 10.1. *VBA macro that checks for a subject on an outgoing e-mail*

```
Private Sub Application_ItemSend(ByVal Item As Object, _
    Cancel As Boolean)

    Dim sendMessage As Integer

    If Item.Class = olMail Then
        If Item.Subject = "" Then
            sendMessage = MsgBox("Subject text is missing." & _
                vbCrLf & vbCrLf & "Do you want to send this" & _
                " message?", vbYesNo, "Missing Subject")
```

```
        If sendMessage = vbNo Then
            Cancel = True
            Item.Display
        End If
      End If
    End If
End Sub
```

To convert this to a VSTO add-in, you'll first create an add-in project, as described earlier in this chapter.

1. Create an Outlook add-in project with VSTO.

2. Right-click ThisApplication in Solution Explorer, and click View Code.

3. In the Class Name drop-down, select (ThisApplication Events), and then select ItemSend in the MethodName drop-down, as shown in Figure 10.6.

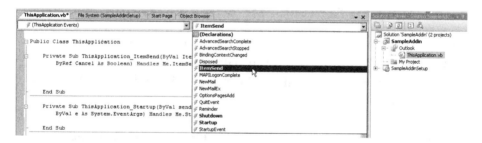

Figure 10.6. *ItemSend event handler*

4. Add the code in Listing 10.2 to the ItemSend event handler. Note that the only change necessary to the code is displayed in bold font.

Listing 10.2. *VSTO add-in that checks for a subject on an outgoing e-mail*

```
Private Sub ThisApplication_ItemSend(ByVal Item As Object, _
    ByRef Cancel As Boolean) Handles Me.ItemSend
```

```
Dim sendMessage As Integer

If Item.Class = Outlook.OlObjectClass.olMail Then
    If Item.Subject = "" Then
        sendMessage = MsgBox("Subject text is missing." & _
            vbCrLf & vbCrLf & "Do you want to send " _
            & "this message?", vbYesNo, "Missing Subject")
        If sendMessage = vbNo Then
            Cancel = True
            Item.Display()
        End If
    End If
End If
End Sub
```

5. Press F5 to run the code.

6. Create an e-mail without filling in the Subject text box, and then
    click Send. The message box (indicating that there's no Subject
    text) should appear and give you the opportunity to add the text or
    send the message as is.

You can also make further modifications to the code to use some of the
features of Visual Basic 2005, as shown in Listing 10.3.

Listing 10.3. *Further modifying the VSTO add-in code*

```
Private Sub ThisApplication_ItemSend(ByVal Item As Object, _
    ByRef Cancel As Boolean) Handles Me.ItemSend

    Dim myMailItem As Outlook.MailItem = _
        TryCast(Item, Outlook.MailItem)

    If myMailItem IsNot Nothing AndAlso myMailItem.Subject = _
        String.Empty Then

        If MsgBox("Subject text is missing." & vbCrLf & _
            vbCrLf & "Do you want to send this message?", _
            MsgBoxStyle.YesNo, "Missing Subject") = _
            MsgBoxResult.No Then
```

```
            Cancel = True
            myMailItem.Display()

        End If
    End If
End Sub
```

Here, we cast the Item (which is of type Object) to a MailItem. We used TryCast because if the attempt to cast the object fails, TryCast returns Nothing instead of an InvalidCastException error that we'd have to handle. With TryCast you can test to be sure that the object is not Nothing before performing additional operations on it.

The code also uses AndAlso to first check whether myMailItem is Nothing and, if it isn't, whether the Subject property is empty; only then does it execute the remainder of the code. Instead of using nested If statements or using the And operator (which would always check both conditions), we use AndAlso, which checks the second condition only if the first condition is True, thus preventing the exception that would otherwise occur. Finally, the code checks the DialogResult of the message box directly. In this way, we don't need to create a separate variable for an integer that represents the VBA constants vbNo and vbYes.

Creating a Simple Add-in

You can also have code run as soon as the Outlook application opens and the add-in is loaded. To do this, you add code to the Startup event handler of ThisApplication.

1. Right-click ThisApplication in Solution Explorer, and click View Code.

2. Add the CreateTask method in Listing 10.4 to the ThisApplication class, and then add a call to CreateTask in the Startup event handler.

Listing 10.4. *Adding code to the Startup event handler of an Outlook add-in*

```
Private Sub ThisApplication_Startup(ByVal sender As Object, _
    ByVal e As System.EventArgs) Handles Me.Startup
    CreateTask()
End Sub


Private Sub CreateTask()
    Dim NewTask As Outlook.TaskItem = TryCast( _
        Me.CreateItem(Outlook.OlItemType.olTaskItem), _
        Outlook.TaskItem)

    If NewTask IsNot Nothing Then

        With NewTask
            .Subject = "My new task"
            .DueDate = System.DateTime.Now
            .Body = "This is my new Task which is due right now!"
            .Status = Outlook.OlTaskStatus.olTaskInProgress
            .Display()
        End With
    End If
End Sub
```

3. Add the code in Listing 10.5 to the Shutdown event handler of ThisApplication.

Listing 10.5. *Adding code to the Shutdown event handler of an Outlook add-in*

```
Private Sub ThisApplication_Shutdown(ByVal sender As Object, _
    ByVal e As System.EventArgs) Handles Me.Shutdown

    MsgBox("Outlook is closing.  No, really!")

End Sub
```

4. Press F5 to run the code.

When Outlook opens, the Outlook task is created and displayed, as shown in Figure 10.7.

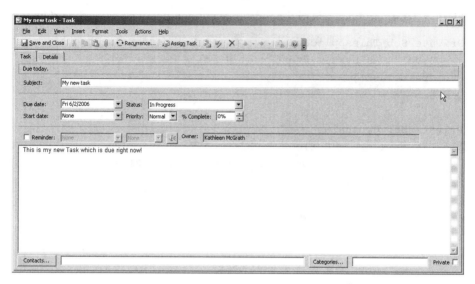

Figure 10.7. *Creating an Outlook task*

You can then click Save And Close to save the task in Outlook and close the Task item. When you close Outlook, the Shutdown event is raised and the message box in Figure 10.8 is displayed.

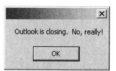

Figure 10.8. *Shutdown event handler*

We chose this text for the message box because one of the issues that VSTO Outlook add-ins have resolved is the problem with Outlook not properly releasing references to Outlook objects in managed shared add-ins.

IntelliSense in Visual Studio

VSTO ships with XML files that enable IntelliSense for the VSTO-specific object model for Word and Excel. However, if you want to have the benefits of an enhanced IntelliSense feature for the Outlook object model (or the Interop object models of Word and Excel), you should install the IntelliSense XML files that are available as a download on www.microsoft.com. In the Download Center, search for "IntelliSense" and select Microsoft IntelliSense XML Files for Microsoft Visual Studio Tools for the Microsoft Office System Solution Developers. You can then download and install VSTOIntelliSenseXML.msi.

After you have installed the IntelliSense XML files, create an Outlook add-in using VSTO to look at the IntelliSense capabilities in the Visual Studio IDE.

1. Create an Outlook add-in project using VSTO.

2. In the Startup event handler of ThisApplication, type the code in Listing 10.6.

Listing 10.6. *Viewing IntelliSense for an Outlook add-in in Visual Studio*

```
Private Sub ThisApplication_Startup(ByVal sender As Object, _
    ByVal e As System.EventArgs) Handles Me.Startup

    Dim NewMail As Outlook.MailItem = _
        Me.CreateItem(Outlook.OlItemType.olMailItem)
    NewMail.
```

When you type *NewMail* and then a period, IntelliSense displays the members available to the mail item as well as a description of what the method does, as shown in Figure 10.9.

If you don't install the IntelliSense XML files, the member list still appears in IntelliSense but doesn't include descriptions, as you can see in Figure 10.10.

In addition to these IntelliSense XML files, you can find IntelliSense code snippets for Outlook by searching on the Download Center of

Figure 10.9. *IntelliSense with descriptions*

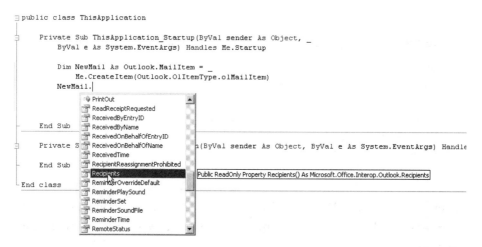

Figure 10.10. *IntelliSense without descriptions*

www.microsoft.com. If you search for Outlook snippets, you can download and install a number of very useful code snippets to use in building your Outlook solutions. Chapter 2 has more about IntelliSense code snippets, and Appendix A has information on how to create your own.

Outlook Object Model Overview

There are several ways to learn about the Outlook object model when you are using VBA. You can look at the objects in the Object Browser of the Visual Basic Editor, and you can use IntelliSense within the VBE. You can also use the Object Browser and IntelliSense (along with other advanced functionality) in Visual Studio when creating Outlook solutions in VSTO. (These features are described in more detail in Chapter 2.) As mentioned earlier, you must install the VSTOIntelliSenseXML.msi file in order to have the rich IntelliSense functionality in Visual Studio for your Outlook solutions. Remember, too, that Help files are available in Outlook and VSTO.

VSTO does not add any functionality to the Outlook object model. VSTO does not create host items or host controls for Outlook solutions (as it does with Word and Excel), because these controls are document-specific. Instead, VSTO provides a thin wrapper around the Outlook Application object so that you can access its members from the ThisApplication class using the Me keyword. Note that the add-in model introduced in VSTO 2005 SE has some architectural differences and does not wrap the Application object. You'll learn more about this in Chapter 14.

As noted in the Preface, we assume that you are a VBA developer who is already familiar with the Office object models and are interested in learning how you can transfer this knowledge to creating solutions with VSTO. Because VSTO doesn't enhance the object model in Outlook as it does in Word and Excel, this section only briefly describes some of the objects in the Outlook object model.

Application Object

The Application object represents the Outlook application and is the topmost object in the Outlook object model. VSTO wraps the Interop Application object and provides a ThisApplication class when you create a new Outlook add-in project. In the ThisApplication class, you can access the properties, methods, and events of the Application object by using the Me keyword, as shown in Figure 10.11. Note that Outlook has restricted methods and properties that can cause an Outlook security warning to be displayed if the object is not accessed through ThisApplication. You'll learn more about this later in this chapter in the section "Security in Outlook Add-ins Created with VSTO."

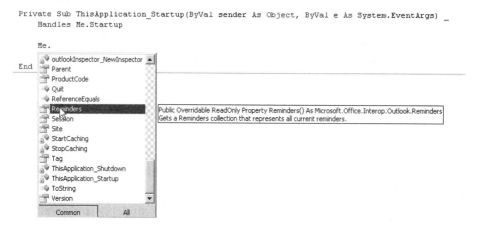

Figure 10.11. *Using the Me keyword to access methods and properties of the Application object in the ThisApplication class*

NameSpace Object

The Session property returns a NameSpace object that enables you to access the underlying Outlook data store and gives you access to the default folders. For example, you can access the NameSpace object by using the Application's Session property and then access the inbox, as shown in Listing 10.7.

> ❖**Note** Do not confuse the Outlook NameSpace object with a
> .NET namespace. These are two completely separate concepts
> that unfortunately have the same name.

Listing 10.7. *Accessing NameSpace to display the number of items in an inbox*

```
Dim Inbox As Microsoft.Office.Interop.Outlook.MAPIFolder
Inbox = Me.Session.GetDefaultFolder( _
    Outlook.OlDefaultFolders.olFolderInbox)
MsgBox(String.Format("Inbox contains {0} items.", _
    Inbox.Items.Count))
```

This code displays the total number of items in the inbox. Notice that this example uses the Format method of the String class to display the information, making it easier to work with the string. To display this same message using VBA, you'd have to concatenate strings, as shown in Listing 10.8.

Listing 10.8. *Using VBA to display the number of items in an inbox*

```
Dim ns As Outlook.NameSpace
Set ns = Application.Session
Dim inbox As Outlook.MAPIFolder
Set inbox = ns.GetDefaultFolder(olFolderInbox)
MsgBox ("Inbox contains " & inbox.Items.Count & " items.")
```

Explorer Object

The Explorer object is the window where a folder's contents are displayed. Folders contain items, such as mail items. The code in Listing 10.9 displays the name of the current folder in the active Explorer. The code is added to the Startup event handler of ThisApplication; therefore, the inbox should be the default current folder.

Listing 10.9. *Displaying the name of the current folder in the active explorer*

```
Private Sub ThisApplication_Startup(ByVal sender As Object, _
    ByVal e As System.EventArgs) Handles Me.Startup

    MsgBox(Me.ActiveExplorer.CurrentFolder.Name)

End Sub
```

Inspector Object

The Inspector object is the window where an Outlook item (such as an individual appointment item, e-mail item, and contact item) is displayed. You can capture the NewInspector event so that you can take action each time an inspector is opened. For example, the code in Listing 10.10 displays the caption of the Inspector in a message box each time a new Inspector is opened.

Listing 10.10. *Displaying the caption of an inspector when the NewInspector event is raised*

```
Dim WithEvents myInspectors As Outlook.Inspectors

Private Sub ThisApplication_Startup(ByVal sender As Object, _
    ByVal e As System.EventArgs) Handles Me.Startup

        myInspectors = Me.Inspectors

End Sub

Private Sub myInspectors_NewInspector(ByVal Inspector As _
    Microsoft.Office.Interop.Outlook.Inspector) _
    Handles myInspectors.NewInspector

        MsgBox(Inspector.Caption)

End Sub
```

Outlook Folders

Outlook folders are used to store items. You can create your own folders, but there are a number of default folders that are members of the MAPIFolder object. These default folders are listed in Table 10.1.

Table 10.1. *Outlook Folders*

Folder	Items Folder Contains	Enumeration
Calendar	AppointmentItem, MeetingItem	OlDefaultFolders.olFolderCalendar
Contacts	ContactItem, DisListItem	OlDefaultFolders.olFolderContacts
Deleted Items	Any	OlDefaultFolders.olFolderDeletedItems
Drafts	MailItem	OlDefaultFolders.olFolderDrafts
InBox	MailItem, DocumentItem, TaskRequestItem, TaskRequestUpdateItem	OlDefaultFolders.olFolderInbox
Journal	JournalItem	OlDefaultFolders.olFolderJournal
Junk e-mail	MailItem	OlDefaultFolders.olFolderJunk
Notes	NoteItem	OlDefaultFolders.olFolderNotes
Outbox	MailItem	OlDefaultFolders.olFolderOutbox
Sent Items	MailItem, DocumentItem, TaskRequestAcceptItem, TaskRequestDeclineItem	OlDefaultFolders.olFolderSentMail
Tasks	TaskItem	OlDefaultFolders.olFolderTasks
Public Folders	PostItem	OlDefaultFolders.olPublicFoldersAllPublicFolders

Outlook Items

Items in Outlook are contained within folders. Outlook has an Items collection that can contain multiple types of objects. The Items collection always returns an Object type, which must be cast into the specific Outlook item before you can use it in your code. Table 10.2 lists the Outlook items available in Outlook.

Table 10.2. *Outlook Items*

Item	Description	Enumeration
AppointmentItem	A meeting or appointment in the Calendar folder.	OlitemType.olAppointmentItem
ContactItem	A contact containing information about a person in the Contacts folder.	OlitemType.olContactItem
DistListItem	A distribution list containing several contacts in the Contacts folder.	OlitemType.olDistributionListItem
JournalItem	A journal entry in the Journal folder.	OlitemType.olJournalItem
MailItem	An e-mail message in the Inbox, Outbox, or SentItems folder.	OlitemType.olMailItem
MeetingItem	An item in the Inbox folder that contains information about a scheduled meeting to be added to the Calendar folder. An AppointmentItem becomes a MeetingItem when received in the inbox.	Outlook.MeetingItem
NoteItem	A note in the Notes folder.	OlitemType.olNoteItem
PostItem	A post in a public folder or a mail folder.	OlitemType.olPostItem
RemoteItem	A remote item in the inbox; similar to a MailItem but contains a subset of the information. For example, only the first 256 characters of the message body are available before the message is downloaded.	Outlook.RemoteItem

(continues)

Table 10.2. *Outlook Items (Continued)*

Item	Description	Enumeration
ReportItem	A report in the inbox; similar to a MailItem but also contains a report. These items are generated automatically when an error occurs.	Outlook.ReportItem
TaskItem	A task in the Task folder; the task can be created by the owner or assigned by another person.	OlitemType.olTaskItem
TaskRequestAcceptItem	A response in the inbox that accepts a task request.	Outlook.TaskRequestAcceptItem
TaskRequestDeclineItem	A response in the inbox that declines a task request.	Outlook.TaskRequestDeclineItem
TaskRequestItem	An object that represents a task that has been assigned.	Outlook.TaskRequestItem
TaskRequestUpdateItem	An object that represents an update of information for a task that has been previously assigned.	Outlook.TaskRequestUpdateItem

Events

There are a number of events on the Application object. You can write code in the ItemSend event handler to perform actions or verify data before an item (such as an e-mail message, task, or meeting request) is sent. Or you can use either the NewMail event or the NewMailEx event to perform actions when a new mail item is received and added to the inbox. The main difference between these two events is that with NewMailEx, you can get information about each of the items received based on its ID. Figure 10.12 shows all the events available on the ThisApplication class.

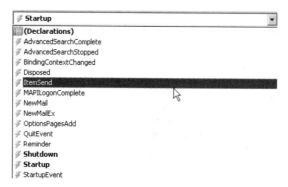

Figure 10.12. *Events available on the ThisApplication class*

You should use the Shutdown event handler rather than QuitEvent, because the add-in is unloaded before this event is raised (and thus the event cannot be raised).

There are a number of events for Inspectors and Explorers as well as for the items that are available to your VSTO add-in solution. You can use the Activate and Deactivate events for either an Inspector or an Explorer. For example, there are additional events for Inspectors and Explorers related to size and position, such as BeforeMinimize, BeforeSize, and BeforeMove. Collections, such as Folders, have events when folders are added, removed, or changed, and Items have events when items are added, removed, or deleted.

Customizing Menus and Toolbars in Outlook

One of the main points of entry to code in Microsoft Office 2003 applications is through their menus and toolbars. Using the code you created in the preceding section to add a task, you can add additional code to call this code from a menu item that you create. In this example, you will delete the toolbar if it already exists and then re-create it.

We take this approach instead of setting a reference to the existing toolbar (if found) because we don't know what state the toolbar was in when Outlook last closed, and whether the toolbar buttons were created correctly. Rather than check for the toolbar's existence and the functionality of each button, it is easier to delete and re-create the toolbar. This happens only once during application startup.

1. Create an Outlook add-in project in VSTO.

2. In Solution Explorer, right-click ThisApplication and click View Code.

3. Add the code in Listing 10.11 to the Startup event handler of ThisApplication. Note that the variables are created outside the Startup event handler, at the class level.

Listing 10.11. *Checking for existing menus and re-creating them*

```
Private menu As Office.CommandBar
    Private menuPopup As Office.CommandBarPopup
    WithEvents CreateTask As Office.CommandBarButton

    Private Sub ThisApplication_Startup(ByVal sender As Object, _
        ByVal e As System.EventArgs) Handles Me.Startup

    ' Check whether menu exists and, if it does, remove it.
    Dim checkMenu As Office.CommandBarPopup = _
        Me.ActiveExplorer().CommandBars.ActiveMenuBar. _
        FindControl(Office.MsoControlType.msoControlPopup, _
        System.Type.Missing, "Tasks", True, True)

    If checkMenu IsNot Nothing Then
       checkMenu.Delete(True)
    End If

    ' Call code to create new menu.
    AddMenuBar()

End Sub
```

4. Add the code for the AddMenuBar method, as shown in Listing 10.12. This code adds a menu named Tasks and a menu item that displays the caption "Create Task." The FaceID 837 is the icon for Outlook tasks.

Listing 10.12. *Creating a new menu*

```
Private Sub AddMenuBar()
    Try
        menu = Me.ActiveExplorer().CommandBars.ActiveMenuBar
        menuPopup = menu.Controls.Add( _
            Office.MsoControlType.msoControlPopup, _
            Temporary:=True)
        If menuPopup IsNot Nothing Then
            menuPopup.Caption = "Tas&ks"
            menuPopup.Tag = "Tasks"
            CreateTask = menuPopup.Controls.Add( _
                Office.MsoControlType.msoControlButton, _
                Before:=1, Temporary:=True)

            With CreateTask
                .Style = Office.MsoButtonStyle _
                    .msoButtonIconAndCaption
                .Caption = "Create Task"
                .FaceId = 837
                .Tag = "CreateTask"
            End With

            menuPopup.Visible = True
        End If
    Catch Ex As Exception
        MsgBox(Ex.Message)
    End Try
End Sub
```

5. Add the code in Listing 10.13 to the Click event handler of the CreateTask menu item.

Listing 10.13. *Creating a task from the Click event of the menu item*

```
Private Sub CreateTask_Click(ByVal Ctrl As _
    Microsoft.Office.Core.CommandBarButton, _
    ByRef CancelDefault As Boolean) Handles CreateTask.Click
    Dim NewTask As Outlook.TaskItem = _
    Me.CreateItem(Outlook.OlItemType.olTaskItem)

    With NewTask
        .Subject = "My new task"
        .DueDate = System.DateTime.Now
        .Body = "This is my new Task which is due right now!"
        .Status = Outlook.OlTaskStatus.olTaskInProgress
        .Display()
    End With
End Sub
```

6. Press F5 to run the code. When Outlook opens, a new Tasks menu appears, as shown in Figure 10.13. When you click the menu item Create Task, the new task item is created and displayed.

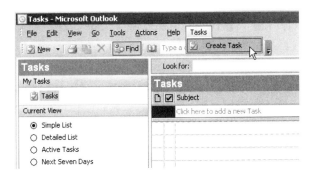

Figure 10.13. *Menu and menu item*

This code is very similar to the code you would use to create a menu and menu item in Word and Excel, except that you use the Explorer object. Outlook also enables you to add menus and toolbars to individual Inspectors, such as an e-mail item, a task item, or a meeting request. It can be particularly challenging to ensure that the code behind your buttons works correctly when you open multiple Inspectors. This is because the menu is added only to the first Inspector that is opened. Appendix B explains how to resolve this issue.

Debugging Add-ins

It can be challenging to debug Outlook add-ins that are created with VSTO if you haven't set your debugger to stop on all exceptions. This is because Outlook often swallows the exceptions that are thrown (meaning that they are not bubbled up from the Outlook application to your Visual Studio debugging session); by default, the code will not break into the debugger. Either you can set the debugger to break on all exceptions, or you can use Try Catch blocks to trap and handle the errors. For more about debugging VSTO solutions, see Chapter 2, and for more on using Try Catch statements, see Chapter 3.

Another way to troubleshoot problems with add-ins is to write errors to a log file. By default, Outlook does not automatically log errors. You can change this by adding an environment variable called VSTO_LOGALERTS and setting its value to 1. The log is created in the same folder that contains the application manifest for the Outlook add-in. If you prefer to display the error in a message box, you can create an environment variable called VSTO_SUPRESSSDISPLAYALERTS and set its value to zero.

To modify environment variables, click Environment Variables in the System Properties dialog box, and then click New in the Environment Variables dialog box, as shown in Figure 10.14.

Keep in mind that you should always close the debug sessions by closing Outlook so that any cleanup code is called correctly. When you stop debugging from VSTO, it shuts down Outlook, potentially damaging the .OST file (Outlook's offline store). Normally, Outlook can repair this damage, but it could take a few minutes at startup. Thus, it is always

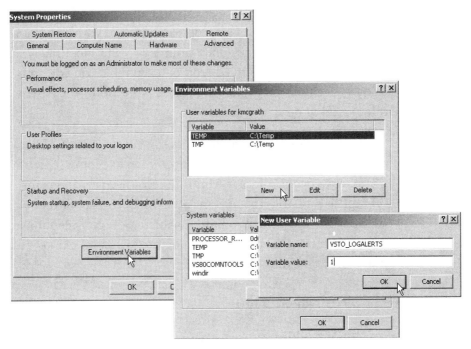

Figure 10.14. *Creating environment variables to log VSTO errors*

advisable to stop debugging by closing the host application (Outlook). You might also want to run Clean on the add-in if you want to unload it from outside Outlook. To do this, right-click the project and then select Clean in the context menu. Also, keep in mind that Outlook disables any add-ins that fail during startup.

Disabled Add-ins

If an add-in fails when it is being loaded, Outlook can disable the add-in in one of two ways. The first way, known as *hard disabling,* is to disable the add-in and AddinLoader.dll, the loader that VSTO uses to load add-ins. If this loader is disabled, any add-in created by VSTO will also be disabled and cannot be loaded until the disabled add-ins are reenabled. Typically, hard disabling occurs when Outlook closes unexpectedly, but it can also occur if you manually stop the debugger when code in the Startup event is executing. Also, if you stop execution of your program when the Startup event handler code is running, you will most likely experience a hard disable of the add-in. You can reenable the add-in by clicking Enable in the Disabled Items list, which is found in the About Microsoft Outlook dialog box.

The second way Outlook disables an add-in is known as *soft disabling*. Outlook soft-disables the add-in when an unhandled exception occurs in the add-in's Startup event handler. You must first correct the error before you attempt to reenable the add-in; otherwise, the act of reenabling will fail, and the add-in will remain disabled. You can reenable a soft-disabled add-in in the COM Add-ins dialog box. Let's take a look at both types of disabled add-ins.

Reenabling a Soft-Disabled Add-in

1. Create an Outlook add-in project with VSTO.

2. In the Startup event handler of ThisApplication, add the code in Listing 10.14.

Listing 10.14. *Creating an error at startup*

```
Private Sub ThisApplication_Startup(ByVal sender As Object, _
    ByVal e As System.EventArgs) Handles Me.Startup

    Dim first As Integer = 12
    Dim second As Integer = 0
    Dim DivideByZero As Integer = first / second
    MsgBox(DivideByZero)

End Sub
```

3. Press F5 to run the code. The message box does not display; the code throws a divide-by-zero exception, and, because it is not handled, the add-in is soft-disabled.

4. On the Tools menu in Outlook, click Options.

5. Select the Other tab in the Options dialog box, and then click Advanced Options.

6   In the Advanced Options dialog box, click COM Add-ins. The COM Add-ins dialog box will appear, as shown in Figure 10.15.

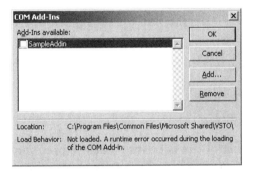

Figure 10.15. *Soft-Disabled add-ins*

Because the divide-by-zero error is hard-coded, you need to fix the error before reenabling the add-in. Otherwise, you could simply select the check box next to the disabled add-in to reenable it. If you just reenable it in this case, the code will attempt to run again, and the add-in will be disabled again. You can change the variable "second" to equal 4 and rerun the code. This time, a message box displays the value of the DivideByZero variable (which now divides by 4).

Reenabling a Hard-Disabled Add-in

We use the code in Listing 10.14 to show an example of hard-disabling an Outlook add-in.

1. Add a breakpoint to the line of code that divides the first number by the second number, as shown in Figure 10.16.

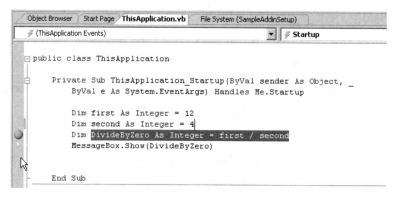

Figure 10.16. *Setting a breakpoint in the Startup event handler of an Outlook add-in*

2. Press F5 to run the code.

3. When execution of the code stops at the breakpoint, as shown in Figure 10.17, click the Stop Debugging button.

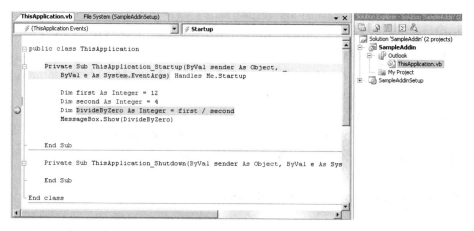

Figure 10.17. *Stopping code execution in the Startup event handler of an Outlook add-in*

4. Press F5 to run the code again. This time a dialog box informs you that Outlook has experienced an error and asks whether you want

to disable the add-in, as shown in Figure 10.18. In some cases the add-in is automatically disabled.

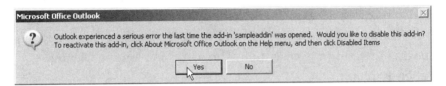

Figure 10.18. *Dialog box where you can disable an add-in*

5. For this example, click Yes.

6. To reenable the add-in, click About Microsoft Office Outlook from the Help menu.

7. In the About Microsoft Office Outlook dialog box, click Disabled Items.

8. In the Disabled Items dialog box, select the add-in you created. Then click Enable, as shown in Figure 10.19. The add-in will run when you close and then reopen Outlook.

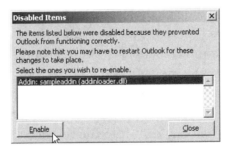

Figure 10.19. *Enabling a disabled Outlook add-in*

If a VSTO add-in is hard-disabled, any add-in that was loaded by addinloader.dll will also be disabled; in other words, all VSTO add-ins are disabled. This issue is resolved in VSTO 2005 SE because only the particular add-in that caused the problem is disabled. For more information, see Chapter 14.

You can soft-disable an add-in yourself by navigating to the COM Add-in dialog box and deselecting the check box next to the add-in; or you can permanently remove the add-in by selecting it and clicking Remove. Removing the add-in is essentially the same as running Clean from Solution Explorer.

Security in Outlook Add-ins Created with VSTO

The security requirements of Outlook add-ins match those of document-level customizations for Word and Excel created with VSTO. By default VSTO solutions are very secure, using code access security (CAS). Additionally, in order for AddinLoader.dll to load a VSTO add-in, it must have the proper .NET Framework security policies applied. In Chapter 11 you will learn more about security requirements for Outlook add-ins created with VSTO.

Outlook 2003 improved its security model through the Outlook e-mail security update, which helps protect users from e-mail viruses. This security model (often referred to as the Outlook *object model guard)* prevents access to certain members of the Outlook object model. But it automatically trusts all installed COM add-ins, provided that you access any Outlook objects through the Outlook Application object that is referenced by ThisApplication. If you create a new instance of the Application object, then any calls into the restricted object model will cause a security warning to be displayed, as shown in Figure 10.20.

It is important to note that if a user clicks No on this dialog box, thereby denying access to a restricted property or method, it will cause an exception. You can avoid this type of error if you always access objects through the ThisApplication class rather than create a new instance of

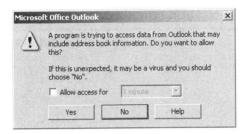

Figure 10.20. *Security warning (Outlook object model guard warning dialog box)*

an Application object. Note, however, that when Outlook is used with Exchange server, administrators can specify that all VSTO add-ins be trusted, because they can specify that AddinLoader.dll be trusted. This means that if any AddinLoader.dll add-in attempts to access the restricted objects of Outlook's object model, the security warning shown in Figure 10.20 would not be displayed. Keep in mind that the security warning might still be displayed if Outlook has been configured to deny access to information within the object model.

If the end user has the Outlook macro security setting set to Very High or High, only add-ins that are signed with certificates are trusted and allowed to run. The AddinLoader.dll that shipped with VSTO was not signed, but if you install VSTO 2005 SE, a signed version of the DLL will replace the unsigned version.

Restricted Methods

Table 10.3 lists the restricted Outlook object model methods that will cause the Microsoft Office Outlook object model guard warning to display.

Table 10.4 lists the restricted Outlook object model properties that will cause the Microsoft Office Outlook object model guard warning to display.

Table 10.3. *Restricted Methods*

Method Name	Object
Execute	Action
Find	UserProperties
GetMember	DistListItem
SaveAs	AppointmentItem ContactItem DistListItem JournalItem MailItem MeetingItem PostItem TaskItem
Send	AppointmentItem MailItem TaskItem
Respond	AppointmentItem
Any method within these particular objects	AddressEntries AddressEntry Recipient Recipients

Table 10.4. *Restricted Properties*

Object	Property
AddressEntries AddressEntry	Any property
AppointmentItem	Body NetMeetingOrganizerAlias OptionalAttendees Organizer RequiredAttendees Resources

(continues)

Table 10.4. *Restricted Properties (Continued)*

Object	Property
ContactItem	Body Email1Address Email2Address Email3Address Email1AddressType Email2AddressType Email3AddressType Email1DisplayName Email2DisplayName Email3DisplayName Email1EntryID Email2EntryID Email3EntryID IMAddress NetMeetingAlias ReferredBy
DistListItem	Body
Inspector	HTMLEditor WordEditor
ItemProperties	Any restricted property
MailItem	Body Bcc Cc HTMLBody SenderEmailAddress SenderEmailType SenderName SentOnBehalfOfName ReceivedByName ReceivedOnBehalfOfName ReplyRecipientNames To
MeetingItem	Body SenderName

(continues)

Table 10.4. *Restricted Properties (Continued)*

Object	Property
NameSpace	CurrentUser GetRecipientFromID
PostItem	Body HTMLBody SenderName
Recipient Recipients	Any property
TaskItem	Body ContactNames Contacts Owner StatusOnCompletionRecipients StatusUpdateRecipients
UserProperty	Formula

Summary

In this chapter you looked at the functionality of a VSTO Outlook add-in and learned why VSTO add-ins are preferred over shared add-ins. The main reason is that VSTO loads add-ins into separate application domains, thereby reducing the possibility that a problematic add-in will adversely affect other VSTO add-ins. VSTO also addresses the shutdown problem that occurs with managed shared add-ins that implement the IExtensibility2 interface. You also learned about the new architecture of VSTO Outlook add-ins when you install VSTO 2005 SE. Next, you looked at the basic objects in the Outlook object model hierarchy, and then you learned how to create menus and menu items in the main Outlook window.

We also looked at how you can debug an Outlook add-in, and you learned how to set environmental variables that let you display errors in a message box or write them to a log file. You also saw how you can reenable add-ins that have been soft-disabled or hard-disabled. Finally, we looked at the Outlook object model guard, and you discovered how you can avoid displaying the security warning when you access restricted properties and methods.

Review Questions

1. What is the shutdown problem that Outlook add-in developers often face, and how does VSTO remedy it?

2. Why is it important for each Outlook add-in to be loaded into a separate application domain?

3. What objects in the Outlook object model are enhanced by VSTO?

4. What is the difference between an Inspector object and an Explorer object in Outlook?

5. What is the Outlook object model guard?

Security and Deployment

The only truly secure system is one that is powered off, cast in a block of concrete and sealed in a lead-lined room with armed guards.
—GENE SPAFFORD

Topics Covered in This Chapter

VSTO Security Model

Deploying Word and Excel Solutions

Deploying Outlook Solutions

Summary

Review Questions

VSTO Security Model

VSTO makes it easy for you to create great Office solutions. Of course, after you have completed your solution, you must deploy it to end users in a secure, maintainable way. VSTO has a powerful, flexible security model that is built on top of .NET code access security, giving you control over which code you allow to run on your machine.

One of the key security design principles of VSTO is that it is secure by default. This means that no code runs without having been given specific permission to run. You may be thinking that throughout this book you have been creating VSTO solutions and haven't had to think about security; when you pressed F5, the code just ran. That is because when you create a new VSTO solution, the IDE automatically gives explicit permission for your solution to run on your development machine. We will take a look at how this permission is granted, but first you need to understand a little about CAS.

Another key security design principle of VSTO is that the document does not contain the code. Unlike VBA solutions, which are embedded in the document (or in a global template), VSTO assemblies are contained in a separate code file. This makes it more difficult to propagate macro viruses because virus writers cannot simply use e-mail to distribute document viruses. The document solution must be installed to a trusted location before it will run. Although this is a very secure system, it makes deployment a little more challenging.

Code Access Security

CAS is the security system for the .NET Framework. Although a complete explanation of CAS is outside the scope of this book, we cover a few basic concepts. CAS is different from Windows security, which is a role-based system. Role-based security grants permissions based on the user's role—for example, being a member of the administrators group or the power users group. In contrast, CAS grants permissions based on what the code is allowed to do, regardless of the role of the user running the code.

CAS uses *code groups* to manage permissions. There are two things you should understand about code groups: evidence and permissions. *Evidence* determines whether the code belongs in the group. For example, you can specify that all code in a particular folder belongs in a group. This is known as *URL evidence,* which is the evidence most commonly used by VSTO. Strong name evidence is another type. *Strong name* signing gives the component a unique ID that can be used to identify that exact component. You can specify that all code that is signed with a strong name key belongs in a code group. Other kinds of evidence include certificates and custom evidence. Later you will see how to extend the security system using custom evidence.

Now that you know which code belongs in the code group, the next step is to assign permissions to the code group. This is the easy part, because all VSTO solutions require *full trust.* VSTO solutions require full trust because they interact with Office using COM interop and because the Office object model was designed for full trust only. Consider, for example, something simple: using the Save method to save a document called c:\windows\system\system32.dll, something that could corrupt the operating system. This is why an API needs to be designed to operate with restricted permissions and why Office is not designed to use partial trust.

There are two ways to define a code group. One is to use the command-line tool Code Access Security Policy (CASPOL.exe). This tool is located in \WINDOWS\Microsoft.NET\Framework\v2.0.50727\Caspol.exe. The other way is to use a Microsoft Management Console (MMC) tool called .NET Framework 2.0 Configuration (shown in Figure 11.1). You can locate this tool by opening Administrative Tools in the Control Panel, selecting Performance and Maintenance, and then clicking Microsoft .NET Framework 2.0 Configuration.

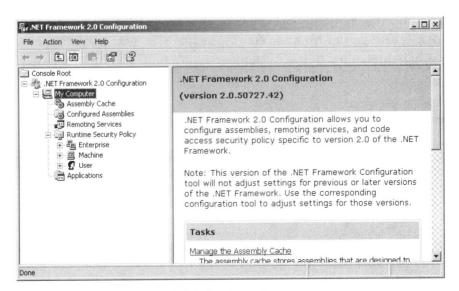

Figure 11.1. *.NET Framework 2.0 Configuration*

As mentioned earlier, VSTO automatically creates a code group for any project. Let's look at exactly how this code group is set up. If you open the .NET Framework 2.0 Configuration console and expand the My Computer node and the Runtime Security Policy node, you will see that there are three levels: Enterprise, Machine, and User. VSTO creates the code group under the user level, meaning that this code group applies only to the user who created it.

As you can see in Figure 11.2, if you expand the User node, there is a Code Groups node, and under that an All_code node. Under the All_code node is the VSTOProjects node. Under the VSTOProjects node, VSTO creates a code group for each project that you create, using a GUID so that each code group name is unique.

If you drill down a little further, you get to the code group that actually grants the permissions. This code group is named after the VSTO assembly name; in this example, ExcelWorkbook1.dll is the name of the code group. When you select this code group in the .NET Framework 2.0 Configuration console, you can see the description to the right. It contains the code group's evidence and the permissions.

To see the details, right-click the code group (as shown in Figure 11.2) and select Properties from the context menu. The code group Properties page has three tabs: General, Membership Condition, and Permission Set.

General Tab

The General tab enables you to set the code group's name and description, as shown in Figure 11.3.

Membership Condition Tab

The Membership Condition tab is where you define the evidence for the code group. As shown in Figure 11.4, the type of evidence in our example is URL, which is the path to the assembly, including the assembly

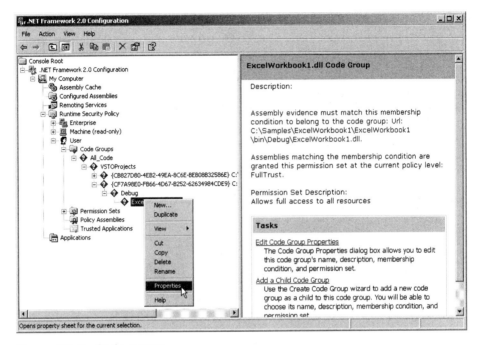

Figure 11.2. *Code groups*

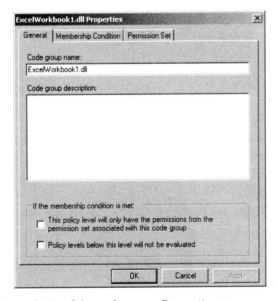

Figure 11.3. *General tab of the code group Properties page*

name. You can use an asterisk (*) to give permission to all files and folders under the path specified. The VSTO project system tries to be as secure as possible when it creates entries during the build process, so it grants explicit permission only to the one assembly in your solution.

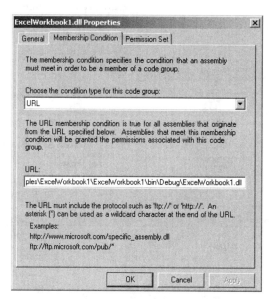

Figure 11.4. *Membership Condition tab of the code group Properties page*

Permission Set Tab

In the Permission Set tab, you define the permissions that the code group grants as shown in Figure 11.5. VSTO solutions must be given full trust in order to run.

The default behavior is for the VSTO project system to grant trust to your project, but you can turn off this behavior using your project's Trust Assemblies Location property, as shown in Figure 11.6.

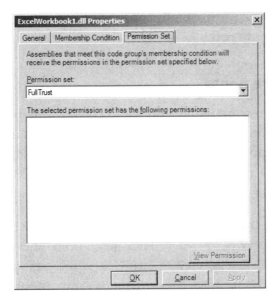

Figure 11.5. *Permission Set tab of the code group Properties page*

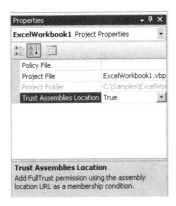

Figure 11.6. *Trust Assemblies Location property*

Deploying Word and Excel Solutions

A few basic steps are necessary to deploy VSTO solutions. The first step is to correctly set up the client machine with all the required software or prerequisites. The next step is to deploy all the solution files to the server or client machines. Finally, you set up security to allow your deployed solution to run.

Client Requirements

VSTO solutions require that a number of components be installed on the client machine. You may not have thought a lot about this. The code just works on your development machine because VSTO installs and checks for all the required software when you install VSTO on your machine. Let's take a look at what is required and how to install it.

- **Microsoft Office System 2003 Professional SP1 or later.** Office 2003 Pro Service Pack 1 or later is required. Many users may have only Office 2003 Standard Edition, so pay special attention to the edition of Office they are using. You may also install a stand-alone version of Word, Excel, or Outlook.

- **Primary interop assemblies.** The PIAs enable managed code (your VSTO assembly) to communicate or interoperate with unmanaged code (the Office object model). The PIAs come on the Office CD but are not installed by default. If the PIAs have not been installed, you can rerun your Office setup and choose the Add or Remove Features option to install the Office PIAs. Another option is to install the redistributable version of the Office PIAs. This is a Microsoft Installer (MSI) package that you can freely download. This option has the advantage of not requiring you to rerun the Office setup, something that may be difficult to do in an enterprise environment.

- **.NET Framework 2.0.** VSTO solutions are managed code solutions, and they require that .NET Framework 2.0 be installed on the client machine, and it must be installed before the Office PIAs are installed. Often, this is the reason that the Office PIAs are not installed with the Office installation even though the administrator has done a full install.

- **VSTO 2005 Runtime.** The VSTO runtime component must be installed on all end-user computers that will run VSTO solutions.

Microsoft PSS VSTO 2005 Client Troubleshooter

It can be difficult to verify that you have configured the client machine correctly with all the requirements. Some of this difficulty can be attributed to the different ways Office can be installed. You cannot always assume that Office has been installed to allow .NET programmability. However, you can use a tool created by the VSTO product support team that will analyze a client machine to determine whether the correct software is installed to run a deployed VSTO solution. This Microsoft PSS VSTO 2005 Client Troubleshooter can be located in the Download Center on www.microsoft.com.

Figure 11.7 demonstrates the results you might receive when using this tool. It reports a lot of detailed information about what is installed on the client machine. If everything is installed correctly, you need look only at the top section. If you see all green (check mark) symbols across the top section, it indicates that the client machine has all the required software installed and there is no need to drill into the details. However, if there is a yellow ("!") symbol in the top section, the tool provides detailed information to pinpoint and correct the problem. The details are divided into three sections. The first section gives details about the operating system and the version of the .NET Framework installed.

The middle section displays the Office products and PIAs installed, as shown in Figure 11.8. The PIAs are those that are installed as part of the Office installation. You can learn more about the Office PIAs in Chapter 3.

As Figure 11.9 shows, the bottom section, Miscellaneous, contains information about the VSTO runtime components and the PIAs installed via the redistributable MSI.

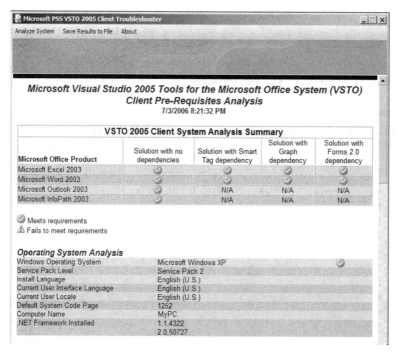

Figure 11.7. *PSS Client Troubleshooter*

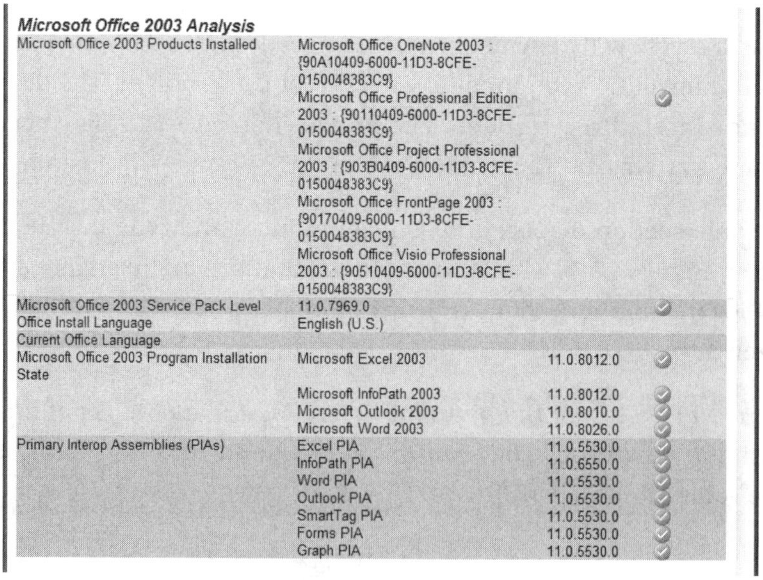

Figure 11.8. *Analysis of installed Office products*

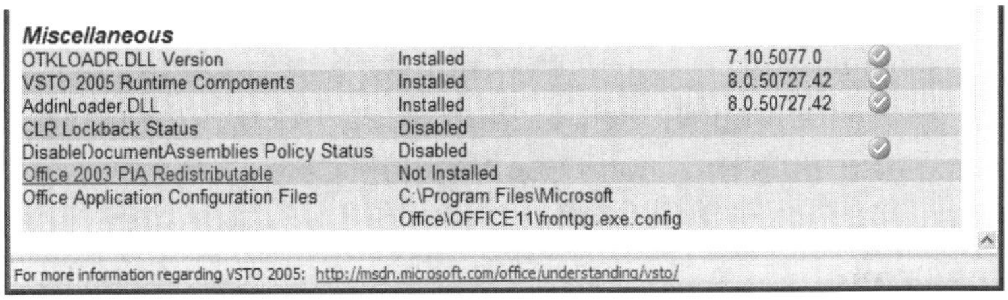

Figure 11.9. *Miscellaneous prerequisites*

Deployment Models

VSTO supports a number of conceptual deployment models, which can be defined as local/local, local/remote, and remote/remote. These models are useful to describe the deployed location of the document and the assembly and are grouped based on three common deployment scenarios.

Local/Local

In this model the document and the assembly are installed locally on the user's machine. This model is most similar to a standard application and is normally installed using the MSI. (Later in this chapter you will see how to deploy using an MSI.) The local/local model has the advantage of being available even if the user is offline and not connected to the network. Also, if the application is installed with an MSI, it can be repaired or uninstalled from the Add or Remove Programs tool in the Control Panel. One disadvantage of this model is that the application is more difficult to update because the document and assembly are located on the client machine, and an update requires that you update every client.

Local/Remote

This is the most common model. A copy of the document is on the local machine, and the assembly is on the server or file share. This model allows the user to make changes to the document and still be linked to the latest assembly on the server. Administrators can update or roll back the application on the server, with all clients picking up the latest version the next time they open the document.

Remote/Remote

In this model, both the document and the assembly are located on the server. To implement this model, you usually use a template—for example, a .dot or an .xlt file. Using a template allows each user to create a new document instance from the centrally located template. After the user has created a document from the template, the user often saves a local copy, which brings us conceptually back to the local/server model. Using Microsoft SharePoint to store the document is a good example of a pure remote/remote model. It is also important to note that using this model you must explicitly trust the document as well as the assembly when the document is located remotely. To explicitly trust the document, either it must be in a location to which you grant full trust permissions, or the document itself must be granted full trust permissions.

Application and Deployment Manifests

A VSTO solution consists of a document that is linked to an assembly. This enables you to easily update solutions distributed to your users in the enterprise. By contrast, VBA code is embedded in the document, so you distribute the document by making a copy of the code for each copy of the document. This makes it almost impossible to update the code if a bug or security vulnerability is discovered.

Using VBA and Word, you could use a global template containing VBA code that is available to any open document. To update this global template code, you must do one of two things. You either deploy an updated template to each user machine, or, if the template is stored on a server, you must ensure that each user has closed any document that is based on that template before you update the template code.

In the VSTO model, you can deploy the assembly to a share and then e-mail the document to your users. To update the solution, you can deploy the updated assembly to the server; all your end users get the updated code automatically the next time they open the document. You can even roll back to a previous version if something goes wrong with your update.

Application and deployment manifests enable automatic updating and rollback. VSTO uses XML manifest files that are similar to ClickOnce manifest files. ClickOnce is an update and deployment technology used by the .NET Framework. This version of VSTO does not use ClickOnce but is conceptually very similar. Let's look at how manifests work in VSTO. An application manifest tells VSTO which assembly to load and where it is located. The application manifest, which is embedded in the Word or Excel document, also points to a deployment manifest. The deployment manifest is normally deployed to a server and contains a pointer to the current version of the application manifest on the server.

Loading the correct version of your application involves a series of steps that starts when you open your VSTO document. The VSTO runtime reads the location of the deployment manifest from the application manifest embedded in the document. Next, the runtime compares the version of the application manifest with the version of the application manifest pointed to by the deployment manifest. If the two do not match, the new application manifest is downloaded and replaces the application manifest in the document. After the runtime ensures that you have the correct manifest, it reads the location of the assembly from the embedded application manifest, which may have just been updated, and loads the assembly. Your solution is now running. This process is illustrated in Figure 11.10.

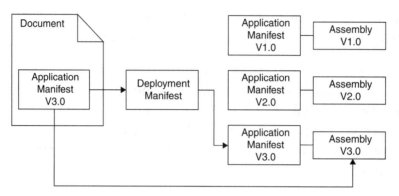

Figure 11.10. *Manifest-based update model*

Deployment Tasks

Deploying VSTO solutions consists of a few tasks, and the final result of a successful deployment is to have all these tasks completed. Some of these tasks may be optional, depending on your scenario. There are many ways to accomplish these tasks, depending on how you deploy the solution. Some tasks are automatic—for example, when you use the Publish Wizard—and others must be done manually.

Following is a high-level overview of the steps required to deploy your solution. Later in the chapter, we describe the manual steps in a deployment walkthrough.

1. Ensure that the client meets all the VSTO client requirements. The PSS Troubleshooter tool can make it easy for you to verify that you have this client set up correctly.

2. Copy the solution files to deploy them to the end user machine or server location. This also includes deploying the application and deployment manifest files.

3. Update the application manifest embedded in the document to point to the deployed deployment manifest. At a minimum, you must point to the correct assembly location.

4. Grant full trust to the VSTO solution, including the document if it is located on a server.

Publish Wizard

Using the Publish Wizard is the easiest way to deploy your application. The Publish Wizard creates your application and deployment manifests, copies your project output to the publish location, and updates the embedded application manifest. Using the preceding section as a guide, you can see that the Publish Wizard does two of the four required tasks. The two remaining tasks are verifying the client prerequisites and granting permissions. Let's take a look at a simple publishing example.

Using the Publish Wizard

1. Create an Excel Workbook project with VSTO.

2. Add the code in Listing 11.1 to the ThisWorkbook_Startup method. This action creates an empty actions pane with a blue background. The background color makes it easy for you to see that your code is running.

Listing 11.1. *Creating an empty actions pane with a blue background*

```
ActionsPane.BackColor = Color.Blue
ActionsPane.Visible = True
```

3. Set the publish version.

You control the publish version of the application from the Publish tab of the project Properties page. Double-click the My Project node in Solution Explorer, and select the Publish tab to view the Publish Wizard properties, as shown in Figure 11.11. The publish version number is different from the file or assembly version number, which is the version of an individual file within your application. The publish version is the overall version of your solution; it is the one number that represents all the individual files, each of which may have a different version number. The publish version is a four-dot number: *Major.Minor.Revision.Build.* By default, VSTO sets the Publish Wizard to automatically increment the build part of the version number starting at 1.0.0.0. So the second time you publish, the publish version number will be 1.0.0.1, and then 1.0.0.2, and so on.

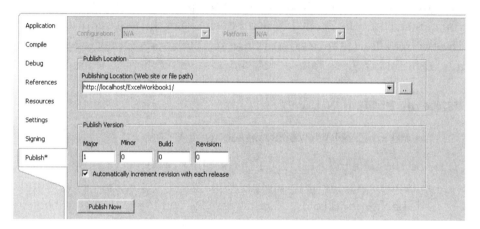

Figure 11.11. *Setting the Publish Location and Publish Version*

4. Set the default Publish Location.

    You can instead change this in the Publish Wizard, but it is a good idea to set it here so that each time you run the wizard the correct value will be set. This path can be either an HTTP URL to which you have permission, or a local file or universal naming convention (UNC) path, as shown in Figure 11.12.

5. Publish the solution with the Publish Wizard.

    You can launch the Publish Wizard in a number of ways. One way is to click the Publish Now button on the Publish tab. This action publishes the solution using the settings from the Publish tab and does not display the Publish Wizard. Or you can run the Publish Wizard by clicking Publish ExcelWorkbook1 from the Build menu. You can also launch the Publish Wizard by right-clicking the project in Solution Explorer and choosing Publish from the Project context menu.

The Publish Wizard opens, and you can set the Publish Location. In this case, you've already set it in the Publish tab, so you do not need to make any changes.

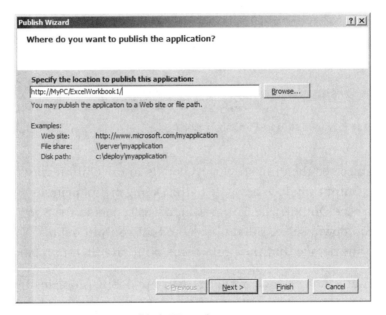

Figure 11.12. *First step in Publish Wizard*

6. Click Next.

7. Click Finish to confirm the publish location and publish the project, as shown in Figure 11.13.

When you click Finish on the Publish Wizard, the wizard closes and the confirmation that it completed successfully is shown in the status bar.

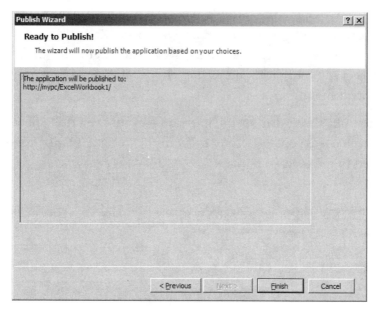

Figure 11.13. *Final step in Publish Wizard*

You can also see the Publish Wizard details in the Output window. To open the Output window, navigate to the Debug menu, point to Windows, and then click Output. The Output window will open. In the Show Output From drop-down, select Build to see the build output details. You can see from the details that the project was built and then published.

The Output window is one of the few ways to debug problems using the Publish Wizard. For example, if you cannot find or connect to the publish location, you see an error in the Output window. Figure 11.14 shows the successful publishing of an application.

The Publish Wizard has succeeded, and now let's verify that everything is correct and confirm what was published. The first step is to verify the published location. In this case, you published to http://localhost/ExcelWorkbook1. This location might translate into, for example, C:\Inetpub\wwwroot\ExcelWorkbook1. This is the virtual folder of your publish Web site on your machine.

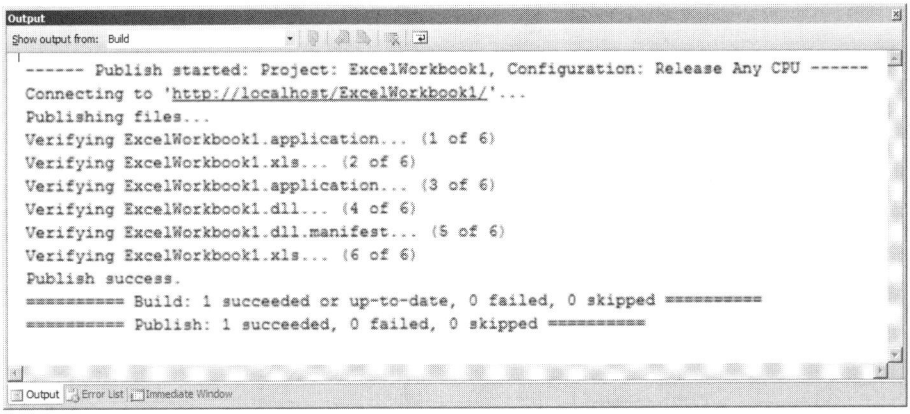

Figure 11.14. *A published application in the Output window*

You can see that the Publish Wizard has created a directory that contains your application. This folder is the name of the project followed by an underscore and the version number—for example, ExcelWorkbook1_1.0.0.0. Two files are published at the root: the Excel document and the deployment manifest. The deployment manifest ends with the .application extension. This is an unfortunate extension, and the file is even misidentified by Windows Explorer as the application manifest, as shown in Figure 11.15.

The Excel document, ExcelWorkbook1.xls, has an embedded application manifest that points to the deployment manifest in this directory. The deployment manifest, ExcelWorkbook1.application, points to the current version of the application manifest. In our case we have only one version, so it points to the application manifest, ExcelWorkbook1.dll.manifest, in the ExcelWorkbook1_1.0.0.0 directory. As shown in Figure 11.16, the published application directory contains a copy of the Excel document and the assembly. There are also two manifest files here. The application manifest ends with the .manifest extension and is the same file as the manifest that is embedded in the Excel document. There is also a copy of the deployment manifest, a convenience to administrators to enable easy rollback.

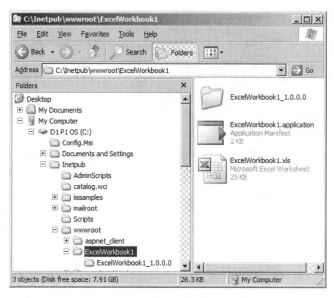

Figure 11.15. *Deployment manifest (not application manifest)*

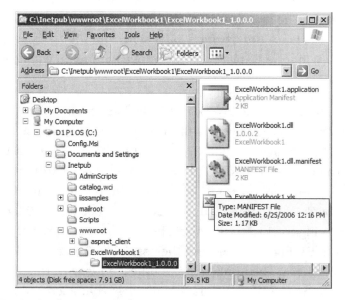

Figure 11.16. *Application manifest*

For the solution to run, you must set the CASPOL. The Publish Wizard does not check that the client machine is set up correctly, and it does not set the security policy to allow your solution to run. You should assume for this example that your machine is set up correctly. You will use the .NET 2.0 Configuration tool to give your solution full trust permissions based on the published location.

1. Open the .NET 2.0 Configuration tool.

2. In the Control Panel, select Performance and Maintenance, and then select Administrative Tools.

3. In the Administrative Tools window, open the Microsoft .NET Framework 2.0 Configuration tool, as shown in Figure 11.17.

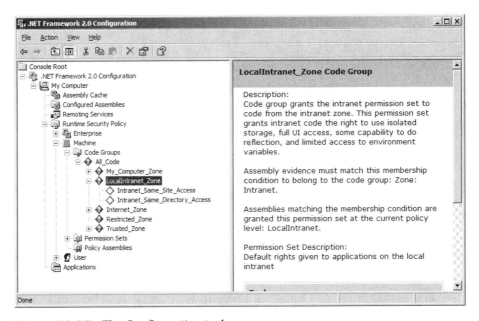

Figure 11.17. *The Configuration tool*

4. Create a new security code group to define your solution, and specify the permissions it is granted. In the .NET Framework 2.0 Configuration tool, expand the tree My Computer | Runtime Security Policy | Machine | Code Groups | All_Code | LocalIntranet_Zone.

5. Right-click LocalIntranet_Zone, and click New. This action opens the Create Code Group Wizard, as shown in Figure 11.18.

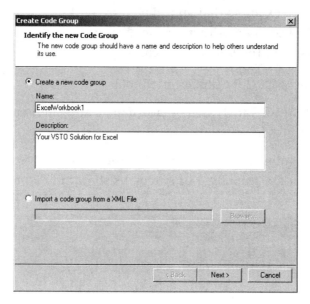

Figure 11.18. *Create Code Group Wizard*

6. Type a name for your code group, and add an optional description.

7. Select Next to continue.

8. In the second step in the Create Code Group Wizard, define the evidence that allows code to belong to this group, as shown in Figure 11.19. Choose URL as the condition type, and type the URL of your solution as the published path. By adding the asterisk (*) to the end of the path, you allow all code under this path to belong to the group. Keep this group as small as possible, and make sure that only trusted users have rights to add code to this directory.

9. Click Next.

10. Define the permissions used by the code belonging to this group, as shown in Figure 11.20. All VSTO solutions require full trust, which is the default.

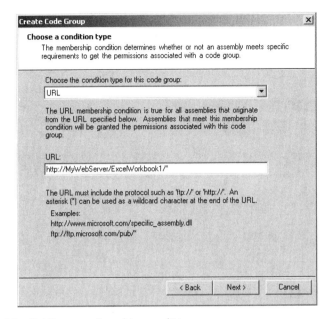

Figure 11.19. *Setting membership conditions*

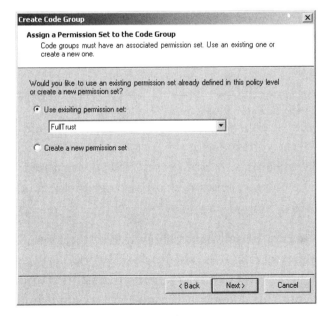

Figure 11.20. *Assigning a permission set*

11. The final step in the Create Code Group Wizard is a confirmation screen, as shown in Figure 11.21. Click Finish to create the new code group.

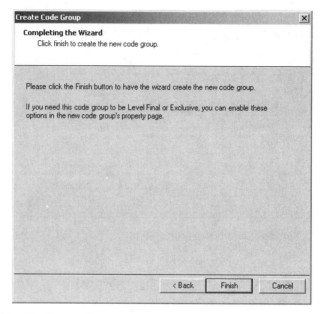

Figure 11.21. *Final step of Create Code Group Wizard*

Figure 11.22 shows your newly created code group. If you click the name of the code group, you will see its details in the right pane. Note that there is a known issue with the tool that adds "Copy of" to the name of your code group. To keep your CASPOL organized, you should rename it to the correct name. You can also see the details of the code group in the right pane when you select a node.

Now it's time to run the solution. Using Internet Explorer, browse to the http://MyWebServer/ExcelWorkbook1/ExcelWorkbook1.xls file. The result is that your VSTO Excel document opens and your code runs. You can also copy this document to your local machine and run it from there. When you open the document, the VSTO loader finds the assembly in the published location and runs it.

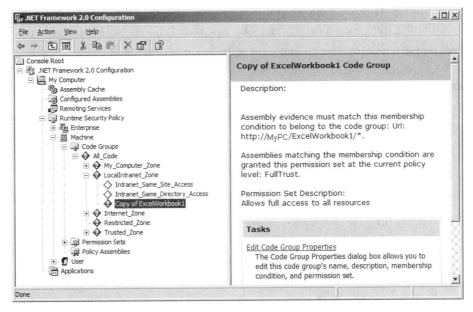

Figure 11.22. *Code group details*

Update and Rollback

Unlike VBA solutions, VSTO solutions are easy for developers and administrators to update because of VSTO's manifest-based deployment model. Let's look at updating the solution you just published.

Each time you publish your solution, VSTO creates a new folder that contains your entire solution. This separation of versions enables you to roll back or forward to a different version. VSTO does not manage the versions that have been published, so you need to remove old versions as you see fit.

Updating

1. On the Publish tab, change the publish version number to 2.0.0.0. Double-click the My Project node in Solution Explorer, and select the Publish tab to view the Publish Wizard properties, as shown in Figure 11.11.

2. Modify ThisWorkbook_Startup with the code in Listing 11.2. This action creates an empty actions pane with a red background, making it easy for you to see that your code is running.

Listing 11.2. *Creating an empty actions pane with a red background*

```
ActionsPane.BackColor = Color.Red
ActionsPane.Visible = True
```

3. Click Publish Now on the Publish tab to publish the new version.

4. Press F5 to run the solution.

5. Using Internet Explorer, browse to the http://MyWebServer/ ExcelWorkbook1/ExcelWorkbook1.xls file. The result is that your VSTO Excel document opens and your code runs. This time you see that the actions pane is red, and this tells you that the new version of the application is running.

Rollback

The VSTO Publish Wizard makes it easy to roll back to another version. Each time you publish, VSTO creates a copy of your document and a copy of the deployment manifest.

1. Copy the old deployment manifest from the folder version that you want to roll back to. In this case you will roll back to version 1.0.0.0, so copy the ... | ExcelWorkbook1 | ExcelWorkbook1_1.0.0.0 | ExcelWorkbook1.application file, and paste it over the file that is in the root of your folder.

    Now when the document is opened, the deployment manifest points to version 1.0.0.0 of your solution. When you publish, VSTO copies the entire solution to the published location. This includes a copy of the document at the time the solution was published. You can use this copy of the document if changes in the document require a specific solution. For example, if version 1 of the solution depends on a bookmark called TotalBookmark that does not exist in version 2, rolling back the code would break the solution.

2. Press F5 to run the solution.

3. Using Internet Explorer, browse to the http://MyWebServer/ ExcelWorkbook1/ExcelWorkbook1.xls file. The result is that your VSTO Excel document opens and your code runs. This time you see that the actions pane is blue, and this tells you that the old version of the application is running.

Microsoft Installer Project

Another approach to deploying your VSTO solutions is to use a Visual Studio Setup project. The Visual Studio Setup project creates a Microsoft installer file, which has the extension .msi. The MSI files are standard Microsoft installer files. MSI files display an Install Wizard and add an entry to the Add And Remove Programs feature in the Control Panel to allow you to repair and uninstall the application.

Earlier in this chapter you learned about some of the shortcomings of the Publish Wizard, such as not checking for or installing client prerequisites and not configuring the client's security policy. Out of the box, the Visual Studio Setup project is missing a few features that you need to install your projects. The Setup project is extensible, but doing so is complicated and beyond the scope of this book. Microsoft has provided an article that explains in depth how to modify the Setup program. Following the steps outlined in the article will get your development machine configured correctly to create MSIs to install your VSTO projects. You can locate this article on MSDN at http://msdn.microsoft.com/library/ en-us/odc_vsto2005_ta/html/OfficeVSTOWindowsInstallerOverview.asp or by searching for the title "Deploying Visual Studio 2005 Tools for Office Solutions Using Windows Installer (Part 1 of 2)."

The Setup project does not check for prerequisites needed by VSTO. These checks are done as part of the Visual Studio *bootstrapper*, the setup.exe that is created by the Setup project to check for and optionally install the required software (see Figure 11.23). The bootstrapper is extensible using XML files, which you can copy from the deployment article.

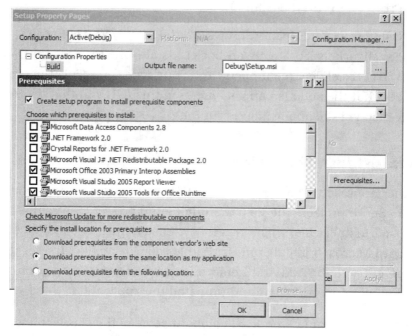

Figure 11.23. *Setting prerequisites in the Setup Property Pages dialog box*

Next, you update the application manifest that is embedded in the document by using the ServerDocument API (discussed in Chapter 13) in a custom action. As you can see in Figure 11.24, the UpdateManifest custom action is called from the Custom Actions tab of the Setup project. You use the CustomActionData property to pass parameters that are required by the custom action. The custom action is called when the user is doing an install, repair, or uninstall.

Now you update the CASPOL security on the client machine to give the code permission to run. You do this using a custom action. You can find an example of how to write the UpdateManifest custom action project and the SetSecurity custom action project that is added to your VSTO

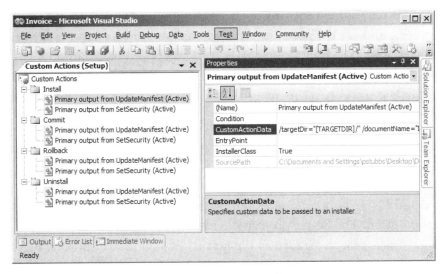

Figure 11.24. *Custom action to update the manifest*

solution in the deployment article described earlier. Figure 11.25 shows that the SetSecurity custom action is called from the Custom Actions tab of your Setup project.

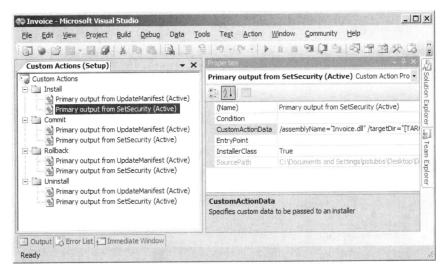

Figure 11.25. *Custom action to set the security*

After you have added the prerequisite checks, updated the application manifest, and set the security permissions, you are ready to build the Setup project. The build from the Setup project produces an .msi file and a setup.exe file. Normally you run setup.exe to install your solution. Although you can run the .msi directly, the setup may stop if the client dependencies are not met.

Deploying Outlook Solutions

By default, the Outlook project template includes a Setup project in your solution. The Setup project is a standard one, and it includes the correct registry keys needed to register a set of Outlook add-ins. Figure 11.26 shows the keys added by the Setup project.

Like the Publish Wizard, the Outlook Setup project creates an .msi with similar features. It copies the add-in to the correct location and regis-

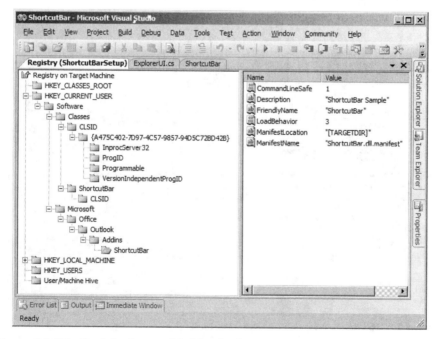

Figure 11.26. *Registry keys added by the Setup project*

ters the add-in with Outlook, but it does not check that the client is set up correctly and does not set the security permissions for the add-in to run. You need to add prerequisite checks to the Setup bootstrapper and add the SetSecurity custom action, as mentioned earlier. In this case, you do not need to update the application manifest because Outlook does not embed the application manifest.

Also note that when you build your Outlook project, there are some custom build tasks that are part of the project file that deploys your add-in on your developer machine. This can make it difficult to test your Setup project, because building the solution installs the add-in. One workaround is that after you build your solution, you can uninstall the add-in by right-clicking the add-in project and clicking Clean from the context menu. Running Clean on your Outlook project uninstalls the add-in.

Summary

We started this chapter by looking at the VSTO security model and describing code access security. You looked at the client requirements and learned how to verify them using the PSS Client Troubleshooter tool. You then looked at how to use the Publish Wizard to deploy your solution. You saw that VSTO manifests enable easy updating and roll-back of your deployed solutions. You learned the basics of using the Windows installer to deploy your solution as an .msi file. You finished by discovering how to deploy Outlook add-ins in an .msi file.

Review Questions

1. What are the two ways that code access security can be set?

2. What permission sets do VSTO solutions require?

3. Name the three deployment models.

4. Explain how VSTO uses the application and deployment manifest to update a solution.

5. Explain how deploying Outlook solutions is different from deploying Word and Excel solutions.

12

Migrating VBA Solutions to VSTO

We always overestimate the change that will occur in the next two years and underestimate the change that will occur in the next ten.
—BILL GATES

Topics Covered in This Chapter

Migration Overview

VBA has been around for a long time, and many people have existing VBA projects. Still, using VSTO and managed code offers advantages for creating customizations for Word, Excel, and Outlook:

- Code that is managed by the .NET Framework and includes automatic garbage collection

- Access to thousands of classes in the .NET Framework class library

- Use of an object-oriented programming language

- Improved security model

- More manageable update and rollback model

- Better development, environment, and debugging tools

- Enhanced object models that enable data binding and expose events on native Office objects

- Data caching and offline capabilities

- Ability to create document-specific Word and Excel smart tags

- Simplified coding for creating customized Word and Excel task panes

- Stable loading of managed add-ins

You have seen the power that VSTO and the .NET Framework bring to Office development. If you've decided to make the move to Visual Basic 2005 and VSTO, you should consider the discussion in this chapter before migrating your existing code.

Migration Strategies

You should consider a number of factors when determining how to move your VBA applications to VSTO. First, it's a good idea to take an inventory of your VBA applications to judge their complexity and their dependencies. Does a given VBA application consist mainly of recorded macro code, or is it all high-end, handwritten VBA that uses features like UserForms, Web services, and native Windows API calls? The answer to this question will assist you in determining your migration strategy.

Next, inventory your skills. Do you have advanced VBA and Visual Basic knowledge, and do you understand the business problem that the VBA application is trying to solve? Part of the migration process is migrating your programming skills.

The easiest way to convert an application from VBA to VSTO is to convert the VBA syntax to Visual Basic syntax. This is the approach that you will take in the next section (refer to Chapter 4 to learn about the language differences between VBA and Visual Basic 2005). Converting syntax is easy for simple to moderately complex VBA projects, even if you have little knowledge of VBA or VSTO and little domain knowledge. Although this approach will get your VBA application converted, it will not take advantage of the features of VSTO. If you start with a poorly written VBA application, you will end with a poorly written VSTO application.

The next choice is to take a balanced approach. You convert much of your VBA code line by line, exploiting VSTO features where applicable. For example, in "Advanced Migration of a Word VBA Project" later in this chapter you will use an actions pane instead of a simple Windows Forms dialog box to collect user information. You could use XML nodes instead of bookmarks, and data caching instead of hidden worksheets. It requires more VSTO and domain knowledge to redesign the relevant parts of an application.

The most advanced way to migrate your VBA project is to completely redesign the entire solution. This approach requires the most VBA and VSTO knowledge and the most domain knowledge. The advantage is that you can focus on end-user goals, and you are not bound to the requirements that were specified when the application was originally written. User requirements change frequently, and redesigning the application gives you the opportunity to address many user needs. However, this approach is the most costly and time-consuming. Depending on the size or complexity of the application, you may want to purchase a third-party conversion tool to automate part of the conversion. You might also want to use interop to convert parts of the application in stages. This method allows you to incrementally add VSTO functionality to an existing VBA application.

Another advanced approach is to use VBA-to-VSTO interoperability, calling VSTO functions from VBA and calling your VBA functions from

VSTO. In this way, you can migrate your applications to VSTO in phases. For example, if you need to call a Web service, you can do it very easily in VSTO. But if your application uses a complex VBA macro, it might be easier to reuse it than to rewrite it.

Whichever approach you take, the benefits of moving to VSTO and managed code will pay off in the long term with increased developer productivity, quicker time to market, and advanced user features. However, if your VBA solution is working and meets your business requirements, you are not required to migrate the solution. VBA will be supported by Microsoft for the foreseeable future, giving you time to carefully plan your migration when it makes sense for your business.

Simple Migration of a Word VBA Project

In this section, you will migrate a sample Word VBA application to VSTO. As shown in Figure 12.1, the application is a simple memo template that prompts users for information when they create a new document. After users enter information into the fields of the VBA UserForm and click OK, the bookmarks on the document are populated with the information.

The New event fires when a new document is created from a template. It is here that you will write the code to show the UserForm, because the form is displayed only when the document is created. You also set other properties of the document, such as the caption. The frmMain.Show code in Listing 12.1 displays the UserForm in Figure 12.1.

Listing 12.1. *Displaying a UserForm when a new document is created*

```
Private Sub Document_New()

    With ActiveDocument
        .SpellingChecked = True
        .GrammarChecked = True
        .ActiveWindow.Caption = _
```

```
        .ActiveWindow.Caption & " - Memo"
        .ActiveWindow.View.ShowFieldCodes = False
    End With

    ' Show the form.
    frmMain.Show
End Sub
```

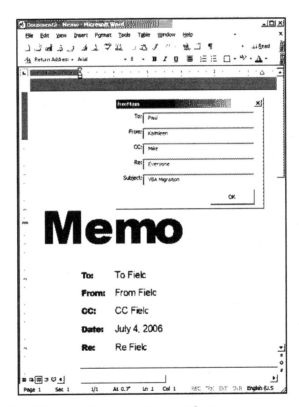

Figure 12.1. *Word VBA application with input form*

Figure 12.2 shows the UserForm in the design view of the VBA Editor.

As shown in Listing 12.2, the VBA code handled by the Click event of the OK button sets the text box values to the correct bookmark and then closes the form.

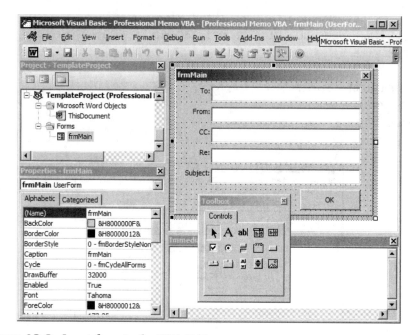

Figure 12.2. *Input form in the VBA Editor*

Listing 12.2. *Populating bookmarks on a UserForm Click event*

```
Private Sub btnOK_Click()

    ' Insert the fields into the bookmarks.
    With ActiveDocument
        .Bookmarks("To").Range = txtTo
        .Bookmarks("From").Range = txtFrom
        .Bookmarks("CC").Range = txtCC
        .Bookmarks("Re").Range = txtRe
        .Bookmarks("Subject").Range = txtSubject
    End With

    Unload Me
End Sub
```

Figure 12.3 shows the expected results of your VBA project. The bookmarks have been populated with the correct information from your UserForm.

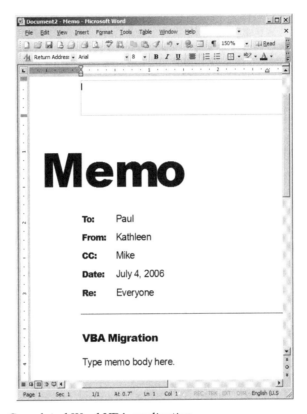

Figure 12.3. *Completed Word VBA application*

Advanced Migration of a Word VBA Project

You will now convert the VBA memo project that you created in the preceding section. You will convert the project to VSTO using the easiest conversion path without changing any semantics of the original VBA program.

Copying the Word Template

Copy the existing Word template file so that you have a template to use for your VSTO solution. Name the new template Professional Memo VSTO.dot.

Removing the VBA Code and the UserForm from the Template

1. Open the template in Word by clicking Open on the File menu. Then press ALT+F11 to open the VBA Code Editor.

2. In the Forms folder, delete the frmMain form.

3. In the Microsoft Word Objects folder, open the ThisDocument code. Delete all the code by selecting the code with the mouse and pressing the DELETE key.

4. Save the file as Professional Memo VSTO.dot.

Now that you have removed all the VBA code, you are ready to use the template to create your VSTO project.

1. Create a new VSTO Word project.

2. Start VSTO and create a new Word Template project. Name the new project "Professional Memo VSTO," and then click OK to start the VSTO Project Wizard.

3. Select Copy An Existing Document, and type the path to Professional Memo VSTO.dot, as shown in Figure 12.4. Click OK to create the VSTO project.

Creating a Windows Form

VSTO does not use the same forms system used by VBA, so you need to re-create your VBA form using Windows Forms. Add a new Windows Form to the VSTO project by right-clicking the project, pointing to Add,

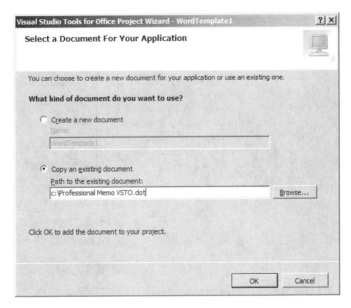

Figure 12.4. *Using an existing document template*

and then clicking Windows Form. In the Add New Item dialog box, name the form frmMain.vb. A new Windows form is added to your project, and the designer is opened.

You can now drag and drop controls onto your document to create a form that looks like your VBA UserForm. You can see in Figure 12.5 that the Windows Form is nearly identical.

You are now ready to populate the bookmarks when the user selects OK. Double-click the OK button on frmMain to create a Click event handler for the OK button. Type the code in Listing 12.3. You can see that it is almost identical to the VBA code. One difference is that you get a reference to the Document object in the With statement. In this case, because you are in a Windows Form you use the Globals object to reference the ThisDocument object. In addition, Visual Basic 2005 does not support default properties so you must specify the text property in all cases. You close the Windows Form using its Close method.

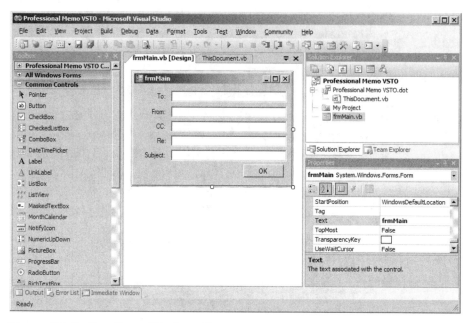

Figure 12.5. *Creating a Windows Form*

Listing 12.3. *Populating bookmarks on an OK button Click event*

```
Public Class frmMain

    Private Sub btnOK_Click(ByVal sender As System.Object, _
        ByVal e As System.EventArgs) Handles btnOK.Click

        ' Insert the fields into the bookmarks.
        With Globals.ThisDocument
            .Bookmarks("To").Range.Text = txtTo.Text
            .Bookmarks("From").Range.Text = txtFrom.Text
            .Bookmarks("CC").Range.Text = txtCC.Text
            .Bookmarks("Re").Range.Text = txtRe.Text
            .Bookmarks("Subject").Range.Text = txtSubject.Text
        End With

        ' Close the form.
        Me.Close()
    End Sub
End Class
```

Starting the Form

Now that you have created your form, you are ready to launch it when the user creates a new document from the template. The New event of the document fires when a new document instance is created. Right-click ThisDocument.vb in Solution Explorer, and click View Code. In the Class Name drop-down box (left), select ThisDocument Events. The Method Name drop-down box (right) now displays all the events of the Document object.

Select New in the right drop-down to create an event handler to handle the New event. Type the code in Listing 12.4 in the New event handler. This code is very similar to the VBA code. The first thing you change is the way you reference the Document object. Instead of using Active-Document, you use the Me keyword. Also, the way you launch the Windows Form is a little different. Because Visual Basic 2005 is an object-oriented language, you create a new instance of the frmMain object.

Listing 12.4. *Displaying a Windows Form when a new document is created*

```
Public Class ThisDocument

    Private Sub ThisDocument_New() Handles Me.New
        Me.SpellingChecked = True
        Me.GrammarChecked = True
        Me.ActiveWindow.Caption = _
          Me.ActiveWindow.Caption & " - Memo"
        Me.ActiveWindow.View.ShowFieldCodes = False

        ' Show the UserForm.
        Dim frmMain As New frmMain
        frmMain.Show()
    End Sub

    Private Sub ThisDocument_Startup(ByVal sender As Object, _
        ByVal e As System.EventArgs) Handles Me.Startup

    End Sub
```

```
Private Sub ThisDocument_Shutdown(ByVal sender As Object, _
    ByVal e As System.EventArgs) Handles Me.Shutdown

End Sub

End Class
```

Running the Solution

You have completed migrating your VBA code, and you're ready to run your new VSTO solution. Press F5 to run the solution. You can see in Figure 12.6 that the VSTO solution works the same as the VBA application did.

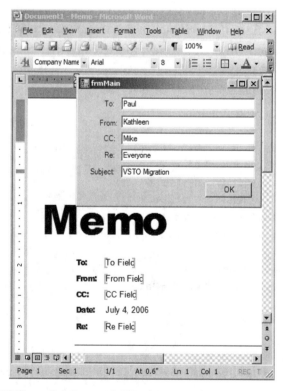

Figure 12.6. *VSTO application with Windows Form*

Converting your VBA to VSTO is not difficult, but this solution doesn't take advantage of the VSTO features. In the next section, you will change some things in your solution to make it more like .NET and to use more features of VSTO.

Redesigning the Solution

Now let's go beyond a simple conversion to use more of the power of VSTO and the .NET Framework. You will upgrade your project to use the Bookmark view control to program against the Word bookmarks as first-class .NET objects. You will then convert your Windows Form to use the Document Actions task pane.

Bookmark View Controls

As you learned in Chapter 6, when you create a bookmark in Word while in the Visual Studio IDE, a wrapper object is created called a view control. The Bookmark view control shows up in IntelliSense as a programmable object. And unlike regular Bookmark objects, Bookmark view controls are not late bound; thus, you do not need to refer to the bookmark using its string name from the Bookmarks collection.

Using late-bound objects can cause problems because typographical errors in the name are not found until run time. The names of the Bookmark view controls will be the same names as the bookmarks they wrap. To make the code more readable, you will append the type name to the names of all the view controls. For example, To becomes ToBookmark. The code also updates the Windows Form field names so that instead of using the Hungarian notation of VBA, you use a more .NET-style naming convention, as shown in Listing 12.5. The sample is not only more resilient to document changes but also easier to read and program.

Listing 12.5. *Populating Bookmark view controls on an OK button Click event*

```
Public Class MainForm

    Private Sub btnOK_Click(ByVal sender As System.Object, _
        ByVal e As System.EventArgs) Handles OkButton.Click

        ' Insert the fields into the bookmarks.
        With Globals.ThisDocument
            .ToBookmark.Text = ToTextBox.Text
            .FromBookmark.Text = FromTextBox.Text
            .CCBookmark.Text = CCTextBox.Text
            .REBookmark.Text = ReTextBox.Text
            .SubjectBookmark.Text = SubjectTextBox.Text
        End With

        ' Close the form.
        Me.Close()
    End Sub
End Class
```

Using the Actions Pane

You will now convert your sample from showing a modal dialog box to showing an actions pane that will enable the user to update the bookmarks. As described in Chapter 5, the actions pane is docked and does not obstruct users' view of the document as a Windows Form does. This helps the users understand the context of the fields they are adding.

Converting a Windows Form to a User Control

It is super easy to make this conversion. A user control can be placed in other controls or forms. In the example, you will put your user control onto the actions pane. You need to change the type that your form derives from. It's now System.Windows.Forms.Form, and you need to change it to System.Windows.Forms.UserControl.

To do this, click on the Show All Files button at the top of Solution Explorer. Expand the MainForm.vb node in Solution Explorer to see the code-behind files. Open the MainForm.Designer.vb class, and change the type that the form inherits from, as shown in Listing 12.6. Save and close the MainForm.Designer.vb class, and click the Show All Files icon again to hide the code-behind files. Open the MainForm.vb class, and notice that it is now a user control and does not have a title bar.

Listing 12.6. *Change the Windows Form to a user control type*

```
<Global.Microsoft.VisualBasic.CompilerServices. _
DesignerGenerated()> _
Partial Class MainForm
    Inherits System.Windows.Forms.UserControl
```

Let's look at how to show the MainForm UserControl inside of the ActionsPane when the document is started.

1. Right-click the ThisDocument.vb file in Solution Explorer, and click View Code.

2. Change the New event handler to the code in Listing 12.7. The only change is the way you open the form. You are creating a new instance and adding it to the actions pane's Controls collection in one line, shown in Listing 12.7 in bold.

Listing 12.7. *Displaying a user control in the actions pane when a new document is created*

```
Public Class ThisDocument

    Private Sub ThisDocument_New() Handles Me.New
        Me.SpellingChecked = True
        Me.GrammarChecked = True
        Me.ActiveWindow.Caption = _
          Me.ActiveWindow.Caption & " - Memo"
        Me.ActiveWindow.View.ShowFieldCodes = False
```

```
            ' Show the user form.
            ActionsPane.Controls.Add(New MainForm())
        End Sub


        Private Sub ThisDocument_Startup(ByVal sender As Object, _
            ByVal e As System.EventArgs) Handles Me.Startup

        End Sub


        Private Sub ThisDocument_Shutdown(ByVal sender As Object, _
            ByVal e As System.EventArgs) Handles Me.Shutdown

        End Sub

End Class
```

3. Change the MainForm control code to the code in Listing 12.8. The only line that changes is the line Me.Visible = False. This code hides the form after the fields are inserted into the document.

Listing 12.8. *Populating bookmark view controls on an OK button Click event*

```
Public Class MainForm

    Private Sub btnOK_Click(ByVal sender As System.Object, _
        ByVal e As System.EventArgs) Handles OkButton.Click

        ' Insert the fields into the bookmarks.
        With Globals.ThisDocument
            .ToBookmark.Text = ToTextBox.Text
            .FromBookmark.Text = FromTextBox.Text
            .CCBookmark.Text = CCTextBox.Text
            .REBookmark.Text = ReTextBox.Text
            .SubjectBookmark.Text = SubjectTextBox.Text
        End With

        'Hide the form.
        Me.Visible = False
    End Sub
End Class
```

4. Run the solution by pressing F5. You now have an actions pane docked to the right side of the document that contains the MainForm user control, as shown in Figure 12.7.

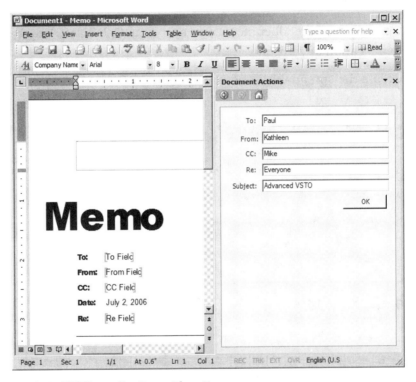

Figure 12.7. *VSTO application with actions pane*

VBA and VSTO Interoperability

VBA and VSTO interop is not a built-in feature of VSTO or VBA, so you must manually connect the two programming environments. Connecting VBA and VSTO allows you to call user defined functions (UDFs), which can be written only in VBA. A UDF is a VBA function that can be used in Excel formulas and other places. In Chapter 7, you learned how to create a simple UDF. In this section you will create a UDF to calculate the distance between two points.

Creating an Interop Excel Application

To create the sample Excel application, which calculates the distance between two points in two-dimensional space, you will use a user defined function written in VBA.

1. Open a new Excel document, and save it as CalculateDistance.xls to a location of your choice.

2. Create the spreadsheet shown in Figure 12.8.

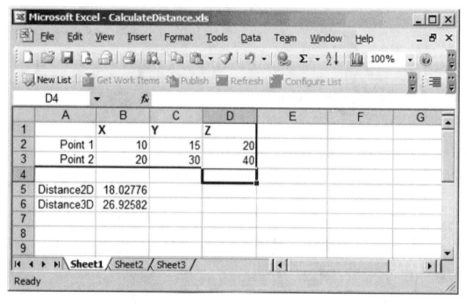

Figure 12.8. *Calculating the distance between two points*

3. Select cell B5 and enter the formula to call the UDF that you will create in the next section.

    ```
    =VBA_CalculateDistance2D(B2,C2,B3,C3)
    ```

4. Select cell B6 and enter the formula to call the UDF that you will create in the next section.

    ```
    =VSTO_CalculateDistance3D(B2,C2,D2,B3,C3,D3)
    ```

Creating the User Defined Functions in VBA

Because Excel supports UDFs only in VBA (and automation DLLs, a topic outside the scope of this book), you must create your UDFs in a VBA module. You will also use this module to call your VSTO functions.

1. Press ALT+F11 to open the VBA Editor.

2. Right-click the Modules node under VBA Projects (CalculateDistance.xls), and choose Insert | Module from the context menu. This action creates a new module with the default name Module1.

3. Add the code in Listing 12.9 to Module1.

Listing 12.9. *Creating UDFs and implementing VSTO interop in VBA*

```
Public Class MainForm

    Dim VSTOFunctions As Object

    ' VSTO will call this function to connect to VBA.
    Public Sub RegisterVSTOFunctions(VSTOFunctionsReference _
        As Object)

        Set VSTOFunctions = VSTOFunctionsReference

    End Sub

    Public Function VBA_CalculateDistance2D( _
        X1 As Integer, Y1 As Integer, _
        X2 As Integer, Y2 As Integer) As Double

        Dim Distance2D As Double
        Distance2D = Sqr((X2 - X1) ^ 2 + (Y2 - Y1) ^ 2)

        VBA_CalculateDistance2D = Distance2D

    End Function

    ' Calculate the 3D distance in VSTO.
    Public Function VSTO_CalculateDistance3D( _
```

```
        X1 As Integer, Y1 As Integer, Z1 As Integer, _
        X2 As Integer, Y2 As Integer, Z2 As Integer) _
        As Double

        Dim Distance3D As Double
        Distance3D = VSTOFunctions.CalculateDistance3D( _
            X1, Y1, Z1, X2, Y2, Z2)

        VSTO_CalculateDistance3D = Distance3D

    End Function

End Class
```

The first thing we add to the module is a variable called VSTOFunctions, which will hold a reference to the VSTO object. It is passed when VSTO calls the RegisterVSTOFunctions subroutine during the document's Open event. When you have a reference to this object, you can call public methods on this object from VBA. Note that VBA uses late binding to call the methods, so you do not see IntelliSense for this object.

In this example, you have created two UDFs. The first of these, VBA_CalculateDistance2D, is implemented in VBA. The other UDF, VSTO_CalculateDistance3D, is a pass-through to the VSTO function CalculateDistance3D. These functions complete the VBA side of the interop.

Note that the VBA functions are wrappers around the VSTO functions, allowing you to create managed UDFs. Now let's look at the VSTO side.

Creating a VSTO Excel Project

You now need to create a VSTO project that uses the CalculateDistance.xls file that you built earlier. Create a new Excel Workbook project. In the Create New Project Wizard, select Copy An Existing Document. Browse to and select CalculateDistance.xls.

Creating the VSTOFunctions Class

You will now create a class called VSTOFunctions. This class contains the functions that will be called by VBA.

1. On the Project menu, click Add Class. Name the class VSTOFunctions.vb.

2. Add the code in Listing 12.10.

Listing 12.10. *Creating the VSTOFunctions class*

```vb
<System.Runtime.InteropServices.ComVisible(True)> _
Public Class VSTOFunctions

    ' Called by VBA.
    Public Function CalculateDistance3D( _
    ByVal X1 As Integer, ByVal Y1 As Integer, _
        ByVal Z1 As Integer, ByVal X2 As Integer, _
        ByVal Y2 As Integer, ByVal Z2 As Integer) _
        As Double

        Dim Distance3D As Double

        If Z1 + Z2 = 0 Then
            'This is 2D so call CalculateDistance2D (in VBA).
            Return CalculateDistance2D(X1, Y1, X2, Y2)
        End If

        ' Calculate the 3D distance.
        Distance3D = Math.Sqrt((X2 - X1) ^ 2 + (Y2 - Y1) ^ 2 + _
            (Z2 - Z1) ^ 2)

        Return Distance3D

    End Function

    ' Call the VBA function.
    Public Function CalculateDistance2D( _
    ByVal X1 As Integer, ByVal Y1 As Integer, _
    ByVal X2 As Integer, ByVal Y2 As Integer) As Double
```

```
    ' Use the existing CalculateDistance2D written in VBA.
    Return Globals.ThisWorkbook.Application.Run( _
        "VBA_CalculateDistance2D", X1, Y1, X2, Y2)
    End Function
End Class
```

The first thing you add to the class is an attribute called ComVisible, whose value you set to True. This attribute allows you to pass this class to VBA. Next, you create two functions. The CalculateDistance3D function is implemented in Visual Basic 2005 and is called from the VBA VSTO_CalculateDistance3D function you created earlier. The CalculateDistance2D function calls VBA_CalculateDistance2D in VBA. The CalculateDistance2D function is called by the CalculateDistance3D function if the values of Z1 and Z2 are zero.

This example demonstrates calling VSTO from VBA, and calling VBA from VSTO. The final step is to connect VSTO and VBA when the workbook opens.

Connecting VBA and VSTO When the Workbook Opens

When the workbook opens, you call the RegisterVSTOFunctions subroutine in VBA, passing a reference to an instance of the VSTOFunctions class you created earlier.

1. Add the code in Listing 12.11 to the ThisWorkbook.vb class.

Listing 12.11. *Calling the RegisterVSTOFunctions subroutine in VBA when the workbook opens*

```
Public Class ThisWorkbook

    Private Sub ThisWorkbook_Open() Handles Me.Open

        ' Connect VSTO and VBA.
        Me.Application.Run("RegisterVSTOFunctions", _
            New VSTOFunctions)

    End Sub
```

```
Private Sub ThisWorkbook_Startup(ByVal sender As Object, _
    ByVal e As System.EventArgs) Handles Me.Startup

End Sub

Private Sub ThisWorkbook_Shutdown(ByVal sender As Object, _
    ByVal e As System.EventArgs) Handles Me.Shutdown

End Sub

End Class
```

2. Press F5 to run the VSTO solution.

3. When the workbook opens, type some values for the two points. You may need to press CTRL+ALT+F9 to get Excel to recalculate the formulas.

As you have seen, implementing VBA and VSTO interoperability is not very complicated. This technique can be a powerful part of your migration strategy because it lets you migrate individual functions to VSTO one at a time.

Summary

We started this chapter by discussing VBA migration and explained what is involved in migrating to VSTO. You then looked at various strategies for this migration. You saw how to migrate Word and Excel VBA projects to VSTO, and you learned about some of the issues that are involved in converting VBA forms to Windows Forms. Finally, you saw how to implement interoperability between VSTO and VBA.

Review Questions

1. What are some of the reasons to migrate VBA solutions to Visual Basic 2005 and VSTO?

2. What are some of the strategies for migrating VBA solutions to VSTO?

3. How can the actions pane be used to replace dialog boxes?

4. What types of forms are used in VBA and VSTO?

5. Name one advantage of using the actions pane instead of a Windows Form.

13

Advanced Topics in VSTO

A little knowledge that acts is worth infinitely
more than much knowledge that is idle.
—KAHLIL GIBRAN

Topics Covered in This Chapter

ServerDocument Overview

Attaching and Detaching Document-Based Customizations

Reading and Writing the Data Cache

Clearing the Data Cache

Summary

Review Questions

ServerDocument Overview

VSTO provides a class called ServerDocument to read from and write to the data cache, and to attach and detach solutions that are associated with the document. As discussed in Chapter 11, VSTO document-based solutions have an application manifest and a data cache embedded in the document. The application manifest is used to locate the solution assembly and is linked to the deployment manifest.

The document also contains a data cache that is used by the VSTO runtime to store data when the user is offline. VSTO embeds the application manifest and the data cache into the document by inserting a special ActiveX control called the Runtime Storage Control. It is this control that the ServerDocument class manipulates.

Attaching and Detaching Document-Based Customizations

You can think of a VSTO document solution as a Word or Excel document with an attached VSTO assembly. When you create a new VSTO project in Visual Studio, the VSTO project system attaches the assembly for you automatically as part of project creation. This is the most common scenario for developers, but in other scenarios you will attach the solution to (or detach it from) the document.

Detaching a Solution from a Document Using ServerDocument

A common detaching scenario involves document generation. For example, imagine that you have created a VSTO solution that pulls data from a database to generate an invoice document. The user opens the VSTO template file, which creates a new VSTO document instance. The user then uses the actions pane, data binding, and other VSTO features to generate the invoice. When you send a document in e-mail, you're not sending the assembly along with it. Even if you did, the user wouldn't have permission to run the solution.

The customer requires that you send the invoice as an uncustomized Word or Excel document. The solution is to detach the VSTO solution from the document before you send it. Listing 13.1 shows how to detach a VSTO solution from a document using a Console application. After you detach the VSTO solution, the customization is no longer associated with the document, and it can be opened and used by any user who has any version of Office 2003 or the Office 2003 viewers.

Listing 13.1. *Detaching a VSTO solution from a document*

```
Imports Microsoft.VisualStudio.Tools.Applications.Runtime

Module Module1
```

```
Sub Main()

    ' Path to VSTO document.
    Dim documentPath As String = "C:\Invoice\Invoice.xls"
    'Detach the VSTO solution from the document.
    DetachSolution(documentPath)

End Sub

Sub DetachSolution(ByVal documentPath As String)

    ' Check to see whether the document is a VSTO solution.
    If ServerDocument.IsCustomized(documentPath) Then

        ' Remove VSTO solution to make a normal document
        ' again.
        ServerDocument.RemoveCustomization(documentPath)

    End If

End Sub

End Module
```

Attaching a Solution to a Document Using ServerDocument

A common attaching scenario involves document processing. In this scenario, you receive an invoice from a customer and need to process it by uploading the data to a database in your company. The customer sends you an Office document, and you then attach an existing VSTO solution to the document. Now the VSTO customization runs whenever you open the document.

Or suppose you've created functionality that you want to use on any document. For example, if you have created a customization for formatting financial tables in a Word document, you can attach this code to any document and use these tools. Listing 13.2 shows how to attach a VSTO solution to a document.

> ❖ **Note** If the document does not have the Runtime Storage Control embedded, then the Word or Excel application will be started. This is important to keep in mind if you are attaching the solutions on a server where Office may not be installed.

Listing 13.2. *Attaching a VSTO solution to a document*

```vb
Imports Microsoft.VisualStudio.Tools.Applications.Runtime

Module Module1

    Sub Main()

        ' Path to VSTO document.
        Dim documentPath As String = "C:\Invoice\Invoice.xls"
        Dim assemblyName As String = _
            "C:\Invoice\Invoice_1.0.0.0\Invoice.dll"
        Dim deploymentManifestPath As String = _
            "C:\Invoice\Invoice.application"
        Dim applicationVersion As String = "1.0.0.0"
        Dim makePathsRelative As Boolean = False

        ' Attach the VSTO solution to the document.
        AttachSolution( _
                documentPath, _
                assemblyName, _
                deploymentManifestPath, _
                applicationVersion, _
                makePathsRelative)
    End Sub

    Sub AttachSolution( _
        ByVal documentPath As String, _
        ByVal assemblyName As String, _
```

```
        ByVal deploymentManifestPath As String, _
        ByVal applicationVersion As String, _
        ByVal makePathsRelative As Boolean)

        ' Check whether it is already attached.
        If Not ServerDocument.IsCustomized(documentPath) Then

            ' Attach the solution to the document.
            ServerDocument.AddCustomization( _
                documentPath, _
                assemblyName, _
                deploymentManifestPath, _
                applicationVersion, _
                makePathsRelative)

        End If
    End Sub
End Module
```

Attaching a Solution to a Document Using Custom Document Properties

There is another way to attach a VSTO solution to your document without programming. You might use this technique when you have an existing VSTO solution that is pointing to a deployment manifest on a particular server. If the server goes down and you need to load the assembly from a different server, you can easily change the custom document properties to reference the new location.

There are two custom document properties: _AssemblyName and _AssemblyLocation. In this section, you will modify the custom document properties of a Word or Excel document.

1. Open the Word or Excel document.

2. On the File menu, click Properties, and then click the Custom tab to open the Custom Properties dialog box.

3. Set the _AssemblyLocation to the path of the deployment manifest file. This can be a file, a UNC, or an HTTP path. As in Listing 13.2, you can set the property to *C:\Invoice\Invoice.application*. If this is not a VSTO document, you must first create this property.

4. Set _AssemblyName to an asterisk (*). If this is a VSTO document, you must first create this property.

5. Click OK to close the Properties dialog box.

6. Save the document.

When the document is opened after the custom properties have been set, the VSTO runtime attaches the solution to the document. The runtime embeds the Runtime Storage Control, embeds the application manifest, and loads the assembly.

Reading and Writing the Data Cache

VSTO's data caching feature enables you to embed data in the document. The data cache travels with the document when you copy or send it. The embedded data cache also enables the offline scenario by storing the data locally when you are not connected to the server. Users seldom need to think about how the data is stored. VSTO makes client programming of the data cache very easy. Often it is as simple as setting the CacheInDocument property to True. You can also add the Cached attribute to variables you want VSTO to store in the data cache.

Cached Data Structure

The cached data is stored in the document in a hierarchy. You can see this hierarchy in Figure 13.1, which shows the types and names of the objects in this example.

Let's look at a simple example of reading and writing the data cache from outside Word or Excel.

```
ServerDocument
    CachedData
        CachedDataHostItemCollection
            CachedDataHostItem ("ExcelWorkbook1.Sheet1")
                CachedDataItemCollection
                    CachedDataItem ("FirstName")
                    CachedDataItem ("LastName")
```

Figure 13.1. *Sample cached data structure*

Creating a Test Document with Cached Data

1. Using VSTO, create an Excel workbook project called CachedDataSample.

2. In cell A1, type *First Name*, and in cell A2, type *Last Name*.

3. Select cell B1, and create a named range called FirstName. Select cell B2, and create a named range called LastName. The document should look like the one in Figure 13.2.

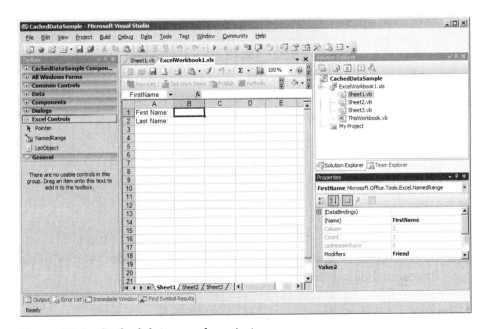

Figure 13.2. *Cached data sample project*

4. Right-click Sheet1.vb in Solution Explorer or Sheet1 in the designer, and click View Code. Add the code in Listing 13.3 to the Sheet1 class. This code adds public cached fields to class Sheet1.

Listing 13.3. *Adding cached fields to the Sheet1 class*

```
<Cached()> _
Public CachedFirstName As String
<Cached()> _
Public CachedLastName As String
```

This action creates two public string fields. You add the Cached attribute to tell the VSTO runtime to cache these fields. It is important that you make these fields public. If you do not explicitly specify the visibility of the field, Visual Basic will mark them Private by default. The data will be cached only if it is marked Public. If it is not public, you may not see an exception message.

5. On Startup set the named range values to the values that are cached in the document. Add the code in Listing 13.4 to initialize the named ranges you created earlier.

Listing 13.4. *Initializing named ranges with cached data values*

```
Private Sub Sheet1_Startup(ByVal sender As Object, _
    ByVal e As System.EventArgs) Handles Me.Startup

    ' Set the FirstName and LastName to the value in the cache.
    FirstName.Value = CachedFirstName
    LastName.Value = CachedLastName
End Sub
```

6. Update the cached values when the named range changes. You will handle the Change event of the named range to update the value of the cached data fields. Add the code in Listing 13.5.

Listing 13.5. *Updating cached data values on the named range Change event*

```
Private Sub FirstName_Change(ByVal Target As _
    Microsoft.Office.Interop.Excel.Range) Handles _
    FirstName.Change
```

```
    CachedFirstName = FirstName.Value

End Sub

Private Sub LastName_Change(ByVal Target As _
    Microsoft.Office.Interop.Excel.Range) Handles _
    LastName.Change

        CachedLastName = LastName.Value

End Sub
```

7. Press F5 to run the solution. When the solution opens for the first time, the named ranges will be empty because the data cache is not yet set. Fill the named ranges with data. You can see the results in Figure 13.3.

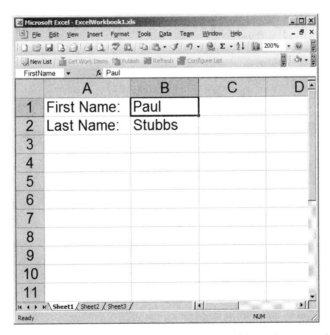

Figure 13.3. *Create the cached data on first run by filling the named ranges.*

8. Save and close the document.

Reading and Writing the Document Data Cache

In the preceding section you created the test document that you will use to read and write the data using the ServerDocument API. In the following steps, you will create a new Console application that will read and write the cached data fields from the document.

1. Create a new Visual Basic Console application project.

2. Add a reference to the VSTO runtime, as shown in Figure 13.4. On the Project menu, click Add Reference. In the .NET tab of the Add References dialog box, select Microsoft.VisualStudio.Tools.Applications.Runtime.

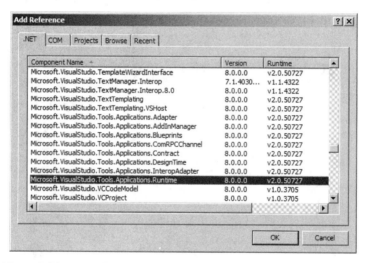

Figure 13.4. *Adding a reference to the VSTO runtime*

3. Add an Imports statement for the runtime to the Module1.vb class file. Use the code in Listing 13.6.

Listing 13.6. *Adding an Imports statement for the VSTO runtime*

```
Imports Microsoft.VisualStudio.Tools.Applications.Runtime
```

4. Create a ServerDocument object by passing the path to the document in the constructor, as shown in Listing 13.7. In this example you use a Console application, but this could also be called on the server in an ASP.NET application, in a Windows Forms application on the client, or even in the VSTO application itself.

Listing 13.7. *Creating an instance of the ServerDocument class*

```
Dim documentPath As String = _
    "C:\CachedDataSample\CachedDataSample\bin\Debug\" & _
    "ExcelWorkbook1.xls"

'Create the ServerDocument class.
Dim myServerDocument As New ServerDocument(documentPath)
```

5. Add the code in Listing 13.8 to create a CachedData object from the ServerDocument object.

Listing 13.8. *Getting an instance of the CachedData class*

```
' Get the cached data from the document.
Dim myCachedData As CachedData = myServerDocument.CachedData
```

6. Add the code in Listing 13.9 to create a CachedDataHostItem object from the CachedData object.

Listing 13.9. *Getting an instance of the CachedDataHostItem class*

```
' Get the cached data for Sheet1.
Dim sheet1CachedData As CachedDataHostItem = _
    myCachedData.HostItems("ExcelWorkbook1.Sheet1")
```

7. Add the code in Listing 13.10 to get the CachedDataItem objects from the CachedDataHostItem object. The CachedDataItem object represents the individual cached items in the data cache. Each item that you mark as cached in the document solution will have one CachedDataItem.

Listing 13.10. *Getting the instances of the CachedDataItem class*

```
Dim FirstNameCachedData As CachedDataItem = _
    sheet1CachedData.CachedData("CachedFirstName")
Dim LastNameCachedData As CachedDataItem = _
    sheet1CachedData.CachedData("CachedLastName")
```

Next, you need to convert the CachedDataItem Xml objects to String objects to get the cached values, a process known as *deserialization*. The CachedDataItem class has a property called Xml that contains the XML serialized data. It also has a DataType property, which is the type of the data that is serialized in the Xml property. There is also a property called Schema, which contains the schema for the Xml property, but only if the type is a DataTable or a DataSet.

The CachedDataItem object does not provide any methods to deserialize the data that is stored in the Xml property. You need to implement this functionality because this API is designed to be run on the server.

When you use XmlSerializer to deserialize the data, you might not get optimum performance. You also need to consider issues with versioning. For example, if you serialize the data on the client using version 1 of your solution and then try to deserialize it using version 2, problems may arise. For best performance, you should use System.Xml's document object model (DOM) to parse the XML manually and extract the values. This approach works for any type and version and doesn't require that the client types and assemblies be installed on the server.

In this example, you use XmlSerializer because these are simple string types. To deserialize the FirstName and LastName values, add the code in Listing 13.11 to the top of the module, followed by the code in Listing 13.12. In this example you don't use the deserialized values after you create them.

Listing 13.11. *Namespaces needed to deserialize the data cache*

```
' Namespaces for deserialization.
Imports System.Xml.Serialization
Imports System.IO
```

Listing 13.12. *Deserializing the instances of the CachedDataItem class*

```
' Get the FirstName value.
Dim FirstNameSerializer As New XmlSerializer( _
    Type.GetType(FirstNameCachedData.DataType))
Dim FirstNameXml As New Xml.XmlTextReader( _
    New StringReader(FirstNameCachedData.Xml))
Dim FirstName As String = _
    FirstNameSerializer.Deserialize(FirstNameXml)


' Get the LastName value.
Dim LastNameSerializer As New XmlSerializer( _
    Type.GetType(LastNameCachedData.DataType))
Dim LastNameXml As New Xml.XmlTextReader( _
    New StringReader(LastNameCachedData.Xml))
Dim LastName As String = LastNameSerializer.Deserialize( _
    LastNameXml)
```

Now you can set the FirstName and LastName CachedDataItems. The CachedDataItem class provides a method to automatically serialize the data into the Xml property. You call the SerializeDataInstance method, passing as the parameter the object to store. In this example, you are passing a string to update the cached data values. Add the code in Listing 13.13 to set the cached data values.

Listing 13.13. *Setting the instances of the CachedDataItem class*

```
FirstNameCachedData.SerializeDataInstance("Kathleen")
LastNameCachedData.SerializeDataInstance("McGrath")
```

The final step is to save and close the document to persist the changes. Add the code in Listing 13.14 to save and close the document.

Listing 13.14. *Saving and closing the document*

```
myServerDocument.Save()
myServerDocument.Close()
```

Running the Solution

Now you can run the console application to test whether the data was cached in the document.

1. Press F5 to run the Console application and update the cached values in the document with the new first and last names.

2. Open the cached data sample document that you just updated, as shown in Figure 13.5. Browse to <drive>:\ CachedDataSample\ CachedDataSample\bin\Debug\ExcelWorkbook1.xls and open the workbook. You will see the new values populated in the named ranges.

Figure 13.5. *Sample cached data document after the cached data is updated*

Listing 13.15 contains the complete listing. Two For Each loops assist with development and debugging. The CachedDataHostItems and the CachedDataItems classes are referenced by a string, but there isn't an easy way to determine what the name is. The For Each loops print all the names, and you can use the printout to find the cached data object you are looking for. To list all the names, uncomment the code.

Listing 13.15. *Complete listing for reading and writing the data cache*

```
Imports Microsoft.VisualStudio.Tools.Applications.Runtime

' Namespaces for deserialization.
Imports System.Xml.Serialization
Imports System.IO

Module Module1

    Sub Main()
        Dim documentPath As String = "C:\CachedDataSample\" _
            & "CachedDataSample\bin\Debug\ExcelWorkbook1.xls"

        ' Create the ServerDocument class.
        Dim myServerDocument As New ServerDocument(documentPath)

        ' Get the cached data from the document.
        Dim myCachedData As CachedData = _
            myServerDocument.CachedData

        ' Uncomment to display in the output window the host
        ' item IDs of all cached host items.
        'For Each cdhi As CachedDataHostItem In _
        '    myCachedData.HostItems
        '    Debug.Print(cdhi.Id)
        'Next

        ' Get the cached data for Sheet1.
        Dim sheet1CachedData As CachedDataHostItem = _
            myCachedData.HostItems("ExcelWorkbook1.Sheet1")

        ' Uncomment to display in the output window the
        ' cached data item IDs of all cached data items
        ' in the cached host item.
```

```vb
' Get the FirstName and LastName from the cache
'For Each cdi As CachedDataItem In _
'    sheet1CachedData.CachedData
'    Debug.Print(cdi.Id)
'Next

Dim FirstNameCachedData As CachedDataItem = _
    sheet1CachedData.CachedData("CachedFirstName")
Dim LastNameCachedData As CachedDataItem = _
    sheet1CachedData.CachedData("CachedLastName")

' Get the FirstName value.
Dim FirstNameSerializer As New XmlSerializer( _
    Type.GetType(FirstNameCachedData.DataType))
Dim FirstNameXml As New Xml.XmlTextReader( _
    New StringReader(FirstNameCachedData.Xml))
Dim FirstName As String = FirstNameSerializer _
    .Deserialize(FirstNameXml)

' Get the LastName value.
Dim LastNameSerializer As New XmlSerializer( _
    Type.GetType(LastNameCachedData.DataType))
Dim LastNameXml As New Xml.XmlTextReader( _
    New StringReader(LastNameCachedData.Xml))
Dim LastName As String = LastNameSerializer _
    .Deserialize(LastNameXml)

FirstNameCachedData.SerializeDataInstance("Kathleen")
LastNameCachedData.SerializeDataInstance("McGrath")

myServerDocument.Save()
myServerDocument.Close()

    End Sub

End Module
```

Clearing the Data Cache

Using ServerDocument, you can clear the cached data from the document. For example, suppose you have a VSTO solution that you want to deploy to an end user, but you don't want to remove the solution or the Runtime Storage Control because the user will run the VSTO solution. You do want to clear the data cache so that your test data does not go to the end user. Listing 13.16 shows how to clear the data cache from the document.

Listing 13.16. *Clearing the data cache in a VSTO document*

```
Imports Microsoft.VisualStudio.Tools.Applications.Runtime

Module Module1

    Sub Main()
        ' Path to VSTO document.
        Dim documentPath As String = "C:\Invoice\Invoice.xls"

        ' Clear the data cache.
        ClearDataCache(documentPath, True)

    End Sub

    Sub ClearDataCache(ByVal documentPath As String, _
        ByVal ClearDataOnly As Boolean)

        ' Create the ServerDocument class.
        Dim myServerDocument As New ServerDocument(documentPath)

        ' Get the cached data from the document.
        Dim myCachedData As CachedData = myServerDocument _
            .CachedData

        If ClearDataOnly Then
            ' Clear only the data but leave the description.
            myCachedData.ClearData()
```

```
      Else
          ' Alternatively, you can call Clear to completely
          ' remove the data cache.
          myCachedData.Clear()
      End If

      myServerDocument.Save()
      myServerDocument.Close()
   End Sub

End Module
```

In the ClearDataCache subroutine you create a new instance of the ServerDocument class using the path to the document. You get a reference to the CachedData object in ServerDocument. You can then call Clear or ClearData. The Clear method clears all the data and removes the data cache description from the manifest. Calling the ClearData method clears only the data; it does not remove the description from the manifest. In Listing 13.16 a ClearDataCache subroutine takes a Boolean value that enables you to choose how you want the data cache cleared.

Summary

You started this chapter by learning about application manifests, and you saw how to attach and detach them from a document. You also looked at how solutions can be attached to a document using custom document properties. You saw how you can easily update the application manifest regardless of your knowledge of XML or the application manifest schema. Finally, you looked at how to read and write data to and from the data cache from an external program.

Review Questions

1. What is the main purpose of the ServerDocument class?

2. How are the application manifest and data cache embedded in a document?

3. What API is used to manipulate the embedded data?

4. Explain how the data cache is structured.

5. Why might you want to clear the data cache?

6. Explain how to clear the data cache.

14

VSTO 2005 SE and the 2007 Microsoft Office System

The best way to predict the future is to invent it.
—ALAN KAY

Topics Covered in This Chapter

Introduction to VSTO 2005 SE

Creating Add-ins

Customizing the Ribbon

Creating Custom Task Panes

Creating a Custom Form Region

Summary

Review Questions

Introduction to VSTO 2005 SE

You can install a free, fully supported add-on for Visual Studio that lets you develop application-level solutions for several 2007 Microsoft Office system and Microsoft Office 2003 applications. This add-on is available as a free download in the Microsoft Download Center.

This download is Visual Studio 2005 Tools for the 2007 Microsoft Office System. In this book, it is referred to as Visual Studio Tools for Office Second Edition (VSTO 2005 SE) to distinguish it from Visual Studio Tools for Office (VSTO).

VSTO 2005 SE provides an add-in model that enables you to create application-level customizations (add-ins) for six 2007 Microsoft Office system applications: Microsoft Word, Excel, Outlook, InfoPath, Power-Point, and Visio. You can also create add-ins for five Microsoft Office 2003 applications: Microsoft Word, Excel, Outlook, PowerPoint, and Visio. VSTO 2005 SE also ensures that solutions you've built with VSTO for Office 2003 will run on the 2007 release of Office, provided that you deploy the VSTO 2005 SE runtime (VSTOR.exe) to your end-user machines.

If you install VSTO 2005 SE on a machine that has VSTO or Visual Studio Team System edition installed, you will have all the functionality of VSTO and VSTO 2005 SE. If you install VSTO 2005 SE on a machine that has Visual Studio Professional installed, you will have only the VSTO 2005 SE features, because VSTO does not ship as part of Visual Studio Professional. This means that even if you don't have VSTO installed, you can still get this add-on for Visual Studio and create add-ins for the 2007 release of Office, as well as add-ins for Office 2003. Unlike solutions you may have developed with VSTO, one of the benefits of using VSTO 2005 SE is that you can develop solutions that will run in all editions of the 2007 Microsoft Office system, including the Standard edition.

Additional features available in VSTO 2005 SE include run-time support for customizing the new UI feature in the 2007 release of Office: the Ribbon (shown for PowerPoint in Figure 14.1), the custom task pane, Outlook form regions, and InfoPath 2007 forms. Excel add-ins created with VSTO 2005 SE also have the benefit of the Excel locale issue fix (the transparent proxy), which was available for document-level customizations in Excel 2003. You can learn more about the transparent proxy in Chapter 7.

Features in All Releases

The main difference between VSTO and VSTO 2005 SE is that the latter contains application-level add-in support for Office (2003 and 2007) applications; there is no document-level customization support in VSTO

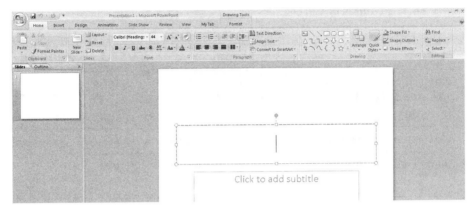

Figure 14.1. *The Ribbon in PowerPoint*

2005 SE (except for support for managed code behind InfoPath 2007 forms).

> ❖ **Note** You cannot simultaneously develop VSTO solutions for the 2003 and 2007 releases of Office. Side-by-side installations of these applications are not supported in a development environment.

Table 14.1 shows the differences between the VSTO features and those of VSTO 2005 SE. This table doesn't represent a comprehensive feature list for VSTO 2005 SE. However, it gives you a general idea of what you can expect from VSTO 2005 SE.

> ❖ **Note** If you've installed VSTO 2005 SE on a version of Visual Studio 2005 that doesn't contain VSTO, you will have only the functionality listed in the VSTO 2005 SE column. If you've installed it on top of VSTO, you will have the features listed in both columns.

Table 14.1. *Features of VSTO*

Feature	Scope	VSTO	VSTO 2005 SE
Managed code extensions for Office 2003 (Word, Excel, InfoPath)	Document-Level	✔	
Actions pane for Office 2003	Document-Level	✔	
Smart tags for Office 2003	Document-Level	✔	
Document designer for data-bindable Windows Forms controls and host controls	Document-Level	✔	
InfoPath 2007 Forms	Document-Level		✔
Add-in Support			
Outlook 2003	Application-Level	✔	✔
Outlook 2007	Application-Level		✔
Word 2003	Application-Level		✔
Word 2007	Application-Level		✔
Excel 2003	Application-Level		✔
Excel 2007	Application-Level		✔
InfoPath 2007	Application-Level		✔
PowerPoint 2003	Application-Level		✔
PowerPoint 2007	Application-Level		✔
Visio 2003	Application-Level		✔
Visio 2007	Application-Level		✔
Ribbon	Application-Level		✔
Custom task pane	Application-Level		✔
Outlook form region	Application-Level		✔

Here's an easy way to understand which edition of VSTO to use with Office. If you want to develop solutions for Office 2003, use VSTO for document-level customizations and VSTO 2005 SE for add-ins. If you want to develop solutions for the 2007 release of Office, use VSTO 2005 SE. Note that VSTO 2005 SE does not support document-level customization for either the 2003 or the 2007 release of Office, with one exception: InfoPath 2007 Forms.

VSTO 2005 SE Add-in Model

VSTO 2005 SE provides safe loading, unloading, and management of add-ins created with managed code (Visual Basic and C#). The architecture of VSTO 2005 SE add-ins described here is identical for all the supported Office (2003 and 2007) applications but differs from add-in development of Outlook 2003 with the full version of VSTO. If you create a new project using VSTO 2005 SE, you'll see the six supported add-ins in the 2007 Add-ins node, as shown in Figure 14.2, as well as five supported add-ins in the 2003 Add-ins node.

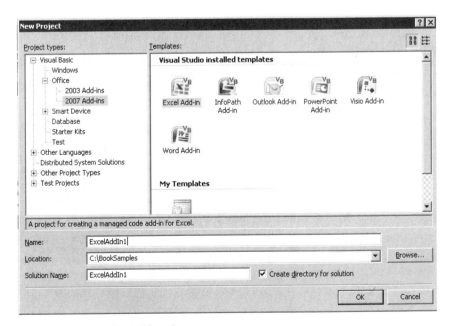

Figure 14.2. *The ThisAddin class*

As with VSTO add-ins, VSTO 2005 SE add-ins provide application domain isolation for each add-in that is loaded, but a different architecture is employed in VSTO 2005 SE add-ins. When you create a new VSTO 2005 SE add-in, you'll notice that a ThisAddin (not ThisApplication) code file and class are generated. The Application object in VSTO 2005 SE add-ins is not wrapped; you will no longer find the Microsoft.Office.Tools.Outlook.Application namespace. Instead, VSTO 2005 SE add-ins reference the Interop Application object (Microsoft.Office.Interop.Outlook.Application).

So the main difference in writing code for a VSTO 2005 SE add-in is that you access the Application object through the ThisAddin class. For example, if you want to display the version of the application in a message box you no longer write

```
MsgBox(Me.Version.ToString())
```

Instead, you write

```
MsgBox(Me.Application.Version.ToString())
```

As shown in Figure 14.3, the ThisAddin class exposes a Shutdown and a Startup event and creates the event handlers, maintaining its consistency with VSTO add-ins and document-level customization projects. Even though the Application object is not wrapped, the add-in is strongly typed.

All VSTO 2005 SE add-ins follow this same pattern; however, in Excel add-ins, VSTO 2005 SE generates initialization code that wraps the Application object in the transparent proxy class, as shown in Figure 14.4. This class fixes the Excel locale issue described in Chapter 7.

Office 2007 provides a new interface for add-ins that displays specific information about the add-ins you have loaded. Any loaded shared add-in is referenced by mscoree.dll, whereas VSTO 2005 SE add-ins refer-

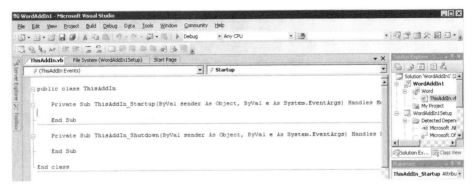

Figure 14.3. *The ThisAddin class for Word*

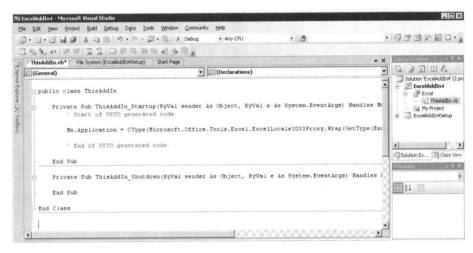

Figure 14.4. *The ThisAddin class*

ence the path to the manifest for the add-in, as shown in Figure 14.5. This reference enables you to easily identify add-ins. What's more, only a specific add-in that causes problems need be disabled.

VSTO add-ins are loaded by AddinLoader.dll and act as a shim between the add-in and the Outlook application. Because Office 2003 shipped before VSTO, it is not aware of the AddinLoader.dll file. As described in Chapter 11, VSTO add-ins require registry entries that specify the

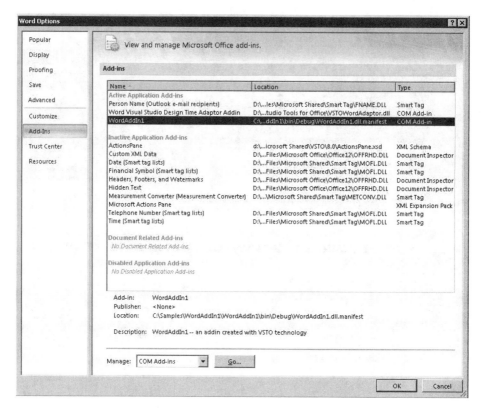

Figure 14.5. *Add-in interface*

ManifestLocation and the ManifestName. With VSTO 2005 SE add-ins, on the other hand, these registry keys are combined into one entry named Manifest. Also, the COM-specific registration is now omitted. There is no ProgId or CLSID registration under HKEY_CLASSES_ROOT, resulting in faster startup time for VSTO 2005 SE add-ins.

VSTO 2005 SE adds a new bootstrapper component, VSTOEE.dll, to the VSTO runtime. When Office sees the Manifest entry in the registry, it loads VSTOEE.dll, which then loads the proper version of the Addin-Loader.dll to load the add-in. The location of the add-in assembly is then listed in the new Add-in interface of Office 2007.

Because detailed information about the add-in is known, Office can limit hard-disabling to a specific, badly behaving add-in rather than disable the entire VSTO loader and thereby add all VSTO add-ins to the Exclusion list. As a result, VSTO 2005 SE add-ins are much more stable than VSTO add-ins or managed shared add-ins.

Figure 14.6 shows an example of a disabled add-in. In VSTO add-ins for Outlook 2003, an add-in can be disabled whenever an error occurs during startup. With VSTO 2005 SE, errors that occur in startup do not disable the add-in because the event sequencing in VSTO 2005 SE is different from that in VSTO add-ins.

Figure 14.6. *Add-ins in the Exclusion list*

Figure 14.6 shows two VSTO 2005 SE add-ins. ExcelAddin3 is listed under Active Application Add-ins, and ExcelAddin2 is listed under Disabled Application Add-ins. Each of these add-ins was created with VSTO 2005 SE, but only the problematic add-in has been disabled.

Because VSTO 2005 SE add-ins differ architecturally from and are more stable than VSTO add-ins, you might want to consider migrating existing VSTO add-ins for Outlook 2003 to VSTO 2005 SE add-ins.

Creating Add-ins

As mentioned earlier, VSTO 2005 SE supports the creation of add-ins for the six most popular applications in the 2007 Microsoft Office system and add-ins for five Office 2003 applications. If you're wondering why you can't create an add-in for InfoPath 2003 with VSTO 2005 SE, it is simply because InfoPath 2003 does not support add-ins of any type. The ability to create add-ins for the remaining applications is great news if you have found the document-level customizations of VSTO restrictive. Keep in mind, however, that the VSTO 2005 SE add-ins are not designed to work with document-level customization; the add-ins are loaded into a separate application domain and are isolated from code running in other application domains (such as document-level customizations). This isolation is similar to the way each document-level solution is loaded into a separate application domain, and thus it is difficult to implement communication between solutions.

Add-ins enable you to provide functionality for your solution that is available at the application level. For applications that have the concept of documents, such as Word, Excel, and PowerPoint, this means that the customization is available to any document, workbook, or slide presentation that you open.

Creating an Add-in

In this section, you'll create a simple "hello world" add-in so that you can become familiar with the VSTO 2005 SE add-in programming model.

1. Open Visual Studio and create a new project by clicking File | New Project.

2. Select the 2007 Add-in node, and in the New Project dialog box, select PowerPoint Add-in.

3. Keep the default name for the add-in, and click OK.

4. Right-click ThisAddin.vb in Solution Explorer, and click View Code.

5. Add the code in Listing 14.1 to the Startup event handler of ThisAddin.

Listing 14.1. *Adding code to the Startup event handler of a PowerPoint add-in*

```
Private Sub ThisAddIn_Startup(ByVal sender As Object, _
    ByVal e As System.EventArgs) Handles Me.Startup

    MsgBox(Me.Application.Name & " " & _
        Me.Application.Version)

End Sub
```

6. Press F5 to run the code. When the application opens, the product name and version should appear in a message box.

Now that you know how to create an add-in using VSTO 2005 SE, you can extend the add-in by adding code to customize the Ribbon, create a Custom task pane, or create an Outlook form region.

Customizing the Ribbon

The 2007 Microsoft Office system provides a new UI feature called the Ribbon. The *Ribbon* replaces the traditional menu and toolbars, making it easier for end users to find the functionality they need because related features are grouped. The idea is that these applications had a lot of functionality that users didn't know existed because it was buried deep in a submenu of a menu. After time spent learning to find familiar functionality, users will be able to more easily find useful functionality that has been present in earlier versions but was not easily discoverable.

Applications available in VSTO 2005 SE that support the Ribbon include Word, Excel, Outlook, and PowerPoint. Note that although Outlook supports the Ribbon on its Inspectors (the smaller windows that pop up when you create new mail, add a task, send a meeting request, etc.), it does not support Ribbons on the main Outlook window (the Explorer). This window uses Office 2003-style menus and toolbars.

The Ribbon Item

The Ribbon is often used as an entry point into your code. For example, your PowerPoint add-in might add a design Ribbon that contains controls that enable end users to design new PowerPoint themes. When you create an add-in to customize the Ribbon using VSTO 2005 SE, a generic "Hello world" tab, a group, and a toggle button are added to the Ribbon by default. This gives you the basic XML and code necessary to customize the Ribbon, which you can then modify to your liking. First we look at customizing the generic Ribbon.

1. Create an Excel 2007 add-in project using VSTO 2005 SE.

2. In Solution Explorer, right-click the project file, point to Add, and then click New Item.

3. In the New Item dialog box, select Ribbon Support.

4. Leave the default name Ribbon1.vb, and click Add, as shown in Figure 14.7.

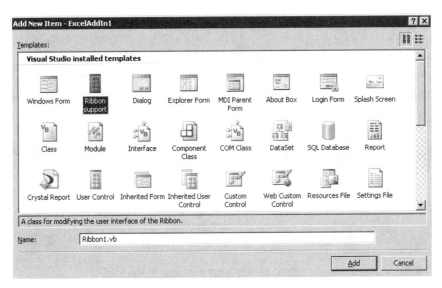

Figure 14.7. *Adding a Ribbon item to an Excel add-in project*

A new class named Ribbon1.vb and an XML file named
Ribbon1.xml are added to the project, as shown in Figure 14.8.
Later in this chapter you'll take a closer look at these files.

Figure 14.8. *Ribbon class and XML file displayed in Solution Explorer*

5. Uncomment the code at the top of the Ribbon1.vb code file, as shown in Figure 14.9. This code handles the service request to hook up the custom Ribbon. It is commented out because you might already have a class in your project that overrides the RequestService method.

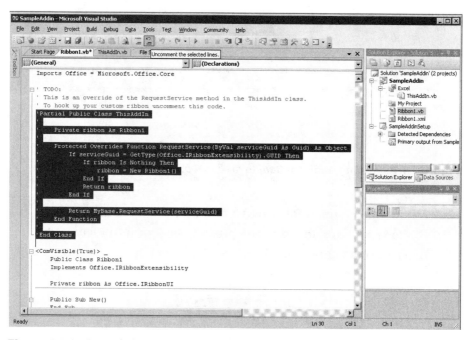

Figure 14.9. *Partial class to override the RequestService method*

6. Press F5 to run the code.

Even though you haven't written any code, VSTO 2005 SE generates the required class files, code, and XML markup to display a toggle button in a group named My Group, on a tab named Add-Ins, as shown in Figure 14.10.

To understand how the tab, group, and button were created, you can look at the code in the Ribbon1.vb and Ribbon1.xml files.

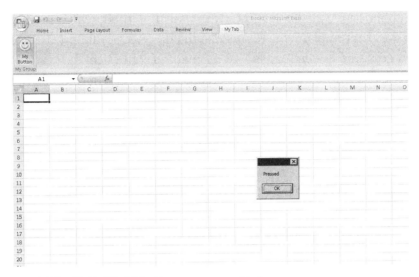

Figure 14.10. *Hello World button, group, and tab*

1. Close Excel.

2. In Solution Explorer, right-click Ribbon1.vb and then click View Code. Ribbon1.vb opens in code view in Visual Studio. Expand the Ribbon Callbacks region, as shown in Figure 14.11.

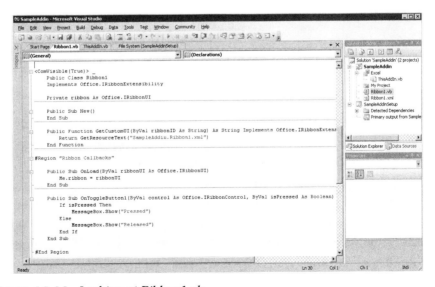

Figure 14.11. *Looking at Ribbon1.vb*

The Ribbon1.vb code file has a GetCustomUI method, which is required in classes that implement IRibbonExtensibility. The Ribbon Callbacks region contains an OnToggleButton1 method that checks the state of the toggle button (on or off) and displays text accordingly. You can write code to handle the events of the buttons you add to the Ribbon in this region.

Next, open the XML file to see the XML that was generated for the Ribbon. This XML markup is what tells the application which additional customizations to display on the Ribbon. In Solution Explorer, right-click Ribbon1.XML and then click Open. The Ribbon1.xml file opens in code view in Visual Studio, as shown in Figure 14.12.

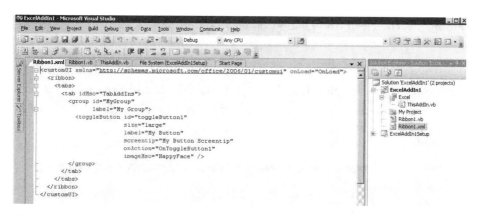

Figure 14.12. *Looking at Ribbon1.xml*

In the first node under customUI, you'll see the <ribbon> node. This represents the area on which the tabs and controls reside. The next node, <tabs>, contains all the <tab> nodes that you are adding to the Ribbon. In this case, VSTO 2005 SE uses the built-in Add-Ins tab. The next node is the <group> node. You can have multiple groups on a tab, but by default VSTO 2005 SE adds a single group that is labeled "My Group." Any buttons that are to appear in the group would be listed as child nodes of <group>. VSTO 2005 SE adds a single toggle button labeled "My Button" to MyGroup. Notice that the onAction attribute is set to OnToggleButton1, the name of the method that exists in the Ribbon1.vb file. This method is called each time the end user clicks the toggle button.

The idMso qualifier is for built-in tabs, groups, and controls. You use the id qualifier for custom tabs, groups, and controls that you create. You can use the idQ qualifier when you want to share the same custom group in two different add-ins.

It is easy to modify the Ribbon. In this section you will change the label of the built-in Add-Ins tab to "Format Tab," change the group label to "Format Group," and add three other toggleButton controls to the group to display default Bold, Italic, and Underline buttons. To do this, change the XML markup in Ribbon1.xml as shown in Listing 14.2.

Listing 14.2. *XML markup in the Ribbon1.xml file*

```
<customUI xmlns=
    "http://schemas.microsoft.com/office/2006/01/customui"
    onLoad="OnLoad">
  <ribbon>
    <tabs>
      <tab idMso="TabAddIns" label="Format Tab">
        <group id="MyGroup"
               label="Format Group">
          <toggleButton id="toggleButton1"
                        size="large"
                        label="My Button"
                        screentip="My Button Screentip"
                        onAction="OnToggleButton1"
                        imageMso="HappyFace" />
          <toggleButton idMso="Bold" />
          <toggleButton idMso="Italic" />
          <toggleButton idMso="Underline" />
        </group>
      </tab>
    </tabs>
  </ribbon>
</customUI>
```

When you press F5 to run the code, Excel displays a group labeled "Format Group" in a tab labeled "Format Tab." The group contains four toggle buttons, as shown in Figure 14.13.

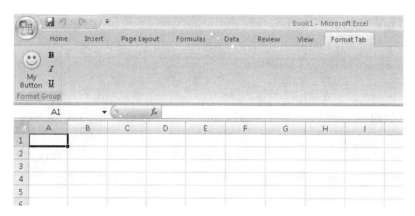

Figure 14.13. *Customizing the Ribbon*

Working with XML

Because XML is case sensitive, it is easy to make errors that might be difficult to find. You can turn on error messages for the Ribbon so that you are notified of the type of error that occurred, rather than the application simply not displaying the customization.

> ❖**Note:** You could have added a new Format tab in addition to the built-in Add-Ins tab, rather than replacing it.

For example, in the XML code shown in Listing 14.2, if you change the case of idMso to idMSO and then run the code, you'll see that this one error causes the entire customization to fail, and the Format Tab tab does not display. Without knowing the cause of the error, you might spend considerable time looking through the XML markup to find it. You can turn on error messages for UI customization as follows:

1. Click the File menu (this is the big round button known as the Microsoft Office button), and then select Options. In this case, it will be for Excel Options, but this particular setting works in all Office applications that support UI customizations.

2. In the left pane, select Advanced, and then scroll down to General in the right pane.

3. Select the Show Add-in User Interface Errors check box, as shown in Figure 14.14, and then click OK.

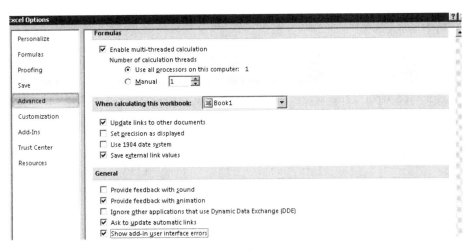

Figure 14.14. *Displaying UI errors for add-ins*

Now when you run the same code, you'll get an error message that indicates that an error was found in the XML description of the custom UI of a particular add-in. It also gives information about what the error was, such as the attribute idMSO not being defined in the schema, as shown in Figure 14.15.

You can enable IntelliSense for the XML markup to help reduce typing errors. Microsoft provides a schema for the Ribbon called CustomUI.xsd that you can reference in your add-in and enable IntelliSense for the XML markup. You can find this schema by searching for "2007 Office System: XML Schema" on the Microsoft Download Center. Save the

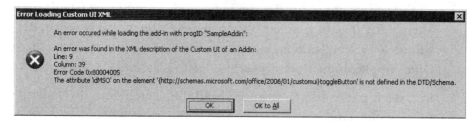

Figure 14.15. *Ribbon error*

CustomUI.xsd file to the \Program Files\Microsoft Visual Studio 8\XML\Schemas directory and add a reference to the file in the Project properties of your add-in.

This schema provides IntelliSense as you work in the XML file in Visual Studio. For example, if you want to add an attribute that enables a screen tip for a control, type *screen,* as shown in Figure 14.16. The IntelliSense drop-down appears and displays the attributes available for the control.

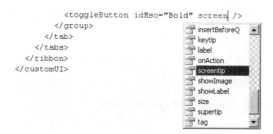

Figure 14.16. *Displaying IntelliSense*

As you saw in Listing 14.2, the idMso attribute of the toggle button you added is set to "Bold"; this name is self-evident, but it can be challenging to figure out the names (or control IDs) for the rest of the buttons. In the application's Options dialog box you can display control IDs for all the built-in controls.

1. Click the File button and then select Options. In this case, it will be for Word Options, but this setting displays the controls and control IDs for each individual application.

2. In the left pane, select Customize. In the right pane, you will see options for customizing the Quick Access toolbar. Later in this chapter you'll learn more about the Quick Access toolbar.

To see the control ID for a control, select a command from the drop-down, and then hold your cursor over a button in the list. The control ID is displayed in a pop-up, as shown in Figure 14.17.

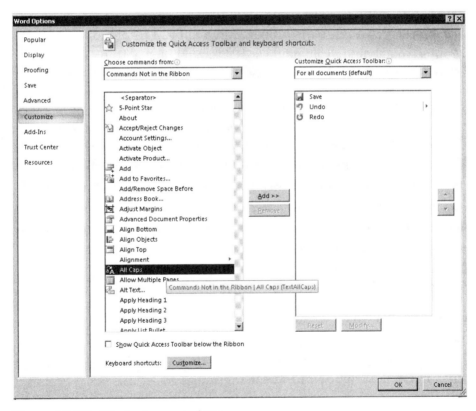

Figure 14.17. *Displaying control IDs*

In this case, the control ID is TextAllCaps. If you want to use one of the built-in icons, but not the default functionality, for your button, you can set your control's imageMso attribute to that same control ID. This eliminates the need to find a control's faceID, because the icon has the same name as the control (the control ID). You can download a list of all the control IDs on the Microsoft Download Center by searching for "2007 Office System: List of Control IDs".

Customizing the Built-In Ribbon

Rather than create your own tab, you might instead want to customize an existing built-in tab. Remember that just because you can do something, it doesn't mean that you should! There are some things to keep in mind as you customize the Ribbon. Although you can hide tabs and groups, you should avoid doing so. Other installed add-ins might rely on these built-in items that you've hidden.

You cannot add buttons to a built-in group. This is unfortunate because in some situations it would make sense to add a new button to an existing group. For example, in Chapter 6 you learned how to create a new button called BoldItalic and place on the same toolbar as the built-in Bold button. This is not possible in Office 2007. You could hide the existing Format tab and then re-create your own, reusing the built-in controls and adding your own controls, but this approach is not recommended (although many people will probably take this approach to place controls logically on the Ribbon). Instead, you can add a new group to a built-in tab and then customize your new group.

In this section, you'll create a Word add-in and use the Ribbon item to add a new group to the Home tab. You'll add two buttons that use existing functionality not currently found on the Ribbon, and you'll add a custom BoldItalic button to this new group.

1. Create a new Word 2007 add-in project using VSTO 2005 SE.

2. Right-click the project, point to Add, and then click New Item.

3. In the New Item dialog box, select Ribbon support.

4. Leave the default name Ribbon1, and click Add. This action adds the Ribbon1.vb code file and the Ribbon1.xml file to your solution.

5. In Solution Explorer, right-click Ribbon1.xml and click Open.

6. Replace the code in Ribbon1.xml with the code in Listing 14.3.

Listing 14.3. *Adding XML markup to Ribbon1.xml*

```
<customUI xmlns=
    "http://schemas.microsoft.com/office/2006/01/customui"
    onLoad="OnLoad">
  <ribbon>
    <tabs>
      <tab idMso="TabHome">
        <group id="NewFont" insertAfterMso="GroupFont"
             label="More Fonts">
          <toggleButton idMso="TextAllCaps" />
    <toggleButton idMso="UnderlineDouble" />
        </group>
      </tab>
    </tabs>
  </ribbon>
</customUI>
```

This XML markup adds a new group labeled "More Fonts" right after the built-in group named GroupFont on the built-in tab named TabHome. On the new group, two toggle buttons are added: one for changing the selected text to all caps, and the other for adding double underlines to the selected text. When you run this code, the new group appears in the Home tab, and it displays the All Caps and Double Underline buttons, as shown in Figure 14.18.

The label for the Double Underline button is quite long, and you can make further revisions to the XML file to modify it. Additionally, Figure 14.19 shows that if you place your cursor over these buttons, the labels are displayed, but no descriptions appear. You can add the descriptions to the control's supertip attribute.

Change the attributes of the toggle buttons, as shown in Listing 14.4, and then press F5 to run the code.

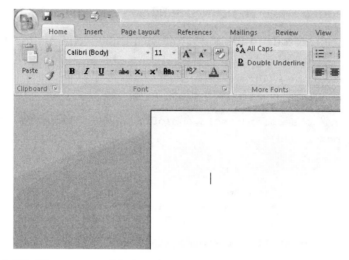

Figure 14.18. *New group added to the Home tab*

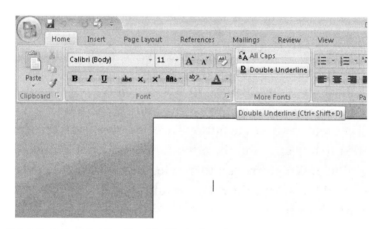

Figure 14.19. *Label for the Double Underline button*

Listing 14.4. *Adding descriptions to controls*

```
<toggleButton idMso="TextAllCaps" supertip="Make the selected
    text all caps." />
<toggleButton idMso="UnderlineDouble" label="Dbl Underline"
    supertip="Double underline the selected text."/>
```

This time, when you place your cursor over the control, a description is displayed, as shown in Figure 14.20.

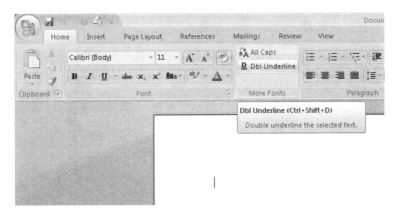

Figure 14.20. *Descriptions added to controls*

Next, you'll add a new toggle button to the More Fonts group and add a custom icon to the button.

1. Create a bitmap to represent the BoldItalic button, as you did in Chapter 8. Name the file BoldItalic.bmp.

2. In Solution Explorer, right-click the solution (e.g. WordAddin1) and select Properties.

3. Click the Resources tab, and then click Add Existing File from the Add Resource drop-down.

4. Navigate to the BoldItalic.bmp file to add it to your project.

5. In Solution Explorer, select the BoldItalic.bmp file and set the Build property to Embedded Resource, as shown in Figure 14.21.

Next, add the code in Listing 14.5 to the end of the Ribbon1.vb code file, after End Class. This action adds a new class to your project that converts bitmaps to a picture type (IPictureDisp) that the Ribbon understands.

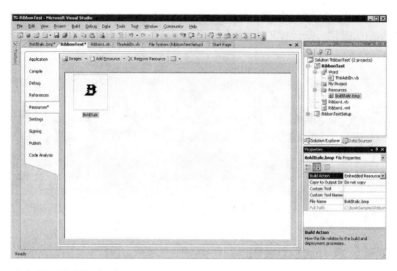

Figure 14.21. *BoldItalic bitmap*

Listing 14.5. *Adding the BitmapToIPicture class*

```
Public Class BitmapToIPicture
    Inherits System.Windows.Forms.AxHost

    Public Sub New()
        MyBase.New(Nothing)
    End Sub

    Public Shared Function Convert(ByVal _
        Image As System.Drawing.Image) As stdole.IPictureDisp

        Convert = GetIPictureFromPicture(Image)

    End Function
End Class
```

In the Ribbon1.vb class, add the code in Listing 14.6 after the
GetCustomUI function.

Listing 14.6. *Adding the GetImage function*

```
Public Function GetImage(ByVal control _
    As Office.IRibbonControl) As stdole.IPictureDisp
```

```
    Return BitmapToIPicture.Convert(My.Resources.BoldItalic)

End Function
```

Now expand the Ribbon Callbacks region, and replace the OnToggleButton1 method (which was auto-generated when you added the Ribbon item) with the ToggleBoldItalic method shown in Listing 14.7.

Listing 14.7. *Adding code to handle the toggle button Click event*

```
Public Sub ToggleBoldItalic(ByVal control As _
    Office.IRibbonControl, ByVal isPressed As Boolean)

    If (isPressed) Then
        Globals.ThisAddIn.Application.Selection.Font.Bold = True
        Globals.ThisAddIn.Application.Selection.Font.Italic _
            = True
    Else
        Globals.ThisAddIn.Application.Selection.Font.Bold = False
        Globals.ThisAddIn.Application.Selection.Font.Italic _
            = False
    End If
End Sub
```

Now you need to indicate in the Ribbon1.xml file that you want the ToggleBoldItalic method to be called when the toggle button is clicked. You do this by assigning the OnAction attribute of the toggle button to the function name. Add the graphic by calling the GetImage function, as shown in Listing 14.8.

Listing 14.8. *Set the getImage attribute to the GetImage method*

```
<customUI xmlns=
    "http://schemas.microsoft.com/office/2006/01/customui"
    onLoad="OnLoad">
  <ribbon>
    <tabs>
      <tab idMso="TabHome">
        <group id="NewFont" insertAfterMso="GroupFont"
          label="More Fonts">
```

```
<toggleButton idMso="TextAllCaps" supertip="Make the
  selected text all caps." />
<toggleButton idMso="UnderlineDouble"
  label="Dbl Underline"
  supertip="Double underline the selected text."/>
<toggleButton id="BoldItalic"
  getImage="GetImage"
  size="normal"
  label="Bold/Italic"
  screentip="Bold and Italic"
  onAction="ToggleBoldItalic"
  supertip="Make the select text bold and italic." />

       </group>
     </tab>
   </tabs>
 </ribbon>
</customUI>
```

Uncomment the code at the top of the Ribbon1.vb code file to handle the
service request to hook up the custom Ribbon, as shown earlier in Figure 14.9.

When you press F5 to run this code, the new Bold/Italic toggle button
appears on the Ribbon in the More Fonts group, as shown in Figure
14.22. Whenever you click the Bold/Italic toggle button, bold and italic
formatting will be applied to (or removed from) the selected text,
depending on its current state.

Adding Other Controls to the Ribbon

So far you've seen examples that show how to create your own toggle
button or use an existing one. You can add a number of other controls
to the Ribbon, and you can see a list of them in IntelliSense, as shown
in Figure 14.23.

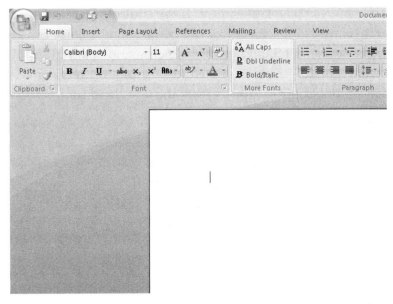

Figure 14.22. *Custom button added to custom group within built-in tab*

Figure 14.23. *Controls displayed in IntelliSense*

In this section, you'll look at some of these controls and learn the event handler signature for each control. We cover only the basic controls: button, check box, combo box, gallery, menu, and split button. You'll create event handlers for each of the buttons, but for the graphics you'll reference existing controls. You'll create the first three controls for Excel.

Button

The Button control is similar to toggleButton, except that Button doesn't have an on and off state; users click the button, and the code in the event handler identified in the onAction attribute runs. Here's the XML markup needed to add a button to the Ribbon.

```
<button id="myButton" label="Printer Setup"
        imageMso="FilePrint" screentip="set up the printer"
        onAction="OnClick" />
```

The code in Listing 14.9 shows the event handler to be written in the Ribbon Callbacks region of the Button1.vb class. When a user clicks the button, the Printer Setup dialog box appears.

Listing 14.9. *Adding a Button control*

```
Public Sub OnClick(ByVal control As Office.IRibbonControl)
    Globals.ThisAddin.Application.Dialogs( _
        Excel.XlBuiltInDialog.xlDialogPrinterSetup).Show()
End Sub
```

CheckBox

Check box controls enable a Boolean state when users select or deselect the control. Here's the XML markup needed to add a check box to the Ribbon.

```
<checkBox id="hideWorksheet" label ="Hide Sheet1"
        onAction="OnCheck"/>
```

The code in Listing 14.10 shows the event handler that hides or shows Sheet1 according to the state of the check box.

Listing 14.10. *Adding a check box control*

```
Public Sub OnCheck(ByVal control As Office.IRibbonControl, _
    ByVal isChecked As Boolean)

    Dim Sheet1 As Excel.Worksheet = _
        Globals.ThisAddin.Application.Sheets(1)
    If isChecked Then
        Sheet1.Visible = Excel.XlSheetVisibility.xlSheetHidden
    Else
        Sheet1.Visible = Excel.XlSheetVisibility.xlSheetVisible
    End If

End Sub
```

ComboBox

A combo box lists items from which users can choose. If you add a combo box to the Ribbon, you need to specify the items for the control to display. Here's the XML markup needed to add a combo box to the Ribbon.

```
<comboBox id="MyCombo" label="Attributes" onChange="OnChange" >
    <item id="Super" label="Superscript"/>
    <item id="Sub" label="Subscript"/>
    <item id="None" label="None"/>
</comboBox>
```

Listing 14.11 illustrates how to handle its events.

Listing 14.11. *Adding a combo box control*

```
Public Sub OnChange(ByVal control As Office.IRibbonControl, _
    ByVal text As String)

    Dim CurrentRange As Excel.Range = Globals.ThisAddin _
        .Application.Selection

    Select Case text
        Case "Subscript"
            CurrentRange.Font.Subscript = True
        Case "Superscript"
            CurrentRange.Font.Superscript = True
```

```
    Case "None"
        CurrentRange.Font.Subscript = False
        CurrentRange.Font.Superscript = False
    End Select
End Sub
```

The Custom group for these controls is illustrated in Figure 14.24.

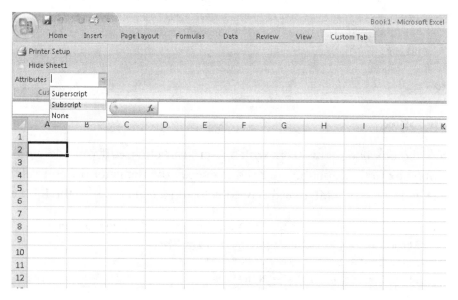

Figure 14.24. *A button, a check box, and a combo box on a Custom tab in Excel*

In the next sections, you'll create a gallery, a menu, and a split button control for Word. If you're creating a new Word 2007 add-in, be sure to uncomment the code in the Ribbon1.vb code file, as shown earlier in Figure 14.9.

Gallery

A gallery is a new type of control that is available for the Ribbon. A *gallery* enables you to add multiple items to a single button. Galleries can be dynamic; for example, you can write code so that the gallery is dynamically populated with items, such as graphics, by reading them from a specified directory at startup. You can also group common functions within a gallery. You will create a gallery of printing choices, as shown in Figure 14.25.

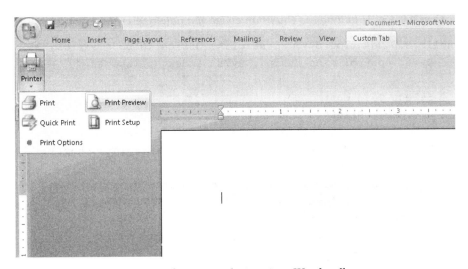

Figure 14.25. *A collection of printing choices in a Word gallery*

To create this gallery, add the XML markup in Listing 14.12 to the Ribbon1.xml file, and add the code in Listing 14.13 to the Ribbon1.vb file.

Listing 14.12. *XML markup for adding a gallery to the Ribbon*

```
<gallery id="galleryPrinter" label="Printer" size="large"
    columns="2" imageMso="FilePrint" onAction="OnAction"
    itemWidth="25" itemHeight="25" >

    <item id="Print" imageMso="FilePrint" label="Print"/>
    <item id="PrintPreview" imageMso="FilePrintPreview"
        label="Print Preview"/>
    <item id="QuickPrint" imageMso="FilePrintQuick"
        label="Quick Print"/>
    <item id="PrintSetup" imageMso="PrintSetupDialog"
        label="Print Setup"/>
```

```
<item id="PrintOptions" imageMso="PrintOptionsMenuWord"
    label="Print Options"/>

</gallery>
```

Listing 14.13. *Handling the OnAction event of a gallery on the Ribbon*

```
Public Sub OnAction(ByVal control As Office.IRibbonControl, _
    ByVal controlID As String, ByVal index As Integer)

    Select Case controlID
        Case "Print"
            Globals.ThisAddin.Application.Dialogs( _
                Word.WdWordDialog.wdDialogFilePrint).Show()
        Case "PrintPreview"
            Globals.ThisAddin.Application.ActiveDocument. _
                PrintPreview()
        Case "QuickPrint"
            Globals.ThisAddin.Application.PrintOut()
        Case "PrintSetup"
            Globals.ThisAddin.Application.Dialogs( _
                Word.WdWordDialog.wdDialogFilePrintSetup).Show()
        Case "PrintOptions"
            Globals.ThisAddin.Application.Dialogs( _
                Word.WdWordDialog _
                .wdDialogToolsOptionsPrint).Show()
    End Select

End Sub
```

Menu

A menu enables you to cascade a list of menu items (or submenu items) from a control. Listing 14.14 creates a menu and adds a number of built-in Word dialog boxes. Notice that you can show either the classic File | New dialog box or the new 2007 version. There is also a submenu that lists some of the font attributes available in the document. In this example, built-in controls are used, so there's no need to add code to the Ribbon1.vb class because the default behavior for these commands will work automatically.

Listing 14.14. *Adding a menu to the Ribbon*

```
<menu id="MyMenu" label="Built-InDialogs" itemSize="normal" >
    <button idMso="FileNewDialogClassic"/>
    <button idMso="FileNew" />
    <button idMso="FontDialog"/>

    <menu id="SubMenu" label="Font Attributes" itemSize="normal">
       <toggleButton idMso="Bold"/>
       <toggleButton idMso="Italic"/>
       <toggleButton idMso="UnderlineDouble"/>
       <toggleButton idMso="Strikethrough"/>
    </menu>

    <button idMso="ZoomDialog"/>
    <button idMso="SortDialogClassic"/>
    <button idMso="ParagraphDialog"/>
    <button idMso="TabsDialog"/>
    <button idMso="WebOptionsDialog"/>
</menu>
```

When you press F5 to run the add-in, this XML markup is passed to Word to display your menu on the Ribbon, as shown in Figure 14.26.

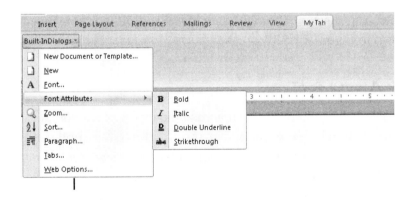

Figure 14.26. *A menu of built-in dialog boxes, along with a submenu*

SplitButton

A split button combines a button and a menu. You can either click the button or click the arrow to the right of the button to reveal a list of items. In this example, you write XML in the Ribbon1.xml file to represent this control, as shown in Listing 14.15. You must specify one button (or toggleButton) and one menu.

Listing 14.15. *Adding a split button to the Ribbon*

```
<splitButton id="MySplitButton" >
    <button idMso="FontDialog"/>
    <menu id="SubMenu2" label="Font Attributes"
        itemSize="normal">
        <toggleButton idMso="Bold"/>
        <toggleButton idMso="Italic"/>
        <toggleButton idMso="UnderlineDouble"/>
        <toggleButton idMso="Strikethrough"/>
    </menu>
</splitButton>
```

If you hold your cursor over the split button, the tool tip displays a thumbnail view of the Font dialog box, as shown in Figure 14.27, and if you click the button, the Font dialog box itself is displayed. When you click the drop-down at the right side of the button, a menu is revealed, as shown in Figure 14.28.

Quick Access Toolbar

The Quick Access toolbar is a customizable toolbar that you see above the Ribbon, to the right of the File menu. As the name implies, this toolbar gives you quick access to the most often used features in the application. By default in Word, you see a Save item, Do and Undo, and a Quick Print item. You can add any built-in command to this menu, or any control that an add-in has added to the Ribbon. To do this, you can use the Customization tab of the Options dialog box or you can right-click a command on the Ribbon and click Add to Quick Access Toolbar, as shown in Figure 14.29.

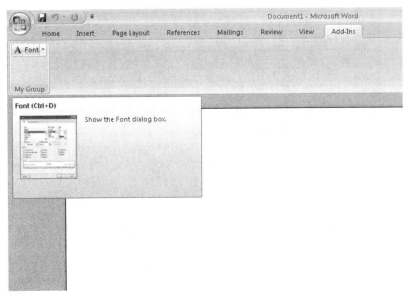

Figure 14.27. *Holding your cursor over the split button control*

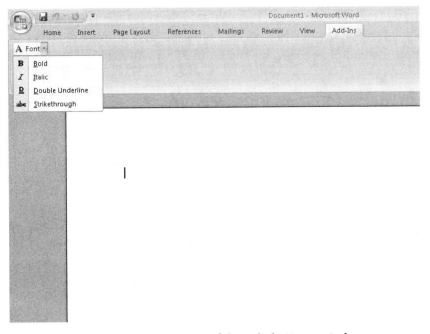

Figure 14.28. *Clicking the drop-down of the split button control*

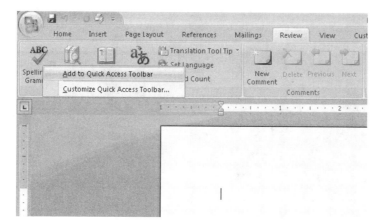

Figure 14.29. *Adding frequently used controls to the Quick Access toolbar*

You cannot programmatically modify the Quick Access toolbar, but end users can manually modify it. Suppose an end user adds a custom control to the Quick Access toolbar and then the add-in that the control was created in is uninstalled. In that case, the button is not removed from the Quick Access toolbar, but it no longer functions. Note that end users can move the Quick Access toolbar so that it appears below the Ribbon instead of above it, as shown in Figure 14.30.

Unsupported Ribbon Functionality

The Ribbon does not support a number of customizations:

- Hiding the File menu button (the large circular button)

- Hiding individual controls in built-in groups

- Adding new controls to built-in groups

- Dynamically adding or removing controls, tabs, or groups (Ribbon items must be statically defined in the XML; you can hide and show them but cannot add them dynamically)

- Modifying built-in menus or galleries

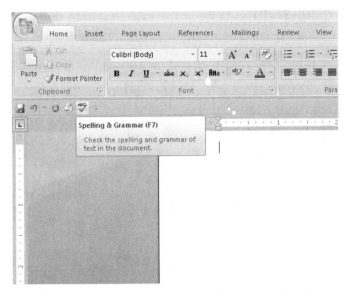

Figure 14.30. *Displaying the Quick Access toolbar below the Ribbon*

- Customizing the mini-toolbar (the toolbar that appears when you select text in the document)

Ribbons in Outlook

The Outlook application supports the Ribbon in individual Inspectors, but not on the main Outlook window (the Explorer). The Explorer has the traditional menu and toolbars that you are familiar with; however, if you open an individual e-mail item, task, meeting request, or other Outlook item (Inspector), the UI displays the Ribbon.

In this section you'll create an Outlook add-in project that has two Ribbons. The first one will be used for the read mail Inspector, and the second one will be used for the contact Inspector.

1. Create an Outlook project using VSTO 2005 SE, and name it SimpleOutlookRibbon. Note that the name is important for the application to read the resources correctly.

2. Press CTRL+SHIFT+A to open the Add New Item dialog, and add a new Ribbon Support item. Name it RibbonHandler.vb.

3. Rename the RibbonHandler.xml file to ReadMailRibbon.xml.

4. Copy the ReadMailRibbon.xml file, and name the copy ContactRibbon.xml.

5. Right-click the ReadMailRibbon.xml file, and select Open, as shown in Figure 14.31.

Figure 14.31. *Opening the ReadMailRibbon.xml file*

6. Add the code in Listing 14.16 to the ReadMailRibbon.xml file.

   There are two ways you can handle the event of pressing the toggle button. The first is to create two separate methods and then assign the appropriate method name to the onAction attribute of the toggle button. The second way is to have a generic method that checks the ID of the control to determine which button was pressed. You can append the name of the XML file to make it easy to identify which button is clicked. In the ReadMailRibbon.xml file, each ToggleButton control defines a separate onAction value.

Listing 14.16. *Changing the ReadMailRibbon XML file*

```
<customUI xmlns="http://schemas.microsoft.com/office/2006/01/
customui"
    onLoad="ReadMailRibbonOnLoad">
  <ribbon>
  <tabs>
    <tab id="ReadMailRibbon.Tab" label="ReadMailRibbon Tab">
      <group id="ReadMailRibbon.Group"
         label="ReadMailRibbon Group">

        <toggleButton id="ReadMailRibbon.toggleButton1"
              label="ReadMailRibbon Toggle Button 1"
              screentip="ToggleButton1 Screentip"
              onAction="ReadMailRibbonOnToggleButton1" />

        <toggleButton id="ReadMailRibbon.toggleButton2"
              label="ReadMailRibbon Toggle Button 2"
              screentip="ToggleButton2 Screentip"
              onAction="OnToggleButton" />

     </group>
    </tab>
  </tabs>
  </ribbon>
</customUI>
```

7. Replace the XML markup in ContactRibbon.xml with the markup in Listing 14.17.

Listing 14.17. *Changing the ContactRibbon XML file*

```
<customUI xmlns="http://schemas.microsoft.com/office/2006/01/
customui"
    onLoad="ContactRibbonOnLoad">
  <ribbon>
    <tabs>
      <tab id="ContactRibbon.Tab" label="ContactRibbon Tab">
        <group id="ContactRibbon.Group"
           label="ContactRibbon Group">
```

```
<toggleButton id="ContactRibbon.toggleButton1"
        label="ContactRibbon Toggle Button 1"
        screentip="ToggleButton1 Screentip"
        onAction="ContactRibbonOnToggleButton1" />

<toggleButton id="ContactRibbon.toggleButton2"
        label="ContactRibbon Toggle Button 2"
        screentip="ToggleButton2 Screentip"
        onAction="OnToggleButton" />

    </group>
   </tab>
  </tabs>
 </ribbon>
</customUI>
```

Next, you will modify the code in RibbonHandler.vb to handle the toggle buttons in each of the Ribbons you created.

1. In Solution Explorer, right-click RibbonHandler.vb, and click View Code.

2. Create two ribbonUI fields to hold a reference to each Ribbon by replacing the existing Ribbon field with the code in Listing 14.18.

Listing 14.18. *Creating the Ribbon fields*

```
Private ReadMailRibbon As Office.IRibbonUI

Private ContactRibbon As Office.IRibbonUI
```

Expand the Ribbon Callbacks region. To set the correct fields, replace the generic OnLoad method with the ReadMailRibbonOnLoad method and the ContactRibbonOnLoad method, as shown in Listing 14.19.

Listing 14.19. *Adding ReadMailRibbonOnLoad and ContactRibbonOnLoad event handlers*

```
Public Sub ReadMailRibbonOnLoad( _
    ByVal ribbonUI As Office.IRibbonUI)
```

```
    ReadMailRibbon = ribbonUI

End Sub

Public Sub ContactRibbonOnLoad( _
    ByVal ribbonUI As Office.IRibbonUI)

    ContactRibbon = ribbonUI

End Sub
```

Next, replace the GetCustomUI function to return the correct Ribbon manifest based on the Ribbon ID. Outlook will pass you the ribbonID, as shown in Listing 14.20.

Listing 14.20. *Returning the Ribbon manifest*

```
Public Function GetCustomUI(ByVal ribbonID As String) As String _
    Implements Office.IRibbonExtensibility.GetCustomUI

    Select Case ribbonID
        Case "Microsoft.Outlook.Mail.Read"
            Return GetResourceText( _
                "SimpleOutlookRibbon.ReadMailRibbon.xml")
        Case "Microsoft.Outlook.Contact"
            Return GetResourceText( _
                "SimpleOutlookRibbon.ContactRibbon.xml")
        Case Else
            Return ""
    End Select

End Function
```

Now you can add the code in Listing 14.21 to the Ribbon Callbacks region to create event handlers for the ToggleButton controls. These methods match the OnAction values you added to the Ribbon XML files.

Listing 14.21. *Adding the ToggleButton handlers*

```
Public Sub ReadMailRibbonOnToggleButton1( _
    ByVal control As Office.IRibbonControl, _
    ByVal isPressed As Boolean)

    If (isPressed) Then
        MessageBox.Show("Pressed!")
    Else
        MessageBox.Show("Released!")
    End If

End Sub

Public Sub ContactRibbonOnToggleButton1( _
    ByVal control As Office.IRibbonControl, _
    ByVal isPressed As Boolean)

    If (isPressed) Then
        MessageBox.Show("Pressed!")
    Else
        MessageBox.Show("Released!")
    End If

End Sub
```

Next, you'll create a generic event handler called OnToggleButton. This handler is called by both ReadMailToggleButton2 and ContactToggleButton2. Even though it is a general handler, you can create specific logic based on the control ID. The logic is the same when the toggleButton is released; however, when the toggleButton is pressed, the results differ depending on the control ID. Add the code in Listing 14.22 to the Ribbon Callbacks region to create event handlers for the other toggleButton controls.

Listing 14.22. *Adding the generic OnToggleButton event handler*

```
Public Sub OnToggleButton(ByVal control As _
    Office.IRibbonControl, ByVal isPressed As Boolean)
```

```
If (isPressed) Then
    If control.Id = "ContactRibbon.toggleButton2" Then
        MessageBox.Show("Contact Toggle Pressed")
    Else
        MessageBox.Show("Pressed!")
    End If
Else
    MessageBox.Show("Released!")
End If

End Sub
```

Finally, uncomment the partial class that handles the service request at the top of the code file, and press F5 to run the code. When you open an existing e-mail, you'll see that the Ribbon contains the ReadMailRibbon Group in the ReadMailRibbon tab, which has two toggle buttons, as shown in Figure 14.32.

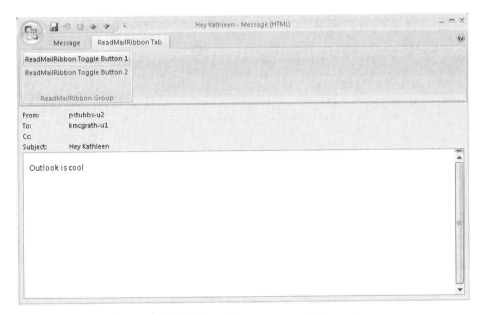

Figure 14.32. *The ReadMailRibbon tab on an e-mail Inspector*

If you click either button, a message box displays "Pressed!" and, when clicked again, displays "Released!" Notice also that this Ribbon appears only when you read an existing mail item, not when you create a new one.

When you open a contact item, the ContactRibbon tab appears, as illustrated in Figure 14.33. This time the behavior of each of the toggle buttons differs. When you click ContactRibbon ToggleButton 1, the generic "Pressed!" message is displayed; however, when you click ContactRibbon ToggleButton 2, the message box displays "Contact Toggle Pressed." The control ID passed to the OnToggleButton method determines which message is displayed.

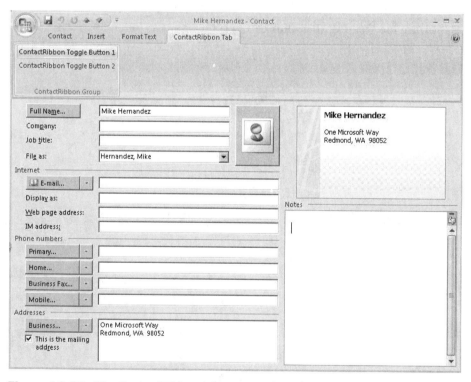

Figure 14.33. *The ContactRibbon tab on a mail Inspector*

Following are all the valid ribbonID values available for Outlook Inspector items.

- Microsoft.Outlook.Mail.Read

- Microsoft.Outlook.Mail.Compose

- Microsoft.Outlook.MeetingRequest.Read

- Microsoft.Outlook.MeetingRequest.Send

- Microsoft.Outlook.Appointment

- Microsoft.Outlook.Contact

- Microsoft.Outlook.Journal

- Microsoft.Outlook.Task

- Microsoft.Outlook.DistributionList

- Microsoft.Outlook.Report

- Microsoft.Outlook.Resend

- Microsoft.Outlook.Response.Read

- Microsoft.Outlook.Response.Compose

- Microsoft.Outlook.Response.CounterPropose

- Microsoft.Outlook.RSS

- Microsoft.Outlook.Post.Read

- Microsoft.Outlook.Post.Compose

- Microsoft.Outlook.DistributionList

- Microsoft.Outlook.Report

- Microsoft.Outlook.Resend

- Microsoft.Outlook.Response.Read

- Microsoft.Outlook.Response.Compose

- Microsoft.Outlook.Response.CounterPropose

- Microsoft.Outlook.RSS

- Microsoft.Outlook.Post.Read

- Microsoft.Outlook.Post.Compose

- Microsoft.Outlook.Sharing.Read

- Microsoft.Outlook.Sharing.Compose

Creating Custom Task Fanes

Creating a Custom task pane in Office 2007 is as easy as creating a document-level actions pane for Word 2003 or Excel 2003. With VSTO 2005 SE, you first create an add-in project for an application that supports the Custom task pane, and then you add a user control to the application's CustomTaskPanes collection. VSTO 2005 SE supports Custom task panes for Word 2007, Excel 2007, Outlook 2007, InfoPath 2007, and PowerPoint 2007. Let's take a closer look at creating a simple Custom task pane for PowerPoint.

Creating an Add-in for PowerPoint

1. Create a new PowerPoint 2007 add-in project.

2. In Solution Explorer, right-click the project, point to Add, and then click User Control.

3. In the New Item dialog box, ensure that User Control is selected, leaving the default name UserControl1, and then click Add.

3. Add a Label control to the user control, and change the text to *View*.

4. Add a ComboBox control below the label.

5. Double-click the user control, and add the code in Listing 14.23 to the Load event of UserControl1.

Listing 14.23. *Filling a ComboBox*

```
Private Sub UserControl1_Load(ByVal sender As System.Object, _
    ByVal e As System.EventArgs) Handles MyBase.Load
```

```
With Me.ComboBox1.Items
    .Add("Normal")
    .Add("Notes Master")
    .Add("Handout Master")
    .Add("Slide Master")
End With

End Sub
```

Next, add the code in Listing 14.24 to the SelectedIndexChanged event handler of the combo box. You'll create the ChangeView method next.

Listing 14.24. *Passing a selected item to the ChangeView method*

```
Private Sub ComboBox1_SelectedIndexChanged(ByVal sender As _
    System.Object, ByVal e As System.EventArgs) Handles _
    ComboBox1.SelectedIndexChanged

        Globals.ThisAddIn.ChangeView(Me.ComboBox1.Text)

End Sub
```

Now you can add the ChangeView method to the Addin class, and also add code to the Startup event handler to add the user control to the CustomTaskPanes collection. One difference from the actions pane here is that you must explicitly set the Visible property to True to make the task pane visible. Add the code in Listing 14.25 to the Addin class.

Listing 14.25. *Displaying the user control on the Custom task pane*

```
Dim myControl As UserControl1

Private Sub ThisAddIn_Startup(ByVal sender As Object, _
    ByVal e As System.EventArgs) Handles Me.Startup

    myControl = New UserControl1
    Me.CustomTaskPanes.Add(myControl, "My Custom Task Pane") _
        .Visible = True
End Sub
```

```
Friend Sub ChangeView(ByVal View As String)

    Dim ViewType As Integer

    Select Case View
        Case "Normal"
            ViewType = PowerPoint.PpViewType.ppViewNormal
        Case "Notes Master"
            ViewType = PowerPoint.PpViewType.ppViewNotesMaster
        Case "Handout Master"
            ViewType = PowerPoint.PpViewType.ppViewHandoutMaster
        Case "Slide Master"
            ViewType = PowerPoint.PpViewType.ppViewSlideMaster
    End Select

    Me.Application.ActiveWindow.ViewType = ViewType

End Sub
```

When you press F5 to run this code, the Custom task pane that contains the combo box becomes visible, as shown in Figure 14.34. You can select the desired master view. You can change the view equally as easily using the Ribbon's View tab, but because a context-sensitive tab becomes visible for each master view, you must continuously switch back to the View tab to see the next view. Showing these options on the Custom task pane eliminates the need to context-switch.

Opening and Closing the Custom Task Pane

If users close this Custom task pane, the only way to reopen it is to close PowerPoint and then reopen it, because you added the code to the Startup event handler. This probably isn't a good approach to take. Instead, you should provide a button on the Ribbon that enables you to toggle the Custom task pane on and off.

1. As shown in Listing 14.26, add a variable for the Custom task pane, and change the code in the Startup event handler of ThisAddin. Remove the code that sets the Visible property to True.

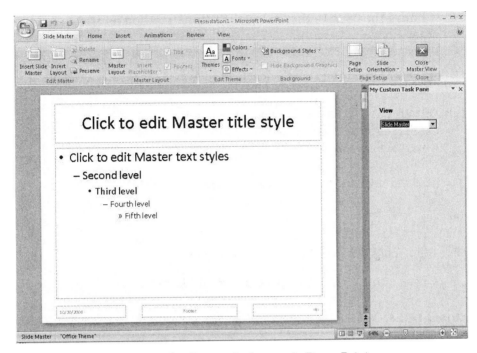

Figure 14.34. *Displaying the Custom task pane in PowerPoint*

Listing 14.26. *Displaying a user control on the Custom task pane*

```
Dim myControl As UserControl1

Public MyTaskPane As Microsoft.Office.Tools.CustomTaskPane

Private Sub ThisAddIn_Startup(ByVal sender As Object, _
    ByVal e As System.EventArgs) Handles Me.Startup

    myControl = New UserControl1
    MyTaskPane = Me.CustomTaskPanes.Add(myControl, _
        "My Custom Task Pane")

End Sub
```

2. Add a Ribbon Support item to the Outlook add-in project.

3. Right-click Ribbon1.vb, and click View Code.

4. Change the code in the OnToggleButton1 method as shown in List-
    ing 14.27.

Listing 14.27. *Controlling the Custom task pane from the Ribbon when the
button is clicked*

```
Public Sub OnToggleButton1(ByVal control _
    As Office.IRibbonControl, _
    ByVal isPressed As Boolean)

    Globals.ThisAddIn.MyTaskPane.Visible = isPressed

End Sub
```

5. Right-click Ribbon1.xml, and click Open.

6. Change the XML markup as shown in Listing 14.28.

Listing 14.28. *XML Markup for controlling the custom task pane from the Ribbon*

```
<customUI xmlns="http://schemas.microsoft.com/office/
  2006/01/customui"
  onLoad="OnLoad">
  <ribbon>
    <tabs>
      <tab idMso="TabAddIns">
        <group id="MyGroup"
              label="My Group">
          <toggleButton id="toggleButton1"
                label="Custom Task Pane"
                screentip="Show and Hide the Custom Task Pane"
                onAction="OnToggleButton1" />
        </group>
      </tab>
    </tabs>
  </ribbon>
</customUI>
```

7. Uncomment the code at the top of the Ribbon1.vb code file to handle the service request to hook up the custom Ribbon, as was shown in Figure 14.9.

8. Press F5 to run the code.

When PowerPoint opens, the Custom task pane is not visible. If you click the Add-Ins tab and then click the Custom Task Pane toggle button, the Custom task pane becomes visible. If you click the Custom Task Pane toggle button again, the task pane is removed.

Managing Task Panes on Multiple Word Documents

The nice thing about the Custom task pane feature is that it is available to any document (PowerPoint slide, worksheet) that you open. However, note that it doesn't work exactly the way you might expect in Word and InfoPath. In these applications, the task pane is parented to the document frame window instead of the main window. When you open a new document in Word, for example, it opens in a separate window. Thus the task pane that you created is still visible only on the original document. To ensure that the task pane is always visible on the active document, you must write additional code.

1. Create a new Word add-in project.

2. Add a user control to the project, leaving the default name UserControl1.

3. Add a couple of controls of your choice to the user control. You will not write any code behind these controls, because our only goal in this example is to show how to handle the Custom task pane with multiple documents.

4. Right-click ThisAddin, and click View Code.

5. Replace the code in the ThisAddin class with the code in Listing 14.29.

Listing 14.29. *Code to handle the Custom task pane in multiple Word documents*

```
Imports System.Collections.Generic

public class ThisAddIn

    Dim AddinCustomTaskPanes As New Dictionary( _
        Of Microsoft.Office.Interop.Word.Document, _
        Microsoft.Office.Tools.CustomTaskPane)

    Private Sub ThisAddIn_Startup(ByVal sender As Object, _
        ByVal e As System.EventArgs) Handles Me.Startup

        CreateCustomTaskPane(Globals.ThisAddIn _
            .Application.ActiveDocument)

    End Sub

    Private Sub ThisAddIn_Shutdown(ByVal sender As Object, _
        ByVal e As System.EventArgs) Handles Me.Shutdown

    End Sub

    Private Sub Application_DocumentBeforeClose(ByVal Doc As _
        Microsoft.Office.Interop.Word.Document, ByRef Cancel As _
        Boolean) Handles Application.DocumentBeforeClose

        ' Delete the attached CustomTaskPane when the document
        ' is closed.
        DeleteCustomTaskPane(Doc)

    End Sub

    Private Sub Application_DocumentOpen(ByVal Doc As _
        Microsoft.Office.Interop.Word.Document) Handles _
        Application.DocumentOpen

        ' Create a new CustomTaskPane when a document is opened.
        CreateCustomTaskPane(Doc)

    End Sub
```

```
Private Sub Application_NewDocument(ByVal Doc As _
    Microsoft.Office.Interop.Word.Document) Handles _
    Application.NewDocument

    ' Create a new CustomTaskPane when a new document
    ' is created.
    CreateCustomTaskPane(Doc)

End Sub

Private Sub CreateCustomTaskPane(ByVal Doc As _
    Microsoft.Office.Interop.Word.Document)

    ' Create a new CustomTaskPane, attaching it to the active
    ' window.
    Dim NewCustomTaskPane As _
        Microsoft.Office.Tools.CustomTaskPane

    NewCustomTaskPane = Me.CustomTaskPanes.Add( _
        New UserControl1, "CustomTaskPane")
    NewCustomTaskPane.Visible = True

    ' Track which document the CustomTaskPane is attached to
    ' so that it can be removed later.
    AddinCustomTaskPanes.Add(Doc, NewCustomTaskPane)

End Sub

Private Sub DeleteCustomTaskPane(ByVal Doc As _
    Microsoft.Office.Interop.Word.Document)

    ' Delete the CustomTaskPane attached to this document.
    Me.CustomTaskPanes.Remove(AddinCustomTaskPanes.Item(Doc))

    ' Remove it from the internal collection.
    Me.AddinCustomTaskPanes.Remove(Doc)

End Sub

End class
```

6. Press F5 to run the code.

When the solution opens, the Custom task pane is visible and contains the controls you added to UserControl1. If you open a new or existing document, a new task pane is created and added to the new document.

This code uses a dictionary to track the Custom task pane with the document. In this way, each time you open a document, the Custom task pane is created and both the pane and the document are added to the dictionary. When you close a document, the DocumentBeforeClose event is raised, and the handler calls the DeleteCustomTaskPane method to remove the Custom task pane from the collection of Custom task panes.

Converting a Document-Level Customization to a VSTO 2005 SE Add-in

In this section, you'll convert a document-level customization that uses the actions pane to a VSTO 2005 SE add-in that uses the Custom task pane. In Chapter 5, you created an Excel solution that displays a custom-made Styles and Formatting task pane. That solution works only for a particular workbook, so let's convert the solution to a VSTO 2005 SE add-in so that it will work with any workbook that is opened.

1. Create a new Excel 2007 add-in project.

2. Add the user control you created for the Styles and Formatting solution in Chapter 5, or create a new one. If you create a new one, follow steps 3 through 11.

3. Resize the control so that its Width is 180 and its Height is 350.

4   Add two label controls, and change the style of the second label to resemble a text box by selecting a white background color and adding a border.

5. Keep the default name (Label1) for the first label, and change its Text property to *Formatting of Active Cell.*

6. Change the name of the second label to *SelectionFont,* and change its AutoSize property to False.

7. Set the Width property of the SelectionFont label to 155, and its Height property to 50, and then clear out any text.

8. Add a Label control to UserControl1, and change the Text property of the label to *Pick formatting to apply.*

9. Add a ListBox control to UserControl1 below the label, leaving the default name ListBox1.

10. Resize the ListBox control so that its Width property is 155, and its Height property is 173.

11. Add a Button control below the ListBox control, and change its Text property to *Reload Styles.*

The user control you created (or copied from the project you created in Chapter 5) should resemble the one in Figure 14.35.

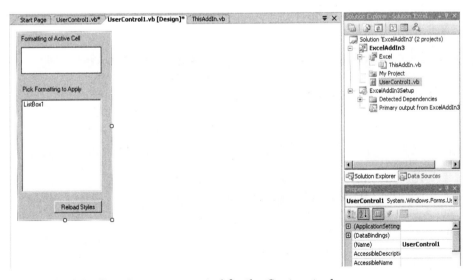

Figure 14.35. *Creating a user control for the Custom task pane*

Next, add the code in Listing 14.30 to the UserControl1 class. You can copy the code from Chapter 5, but note that some changes will be necessary.

Listing 14.30. *Code for user control*

```
Private Sub UserControl1_Load(ByVal sender As System.Object, _
    ByVal e As System.EventArgs) Handles MyBase.Load
    GetCurrentStyles()
End Sub

Private Sub GetCurrentStyles()
    ' Add style names from document to the list box.
    Dim CurrentStyle As Excel.Style

    For Each CurrentStyle In Globals.ThisAddIn.Application _
        .ActiveWorkbook.Styles
        Me.ListBox1.Font = New Font("Times New Roman", 14, _
            FontStyle.Regular)
        Me.ListBox1.Items.Add(CurrentStyle.Name)
    Next
End Sub

Private Sub ListBox1_MouseClick(ByVal sender As Object, _
    ByVal e As System.Windows.Forms.MouseEventArgs) _
    Handles ListBox1.MouseClick

    ' Set the active cell to the style selected in the list box,
    ' and then call ResetStyle to assign style name and
    ' formatting to label.
    Globals.ThisAddIn.Application.ActiveCell.Style = _
        Me.ListBox1.SelectedItem
    ResetStyle()
End Sub

Private Sub ResetStyle()

    ' Retrieve format information from Selected style.
```

```
    Dim CurrentStyle As Excel.Style = _
        Globals.ThisAddIn.Application.ActiveWorkbook. _
        Styles(Me.ListBox1.SelectedItem.ToString)
    Dim FontName As String = CurrentStyle.Font.Name
    Dim FontSize As Single = CurrentStyle.Font.Size
    Dim FontBold As Boolean = CurrentStyle.Font.Bold
    Dim FontItalic As Boolean = CurrentStyle.Font.Italic
    Dim FontAttribute As FontStyle = FontStyle.Regular

    If FontBold = True Then
        FontAttribute = FontStyle.Bold
    End If

    If FontItalic = True Then
        FontAttribute = FontStyle.Italic
    End If

    If CurrentStyle.Font.Underline = _
        Excel.XlUnderlineStyle.xlUnderlineStyleSingle Then

        FontAttribute = FontStyle.Underline

    End If

    ' Set the text of the label to the style and formatting
    ' selected in the list box.
    Me.SelectionFont.Text = Me.ListBox1.SelectedItem.ToString()
    Me.SelectionFont.Font = New Font(FontName, _
        FontSize, FontAttribute)

End Sub

Private Sub Button1_Click(ByVal sender As System.Object, _
    ByVal e As System.EventArgs) Handles Button1.Click

    Me.ListBox1.Items.Clear()
    GetCurrentStyles()

End Sub
```

Add the code in Listing 14.31 to the ThisAddin class, replacing the auto-generated Startup and Shutdown event handlers.

Listing 14.31. *Code to read worksheet styles and populate the Custom task pane*

```
Dim WithEvents worksheet As Excel.Worksheet
Dim myCustomTaskPane As Microsoft.Office.Tools.CustomTaskPane
Dim myControl As UserControl1

Private Sub ThisAddIn_Startup(ByVal sender As Object, _
    ByVal e As System.EventArgs) Handles Me.Startup

    ' Start of VSTO-generated code
    Me.Application = CType(Microsoft.Office.Tools.Excel _
        .ExcelLocale1033Proxy.Wrap(GetType( _
        Excel.Application), Me.Application), Excel.Application)
    ' End of VSTO-generated code

    worksheet = Globals.ThisAddIn.Application.ActiveSheet

    myControl = New UserControl1
    Me.CustomTaskPanes.Add(myControl, _
        "Styles and Formatting").Visible = True

End Sub

Private Sub ThisAddIn_Shutdown(ByVal sender As Object, _
    ByVal e As System.EventArgs) Handles Me.Shutdown

End Sub

Private Sub worksheet_SelectionChange(ByVal Target As _
    Microsoft.Office.Interop.Excel.Range) Handles _
    worksheet.SelectionChange

    ' Set a variable to the label on the actions pane control.
    Dim Actions As System.Windows.Forms.Label = _
        myControl.SelectionFont
```

```
' Retrieve font information from currently selected cell.
Dim FontName As String = Application.ActiveCell.Font.Name
Dim FontSize As Short = CType( _
    Application.ActiveCell.Font.Size, Short)
Dim FontBold As Boolean = Application.ActiveCell.Font.Bold
Dim FontItalic As Boolean = _
    Application.ActiveCell.Font.Italic
Dim FontAttribute As FontStyle = FontStyle.Regular
Dim ExcelStyle As Excel.Style = Application.ActiveCell.Style
Dim StyleName As String = ExcelStyle.Name

' Apply Bold, Italic, and Underline styles to label if they
' are applied to the active cell.
If FontBold = True Then
    FontAttribute = FontStyle.Bold
End If

If FontItalic = True Then
    FontAttribute = FontStyle.Italic
End If

If Application.ActiveCell.Font.Underline = _
    Excel.XlUnderlineStyle.xlUnderlineStyleSingle Then
    FontAttribute = FontStyle.Underline
End If

' Add the Style name and formatting of the active cell to the
' label on the actions pane.
Actions.Text = StyleName
Actions.Font = New Font(FontName, FontSize, FontAttribute)

End Sub
```

When you press F5 to run this code, you'll notice that a number of styles are listed in the ListBox. You can add some text and then apply the style by clicking the style name, as shown in Figure 14.36.

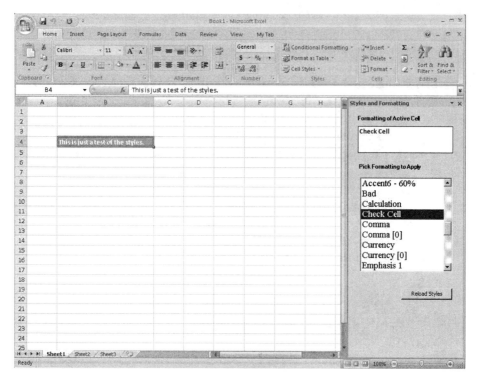

Figure 14.36. *Styles and Formatting Custom task pane*

As long as this add-in is loaded, this Styles and Formatting task pane will be available to any workbook that you open.

Displaying Multiple Task Panes

You can add multiple Custom task panes to an application. As shown in Figure 14.37, each task pane is opened next to the last one added (tiled). You'll use the code from our Styles and Formatting task pane example.

1. Add a new user control to the project.

2. Add a button to the user control.

3. Append the code in Listing 14.32 to the Startup event handler of ThisAddin, and press F5.

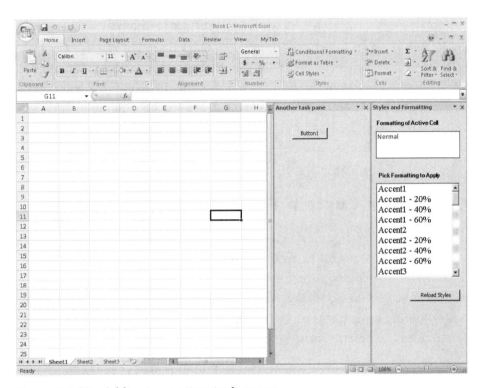

Figure 14.37. *Adding two custom task panes*

Listing 14.32. *Adding another task pane*

```
Dim newControl As New UserControl2
Me.CustomTaskPanes.Add(NewControl, _
    "Another task pane").Visible = True
```

You might also want to control the number of task panes that can be visible at one time. Because the Custom task panes tile, theoretically you could add enough task panes to take up the application's entire screen real estate. To avoid this problem, you could first check whether other Custom task panes in the collection are visible before you make your Custom task pane visible. Remember that users may have any number of add-ins loaded that might display a Custom task pane.

Outlook handles Custom task panes a little differently than other Office applications. As an internal optimization, Outlook might reuse a Custom task pane that was associated with an Inspector previously. This could lead to having multiple Custom task panes for the same Inspector. The best practice for avoiding this is to explicitly delete all Custom task panes you add by using the Remove method of the CustomTaskPaneCollection when the Inspector is closed.

Creating a Custom Form Region

Outlook *form regions,* a new feature of Outlook 2007, allow you to create a form that appears within an Outlook Inspector. In the past you added or changed Inspectors' functionality by changing the Inspectors. Now you can use form regions. You add a form region to an Inspector so that it is adjoining (at the bottom of the form), separate (on a separate page), or replaces the default form, or default page.

 In this section you will create an Outlook form region using VSTO 2005 SE. The first step is to create the form region file, a binary file that has the extension .ofs. The only way to create an .ofs file is to use the Visual Form Designer built into Outlook.

Creating an Outlook Form Region File

1. Open Outlook 2007.

2. On the main menu click Tools, point to Forms, and then click Design a Form. The Design Form dialog box opens, as Figure 14.38 illustrates.

3. Select Message, and then click Open.

Figure 14.38. *Designing a form*

Creating a New Form Region

1. On the Design group of the Developer Ribbon, click Form Region, and then click New Form Region in the menu. A new blank form region is created.

2. Add controls to the form region. If the Toolbox is not visible, click the Control Toolbox icon on the Tools group of the Developer Ribbon.

3. Drag and drop a text box and a command button to the form region. Your form region should look like the one in Figure 14.39.

Saving the Form Region

1. To save only the form region, rather than the entire form, click Form Region and then click Save Form Region on the Design group of the Developer Ribbon. The Save dialog box will open.

2. Name the form region MySimpleFormRegion.ofs, and save it to a location of your choice. Later you will import this file into your VSTO project.

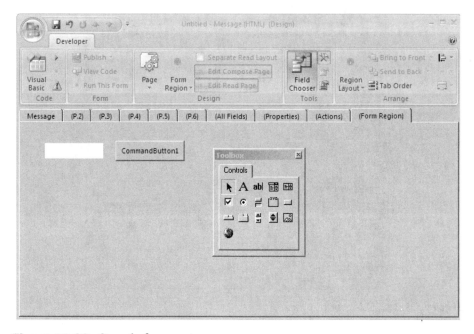

Figure 14.39. *Sample form region*

3. Close the Form Designer and Outlook without saving any other forms.

Creating the VSTO 2005 SE Outlook Add-in Project

You will now create the VSTO 2005 SE add-in project that will create the form region and handle the events.

1. Create a new Outlook 2007 add-in project.

2. Set the name of the project to SimpleFormRegion.

Embedding the Form Region in Your Project

Next, you will add to your project the MySimpleFormRegion.ofs form region that you created earlier.

1. Click Project, and in the main menu click Add Existing Item. You also need to embed the MySimpleFormRegion.ofs as a resource in the assembly.

2. In the main menu, click Project and then SimpleFormRegion Properties.

3. Click the Resources tab, and select Files from the first drop-down menu in the Resources pane.

4. Drag and drop the MySimpleFormRegion.ofs file from Solution Explorer into the Resources pane to embed the file as a resource. You will see the MySimpleFormRegion file in the resources pane, as shown in Figure 14.40.

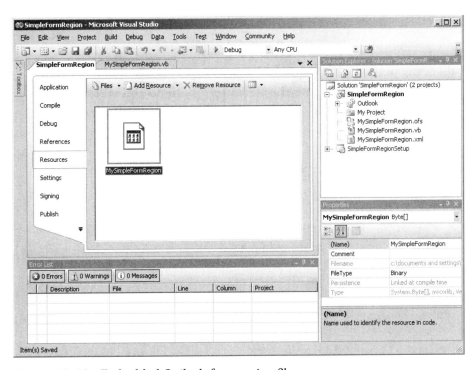

Figure 14.40. *Embedded Outlook form region file*

Creating and Registering the Form Region Manifest

You need to create a form region manifest file and register it in the registry. Let's look at how to do this.

1. To add a form region manifest to your project, click Project, and then in the main menu click Add New Item.

2. In the Templates pane of the Add New Item dialog box, select XML File.

3. Name the new item MySimpleFormRegionManifest.xml, and add the XML in Listing 14.33 to the MySimpleFormRegionManifest.xml file you just added.

4. On the Project menu, click SimpleFormRegion Properties.

5. Click the Resources tab, and select Files from the first drop-down menu in the Resources pane.

6. Drag and drop the MySimpleFormRegionManifest.xml file from Solution Explorer into the Resources pane to embed the file as a resource. You will see the MySimpleFormRegionManifest file in the resources pane.

Listing 14.33. *The form region manifest*

```
<?xml version="1.0" encoding="utf-8" ?>
<FormRegion xmlns=
    "http://schemas.microsoft.com/office/outlook/12/formregion.xsd">
  <name>MySimpleFormRegion</name>
  <title>My Simple Form Region</title>
  <formRegionType>adjoining</formRegionType>
  <showCompose>true</showCompose>
  <showRead>true</showRead>
  <showPreview>false</showPreview>
  <hidden>false</hidden>
  <addin>SimpleFormRegion</addin>
  <version>1.0</version>
</FormRegion>
```

This form region will adjoin the Outlook form, as indicated in Listing 14.33 in the formRegionType node.

Creating the Form Region Registration

Next, you should add a form region registry file to your project. You will not run this file from the project, but it makes a convenient place to store the file so that you can edit it later if you need to.

1. Click Project, and then in the main menu click Add New Item.

2. In the Templates pane of the Add New Item dialog box, select Text File.

3. Name the new item MySimpleFormRegion.reg, and add the text in Listing 14.34 to the MySimpleFormRegion.reg file you just added.

Listing 14.34. *Registering the form region in the registry*

```
Windows Registry Editor Version 5.00

[HKEY_CURRENT_USER\Software\Microsoft\Office\Outlook\FormRegions\
IPM.Note]
"SimpleFormRegion"="=SimpleFormRegion"
```

4. Using Windows Explorer, browse to and run the MySimpleFormRegion.reg file. This adds the correct registry key to the registry.

Creating a Form Region Startup Class

In this section you will add a class that implements FormRegionStartup.

1. Click Project, and then in the main menu click Add Class.

2. Name the class MySimpleFormRegion.vb, and add the code in Listing 14.35 to the MySimpleFormRegion.vb file.

Listing 14.35. *Creating a form region startup class*

```
Public Class MySimpleFormRegion
    Implements Outlook.FormRegionStartup


    Public Sub BeforeFormRegionShow( _
        ByVal FormRegion As Outlook.FormRegion) _
        Implements Outlook._FormRegionStartup _
        .BeforeFormRegionShow

    End Sub

    Public Function GetFormRegionIcon( _
        ByVal FormRegionName As String, _
        ByVal LCID As Integer, _
        ByVal Icon As Outlook.OlFormRegionIcon) As Object _
        Implements Outlook._FormRegionStartup.GetFormRegionIcon

    End Function

    Public Function GetFormRegionManifest( _
        ByVal FormRegionName As String, _
        ByVal LCID As Integer) As Object _
        Implements Outlook._FormRegionStartup _
            .GetFormRegionManifest

    End Function

    Public Function GetFormRegionStorage( _
        ByVal FormRegionName As String, _
        ByVal Item As Object, _
        ByVal LCID As Integer, _
        ByVal FormRegionMode As Outlook.OlFormRegionMode, _
        ByVal FormRegionSize As Outlook.OlFormRegionSize) _
        As Object Implements Outlook._FormRegionStartup _
        .GetFormRegionStorage

    End Function
End Class
```

3. Implement GetFormRegionStorage by adding the code in Listing 14.36. This function is called when Outlook is ready to load the form region, and it returns the embedded form region file.

Listing 14.36. *Returning the embedded form region file*

```
Public Function GetFormRegionStorage( _
    ByVal FormRegionName As String, _
    ByVal Item As Object, _
    ByVal LCID As Integer, _
    ByVal FormRegionMode As OlFormRegionMode, _
    ByVal FormRegionSize As OlFormRegionSize) _
    As Object Implements _FormRegionStartup.GetFormRegionStorage

    ' Read the embedded .ofs file out of the assembly.
    Dim MySimpleFormRegion_OFS As Byte() = _
        My.Resources.MySimpleFormRegion
    Return MySimpleFormRegion_OFS

End Function
```

4. Implement GetFormRegionManifest by adding the code in Listing 14.37. This function is called when Outlook is ready to load the form region manifest, and it returns the embedded form region manifest file.

Listing 14.37. *Returning the embedded form region manifest file*

```
    Public Function GetFormRegionManifest( _
    ByVal FormRegionName As String, _
    ByVal LCID As Integer) As Object _
    Implements Outlook._FormRegionStartup.GetFormRegionManifest

        ' Read the embedded manifest file out of the assembly.
        Dim MySimpleFormRegionManifest As String = _
            My.Resources.MySimpleFormRegionManifest
        Return MySimpleFormRegionManifest

    End Function
```

5. Implement GetFormRegionIcon by adding the code in Listing
    14.38. This function is called when Outlook is ready to load the
    form region icon, and it returns the embedded form region icon
    file.

Listing 14.38. *Returning the embedded form region icon file*

```
Public Function GetFormRegionIcon( _
ByVal FormRegionName As String, _
ByVal LCID As Integer, _
ByVal Icon As Outlook.OlFormRegionIcon) As Object _
Implements Outlook._FormRegionStartup.GetFormRegionIcon

    ' There are no custom icons so just return nothing.
    Return Nothing

End Function
```

Hooking Up Form Region Controls

You need to hook up the form region controls so that you can handle
the control events. Outlook 2007 calls BeforeFormRegionShow, passing
a reference to the form region. This is where you will hook up the
controls.

1. In the main menu click Project, and then click Add Reference.

2. In the COM tab of the Add References dialog box, select Microsoft
    Forms 2.0 Object Library. This action adds a reference to
    Microsoft.vbe.Interop.Forms.

3. Add the Imports Microsoft.vbe.Interop.Forms statement to the top
    of the class.

4. Add the code in Listing 14.39 after the class declaration, adding
    fields to store a reference to the form region controls. These fields
    are declared WithEvents to enable you to handle the events.

Listing 14.39. *Adding form region fields*

```
Dim WithEvents TextBox1 As Outlook.OlkTextBox
Dim WithEvents CommandButton1 As Outlook.OlkCommandButton
Dim WithEvents UserForm As UserForm
```

5. Implement BeforeFormRegionShow by adding the code in Listing 14.40. In this function you hook up form region controls to the local fields you created in step 4.

Listing 14.40. *Hooking up the form region controls*

```
Public Sub BeforeFormRegionShow( _
    ByVal FormRegion As FormRegion) _
    Implements _FormRegionStartup.BeforeFormRegionShow

    ' Hold a reference to the user form.
    UserForm = FormRegion.Form

    ' Map the form region controls to the local variables.
    TextBox1 = UserForm.Controls.Item("TextBox1")
    CommandButton1 = UserForm.Controls.Item("CommandButton1")

End Sub
```

Hooking Up the Form Region

You now need to hook up the add-in to the form region. Outlook uses a service-based model. Outlook calls the RequestService method of the ThisAddin class, passing the GUID of the service it is looking for—in this case, a class that implements FormRegionStartup. You also need to declare a local variable to hold a reference to the FormRegionStartup class that you pass to the service request. Add the code in Listing 14.41 to the ThisAddin class.

Listing 14.41. *Hooking up a form region*

```
public class ThisAddin

    Dim MySimpleFormRegion As New MySimpleFormRegion

    Private Sub ThisAddin_Startup(ByVal sender As Object, _
        ByVal e As System.EventArgs) Handles Me.Startup

    End Sub

    Private Sub ThisAddin_Shutdown(ByVal sender As Object, _
        ByVal e As System.EventArgs) Handles Me.Shutdown

    End Sub

    Protected Overrides Function RequestService( _
        ByVal serviceGuid As Guid) As Object

        If serviceGuid = _
            GetType(Outlook.FormRegionStartup).GUID Then

            Return MySimpleFormRegion
        End If

        Return MyBase.RequestService(serviceGuid)
    End Function
End class
```

Running the Project

Press F5 to run the project. Outlook opens, and you will see your form region at the bottom of the mail Inspector. Figure 14.41 shows the results.

The form region also appears in the preview pane of Outlook, as shown in Figure 14.42.

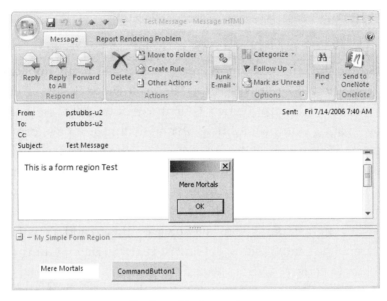

Figure 14.41. *Form region displayed in Inspector*

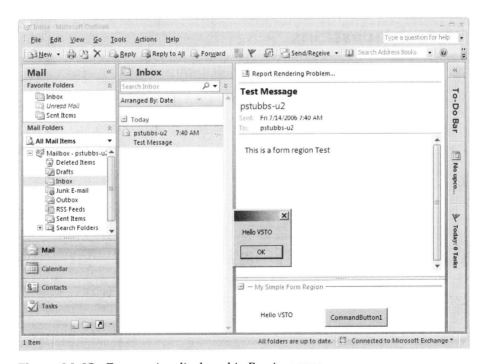

Figure 14.42. *Form region displayed in Preview pane*

Summary

In this chapter you learned about VSTO 2005 SE, a new add-on for Visual Studio that enables you to create add-ins for many applications in the 2003 and 2007 releases of the Microsoft Office System. You learned how to customize the new UI features of the 2007 release of Office by creating your own Ribbon tab and adding groups of controls to existing tabs. You also saw how to repurpose existing Office commands and button icons, as well as how to add your own custom bitmap to a Ribbon control. You ended your Ribbon journey with a look at how to customize the Ribbon on Outlook Inspectors, and then you looked at the new Custom task pane. You saw how easy it is to add a custom task pane, which is available to any document that you open, and you learned how to convert a VSTO document-level customization to a VSTO 2005 SE add-in. Finally, you learned how to create an Outlook form region.

Review Questions

1. What is the main functionality available in VSTO 2005 SE?

2. What does the new Ribbon support item provide?

3. How can you add a button to an existing built-in tab on the Ribbon?

4. How can you display errors that occur in the UI of an add-in?

5. What is the best way to control the opening and closing of the Custom task pane?

6. What must you do to manage the Custom task pane on multiple Word documents?

7. How do you add controls to an Outlook form region?

Creating Code Snippets

Both Visual Basic 2005 and VSTO ship with a number of code snippets you can use in your code. You can also create your own snippets. This appendix shows you how to create a simple XML code snippet that adds a control to the actions pane.

You can use a code snippet editor tool to produce the code snippets, or you can write the code snippet XML file. To download Microsoft's Code Snippet Editor from the Microsoft Visual Basic Developer Center, search for "Code Snippet Editor for Visual Basic 2005." However, for the following example, you'll add XML tags to a file by hand.

1. Create a new text file in Notepad, and then add the XML markup from Listing A.1 to the file.

Listing A.1. *An XML code snippet that adds a control to the actions pane*

```
<?xml version="1.0"?>
<CodeSnippets xmlns="http://schemas.microsoft.com/VisualStudio/
    2005/CodeSnippet">
  <CodeSnippet Format="1.0.0">
    <Header>
      <Title>Add Control to Actions Pane</Title>
      <Author>Kathleen McGrath</Author>
      <Description>
          Adds a control to the actions pane.
      </Description>
      <Shortcut>addcontrol</Shortcut>
    </Header>
    <Snippet>
```

```
        <Declarations>
          <Literal>
            <ID>controlName</ID>
            <Type>Object</Type>
            <ToolTip>
               Replace with the name of the control.
            </ToolTip>
            <Default>DateTimePicker</Default>
          </Literal>
        </Declarations>
        <Code Language="VB" Kind="method body">
          <![CDATA[Me.ActionsPane.Controls.Add(
             New $controlName$())]]>
        </Code>
      </Snippet>
    </CodeSnippet>
</CodeSnippets>
```

2. Replace the text in the <Author> tag with your name.

3. Save the file to the c:\ drive, and name it *myActionsPane.snippet*.

This XML file has two main tags: the <Header> tag and the <Snippet> tag. The <Header> tag contains information about the code snippet, including the title, author, description, and shortcut. The shortcut works in the same way Word's autotext feature works: It is an alias for the snippet's content. Typing the shortcut into the Code Editor and then pressing the TAB key expands the shortcut and inserts the code snippet in place of the shortcut text.

The <Snippet> tag contains variable declarations and code. In the example, the <ID> tag represents the variable name, which is of the type indicated in the <Type> tag. This creates a variable named controlName of the type Object. You can add a tool tip and a default value for the variable by using the <ToolTip> tag and <Default> tag, respectively. The <Code> tag contains the code that you want inserted into the Code Editor. The Language attribute of the <Code> tag indicates that the code example is written in Visual Basic. This code snippet is discoverable only in projects that are created with Visual Basic 2005.

The actual code appears between the brackets after CDATA. In the example, it is a single line of code that adds a control to the actions pane, passing the controlName variable. You can store any number of lines of code in this node. In our example, when this code is inserted into the Code Editor, controlName is highlighted and users can easily replace the default value with any other value.

You can use this simple XML example as a basis for creating other code snippets. We recommend that you also examine the preinstalled XML code snippets for Visual Basic 2005 and VSTO 2005 to learn how to create more complex code snippets.

Importing the Code Snippet

After you have created the code snippet, you must import it into the Code Snippets Manager.

1. On the Tools menu, click Code Snippets Manager.

2. In the Code Snippets Manager dialog box, click Import. Navigate to your newly created code snippet file, and then click Open.

3. Expand the Office Development folder.

4. Expand the Office folder, and select the check box labeled "Environment—Menus, Actions Pane," as shown in Figure A.1.

5. Click Finish, and then click OK to close the Code Snippets Manager.

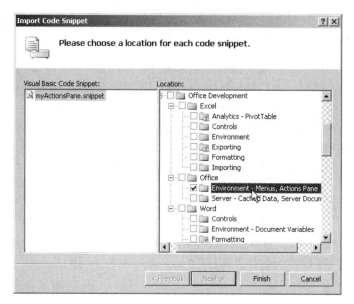

Figure A.1. *Importing a code snippet in the Code Snippets Manager*

Inserting the Code Snippet

In this section you will create a new Excel solution using VSTO and add the code snippet to the Startup event handler of ThisWorkbook.

1. On the File menu, point to New and then click Project.

2. In the Templates pane, select Excel Workbook, leaving all the default settings, and then click OK to create a new workbook project.

3. In the VSTO Project Wizard, select Create a New Document, and then click OK.

4. In Solution Explorer, right-click ThisWorkbook and select View Code.

   The Code Editor opens, and the two default event handlers are visible.

5. In the Startup event handler of ThisWorkbook, type *addcontrol* and then press the TAB key.

Visual Studio inserts the code snippet into the Code Editor with the first variable selected, as illustrated in Figure A.2. In this way, you can replace the default control with the control that you want to add to the actions pane.

```
Me.ActionsPane.Controls.Add(New DateTimePicker())
```

Figure A.2. *IntelliSense code snippet for adding a control to the actions pane*

Using the Code Snippets Manager

You can use the Code Snippets Manager to add your code snippet to the code snippet folder list. To view the Code Snippets Manager, you can select it from the Tools menu. You select the language category for your code snippet in the Language drop-down, and navigate to the folder where you want to store your snippet. To add a code snippet to an existing folder, click Import, and then select your code snippet. To add a folder to the folder list, click Add and navigate to the folder you want to add. When you select a code snippet in the Code Snippets Manager, the description window displays information about the snippet, including a description, shortcut, snippet type, and author, as shown in Figure A.3.

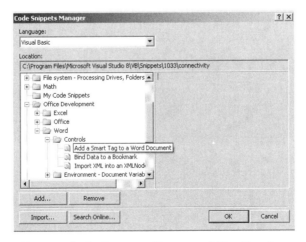

Figure A.3. *IntelliSense Code Snippets Manager, Office Development folder*

B

Creating Inspector CommandBars

In VBA, when you add a button to a CommandBar, you associate a macro with the OnAction property of the button. Using VSTO, you must programmatically create a CommandBarButton and add it to the CommandBar.

Outlook presents some challenges when you're creating CommandBars and CommandBarButtons. For every CommandBarButton that you create, you must hold a reference to it in order for the Click event handler to function properly. In this example, we show you how to create an Inspector CommandBar and add a button to it.

1. Create an Outlook add-in using VSTO.

2. Add the code in Listing B.1 to the Startup event handler of ThisApplication, and add the variables with events at the class level.

Listing B.1. *Creating a variable for an Outlook Inspector*

```
' Create an inspector and CommandBar button object with events.
Dim WithEvents MyInspector As Outlook.Inspectors
Dim WithEvents MyButton As Office.CommandBarButton
Dim MyCommandBar As Office.CommandBar

Private Sub ThisApplication_Startup(ByVal sender As Object, _
    ByVal e As System.EventArgs) Handles Me.Startup

    MyInspector = Me.Inspectors

End Sub
```

3. Add the code in Listing B.2 to the Shutdown event handler of ThisApplication.

Listing B.2. *Releasing objects in the Shutdown event handler*

```
Private Sub ThisApplication_Shutdown(ByVal sender As Object, _
    ByVal e As System.EventArgs) Handles Me.Shutdown

    ' Release the objects.
    MyInspector = Nothing
    MyButton = Nothing

End Sub
```

4. Create a toolbar and add a button, as shown in Listing B.3.

Listing B.3. *Adding a toolbar and button to the Inspector*

```
Private Sub MyInspector_NewInspector(ByVal Inspector As _
    Microsoft.Office.Interop.Outlook.Inspector) _
    Handles MyInspector.NewInspector

    If TypeOf Inspector.CurrentItem Is Outlook.ContactItem Then
        Try
            ' Assign CommandBar to variable if it exists.
            MyCommandBar = Inspector.CommandBars("Sample")
        Catch
        End Try

        ' Otherwise re-create it.
        If MyCommandBar Is Nothing Then
            MyCommandBar = Inspector.CommandBars.Add( _
                Name:="Sample", Temporary:=True)
        End If

        Try
            ' Assign button to variable, if it exists.
            MyButton = MyCommandBar.Controls("Hello")
        Catch
        End Try

        ' Otherwise add the button.
        If MyButton Is Nothing Then
```

```
        MyButton = MyCommandBar.Controls.Add( _
            Type:=Microsoft.Office.Core.MsoControlType. _
            msoControlButton, Temporary:=True)
    End If


    ' Set the style and caption of the button, and then
    ' make it visible.
    With MyButton
        .Style = Microsoft.Office.Core.MsoButtonStyle _
            .msoButtonCaption
        .Caption = "Hello World"
    End With
    MyCommandBar.Visible = True
    MyCommandBar.Position = _
        Microsoft.Office.Core.MsoBarPosition.msoBarTop
    End If
End Sub
```

5. Add the code in Listing B.4 to create an event handler for the button.

Listing B.4. *Handling the button Click event*

```
Private Sub MyButton_Click(ByVal Ctrl As _
    Microsoft.Office.Core.CommandBarButton, _
    ByRef CancelDefault As Boolean) _
    Handles MyButton.Click

    MsgBox("Hello World")

End Sub
```

If you run this code and then open an Inspector (in this case we're checking only for contact items), the button will be added to the Inspector. However, if you open another Inspector, the button is not created for you.

1. Press F5 to run the code.

2. Create a new contact. Notice that the Hello World button has been added to the toolbar of the Contact item.

3. Create another new contact. This time, the Hello World button is not created, as shown in Figure B.1.

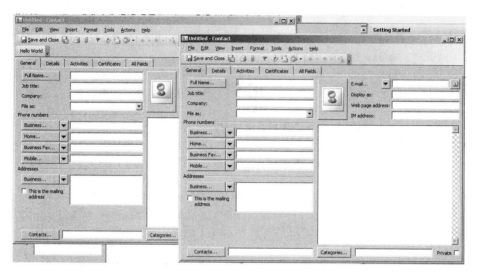

Figure B.1. *Hello World button is added to the first Inspector (left), but not the second.*

You can resolve this issue by creating the class shown in Listing B.5. This class will be used as a base class for creating Inspector CommandBars. Name the class CommandBarBase.vb.

Listing B.5. *Base class for Inspector CommandBars*

```
Imports System.Collections.Generic
Imports Microsoft.Office.Core
Imports Microsoft.Office.Interop.Outlook

' This is an abstract base class for creating your Inspector
' CommandBars.
Public MustInherit Class CommandBarBase

    ' Shared (static) list to hold references to open
    ' Inspectors.
    Private Shared ActiveCommandBars As New List(Of CommandBarBase)
```

```
WithEvents Inspector As Outlook.Inspector
Protected CommandBar As Office.CommandBar

WithEvents cbb As Office.CommandBarButton

Protected Sub New(ByVal Inspector As Outlook.Inspector)

    ' For this example, WordMail is not supported.
    ' Do nothing for WordMail Inspectors; just return.
    If (Inspector.IsWordMail = True) And _
        (Inspector.EditorType = _
            OlEditorType.olEditorWord) Then
        Return
    End If

    ' Keep a reference to this Inspector.
    Me.Inspector = Inspector

    ' Create the CommandBar.
    CommandBar = Me.Inspector.CommandBars.Add( _
        "CommandBarBase", MsoBarPosition.msoBarTop, , _
        True)
    CommandBar.Visible = True

    ' Add the controls.
    CreateControls()

    ' Add to the list.
    ActiveCommandBars.Add(Me)

End Sub

Private Sub Inspector_Close() Handles Inspector.Close

    For Each control As Office.CommandBarControl In _
        CommandBar.Controls

        control.Delete()

    Next
```

```
        ' Remove from the list.
        ActiveCommandBars.Remove(Me)

    End Sub

    Protected ReadOnly Property Tag() As String
        Get
            ' Need a unique name.
            Return Guid.NewGuid.ToString
        End Get
    End Property


    Protected MustOverride Sub CreateControls()

End Class
```

After you have added this CommandBarBase class, you can create a
new class that derives from it and creates the CommandBar and button. Create a new class called ContactCommandBar, and add the code
in Listing B.6 to the class.

Listing B.6. *Derived class for Inspector CommandBars*

```
Public Class ContactCommandBar
    Inherits CommandBarBase

    Public Sub New(ByVal Inspector As Outlook.Inspector)
        MyBase.New(Inspector)
    End Sub

    ' Create CommandBar control with events.
    Dim WithEvents MyButton As Office.CommandBarButton

    Protected Overrides Sub CreateControls()
        MyButton = CommandBar.Controls.Add( _
            Office.MsoControlType.msoControlButton, , , , True)

        With MyButton
            .Style = Microsoft.Office.Core.MsoButtonStyle _
                .msoButtonCaption
```

```
            .Tag = Me.Tag
            .Caption = "Hello World"
            .Visible = True
        End With
    End Sub

    Private Sub MyButton_Click(ByVal Ctrl As _
        Microsoft.Office.Core.CommandBarButton, _
        ByRef CancelDefault As Boolean) Handles MyButton.Click

        MsgBox("Hello World")

    End Sub
End Class
```

Finally, replace the code you previously added to the ThisApplication class with the code in Listing B.7.

Listing B.7. *Creating a new CommandBar*

```
Dim WithEvents MyInspectors As Outlook.Inspectors

    Private Sub ThisApplication_Startup(ByVal sender As Object, _
        ByVal e As System.EventArgs) Handles Me.Startup

        MyInspectors = Me.Inspectors

    End Sub

    Private Sub ThisApplication_Shutdown(ByVal sender _
        As Object, ByVal e As System.EventArgs) _
        Handles Me.Shutdown

    End Sub

    Private Sub MyInspectors_NewInspector(ByVal Inspector As _
        Microsoft.Office.Interop.Outlook.Inspector) _
        Handles MyInspectors.NewInspector
```

```
If TypeOf Inspector.CurrentItem Is _
    Outlook.ContactItem Then
    Dim CommandBar As New ContactCommandBar(Inspector)
End If

End Sub
```

Now when you press F5 to run the code and then open a contact item, the button is created; a button also is created for any contact item that you create or open.

To handle other types of Inspectors, you could create additional classes similar to the ContactCommandBar class that derive from Command-BarBase, or you could create a generic class that handles all Inspectors. Note, however, that this code is not enabled for e-mail items when Word is selected as the editor for e-mail. You can change these settings by deselecting the Use Microsoft Office Word 2003 to Edit E-mail Messages check box and the Use Microsoft Office Word 2003 to Read Rich Text E-mail Messages check box, as shown in Figure B.2. Adding support for Word as the editor is beyond the scope of this example, but you could extend the basic framework of the example to support WordMail.

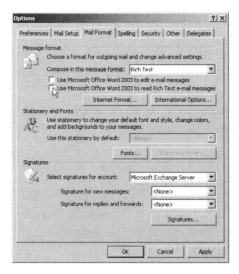

Figure B.2. *Clearing the Use Microsoft Office Word 2003 check boxes*

Index

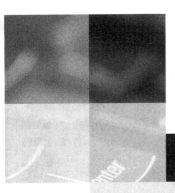

inform**IT**

BOOKS ONLINE
ENABLED

THIS BOOK IS SAFARI ENABLED

INCLUDES FREE 45-DAY ACCESS TO THE ONLINE EDITION

The Safari® Enabled icon on the cover of your favorite technology book means the book is available through Safari Bookshelf. When you buy this book, you get free access to the online edition for 45 days.

Safari Bookshelf is an electronic reference library that lets you easily search thousands of technical books, find code samples, download chapters, and access technical information whenever and wherever you need it.

TO GAIN 45-DAY SAFARI ENABLED ACCESS TO THIS BOOK:

- Go to **http://www.awprofessional.com/safarienabled**

- Complete the brief registration form

- Enter the coupon code found in the front of this book on the "Copyright" page

Addison
Wesley